7/12

Please renew/return items by last date
shown. Please call the number below:

Renewals and enquiries: 0300 123 4049

Textphone for hearing or
speech impaired users: 0300 123 4041

www.hertsdirect.org/librarycatalogue
L32

Hertfordshire

D1626110

Lender to the Lords, Giver to the Poor

1   Samuel Lewis (1838–1901)   *George Plumtre*

Lender to the Lords, Giver to the Poor

GERRY BLACK

 VALLENTINE MITCHELL

First published in 1992 in Great Britain by
VALLENTINE MITCHELL & CO. LTD
Gainsborough House, Gainsborough Road,
London E11 1RS, England

and in the United States of America by
VALLENTINE MITCHELL
c/o International Specialized Book Services, Inc.
5602 N.E. Hassalo Street, Portland, Oregon 97213

Copyright © Gerry Black 1992

British Library Cataloguing in Publication Data
Black, Gerry
    Lender to the Lords, Giver to the Poor
    I. Title
    332.092

    ISBN 0-85303-249-1

Library of Congress CIP Data

Black, Gerry.
        Lender to the lords, giver to the poor / Gerry Black.
        p.   cm.
        Includes index.
        ISBN 0-85303-249-1
        1. Lewis, Samuel, b. 1838. 2. Jewish capitalists and financiers–
    –Great Britain—Biography. 3. Philanthropists—Great Britain–
    –Biography. 4. Usury—Great Britain—History—19th century.
    I. Title.
        HG172.L49B58 1992
        332'.092—dc20
        [B]   91-39878
                                                             CIP

Typeset by Regent Typesetting, London
Printed and bound in Great Britain by
BPCC Wheatons Ltd, Exeter

Contents

Acknowledgements   vii

List of Illustrations   xi

1. The Lewis family   1

2. At school and on the road   11

3. The Davis family: Great Yarmouth, Liverpool and Dublin   20

4. The old moneylenders   29

5. The new moneylenders   48

6. Sam in Cork Street   53

7. Why borrow?   77

8. The favoured eldest sons   87

9. Sir George Lewis, the enemy   96

10. London, Brighton and Maidenhead   117

11. The Turf   132

12. Hugh Lowther and the prairies of Wyoming   145

13. The clubs   155

14. Sam and the fourth marquis of Ailesbury   161

15. Sam and Lord William Nevill   185

16. The Select Committee   205

17. Other clients   255

18. Retirement   279

19. Sam's will   289

20. Ada without Sam   303

21. The lieutenant   318

22. The beneficiaries   343

23. Robin Hood?   367

    Notes on sources   374

    Bibliography   380

    Index   385

Acknowledgements

I first came across the name of Samuel Lewis when writing a thesis on 'Health and medical care of the Jewish poor in the East End of London'. In his will he had left the Jewish Board of Guardians £100,000 to found a convalescent home, and I mentioned this in the draft I submitted to my supervisor, Professor Aubrey Newman of Leicester University. He told me that I would be surprised when I learned the source of Sam's wealth. When I asked him what it was he declined to tell me, saying that it was for me to carry out the research, not him. I knew the approximate date of Sam's death and searched the pages of the *Jewish Chronicle* until I found his obituary notice. This outline of his life intrigued me, for it was a story of rags to riches, involved high society and civil and criminal court appearances, and promised some continuation of my thesis because he had bequeathed large sums to medical charities.

Having completed my thesis, and being deeply bitten by the research bug, I decided to see whether I could discover enough material to write a magazine or newspaper article. Sam had left behind no business or private correspondence. His wife Ada had left several diaries 'all marked inside to whom to be given', but despite every endeavour on my part I have been unable to locate any of them. My fantasy, that one day I would be sitting in a library immersed in a book and someone would tap me on the shoulder, hand me a brown paper parcel containing the diaries, and walk away with the remark 'you might find these interesting', never materialised. I can only hope that they will emerge as a result of the publication of this book.

When I started, my file on the subject consisted of a copy of the *Jewish Chronicle* obituary and the address of the Samuel Lewis Housing Trust. That three and a half years later it has grown into this book is due to the help I have received along the way from individuals and organisations who were kind enough to respond to my letters and requests for facilities to inspect their archives or libraries; to those of my friends, relatives and colleagues who listened to my ramblings on the subject as I discovered yet another twist in the story; and particularly to those who gave me their time to discuss the material and the topics it raised, to suggest lines to follow, and to read and criticise parts of the manuscript. Even those who replied that they had looked through their documents and had nothing relevant helped by enabling me to avoid going off on too many wild goose chases.

I am particularly indebted to librarians and to the professional keepers of archives. Their work and training give them a wide knowledge of a bewildering range of topics, and in addition to providing access to their own books and manuscripts they are full of ideas for further avenues to pursue. My especial thanks therefore to the library staff and keepers of the archives of the Ada Lewis Dublin Winter Distress Fund (at City Hall, Dublin); the Ailesbury family archives (at Wiltshire County Record Office), the Ada Lewis London Winter Distress Fund (held by the City of London Corporation); Anglo-Jewish archives; the Bank of England archives; the Birmingham Hebrew Congregation archives (held in Birmingham Central Library); the Birmingham Hebrew Philanthropic Society Minutes (kept at the offices of the Birmingham Jewish Welfare Board); Brighton Library; the British Library; the Census Office; Dublin Central Library; the Dublin Jewish Board of Guardians; Cheshire County Record Office; the Esher archives (at Churchill College, Cambridge); the Gilbert Library, Dublin; the Grosvenor Estates (their archives are housed in Westminster City Library); the Guards' Boat Club; the Guinness Trust; the Institute of Historical Research; the Irish Jewish Museum in Dublin; Jewish Care (formerly the Jewish Board of Guardians); Jewish Lads' and Girls' Brigade; Jews' College; the King's Fund archives (held at the Greater London Record Office); the Law Society (Solicitors' Record Office); Liverpool Hebrew Congregation records (held in the main library); Maidenhead Library; Midland Bank archives; the Mocatta Library; the Museum of the Duke of Edinburgh Royal Regiment (Berkshire and Wiltshire); the National Monuments Record in Savile Row; the National Portrait Gallery; the National Register of Archives; the Newspaper Library at Colindale; the Public Record Offices at Chancery Lane and Kew; the Public Record Office of Northern Ireland, Belfast; the Rothschild

Acknowledgements

Archives; the Royal Academy of Music; the Royal Archives at Windsor Castle; St Katherine's House; the Samuel Lewis Bequest for the Jewish Poor of Dublin; the Samuel Lewis Trust; the Schoolmistresses' and Governesses' Benevolent Institution; Scottish Jewish archives; the archives of the Shrewsbury family (at Staffordshire County Record Office); Somerset House; University College London Library; University College of North Wales; the Worshipful Company of Musicians; West London Synagogue of British Jews; and the Yorkshire Archaeological Society.

The following all lent a hand, in one or other of the ways indicated above, and I should like to thank each of them: the Marquis of Abergavenny, Gillon Aitken, Sylvia Aron, J. W. Beattie, the Duke of Beaufort, Asher Benson, Doreen Berger, Jim Bradley, his wife Lindy (Ada's great-great-niece), Vera Braynis, Malcolm Brown, the Earl of Cardigan, Melvyn Carlowe, Arthur Chesses, Judy Cook, Michael Croucher, R. A. C. Darmanin, Freddy and Stella Davidson, Shirley and Henry Engelsman, Raymond Foster, Penny Gluckstein, Edward Grayson, Richard W. Hayward, Miss Mollie Hill, Dr Anthony Joseph, Zoe Josephs, Michael and Fay Kaye, Sidney and Shirley Kempner, Anne Kershon, Barbara Levy, Rita Levy, Ronald E. Levy, the Earl of Lonsdale, Simone Mace, Harry Mark, Dr Lara Marks, Barry Myers, Dr Robin Mundill, Professor Aubrey Newman, George Plumptre, Dr Frank Prochaska, Grace Monica Randall, John Randall, John Robinson, Edward Sammes, I. A. Shapiro, Michael Shaw, the Earl of Shrewsbury and Talbot, Anthony Smith, Professor Barry and Mrs Sonia Supple, David Spector, Ettie Steinberg, John Stevens (John Juxon), Charles Tucker, Sheila Watson, Theodore Wilden, Bill Williams, David Henry Wilson and Joe Wolfman.

My particular thanks go to my colleagues at work, who suffered with me the ups and downs encountered during the preparation of the book: Rose Diamond, Peter and Marion Freedman, Irene Leigh, Rose Roth, Leonore Samuels and Gerald and Lily Roland.

Finally my thanks to my daughter Stephanie who solved the numerous problems, almost all self-inflicted, which I encountered with my word processor, and most of all to my wife Anita who so stoically, though not always silently, endured my painful process of gestation, and so perceptively assisted me in every aspect of the preparation of the book.

List of illustrations

1   (frontispiece) Samuel Lewis (1838–1901)

Between pages 34 and 35
2   Samuel Lewis
3   Ada Lewis in Court presentation dress in 1906
4   A fourteenth-century Italian money-lender
5   A Jewish pedlar selling pencils
6   Ada's mother, Sarah Davis, née Mordecai
7   Ada's youngest sister Alice, known as Dotie and as Hope Temple. She married André Messager
8   A lord seeking a loan
9   The West End branch of the Bank of England, Burlington Gardens

Between pages 66 and 67
10 Grosvenor Square. Sam and Ada lived at no. 23 on the north-west corner of the Square from 1880. Ada moved to no. 16 after Sam's death
11 Brunswick Terrace, Brighton. Ada and Sam lived at no. 13
12 Ada at Brighton
13 'Woodside', Maidenhead, near Boulter's Lock. Sam bought it from Lord William Nevill's sister, Lady Cowley, for £11,000 in 1895
14 Sir George Lewis, England's leading solicitor and Sam's greatest enemy
15 Henry Labouchere, Sir George's close friend, a politician and investigative journalist. At first criticised Sam, but later came to admire him
16 The Prince of Wales, later King Edward VII, in 1885. Sam met him on the racecourse and at the Pelican Club

Lender to the lords, giver to the poor

17 The social scene in Hyde Park in the 1880s. Sam and Ada were part of the daily parade

18 Ascot on Gold Cup Day, 1882. Sam rarely missed a meeting

Between pages 258 and 259

19 Hugh Lowther, fifth earl of Lonsdale. One of England's wealthiest men, but frequently in need of cash. He turned to Sam

20 General Owen Williams, member of the Jockey Club and Tory MP, owed Sam more than £140,000 at the time of Sam's death

21 The fourth marquis of Ailesbury. 'If I want money I go and ask Mr Lewis for some ...'

22 The fifth earl of Rosslyn, bankrupt before the age of 30

23 England's premier earl, the twentieth earl of Shrewsbury, found it convenient to deal with Sam. He borrowed more than £367,000

24 Lord Charles Beresford, centre of a Society scandal

25 Sir George Chetwynd, client of and tout for Sam

26 The eighth duke of Beaufort, Sam's highest-ranking client

Between pages 322 and 323

27 The second Viscount Esher, a power behind the throne and government, but a frequent visitor to Sam at Cork Street

28 Sir Edward Guinness, later Lord Iveagh, an important influence on Sam's decision to provide housing for the working classes

29 Lord Farquhar, who persuaded Sam's widow to donate £10,000 a year to the King Edward VII Hospital Fund

30 The dashing Lieutenant William Hill, Ada's second husband

31 The *Samuel Lewis* lifeboat being launched by horses at Skegness just after the First World War. The *Ada Lewis* was based at Newbiggin-on-Sea. Together they saved more than 100 lives.

32 The Ada Lewis drinking trough at Maidenhead

33 The Ada Lewis Homes at Beckenham erected by the Schoolmistresses' and Governesses' Benevolent Institution in 1926 and later sold to fund the building of Queen Mary House at Chislehurst. Ada's legacy of £50,000 to the Institution revolutionised its finances

34 Queen Elizabeth the Queen Mother opening Queen Mary House at Chislehurst in 1967. The young spectator is Lady Diana Spencer, now Princess of Wales

*For Anita, Stephanie, Paul,
Miriam, Shirley and Gerry*

1 · The Lewis family

The proverbial expression 'as rich as a Jew' is not altogether
fulfilled in Birmingham.   William Hutton, 1780

The life of Samuel Lewis, literally one from rags to riches, raises a
host of topics. Though primarily a story of moneylending and
philanthropy in Victorian times, it also contrasts the hard-won
acquisition of money with its easy inheritance. It shows how excessive gambling and extravagant expenditure by certain members of
English aristocratic landed families brought many of them to the
verge of ruin, and caused an unhappy few to topple over the edge –
into bankruptcy, and even into prison.

Samuel Lewis's career highlights the reaction of society to the
rising industrial and commercial plutocrats, and the impact these new
rich had upon the cost of maintaining country seats and engaging in
the increasingly expensive London season; and it helps to explain why
the landed gentry, struggling through an agricultural depression,
needed to resort to borrowing. It reveals the interplay between the
sons of the aristocracy and the street-wise usurers, and requires a
consideration of the role of the Jewish moneylender in particular, the
antisemitism he aroused in the general community, and the alarm and
divisions he caused within the Jewish community.

When the story is placed in its historical setting, it will be seen that
the efforts of the Victorians to control or suppress usury were no
more successful than those of previous generations. The Victorian
attitude towards moneylenders, full of inconsistencies, double standards and hypocrisy, merely reflected attitudes prevalent in earlier
centuries, going back even to medieval times. Much of the criticism
directed at the moneylenders' excesses was made by a class whose
own moral behaviour would not have survived close scrutiny, and
we shall see how many of those who publicly fulminated against

1

the moneylenders and their practices were themselves, directly or indirectly, privately and profitably involved in the business.

Above all, Samuel Lewis's life illustrates the influence of money and what it can buy in terms of power, social position and worldly goods, retaining an influence over events long after the death of those who amassed it. How he dealt with his wealth also raises the question of charitable giving, and the differing views of the aristocracy and the plutocracy towards it. We shall follow the money through to its final resting-place.

Whether he was a saint or a sinner is a question that is considered in the final chapter. The reader may well draw his or her own conclusion before that stage is reached, and is invited to do so.

Sam, the name by which he was to become known, left no diaries, letters or business papers. It is only through official records and the comments of others that we can learn something about him. Fortunately there is enough to build up at least an outline of his life, to flesh out a few of the bones, though inevitably gaps will appear.

Samuel Lewis was born on 14 May 1838 at 1 Lower Hurst Street, Birmingham. It was a back-to-back, grimy, bug-infested slum, in the heart of the area inhabited by the very poorest of the 60 or 70 families which then constituted the Jewish community in the city. At first sight this would appear to be an unpropitious start for one who was to meet, and affect the lives of, some of the highest in the land, men whose own biographies were to be found in the pages of *Burke's Landed Gentry* or *Debrett's Peerage*; one who was to enjoy great wealth, and whose philanthropy to this day benefits thousands. Even the Prince of Wales, born to Queen Victoria in November 1841, and later to be King Edward VII, came to know of Sam and his wealth and, for the best of reasons, tried to lay his hands on part of it.

Paradoxically it was because Sam was born Jewish, poor, and in a provincial city, and specifically that that city was Birmingham, that he was afforded every opportunity to succeed in life. This was largely owing to the structure of the provincial Jewish communities at the time, and the effective institutions they established to preserve and defend their interests. The institutions created in Birmingham were typical of provincial Jewry as a whole. The better-off, through the synagogues, philanthropic societies and schools, supported their poor in times of extreme need, and provided an educational system for their children that in many ways was ahead of its time. This help was given partly for altruistic reasons, and because Jews generally are charitably inclined; but there was another motive. The established among them had fought hard to achieve their positions in society, having to overcome not only normal commercial competition but also prejudice, and they wished to preserve both their own good reputation and that of the Jewish community. They feared a backlash against themselves should anyone be able to raise the accusation that poor Jews were an intolerable burden on the rates, and this they determined to avoid.

It was a further advantage for Sam to have been born in Birmingham, because it meant that he was raised in the midst of a rapidly growing centre of industrial expansion which harboured, in particular, the jewellery trade and its ancillaries, pawnbroking and moneylending. His father, Frederick, born there at the very beginning of the century, described himself variously as a jeweller and as a factor, the latter being a term which, though it could cover a multitude of occupations, could not disguise the fact that he was unsuccessful in all of them. His mother Sarah, née Lyons, was born in Bristol in 1805, and his parents already had a daughter, Gertrude, born on 13 July 1836. Whether they had had any other children is not known, but as Sarah was already in her thirties when Gertrude was born it is quite possible that there had been other children who had died.

To put the Birmingham Jewish community of the 1830s into perspective it must be recalled that it was not until 1656, in the days of Oliver Cromwell, that the Jews officially returned to England after their expulsion by Edward I in 1290. The overwhelming majority of the post-1656 immigrants settled in London, but gradually spread to outlying parts of the country, particularly to the more important provincial centres, market towns and seaports. Most of the pioneers who ventured forth led isolated lives, returning to London, or the nearest large centre which had a synagogue, on High Holydays. Only a minority were ultimately numerous enough to organise themselves in a Jewish sense, and it was not until the 1730s and 1740s that it is possible to trace Jewish communities in the provinces. By 1800 they were established in no fewer than 23 towns, stretching from Dover to Liverpool, from Penzance to Great Yarmouth, and many others followed during the nineteenth century.

3

This penetration into the English countryside and out to the ports was made largely through the activities of the Jewish pedlar. Many a founder of a provincial Jewish community was a pedlar who had made good. By the end of the eighteenth century he, alongside the more numerous non-Jewish pedlars, had become a familiar figure fulfilling a useful economic function, selling scissors and spectacles, coloured handkerchiefs and calendars, leather goods, pens and pencils, cheap jewellery, trinkets, ribbons, laces, watches and the smaller household articles, in fact 'almost everything the village wheelwright and black-smith could not make'. He reached into the furthest corners of the land, and in many places was the only person who brought in goods and ideas from the outside world, thus filling an important gap in the mechanism of distribution. By the 1870s country towns possessed well-stocked shops, but until then the pedlar was a man of some importance. His visits were eagerly awaited by the isolated rural population, by well-to-do farmers and their wives and daughters; and he might hope for a cordial reception even at the mansions of country gentlemen, for he knew the heavy hunting watch that might suit the squire and the brooch and ring that would please his lady. Often he pro-vided villagers with their first glimpse of a Jew. Some who prospered used pony and trap instead of trudging by foot, but for the most part pedlars were exceedingly poor, and glad to settle in any locality which afforded the opportunity of making a modest livelihood.

Jewish pedlars were financed by Jewish shopkeepers who provided them with stock, frequently on a sale or return basis. Accounts were settled once a week, usually on Friday afternoons, after which the shopkeepers and their hawkers would gather for the inauguration of the Sabbath, either in the shop itself or in a hired room. In the centre of almost every provincial congregation was a jeweller or silversmith who performed the service. In Falmouth, for example, the com-munity was founded in the 1740s by Alexander Moses, a silversmith, known as Zender Falmouth, who kept a stock of buckles, cutlery, jewellery and watches. He advanced money to young men to enable them to obtain a hawker's licence, and would then stock them, but only on the condition that they returned on Fridays in order to make up a *minyan* (a group of ten male adult Jews, the minimum required for communal prayer). In Birmingham a Sabbath Meals Society ensured a kosher meal for the benefit of pedlars who happened to be in

4

the town on the Sabbath, and some would be offered hospitality by members of the local community. On Sundays the packs were replenished and the pedlars left to start another weekly round. It was an attractive occupation for the impecunious unskilled, for it needed neither capital nor training, and it is a subject to which we shall return.

It is generally agreed that the Birmingham Jewish community was first established in the 1730s. The earliest settlement was in an area known as 'the Froggery', around the site of the present New Street Station, and there they had a 'rather small but tolerably filled' synagogue. The original settlers were almost entirely of the humblest origins, but by 1800 there were 30 or so families who included among their number two merchants engaged in exporting, though probably not on a very extensive scale, three or four lead-pencil manufacturers, one umbrella-maker and several pawnbrokers and clothiers.

The synagogue was presided over by Rabbi Israel Phillips. By 1809 the congregation had outgrown its building, and the foundation stone of a new synagogue was laid in Severn Street. It was erected at a cost of £1,500, raised partly by donations and partly by a tax imposed by the community on kosher meat and poultry; but that building in turn became too small for the increasing congregation, and it was enlarged in 1827.

This was the synagogue to which Sam was taken by his father. Frederick was not affluent enough to have been a seatholder. He was one of the local poor who, with passing strangers, could attend as worshippers, usually sitting behind the railings. Throughout his life Sam regularly adhered to and observed his Jewish faith – though, as will be seen, some were to accuse him of defiling it.

The importance of the synagogue, for provincial Jews in particular, extended beyond the simple possession of a place of worship. Unlike the proliferation of Christian churches there was in the early days of such communities only one synagogue – there was no choice. It was a focal point and a stabilising factor in the community, though even in Birmingham they were not immune to the Jewish vice of schism. Scarcely a synagogue in the world of any great age can boast a history which does not at least once involve a breakaway group threatening to leave or actually leaving over some grievance, real or imagined, about ritual, or the honorary officers, or the allocation of seats. The story of the Jew stranded on a desert island who built himself two synagogues, the second being the one he would not be seen dead in, has a basis in fact.

Even the rabbis were not immune. One of the early leaders of the Birmingham congregation, Rabbi Myer, took umbrage at the proceedings during a meeting and stormed out, proclaiming that he would have nothing further to do with such people, and that he would convert to Christianity. On the following Saturday morning his wife woke him early so that he would get to the synagogue on time, but he refused to get out of bed. She tried to coax him by telling him that she had his clean shirt all ready, but he told her to save it for the following day when he would wear it for church. He did not put this dire threat into operation, but he still would not attend the synagogue. Eventually a meeting was held to consider his deplorable behaviour towards the community, and it was decided that he could return if he paid a fine equivalent to the price of 18 candles for lighting the synagogue. The fine was paid by Rabbi Myer – paid, but not forgotten. Some two or three years later he became the *Gabai* or treasurer of the synagogue. When his accounts were made up they did not tally with those of the collector. There was a deficiency. 'That,' said Rabbi Myer, 'is for the candles.'

A serious breach occurred in the congregation in 1853. Some members felt that the wealthier elements were drifting away from the poor, and ignoring their duty towards them, so they consecrated their own synagogue in Wrottesley Street because, as they expressed it, 'there is too great a contrast between our present synagogue government and the ancient spirit of Jewish equality ... poor Jews worship almost on sufferance ... The privileges enjoyed by the richer brethren are utterly incompatible with all those purposes of worship, standing, and social intercourse that naturally develop out of the Jewish congregation.' But three years later the community was reunited when a new synagogue, in Singers Hill, was consecrated by the Chief Rabbi, Dr Nathan Adler.

The Minutes of the Birmingham Hebrew Congregation, which are preserved from 1826, show 'a pattern of fierce arguments over the allocation of seats, of insults being hurled and grudgingly retracted', of some conflict between the older established families and the newly arrived immigrants. Despite this, every Jew who lived in the town was entitled to attend and to use the facilities it afforded. The synagogue, together with the Birmingham Hebrew Philanthropic Society and the Hebrew National School, provided the solid base the Birmingham Jews needed to sustain their growth and protect them from any outside hostility.

The provincial Jewish communities had another particular advantage; they did not suffer the breakdown of communication between classes that frequently existed in the outside world. Their rich mostly lived cheek by jowl with their poor, and even when the successful moved to the more pleasant outskirts of the town their businesses often remained in the centres of poverty, and the synagogue, of course, brought them together. When events seemed to be distancing the rich too far, then, as occurred in the Wrottesley Street schism, remedial steps were taken. Even the poorest Jews could feel part and parcel of a warm, close-knit, group. If you had to be born poor, then you might as well be Jewish.

The Lewis family were frequent applicants to the Birmingham Hebrew Philanthropic Society, *Chevra Meshivat Nefesh* (The Society for Restoring the Soul), which had been founded in 1828. The then rudimentary Poor Law system which cared for the general population in the country was on the verge of collapse, particularly in the larger towns, because of growing unemployment and the stress resulting from the agrarian and industrial revolutions. The Jewish attitude towards giving relief to the poor was in stark contrast to that of the overseers of the Poor Law. The Poor Law saved from death but scarcely held life together, relieved poverty but did not attempt to improve the individual's lot. The Torah, on the other hand, teaches that charity should be such as will enable a man to stand on his own feet, and should be given so that the recipient feels no shame in having his wants supplied. The various Jewish organisations set up throughout England in the nineteenth century, led by the Jewish Board of Guardians in London, attempted to follow this path.

It was not unknown, but it was comparatively rare, for a poor Jew to enter the Poor Law workhouse. Quite apart from the consideration that the wealthier Jews strove to avoid any charge that Jews were an undue burden on the rates, there were practical difficulties for an observant Jew. He could not live in the workhouse and keep to his religion. The Rules and Regulations of the Birmingham Guardians of

7

the Poor in 1841 made the daily reading of Christian prayers to *all* inmates compulsory, and the food provided was non-kosher and so considered unfit to eat by the orthodox Jew.

The Birmingham Hebrew Philanthropic Society was inaugurated partly for this very purpose, to keep Jewish inmates of the workhouse to the minimum. The president and the secretary belonged to well-established Birmingham families of pawnbrokers, which profession enjoyed a high reputation and status not accorded to the money-lenders. Pawnbrokers loan money, usually in small amounts, on goods pledged with them. It is lending on security, in contradistinc-tion to the business of moneylending, which is often unsecured. Con-sequently the moneylender takes greater risks and has to charge higher interest proportionate to the risk. Charging high interest rates, however justified, is not a recipe for gaining popularity or esteem.

To become an office-holder of the Society was considered a mark of distinction within the community. The committee met on the first Sunday of the month, and was elected from among the subscribers. Funds were raised by appeals and functions, and proper precautions, never excessive, were taken to ensure that the moneys distributed to the poor were not spent wastefully. Each applicant normally had to obtain a recommendatory note signed by three committee members before his application was considered, though these formalities were waived in cases of emergency. Every application was scrupulously examined, and relief granted, only if it was felt that it would enable the applicant to achieve a level of self-sufficiency. Assistance was not confined to the destitute, but was also given to those who found themselves in unexpected need. Thus a man who was robbed of his savings was helped, and a stranger who needed the fare to Liverpool; a family might be assisted on the occasion of the marriage of a daughter; a young man wishing to earn his living as a pedlar could be provided with sufficient funds to purchase his initial stock.

The impoverished Lewis family belonged to the 15 per cent or so of Jewish families who were able to survive only by obtaining relief from the congregation. Whatever work Frederick Lewis was engaged in at the time Gertrude was born obviously did not produce sufficient income to keep the family, for on 26 October 1836 the Society approved a resolution to relieve him with the sum of 40 shillings 'in consequence of his distressed situation'. This was then a comparatively large sum, sufficient to keep a family for two or three weeks. Their prospects clearly did not improve, for after Sam was born they remained in their slum-dwelling.

Matters came to a head in 1841. Frederick was in such straits that he was quite unable to fend off his creditors any longer, and at that time debtors could still be imprisoned. Courts of Requests dealt with such cases – in Birmingham the Commissioners sat at Old Cross – and Frederick was brought before them. The normal procedure was for seizure and sale of the debtor's goods to take place in the first instance, and if that failed to raise the sum owed, plus costs, the court would order an arrest to be made. The Commissioners were required to make only such order as was 'consonant in equity and good conscience', and their consciences guided them to commit Frederick to prison. Sam, a child of three, who was destined to become one of the richest men in England, saw some of the scanty family furniture being removed from the house, and then watched as his father was led away by the beadle to serve a term of imprisonment, probably at Warwick, for a debt which most likely did not exceed five pounds.

Through the good offices of one of its members an application was made to the Philanthropic Society on 25 July 1841 'by request of Mr. and Mrs. Lewis for a grant of five pounds towards extricating himself from personal distress, he being confined in the Court of Requests, and for the purpose of paying towards the expenses of bailing him through the insolvent court'. The application was refused. The Committee did not consider this was a proper use of its funds. It resolved 'that this Committee cannot make any grant from the funds of this Society for the purpose of aiding any person wishing or intending to avail themselves of this Society in passing through the Insolvent Court'. Their decision was not as hard-hearted as might appear at first sight. They were protecting themselves against the risk of being put in a position where they would effectively be guarantors for any member of the community who failed in business.

There was no such constraint when Sarah appeared before them three days later and made an application on behalf of herself, Gertrude and Sam:

July 28, 1841
Mrs Lewis having put in written application to the President and

9

Committee to take into consideration her personal distress, her husband being in prison and herself being in fear of being driven from her house in consequence of arrears of rent due to the landlord and herself and her family unprovided with shelter, solicits the aid of the Society in her unfortunate situation.

Proposed by Mr I. Cohen, seconded by Mr C. M. Solomon, that two pounds be granted from the funds of the Society. Amendment by Mr Lewis seconded by Mr I. Aaron that the sum of three pounds be granted. The original proposition having been withdrawn, amendment unanimously carried.

In less than a month Frederick was released from prison, but he was still in financial difficulties. He appeared in person before the Committee, and was granted two pounds to avoid having to sell up any more of his chattels.

Far from there being any improvement, the family's troubles increased. On 15 January 1842, Gertrude, at the age of six, died at home of 'water on the brain', no effective medical treatment being available. The family could not even afford the burial fees at the community's cemetery at Beth Olem Row. Their misery and desolation were complete. Fortunately the Committee of the Hebrew Congregation acted swiftly, and the next day called an emergency meeting. On hearing of the family's plight they waived the fees and made a grant of two guineas.

Whether Sam, now nearly four, registered and remembered any of these events is impossible to say. It is most probable that his mother subsequently spoke to him about them, perhaps frequently. What is known, however, is that later in his life Sam used a major part of his wealth specifically to assist those suffering from a lack of medical facilities, and those of the working classes who were unable to rent accommodation at a price they could afford. It is perhaps not too fanciful to suggest that his beneficence in these areas was triggered by the experiences of 1841 and 1842.

2 · At school and on the road

Education has for its object the formation of character.
Herbert Spencer, *Social Statistics* (1831)

Sarah and Frederick now had only one child to rear. How, if at all, was he to be educated? Most fortunately for Sam, the purpose-built Birmingham Hebrew National School opened in 1843 in the very street in which the Lewises lived – it could not have been closer – and it did so when Sam was five years old, the age of admission. He was in exactly the right place at exactly the right time, and this was to recur throughout his career. On this occasion it was clearly a matter of chance, but as his life progressed it happened too frequently for providence alone to have been the cause. Sam recognised an opportunity when he saw one, and grasped it.

So far as education was concerned Jews suffered from disadvantages which had to be overcome by their own efforts, and with their own money. Like all denominations, they wished to retain control over the religious content of the education of their children, and there were as yet no publicly supported non-denominational schools to which their children could be sent. At the elementary level the two main systems of education – the National Society and the British and Foreign Schools Society – were avowedly denominational in the interests of the Church of England and the Nonconformists respectively. Jews were excluded from attending many of the public schools on account of compulsory prayers or regulations in school charters (not that Sam was a candidate for such a school). Fate was to decree, however, that a high proportion of those with whom he conducted business were Old Etonians.

The University of Oxford, by requiring candidates for matriculation

11

tion to subscribe to the Thirty-Nine Articles, excluded all but members of the Church of England. Cambridge allowed Jews to sit the university examinations, but that was the limit of their toleration. They could not be awarded degrees or obtain a scholarship, exhibition or fellowship. Professing Jews could graduate at Edinburgh University and at Trinity College, Dublin, but it was not until 1854 that Oxford allowed non-Anglicans, including Jews, to take lower degrees, and Cambridge deferred the concession until 1856. In England only London University did not require a religious qualification.

The need to establish Jewish schools was thus unavoidable. The earliest Jewish arrivals in England at the time of the Re-settlement, the Sephardim (Jews of Spanish or Portuguese origin), lost no time in establishing schools in London. The Gates of Hope School for Boys claimed descent from one founded in 1664 and the Villareal School for Girls dated from 1730. For the Ashkenazim (Jews of German and East European origin), the Jews' Free School, also in London, held pride of place, in terms of age and size, and was close to the Great Synagogue in Duke's Place. Opened in 1817, it absorbed within itself a school for teaching Torah which had begun in 1732. It was generously supported by the Rothschilds, becoming eventually the largest elementary school in England. It still flourishes, and is now in Camden Town in London.

The first half of the nineteenth century, and particularly the second quarter, witnessed the establishment of several Jewish day schools in the larger provincial communities. One avowed intention was to produce Englishmen and women capable of achieving full citizenship. There was a desire to show the Gentile world that Jews were 'anglicising' their younger generation and fitting them for the full civil rights then being claimed; that they were equipping their children to earn a living in ways other than hawking and peddling.

A Mr Beyfus, who occasionally preached English sermons in Birmingham's Severn Street synagogue, opened a small fee-paying school where secular as well as Jewish religious knowledge was taught, but it seems to have catered for only a few children of the wealthier parents. Then, in November 1840, one of the leading members of the community noticed several Jewish children wandering aimlessly about the streets, and when questioned by him they revealed that their understanding of religious and secular matters was

12

minimal. He thought it a pity that they appeared to be entirely at the mercy of circumstances and without any means of having their ideas properly formed. Later that day he mentioned it to some friends, and said that he would be prepared to donate £10 a year towards founding a Jewish school. His offer was warmly received, and immediately other contributions were pledged. A unanimous resolution was passed at a meeting of the officers of the synagogue that 'the establishment of a National School is essential to the well-being and religion of the Congregation'. They had become alive to the fact that it was a prime, if not the chief, duty of a community to educate its rising generation. A provisional committee was formed, and the synagogue agreed to donate £25 a year, and grant the school the free use of the synagogue vestry for five years. Within a month there were more than 70 pupils, and the *Voice of Jacob* proclaimed that whereas previously the children of the Birmingham community had been ill-provided for in the ordinary schools of the town, now, 'like a flock rallied by the shepherd's horn, they are safely sheltered and protected against the attacks of superstition and infidelity'.

Steps were taken to ensure that the school had every possible support, though they were unsuccessful in their ambitious and rather *chutzpadik* attempt to persuade Queen Victoria to be their patron. They stifled competition by prohibiting members of the Congregation from giving any form of instruction except in the Hebrew National School. At the end of the Saturday services lectures were given by the headmaster, Dr M. J. Raphall, but Beyfus caused problems by leaving with his pupils just before Raphall was about to speak. He was brought to heel by the threat that if such conduct continued he would be deprived of his seat in the body of the synagogue and removed to one near the door. That settled it.

The first Law of the school proclaimed its aims: 'for the study of the Hebrew language and literature of the classics, mathematics, French, English, writing, arithmetic, and all the usual subjects embraced under the head of a commercial education'; and Raphall described his personal aim as 'training the children of the Hebrews in the fear of the God of their fathers, to make them useful citizens, worthy men, loyal subjects, and honourable members of society'. Boys were accepted at the age of five and girls at six, so that it is just possible that Gertrude attended for a short period before her death. By November 1841 it had over 70 pupils, which would have embraced every child of eligible age in the community. Boys were taught from nine till twelve and two till five daily, except on Sunday and Wednesday afternoons when the girls received their Hebrew tuition.

The fees were one shilling per week for boys and sixpence for girls, an impossible expense for some parents, but Law 10 provided that children of necessitous parents could, on application, be admitted as free scholars. Sam clearly came within that category. Additionally the needy were provided with books, the cost being met out of a fund set up for the purpose by the wealthier pupils. Of the 56 boys at the school in 1845, 25 were admitted gratuitously, and there can be no doubt that Sam was one of their number. It was unusual at the time, both in Jewish and non-Jewish schools, for the children of the poor to attend the same schools as the children of the rich, but in this school the sons of all ranks in the community were taught together. This would have stood Sam in good stead later when his life led him into the circles of the rich.

The school was well funded, not only by the local community but also by those outside Birmingham. Sir Moses Montefiore and Messrs N. M. de Rothschild gave £35 each, and there were 93 annual subscribers from all over England, and even one from Jamaica. The school soon outgrew the synagogue vestry, and land at 59 Lower Hurst Street, within just a few yards of the Lewises' home, was purchased for a permanent building. Sam should have been the first to arrive each morning.

The ceremony of laying the foundation stone, performed by Sir Moses Montefiore in August 1843, was a grand occasion. The Mayor of Birmingham and other local dignitaries were present, and a large Jewish contingent travelled from London. The service and the dinner which followed at Dee's Royal Hotel were attended by 'a great number of gentlemen of nearly all religions'. In all, 250 gentlemen and 125 ladies sat down at table for a meal which had been prepared in London by Mr S. Mayers of Cornhill, 'according to the rules of the Jewish dispensation'. A letter of apology for his absence was received from Baron de Rothschild because the event coincided with the anniversary of the death of his late father, Nathan Mayer de Rothschild, which, as the *Birmingham Journal* explained to its readers, was always kept by the relatives of Jewish deceased as a day of mourning. Both he and his wife sent donations of £20, and a total of £500 was raised from the company.

The number and quality of those at the dinner testified to the importance placed by the Jewish community, both in London and the provinces, on the improvement of Jewish schooling. Sir Moses was so deeply affected and overcome with emotion when laying the stone that he was unable to continue with his speech for several minutes. The whole proceedings were reported over several columns in the *Journal*, which appears to have omitted not a single word of the 14 lengthy speeches delivered at the dinner.

In Dr Raphall the school and Sam had a headmaster of great quality, charm and eloquence. It was said of him that 'while the oldest man could find much to learn in his sermons the youngest child would hear no word that he could not understand'. He was also able to assist the school financially. The cost of the new building was £2,000, double that originally estimated, and the deficit caused great anxiety. Jenny Lind, the famed 'Swedish Nightingale', was then at her zenith. A deputation led by Dr Raphall, who was Swedish by birth, called upon her in London and she consented to sing for them without remuneration. The result of her generosity, and their enterprise, was a successful concert at Birmingham Town Hall which netted enough to liquidate the deficit.

In 1847, when Sam was nine, the Chief Rabbi, Dr Nathan Adler, visited the school and examined the pupils. They were all assembled in the hall, and the dais was occupied by the managers and their ladies; the back of the hall was filled by governors, subscribers and parents. The children were called to the dais in turn and questioned on English grammar and on geography, on Roman, French and Grecian history, on Hebrew prayers and the history of the Old Testament. They gave their answers before the whole gathering, a frightening experience for a child. The *Jewish Chronicle*'s reporter particularly noticed 'one lad so small that he had to be placed on the table, but whose ready and correct replies gave the greatest satisfaction to the reverend examiner, and to the numerous audience, and hold out the promise of future excellence'. It could have been Sam. Whether it was or no, the visit of such a distinguished and famous dignitary must have impressed itself on the minds of all the pupils present and been long remembered. At a banquet that evening the Chief Rabbi said:

Your school has another great advantage, it does not recognise the distinction between rich and poor, prevailing in other Jewish schools, a distinction which establishes a barrier between the opulent and the less fortunate; forgetting the exhortation of our sages 'mind the children of the poor, because from them learning cometh forth.' Often, very often, the poor child becomes a star, shining brilliantly for his fellow scholars.

The loudest cheers were reserved for Dr Raphall, who responded to the toast to the School:

... from beginning in a small back room you have gone on and prospered, and now we are assembled in the noblest public rooms that Jews can call their own in Britain. And thank God they are our own. [The speaker was now interrupted by an enthusiastic burst of applause that continued several minutes.] You have cause to cheer; throughout this vast pile there is not a brick, not a foot of timber, not a pane of glass but what is ours, freely, fairly, all our own. [Renewed cheers.] And in these noble rooms, so lofty, so airy, so light, so cheerful, the children find not only comfort which their homes, alas, too often do not afford them, but instruction of which they had this day shown they knew how to profit.

The cheers reflected Jewish insecurity being satisfied, and he was surely right, so far as Sam was concerned, in his reference to 'comfort'. So the opportunity was afforded for Sam to have a sound education. There is no record left of his school attainments, and his later accomplishments provide little reason to think he was of an academic disposition. His signature, as seen on documents executed by him later in life, indicates a person who was literate, but not necessarily intellectual. It could be a good guess, however, that he excelled at arithmetic.

The 1851 census shows that the family had moved to 42 Pershore Street. Sam was now at school-leaving age, and he and his parents must have been giving thought to his career. The most popular trades among the members of the Birmingham Jewish community were tailoring, pawnbroking, glazing, jewellery manufacturing, jewellery retailing and peddling. His father, having had some experience in the jewellery trade, might have guided him towards it. It was rapidly

expanding in Birmingham, and Jewish firms provided a disproportionately high percentage of the total. Though only one per cent of the
population, they carried on five per cent of the jewellery businesses.
Manufacturing was cheap to start up, as rents were low, gas was
freely available, and all else that was required was a leather apron and
a few tools. But to succeed required a long apprenticeship, and Sam
was not to be afforded the necessary luxury of time, for from about
1851 his father no longer lived with the family. Sam's obituary in the
Jewish Chronicle inaccurately refers to his father having died in that
year. The probability is that he simply deserted his wife and child. To
try to make ends meet, Sarah took in lodgers.

Though just 13 years old, Sam had already experienced the loss of
his sister and the abandonment of his father, and had known what it
was to live in squalor and poverty. He had seen his mother reduced to
appealing for charitable aid. In an obituary of Sam written by his
solicitor and friend, Algernon Edward Sydney, Sam was described as
'as devoted a son as ever was born'. Exhibiting great self-confidence,
he determined to be the support of his deserted mother. Probably
influenced by the family lodger, 22-year-old Henry Solomons, and
by Mark Lyons, who also lodged in the house, both commercial
travellers, Sam decided to leave home and earn his living as a pedlar.
He promised to send his mother one pound a week.

He started with a stock, possibly funded by the Philanthropic
Society, of cheap jewellery and steel pen nibs. The hand-made steel
pens previously used were at that time being replaced by those being
manufactured in Birmingham in presses. These were cheaper, and
gave greater uniformity in shape. Better education and cheap postage
increased the demand, and the price fell rapidly enough for a pedlar to
include them in his stock.

There had been pedlars in the country since the Middle Ages. By
the time Sam began, their social status was low, and the work could be
very hard. Their packs were heavy, and street urchins would taunt
them and throw stones; and they were often molested, insulted,
baited and abused. There were more serious dangers. The lonely Jew,
carrying both goods and money, was an obvious target for thieves.
Many innkeepers refused to serve them food, or rent them rooms,
but somehow they managed to survive the week. One pedlar, Joseph
Harris, described his life on the road:

17

On the average my weekly expenses for some time were about five shillings ... My lodgings were from threepence to sixpence per night, and I managed to get a clean change of bed-linen wherever I stayed ... as for food I used to buy 1½ lb of bread, 1 oz of tea, 2 oz of butter and ½lb of sugar. The bread and butter served me for supper and breakfast, and what was left I carried in my pocket for dinner ... The tea lasted me for two days and the sugar for three.

There were, however, some Gentile innkeepers who specialised in catering for Jewish travellers, even keeping a cupboard containing cooking utensils entirely for their use. According to Israel Solomon, writing in 1878 of the situation 30 or so years earlier, one landlord kept the cupboard locked, and guarded the key himself. The Jewish guests would each clean the utensils, and then on the bottom of each write in chalk his name, the day of the month and year, and the portion of the law read in the synagogue on the Sabbath of that week, all in Hebrew, so that the next Jewish guests could be sure the utensils had not been used in the interim and remained pure for kosher purposes.

Some of these specialist hotels were in the centre of populated districts, and the pedlars going the rounds of the district would congregate on a Friday evening and stay over Saturday. They generally formed a club, and one of their number, who was licensed by the rabbi to slaughter animals, was paid one day's loss of profit from his business to get to the hotel on Fridays early enough to kill animal or poultry, or purchase fish, and either cook or superintend the cooking so that it should be quite kosher by the time the brotherhood came there and ushered in the Sabbath. In this way the weekend brought the pedlar the blessed relief of the sight of a friendly Jewish face and the opportunity of communal worship.

No one tramped the country more diligently than Sam, but despite his hard work matters did not go easily for him. He later said that he shed bitter tears on one occasion when he could send his mother only fifteen shillings instead of the promised pound. The very fact that he persevered throws light on some attractive qualities. He obviously did not fear strenuous, difficult work; he was not afraid to travel away from home to earn a living, which at his age showed initiative and courage; he was at ease when talking to those better off than himself;

18

and he was prepared to take a chance on his entrepreneurial skills. To some extent it was a gamble, not in the sense of reckless betting on a horse, but being prepared to take risks in a business venture which could just as easily fail as succeed. He was to remain such a gambler for the rest of his life.

Once again his timing was right. By the end of the century peddling had become an exhausting, fruitless occupation which led nowhere, but in 1850 it could still lead the most successful to wealth. As the retail and railway network gradually covered the land, peddling went into decline, and the 1850s probably afforded the last opportunity for a pedlar to enter upon the career structure which could advance him to a higher calling. The more successful would return to their home town and become stallholders or shopkeepers, or even wholesalers, importers or manufacturers. They then, in their turn, supplied struggling newcomers with goods. Others who, like Sam, started on the road with cheap jewellery and trinkets, sometimes graduated to becoming jewellers and goldsmiths – the most prosperous, bullion merchants and bankers. Some went into what at the time was a closely allied business, moneylending. They would eventually settle down and marry the daughter of their patron, the sister of a colleague, or perhaps the daughter of a member of the Jewish community in one of the towns they visited on their travels.

We know that Sam struggled for many years, because in 1856 we find his mother again making an application to the Birmingham Philanthropic Society for coal and blankets; but that year seems to have been the turning point. There is evidence that he was prospering by the early months of 1857. He had extended his 'round' to Ireland, and visited Dublin at least twice that year, in May and November.

3 · The Davis family: Great Yarmouth, Liverpool and Dublin

In 1857 David Marcus Davis, his wife Sarah, and their four daughters and four sons were living in Dublin. They were to have a fifth daughter in 1858 and a fifth son in 1864. (Some used the surname Davis and others Davies, but here all are referred to as Davis.) The background of the Davis family was on an altogether higher financial and social level than that of the Lewis clan. Sarah Davis, née Mordecai, was born in Great Yarmouth in 1819 or 1820 of a highly respected family. There had been individual Jews in Yarmouth in medieval times, and after the Re-settlement new immigrants were attracted there because of its importance as a centre of trade and industry. The pioneer settler was a silversmith named Simon Hart who arrived in 1760, and the two associates who founded the congregation with him were Joseph Mayers and Henry Mordecai. The dates suggest that Henry Mordecai was Sarah's grandfather. Her father, Isaac, was born in the town in 1778, and became a leader of its small Jewish community. An indication of his standing is shown by the fact that he was one of the trustees appointed by the community to hold the land they rented for use as a burial ground. (Another was Schreiner Woolf, who became the first mayor of Kimberley in South Africa.)

The Yarmouth synagogue was the smallest in England, with seating for only 60 persons, men and women, and the community probably numbered no more than 48. It is noteworthy that several Gentile names figure on its list of contributors, indicating that friendly relations were enjoyed by the Yarmouth Jews with their non-Jewish neighbours. There was even a Jewish candidate in the 1847 election, Francis Goldsmith, the eldest son of Sir Isaac Lyon Goldsmid. He was not successful, but his candidature shows there was a high degree of tolerance in the town.

Isaac Mordecai was variously described as a retail fruiterer, a silversmith and a general dealer. His wife Ann, who was 20 years younger, was also Yarmouth-born. Isaac became Warden of the synagogue, and at the time of his death in March 1853, in his 77th year, he was the oldest member of the congregation and its President, a position he had held for more than ten years. Sarah and her sisters Martha and Elizabeth would have received a solid grounding in how to conduct an orthodox Jewish household which they could then, in turn, pass on to their children.

In so comparatively small a town Isaac must have been a well-known figure, and from the account of the wedding of Sarah to David Marcus Davis, which took place on 12 June 1839, he was highly regarded. The ceremony took place in the town hall, and a report appeared in the *Norfolk Chronicle and Norwich Gazette*:

> On Wednesday afternoon a very large assemblage of ladies and gentlemen attended the Town Hall to witness the ceremony of a Jewish wedding, which was publicly performed. The service was conducted by Rabbi [Lobel Wolffe] Sternberg. The bride, who was elegantly dressed in rich silver drab satinette, and covered with a white lace veil, was an object of considerable attention. Among the spectators were almost all the first families in the town, and a band of musicians attended. After the ceremony, which was concluded by a Hebrew prayer for the royal family, between forty and fifty of the friends of the bride and bridegroom dined together in the card room. In the evening a large party of the votaries of Terpsichore paid their devotions to the goddess, and the dancing was kept up to a very late hour.

The couple went to live in David's house at 11 Mountpleasant, Liverpool, and it was there that their first two children were born, Annette on 9 April 1840 and Clara Emma on 11 April 1841. Their eldest son, Montagu, was probably also born in the same house. They moved to 101 Duke Street and their third daughter, Ada Hannah, was born on 26 June 1844; and their second and third sons, Frank Isaac and Joseph Mayer, on 6 September 1845 and 24 March 1847 respectively. A third move took them to 42 Seel Street and a fourth daughter, Emily Emma, was born on 3 March 1849. Three of Schreiner Woolf's children lived in Liverpool, and this may have been the connection which led David to Sarah.

It is difficult to gauge David's social position, or be sure exactly what his occupation was. On his marriage certificate he described himself as a merchant. In the 1841 census he was most surprisingly recorded as 'gun maker'. The term 'merchant' was used when he registered the births of his children, except that when Emily was born he stated he was a surgeon (then often indicating the profession of dentistry), and on Joseph's certificate he is recorded as a watch manufacturer. In 1858, by which time the family were in Dublin, he is described in *Thom's Directory* as a dealer in jewellery. When Ada married in 1867 he was a merchant again, but by the time of Emily's marriage in 1871 he was once more described as a jeweller. One chronicler of Irish Jewry refers to him as a dentist. Unfortunately, early birth, marriage and death certificates and census returns sometimes display a rather cavalier attitude to accuracy, and perhaps the best indication of his status can be gained from considering the houses he and Sarah occupied.

At one time Mountpleasant was a centre of Liverpool fashion. William Roscoe, the Liverpool poet, historian, banker and Member of Parliament, was born and lived there, as did the sculptor and Royal Academician John Gibson. It was the home of at least three mayors of Liverpool, including Charles Mozeley who was a Jew, and it originally boasted several large mansions. It began to decline in the 1840s, but still contained very commodious dwellings, one of which was in the sole occupation of David and Sarah and their children. In Duke Street and Seel Street they had town houses on three floors and a basement. The conclusion must be that his income from his occupations, whether as merchant, gun maker, surgeon, dentist or jeweller, or from any wealth he may have inherited, established him firmly in the comfortable category of solid middle class.

In the mid-nineteenth century Liverpool housed the largest Jewish provincial community. The Old Hebrew Congregation synagogue was in Seel Street and had a strong Anglo-Jewish consciousness. It had inaugurated addresses from the pulpit in the English language as far back as 1806, and installed the first regular English-speaking minister in the whole of Anglo-Jewry. Its Jewish Philanthropic Society was founded in 1811, and its school in 1842. The Jews in the town were well accepted, and more anglicised than in most Anglo-Jewish communities. There was a 'D. Davis' who was a member of the Hebrew Education Committee, and a 'D. Davis' who was on the Distribution Committee of the Philanthropic Society during the years 1846–7. However, there was at least one other member of that name and Sarah's husband may not have been on either committee; but what is certain is that the Davis family would have been donors to the local Philanthropic Society, in contrast to Sam's parents who were recipients.

The Davis family remained in Liverpool at least until March 1847, when Joseph was born, and at all times lived close to the synagogue and school and within the known Jewish area of settlement. Liverpool's polyglot development as a town made it a particularly tolerant society, and the Davises probably mixed more with their non-Jewish neighbours than would have been the case in most other towns. This meant that the Davis children would benefit in adulthood by being at ease among those of other faiths and upbringing, and this was to reveal itself as the lives of the family progressed, some of them achieving worldly and artistic success.

At some time after 1849 they moved to Dublin and entered into the life of the Jewish community there. They lived successively at 93 Lower Gardiner Street, where Charles was born on 26 November 1855; at 107 Baggot Street, where Alice Maude (also known as 'Dotie' and later in her life as 'Hope Temple') was born on 27 December 1858; and at 39 York Street, where Ernest Henry, the youngest son and last of their children, was born on 30 July 1864, when Sarah was already 46 years old. He qualified as a solicitor and was the last of the family to die, in 1954, at the age of 90.

All three homes were substantial Georgian houses with four floors and a basement. York Street and Baggot Street (where their house still stands) lie close to St Stephen's Green; Gardiner Street (now unfortunately rather run down) is just north of the Liffey. Like most of eighteenth-century Dublin, their houses obtained a pleasing effect by well-designed doorways of one of the classical orders, wrought iron railings, lamps and balconies, and were doubtless luxuriously appointed inside.

There were close connections and ties of kinship between the Dublin community and the Jews of Birmingham. Jacob Phillips (1803–1903), one of the sons of Rabbi Phillips of Birmingham, went to Dublin in 1828, and traded as a watchmaker and jeweller on Ormond Quay before expanding his business to Hong Kong, Shanghai and Australia. Abraham Nerwich, president of the Birmingham Congregation in 1837, was the brother of Meyer Nerwich, styled in the Dublin Directory of 1836 as the 'High Priest'. The Nerwich family were closely allied to the long-established Aarons, the Birmingham pawnbrokers, one of whom married a daughter of Meyer Nerwich. And the Birmingham Hebrew Congregation made contributions to the Dublin community when they sought help. So Sam probably knew, or knew of, some of Dublin's Jews when he first visited there, and may well have been provided with contacts. Insofar as there was a Jewish community in Ireland, it had shared the fate of its English coreligionists, and was expelled by royal decree on 18 July 1290. As in England, re-settlement began after 1656. Perhaps half a dozen Marranos, Jews who were compelled under the Spanish Inquisition to adopt Christianity but who secretly remained faithful to Judaism, came to Dublin in about 1660, and three or four of Polish or German origin settled there. In 1690 one Isaac Pereira, a partner in the firm of Machado & Pereira, was appointed Commissary-General of the Bread for their Majesties' Forces in Ireland. He and his brother took a cadre of London Sephardic Jews over with them, and some stayed. Ashkenazi newcomers, chiefly engaged in peddling and petty trade, began to filter in, and were a striking contrast to the wealthy Sephardic merchants.

The community worshipped together at the sole synagogue, reportedly in Crane Lane and, as occurred in London and other towns, the Ashkenazis soon outnumbered the Sephardim. At the close of the eighteenth century the congregation diminished and the synagogue closed. Thirty years later the community was revived, partly because of the repeal in 1816 of the Irish Naturalisation Act of 1783, which had excluded Jews from the benefits of naturalisation. One of the earliest of the new wave of immigrants was a young 19- year-old Jew, John Michaelis Bernadi, who arrived in 1819. He was born in Hamburg of Sephardic stock, and his father could trace his ancestry back in a direct line for more than 350 years. He traded as a furrier and importer of foreign skins in Upper Gardiner Street. When he was naturalised he changed his name, a minor alteration, to Barnardo – one wonders why he bothered – and it was his son, Thomas John, who founded the Dr Barnardo Homes. Other Polish and German Jews who had mostly been living in England began to arrive, and included several who were to become prominent in Dublin's communal affairs.

From 1836 to 1892 the synagogue was at 12 Mary's Abbey, just north of the Liffey, and close to where the Davises first came to live. The street held an important position in Dublin's commercial life in both the eighteenth and nineteenth centuries, and the Bank of Ireland started there. Indeed, it was the Bank's original premises which, after passing through various hands, including a period as a Baptist chapel, eventually became the synagogue of the Hebrew Congregation. The Davis family attended this synagogue, as did Sam when he was in Dublin on business. It was the natural thing for Sam to worship there. Not only would he have satisfied his requirement for religious observance, but the probability was that some congregant would have invited him to his home, perhaps for a Sabbath meal. He would find himself among people with a common heritage, background and experience, and made to feel at ease in a 'foreign' town.

The Dublin Congregation too made provision for its poor, but help was initially dispensed through the synagogue and not through a philanthropic society; so those who wished to assist the Jewish poor made their donations to the synagogue. The Dublin [Jewish] Board of Guardians was not founded until much later, in 1889, because until then the local community consisted almost entirely of anglicised Jews who were relatively affluent and, like the Davises, had come to Ireland from England. There was no need for a separate organisation, at least not until the arrival of immigrants who had escaped from the pogroms in Russia and Poland in the 1880s. One of the early worshippers at Mary's Abbey was Sir Moses Montefiore, who visited Dublin in his capacity as the London Director of the Provincial Bank of Ireland. He always made a substantial offering when given an *aliyah*, the privilege and honour of being called to participate in the reading of the law in the synagogue. He also never failed to make lavish contributions to several non-Jewish charitable institutions in the town.

When Sam's fortunes took a turn for the better in 1857 he was just

19 years old, and we find the first evidence of his charitable inclinations. On his visits to Mary's Abbey in May and November of that year he was given an *aliyah* and *shnoddered*, that is made offerings, of 5s on each occasion. In June of the following year he is recorded as giving 5s, and in October of 1859 the then grand sum of £2, which he repeated in December. As the combined donations of all the members of the congregation totalled about £2 15s per week Sam's contributions must have made quite a mark on this small community and endeared him to them, particularly as they came from so young a man. His visits would have been noted, and doubtless everyone in the community knew that here was a person of promise and generosity, and would have been very ready to welcome him whenever he came to the town. David Davis and Sam were both describing themselves as jewellers at this time, and the probability must be that they met, and spoke, and that David, who had four daughters to marry, invited Sam to the Davis home. If he did go to Baggot Street, or met the Davises *en famille* at the synagogue, he would have known Annette, then 19, Clara aged 18, Ada aged 15, and Emily just 8 years old.

The question is to be asked – why did Sam give so generously? Was he responding to the duty, the *mitzvah*, of charity, which would have been inculcated in him at home and at school, and because he knew from his own experience just how much such help meant to those in need? Or did he subscribe with a view to making an impression with business advantage in mind? He must be given the benefit of any doubt there might be on this score, as his whole life illustrated that he had genuine charitable leanings. It was to be said of him that, like Sir Moses Montefiore, he too never visited Dublin without leaving behind generous gifts to both Jewish and non-Jewish causes.

It was later stated by the eminent solicitor Sir George Lewis (1833–1911) – no relation of Sam, indeed an enemy, and one who was to play an important part in Sam's life – that Sam initially made money by selling jewellery to officers at Dublin Barracks. Certainly he was doing well enough by 1858 to justify a listing in the *Birmingham Directory* and the *Birmingham General and Trade Directory*, being described as a 'travelling jeweller'. In 1861 we find him and his mother enjoying the luxury of employing a servant, Mary Ann Bartlett, a young girl of 14. They were now at 22 Pershore Street, but occupied only part of the house, the remainder being occupied by a brewer, his wife and their six children. Some years later Sam moved his mother to a new house, at 107 Vyse Street, and there she had a companion/nurse, Agnes Wilton. He made her an allowance sufficient for them both to live in comfort. This arranged, his mother well settled, and his business blossoming, he embarked on certain ambitious steps he had planned for some time. He had made two important decisions; to further his career in London, and to marry.

On 14 August 1867 he wed David and Sarah Davis's third daughter, Ada Hannah. In celebration of the event he *schnoddered* no less than five pounds at Mary's Abbey. The wedding ceremony was performed by the Reverend Sandheim at the Davises' home at 39 York Street, and was duly announced in the London *Jewish Chronicle*. It had hardly been a whirlwind romance; they had been acquainted for probably upwards of ten years, though his visits to Dublin were naturally interspersed by long periods of absence. They had had time to get to know each other well, and it was doubtless a considered decision on both their parts. It gave her an opportunity to be mistress of her own home, and provided him with a suitable wife.

Sam was marrying above his station and entering a family whose whole background and upbringing were socially superior. It perhaps crossed Ada's parents' minds that he was not quite the husband they sought for their daughter. But class differences would have carried less weight than his religion. A presentable, hard-working, Jewish boy, from a respectable, if humble, home, would be more acceptable than a wealthy Gentile. Only Annette, the eldest of the five daughters, was then married, and David and Sarah Davis were doubtless pleased to have another off their hands and rejoiced that Ada had found a decent orthodox young man for a husband.

The couple came to London and lived at the house Sam had prepared at 113 Gower Street, just opposite University College. He was 29 and she was 23, and they were able to afford two living-in servants. We do not know exactly what motivated Sam to come to London, but most probably it was simply his driving ambition to succeed at the highest levels.

By his marriage Sam acquired not only a wife, but a family. After being for so long the only child in his own family he became an integral part of hers. All ten Davis children married, and for most of

27

their lives maintained a close relationship with their parents and with each other. They tended to live near each other. When Ada's parents settled in London, in the 1870s, they lived at 41 Blomfield Road in Little Venice, Maida Vale, close by the canal. In 1876 they joined West London Synagogue in Upper Berkeley Street where Sam and Ada had been members since 1873. Clara was staying with Sam and Ada in 1871 when she married Augustus Jacobs, and that couple made their home in Clifton Gardens just around the corner from Blomfield Road. Frank also lived in Maida Vale, and Ernest in nearby Oxford Terrace. His son Geoffrey Hope-Davis, a favourite nephew of Sam and Ada, was in the West End in Manchester Street. They constantly visited each other, and supported each other when aid was required, and none helped more than Sam. He could not have been more generous had they been his own brothers and sisters, nor was he any less loving and kind to their children. Unfortunately Sam and Ada had no offspring. Given that they were a Jewish Victorian couple it is highly unlikely that this was by choice; it must be assumed that one or both was impotent or infertile.

Ada was an intelligent, handsome, dignified, rather ample young woman; a fine horsewoman and an accomplished violinist and cellist. Although nothing is known of her education, she had clearly had the advantage of a good one. There was no Jewish communal school in Dublin, and it may be that she and her brothers and sisters were privately taught, and quite possibly had a governess. She had more cultivated and cultured interests than Sam – he never did acquire her love for art or music – and, unlike him, she was not a gambler; but she must have discerned many desirable qualities in him. He was of good appearance, neatly dressed, witty of speech, and a rising business man who was clearly destined for further success. They were embarking upon a long and successful marriage, and she was to prove herself to be a woman of determination and courage, and Sam's steadfast support when he came to face sustained attacks on his character from prominent public and communal figures in newspapers and even in Parliament. When their fate led them to a Grosvenor Square mansion she became acknowledged as one of the best and most popular of Mayfair hostesses. In addition to the change in Sam's domestic circumstances, his business career also altered dramatically. He became a moneylender.

4 · The old moneylenders

O Lord, who may lodge in thy tabernacle? Who may dwell on thy
holy mountain? . . . The man of blameless life, who does what is right . . .
who does not put his money out to usury . . .   Psalms 15:1

> Who goeth a borrowing
> Goeth a sorrowing
> Thomas Turser (1524–1580)

The human species, according to the best theory I can form of
it, is composed of two distinct races, the men who borrow and
the men who lend.
Charles Lamb (1775–1834), *The Two Races of Men*

Moneylenders are more sinned against than sinners.
Samuel Lewis, November 1900

There are two words used to describe people who lend money at
interest: 'moneylender' and 'usurer'. The dictionary definition of a
moneylender is simply one whose business it is to lend money at
interest. Nowadays 'usurer' is used mainly in a pejorative sense, as a
term of reproach when describing somebody whose interest charge is
illegal or immoral. It may be illegal either because there is a statute
which forbids it completely or limits the rate of interest which can be
charged; or it may be considered immoral by those whose religious or
personal code forbids it. Different religions have differing views, and
many have altered their views over the centuries, or reinterpreted
them, to take account of changing circumstances. The words 'moneylender' and 'usurer' are here treated as being completely interchange-
able, whether the lending of money is permitted or forbidden, and
whether the rate charged is high or low.

Sam Lewis was entering upon a trade or profession which has
aroused ambivalent attitudes in society throughout the ages, attitudes
frequently inconsistent, intolerant and hypocritical; and to

29

understand the position he found himself in, to set the background against which he operated, it is necessary to delve a little into the history of moneylending.

Should an individual ever be allowed to lend money to another at interest? In these days of widespread credit facilities, when the custom of paying cash for a purchase is becoming outmoded, and when almost every post brings offers of a loan from respectable sources, this may seem a naive question to ask. But it was not ever so. Are those who wish to borrow, for what to them are good reasons, to be prevented from doing so? Are there borrowers who need to be protected by law against entering into loan agreements? Are bankers to be treated differently from moneylenders and, if so, how do you distinguish between the two? Should moneylenders be prohibited from carrying on their trade, or should they at least be restricted in what they do and how much they charge? Does any individual, state or church have the moral right to make such a law, and have any such laws ever been effective?

These problems have occupied statesmen, churchmen and jurists all through civilisation, even until today. The activities of the moneylender have been the object of censure by moralists, persecution by politicians and denunciation by the clergy. In Roman times he was described by Horace as 'a wretch who tempts youths and prodigals to destruction, who bears the hisses of the people, and the hatred of his own relations and neighbours'. In the Dark Ages and the Middle Ages the church, finding its values threatened by the eruption and spread of the monetary economy, and believing that usury was a destabilising factor in society, ruled that usury was one of the foulest offences against God and man, and proclaimed its practice to be a deadly sin against the Divine Law. Even as late as the sixteenth century, Dr Thomas Wilson, a court official in the time of Elizabeth I, said: 'I will wish some penal law of death to be made against these usurers, as well as against thieves or murderers, for that they deserve death much more than such men do. For these usurers destroy and devour up not only whole families, but also whole countries, and bring all folk to beggary that do deal with them.' The borrower was exonerated from blame because, it was argued, his part in the transaction was involuntary and entered into much against his will.

On the other hand, there were those who took the completely

opposite view, and considered that lending money was no different from lending or selling any other commodity, and so should be permitted freely, without restrictions of any kind.

The only time a moneylender is popular is at the moment that he parts with his money – from then on, not. As Jeremy Bentham, the eighteenth-century political economist, expressed it:

> While the money is hoped for, and for a short time after it has been received, he who lends it is a friend and benefactor: by the time the money is spent, and the evil hour of reckoning is come, the benefactor is found to have changed his nature, and to have put on the tyrant and the oppressor. It is a repression for a man to claim his own money: it is none to keep it from him.

The man of dissipation is favoured, and justice often refused to the man of thrift who supplies him. In any popularity contest between a moneylender and an extravagant nobleman, the moneylender would be the loser.

All countries at different times have attempted to regulate the business of the professional moneylender in order to deal with possible abuse. The Romans tackled the problem with the Laws of the Twelve Tables in 500 BC and allowed a rate of 12 per cent; to go above it was a punishable offence equated with theft. Solon, when called upon to give laws to the Athenians, placed no restriction on the rate; it was left to the individuals concerned in the contract, though he did suggest that up to 18 per cent a month was acceptable. In Greece 12 per cent was the rate in ordinary cases, and 18 per cent in commercial affairs. Aristotle, however, argued that all usury was contrary to nature.

The New Testament does not specifically forbid the taking of interest, though some interpret Luke vi: 35 as conclusive against it: 'But you must love your enemies, and do good; and lend without expecting any return.' For Muslims it is, on the face of it, absolutely forbidden, but what is allowed may appear to some to be akin to moneylending by a devious route. There are references in the Torah and Talmud to moneylending, and Talmudists can engage you for hours, if not days, weeks or months, upon their interpretation. The basic Old Testament position is that the taking of interest on a loan to a fellow Jew is prohibited, but it is allowed as regards a stranger:

> You shall not charge interest on anything you lend to a fellow countryman, money or food or anything else on which interest can be charged. You may charge interest on a loan to a foreigner but not on a loan to a fellow countryman, for then the Lord your God will bless you in all you undertake. (Deuteronomy xxiii: 20)

Why should it be right for a Jew to lend money out on interest to a non-Jew but not to a Jew? If it is wrong in one case, how can it be right in the other? Some rabbis say this is because in biblical times there was no Gentile law forbidding the practice of usury by Gentiles, and as Gentiles took interest from Jews it was only equitable that Jews should take interest from Gentiles. However, if the Gentile had fallen into poverty, and stood in need of assistance, the Old Testament emphatically prohibited the taking of interest of any kind whatsoever (Leviticus xxv: 35). This belief that interest should not be charged to a clansman was shared by many self-contained communities. It was so with the Romans and the early Christians. By Muhammadan law a Muslim was forbidden to receive interest from a Muslim. In India it was illegal for the two superior castes, the Brahmins and the Kshattriyas, to engage in such transactions with each other, and even in the case of the lower two castes the code declared 'that the sums lent to a person in distress give rise to no interest, because any such interest to such a clansman would be extortionate'.

In the Dark Ages, and in the Middle Ages, when religion held almost absolute influence over the masses, usury ranked with heresy, incest and adultery. In the fourth century the church forbade the taking of interest by the clergy, and in the fifth century by the laity. The first prohibition in England was in the seventh century. Theodore of Tarsus, the Archbishop of Canterbury, prescribed three years' penance to atone for the sin, including one year on bread and water. The condemnation of usury became the keystone of the political economy of the Middle Ages. As early as the reign of Alfred (871–900), well before the arrival of the Jews in England, penal laws were enacted against usurers. Their chattels were forfeited to the king, their lands went to the lords, and they could not be buried in sanctuary. As late as 1584, usury could bring a sentence of excommunication by a bishop. Moneylenders were repeatedly referred to as declared enemies of society and, as we shall see, 300 years later almost identical words were to be used about Sam.

Various reasons have been suggested to explain why the medieval church so condemned the taking of interest. When trade was in its infancy, money was borrowed, in the vast majority of instances, not for productive purposes but for consumptive. The borrower was either a poor man seeking relief from frequent famines and oppressive taxes, or he was an extravagant man looking for new means of gratification. In either instance the church was concerned; it sought to protect the needy and to curb the spendthrift. Further, the church objected to unearned income, and believed that to live without labour was unnatural. Fears were expressed that should lending and borrowing increase, agriculture would be hampered, the countryside deserted and society destabilised. But the church's efforts were not uniformly successful, and borrowing remained common among both the nobles and the mass of the peasantry.

Credit is essential in any society that has developed beyond its most rudimentary stage, and the church's total opposition to any moneylending whatsoever was impossible idealism. The people of the thirteenth century, still enjoying the fruits of a spectacular expansion of the economy during the twelfth, needed to develop – and did develop – a more sophisticated credit system. The restrictions the church sought to impose were no longer compatible with the reality of society, and the absoluteness of its prohibition corresponded so little to the requirements of the times that it doomed itself to sterility. Further, its position was flawed, first because it was impossible to achieve a standard of perfection by coercion; second, because some of its most illustrious members were in breach, and seen to be in breach, of its own rules; and third, because it offered no adequate alternative to the moneylender.

The acquisitive elements of human nature do not provide generally for lending without a return. A man may lend to a relative or a friend, or even a stranger in need, without interest, but it is not something done to the world at large, that a man will say that anybody who would like to borrow money from him may do so without any interest. For this reason, whenever and wherever there has been a

33

total prohibition against moneylending, by the church or by the state, a way has been found to evade it. If a Roman was forbidden to borrow money from another Roman, he borrowed from a stranger who was not bound by the law. Similarly, when the medieval church imposed an absolute ban on Christians engaging in the practice, borrowers turned to the Jews. In many ways this was inevitable. The Jews were severely restricted from engaging in almost every other occupation. The rise of Christianity had eroded their economic and social life, and the church and the Christian emperors frowned upon their intercourse with true believers on equal terms.

The first Jewish community in England consisted of a group which William the Conqueror (1066–1087) brought over, largely from Rouen, settling them in the City of London in an area around a street still bearing the name Old Jewry. He did so partly because he wanted England to be as prosperous as Normandy, and he knew from his experience there that the Jews, with their heightened commercial sense and understanding of many aspects of monetary economy, could be the key. Indeed, the whole relationship between medieval Anglo-Jewry and the state was dominated by the fiscal purposes of the crown. In England the Jews were not allowed to own land, and other trades were effectively prohibited, since they were ineligible to join the guilds controlling the crafts. Unable to engage in personal enterprise, they had to finance that of others – to lend out their capital at interest, and in this they received the encouragement of the crown, and combined the triple roles of bankers, pawnbrokers, and moneylenders. Canon law did not apply to them; they were not subject to the ecclesiastical punishments imposed on usurers by the popes. Christians gradually came to appreciate the advantage of having a class of men who could provide a reservoir of credit on which they could draw in their hour of need, without that class becoming liable to excommunication. As such the Jews were an ideal choice for Christians who wanted to have their cake and eat it. Christians could benefit from the advantage of a credit sytem, and yet retain their economic innocence and claim not to be implicated in usury. In the forefront of those seeking loans was the king, closely followed by the nobles and, though it still professed to oppose usury, the church itself.

Throughout the thirteenth century, western monarchs generally were plagued by a persistent shortage of funds. England's farming

2 Samuel Lewis

3   Ada Lewis in Court presentation dress in 1906

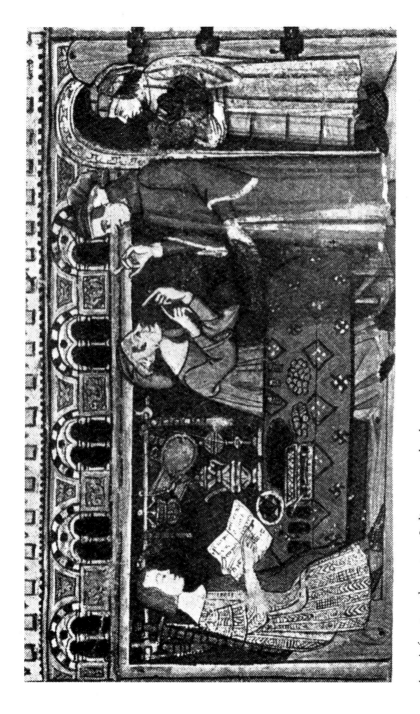

4 A fourteenth-century Italian money-lender

5   A Jewish pedlar selling pencils

6   Ada's mother, Sarah Davis, née Mordecai   *Mrs J.B. Bradley*

7   Ada's youngest sister Alice, known as Dotie and as Hope Temple. She married André Messager   *Mrs J.B. Bradley*

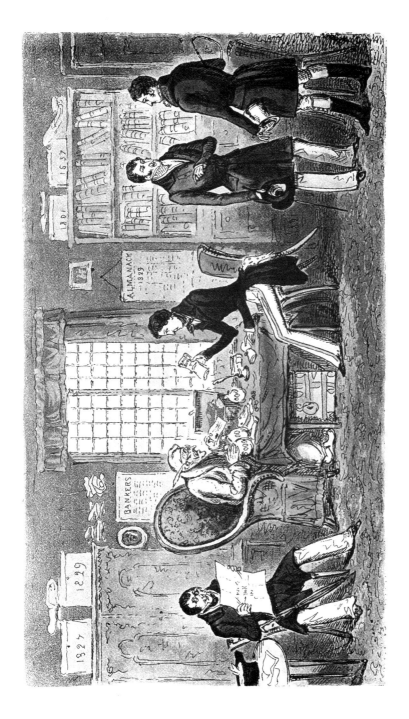

8   A lord seeking a loan

9   The West End branch of the Bank of England, Burlington Gardens. It backed Sam in his business

and commerce ensured a source of revenue because they were strong enough to support taxes, but the king needed cover to bridge the time gap, and cash gap, between raising the tax and collecting it. More magnificent courts and more elaborate administrations staffed by salaried officials, together with the escalating costs of wars, increased the king's needs. If a sudden emergency arose his finances came close to collapse. Consequently royalty were principal clients of the moneylenders and pawnbrokers. The queen mother, Eleanor of Provence, borrowed 600 marks from Rabbi Elijah of London in 1275. Henry III (1216–1272) pledged a painting; Edward III (1327–1377) deposited his crown three times, and in 1339 not only his own, but the Queen's too; and Henry VI (1422–1461) deposited one of the Crown Jewels to pay for his wedding to Margaret of Anjou. She in turn pledged her plate at Rouen to pay the expenses of her journey to England. It was to the Jews that the king regularly resorted for gold for his personal use, so that they to some extent fulfilled a function almost equivalent to official bullion brokers to the crown.

The law provided that on the death of a Jew his estate passed to the king, and this burden was additional to the special taxes raised on Jews during their lifetime whenever the king needed extra money for a war, or a building, or to pay his servants, or for his luxuries. Henry II (1154–1189), Henry III and Edward I frequently drew large sums from the Jewish reservoir without making any recompense. The Jews' non-royal loans were also subject to the will and whim of the king. At any moment he might assign security held by a Jew to a third person, or release a borrower from his bond to a Jew. Indeed, some kings played both ends against the middle, accepting payments from Jews in return for help in enforcing Jewish loans, and from borrowers for release from their debts. In this way the transactions of the Jews could prove doubly rewarding for the crown.

Despite the law's provisions the king rarely confiscated the whole of a Jew's estate. He did not wish to kill the goose which laid golden eggs, and he usually took one-third. This left two-thirds to the Jew's natural heir, who could go on lending at interest and so keep up the king's income. Thus the ultimate beneficiary, and from one point of view the real usurer, was the king, and not the Jew who loaned the money. Between 1066 and 1290 the usual rate was 2d or 3d in the pound per week, equivalent to 43 per cent to 65 per cent per annum, though examples have been found of much higher and much lower charges. If less had gone to the crown, less could have been charged as interest. At the very least, the king should be considered as the Jew's partner.

The household and administration of the great lords approximated, on a somewhat smaller scale, to that of the king, and they shared with royalty the problem of a perennial shortage of cash. It was as though they felt their rank compelled them to keep up standards which were in truth beyond their means, perhaps in itself an inherent defect of the system of nobility, and one which was to recur and manifest itself in the centuries ahead. The landed gentry became heavy borrowers from the Jews, and provided them with the majority of their clients. With their custom came an additional problem. When the king took over the estate of a Jew the debts of the gentry were then owed to the king, which assisted him in keeping them under control. That is why the barons insisted on having a clause in the Magna Carta to the effect that in such cases the king was entitled only to repayment of the capital, and not to the accumulated interest. This relief from interest payments meant that for the barons a dead Jewish moneylender was preferable to a living one. Consequently there was constantly present in the Jewish moneylender's mind the knowledge that his house might be sacked by a mob and he and his family might even be murdered. The classes chiefly responsible for the widespread riots against the Jews in 1189 and 1190, in London, Norwich, York and other towns, were those most deeply indebted to them – the lesser baronage, the knights and the burghers. According to the chronicler William of Newburgh, the well-known attack in York in March 1190, which led to the murder or suicide of most members of its Jewish community, was planned by members of the nobility. 'When the slaughter was over, the conspirators immediately went to the cathedral and caused the terrified guardians, with violent threats, to hand over the records of debts placed there ... and thereupon destroyed these records of profane avarice in the middle of the church with the sacred fire to release both themselves and many others.' Similar action was taken in the other towns where riots occurred.

As for the third class of borrower, the church, the arrival of the Jews in England occurred just when the necessity arose for the erection of many important buildings devoted to religious as well as secular purposes. Without capital, no large building schemes could be under-taken. Notwithstanding its attacks on usury, the church willingly and openly borrowed at interest from Jewish financiers, who advanced money to abbeys and minsters on the security of plate, on vessels used in divine worship and, worst scandal of all, on relics of the saints. Large sums were provided by Jews for the erection and restoration of religious edifices, including Lincoln Cathedral, Peterborough Cathedral and Westminster Abbey. But contrary to popular belief the Jews were by no means the only, or even the main, moneylenders in medieval times, though it would be true to say that the percentage of Jews living by finance was much higher than the percentage of Christians. One still occasionally sees statements that there were no Christian usurers in the Middle Ages because the church forbade usury. It would be equally true to say that there was no immorality in the Middle Ages because the church condemned adultery. Christians overcame the religious prohibitions set by popes and bishops by casuistry of the highest order, subtle distinctions being drawn to justify what was nothing less than blatant usury. Until the twelfth century, the monasteries were the main source of credit. They received consider-able revenues from rents, tolls, from the sale of the produce of their lands and from the offerings of the faithful, and they were always keen to invest their surplus funds. Lending money on interest was one of the methods adopted. The majority of medieval moneylenders throughout Europe were Christian, but the church reserved its accusations of engaging in usury mainly for the Jews.

As the money economy became more widespread, more sophisti-cated bankers and financiers were required. By the middle of the thirteenth century this important economic role was fulfilled by the Knights Templar. Though small in number, they had considerable funds. Despite the fact that the cost of maintaining the war against the Saracens was high, the Temple recovered at least part of this expendi-ture by the rich rewards won in battle, and any deficit was exceeded by the income they generated by acting as the financial representatives of popes and princes. Almost all taxes passed through their hands, including the collection of the contributions sent by the English church to the Holy See, and they acted as a depository where the wealth of kings and princes, the barons, the merchants and the church was held. Their reputation for probity and their international network enabled them to provide facilities for the transfer of deposits, a service originally intended for the use of pilgrims who could deposit in England and collect in the Holy Land to the extent of their credit. The advantages of the system were quickly seized upon by the merchants, and letters of credit issued by the Templars were honoured in every Christian land. Until their influence waned, the Order became the exchange brokers of the day, and loaned money to kings and merchants, collecting their interest under the subterfuge of rent. The popes, whose representatives they were, made no protest at this, even though the church never ceased to denounce the Jewish moneylenders.

If there is one ethnic group which can be associated with the history of moneylending and banking more than any other, it is not the Jews but the Italians. Ambitious princes increasingly sought loans from the companies of Italian merchant bankers who, acting in their capacity as collectors of the various payments owed to the popes, were extending into north-west Europe. The Italians were anxious to invade the wool trade, which was thriving, particularly in England. They had been involved in this trade as early as the reign of Henry II and had made occasional loans to Richard (1189–1199) and John (1199–1216), but it was during Henry III's reign that they really began to flourish. The most numerous of these merchant bankers came from northern Italy and were known by the general title of Lombards. There was a second group, known as the Cahorsins, who most probably emanated from Cahors, the capital of Quercy in south-west France. In time the name Cahorsin came to be used simply as a synonym for a foreign usurer, and the same group can be described by some writers as Lombards and by others as Cahorsins. There was intense competition between the groups, the Jews taking every opportunity to replace the Christians, and the Lombards and Cahorsins trying to squeeze out the Jews and each other. For the most part the advantage in the struggle lay with the Christians, who could rely on the hostility of the local population, open or covert, against the unbelievers.

The Cahorsins and Lombards rapidly replaced the Jews. They transmitted funds to Rome by an early form of bill of exchange, leaving the goods and money they had collected in their own hands. Their surplus they lent to landowners, to the monasteries, to the king himself. According to Matthew Paris, the historian of the period, the 'abominable plague' of Cahorsins raged so fiercely that there was scarcely any man in all England, especially among the prelates, who was not entangled in their nets. So powerful were they that when Roger, Bishop of London, excommunicated them in 1235 and sought to drive them out from his diocese, he was summoned to Rome and forced to give up his attempt. This fostered the strong suspicion that the pope himself was both their accomplice and partner in the spoils. Though banished in 1240 by order of Henry III, these papal usurers were again numerous by 1251, and during the remainder of his reign Italian bankers flourished in England. Though Henry professed to hate their usury, he was in need of their loans. Henry's son, Edward I, having observed how his father had repaid his Italian loans from the proceeds of taxes, made Italian bankers the cornerstone of his financial structure, and the English Jews, financially exhausted by ruinous taxation, were pushed out of the mainstream of the money market. Instead of using several sources of lending, Edward established a special relationship with the Riccardi of Lucca, who effectively became a branch of the English government. They were creditors of broad sections of the upper ranks of society, ranging from earls and archbishops to simple knights and townsmen. For the first 22 years of his reign they acted as his bankers and ensured his liquidity, thus enabling him to carry out his plans in the fields of warfare, foreign affairs, household expenses and royal building. But they ultimately fared no better than the Jews, for in 1294 he had them arrested, and sequestered their assets, asserting that they owed him more than they could pay. They were succeeded by the Frescobaldi of Florence.

Though the behaviour of some Jewish moneylenders attracted continuous complaints, much of it justified, some Christian usurers attracted equally bitter criticisms. The Italians exacted up to 450 per cent per annum and were guilty of the most cruel oppression. They evaded the canon law by charging nothing for the first few months of the loan and 50 per cent interest per month thereafter. They claimed that by so doing they were not guilty of usury because they were effectively lending without interest, as the 50 per cent charge could be avoided by the debtor. However, they always provided that the initial interest-free period was sufficiently short to ensure that the debtor would be unable to repay within its confines. Indeed, by the second half of the thirteenth century it was generally recognised that the terms of business of the Lombards and Cahorsins were more severe than those of the Jews, and their conduct towards their debtors more unscrupulous and less merciful.

By 1290 the Jews of England were no longer of primary importance to the Exchequer. Whereas a century before, the average annual contribution of this small group of people to the royal income has been estimated as 14 per cent of its total, by 1290 it was reduced to little more than one per cent. Economically, too, the function they performed was no longer essential. Not only was the country better developed than at the time of their original settlement during William the Conqueror's reign, when the native middle class had been almost non-existent, but the Cahorsin and Italian usurers, working under the highest patronage, made their presence superfluous. The sums which could be provided by these foreign consortia, specialising in government loans, made the remaining resources of the Jews appear negligible. In 1290 Edward I banished them from the kingdom.

The Anglo-Jewish community has produced three native-born moneylenders who became multimillionaires in present-day terms. Aaron of Lincoln (c. 1125–1186) was probably the richest Englishman of his day, his financial transactions covering the whole country, and his dealings being with many of the leading nobles and churchmen, including the King of Scotland, the Earl of Leicester, the Earl of Chester, the Abbot of Westminster, the Earl of Arundel, the Earl of Northampton, the Bishop of Lincoln and the Archbishop of Canterbury. He was represented by agents in every part of England, and almost all the members of the Jewish community seemed to have had contacts with him. They worked in close collaboration with each other, sometimes amounting to partnership. There was thus an elaborate system of interrelated loan offices prepared to furnish reciprocal assistance for any lucrative transaction – and we shall see that matters were very little different in Victorian England when Sam arrived on the scene. Aaron lent large sums of money to the clergy of at least 25 abbeys and cathedrals. By virtue of his capital the church was enabled to raise several of those 'poems of architecture' that are still the admiration of all who visit them. On Aaron's death, Henry II confiscated the whole of his estate, which was so extensive that a separate department of the Exchequer had to be created to deal with it.

Aaron of York (c.1190–c.1253) was Aaron of Lincoln's thirteenth-century equivalent, but Henry III called on him for assistance whenever a financial crisis arose, which was frequently, and wrung from him every asset he had, and this Aaron ended his days in penury. It was to be a further 600 years before the Jewish community provided its third proven multimillionaire moneylender – Samuel Lewis.

The history of moneylending in England after the Jews were expelled is a chronicle of the conflict between the quest for commercial development of the country and religious dogma, a struggle which has been described as the birth pains of capitalism. The state's position eventually swung from complete prohibition of usury to complete freedom, but this was to take nearly 600 years to achieve. In expelling the Jews Edward did not expel usury; on the contrary, it flourished, and 50 years later a new anti-usury law had to be introduced. Among those who were then in the forefront of usurious activity were such well-known church dignitaries as Walter Langton (d. 1321), Bishop of Coventry, Lichfield and Chester, and William Melton (d. 1340), Archbishop of York. Both these immensely wealthy men served as treasurers of the realm. Melton lent money on hundreds of occasions to knights and barons, to priories and fellow bishops, as well as to simple parishioners, all at interest. The proceedings of Langton's trial in 1307 leave no doubt that his motive was 'nakedly usurious'. This course of conduct continued, and in the sixteenth century there were many bishops who had accumulated wealth from their bishoprics and earlier careers, who were clandestine lenders. Their actions exemplified a flaw in the church's attitude towards usury. It was obvious that it was a house divided against itself. Several of its leading members did not practise what they preached from their pulpits. Their flock was told not to do as they did, but as they instructed them: hypocrisy on a grand scale.

At last, in 1545, in the reign of Henry VIII, the first Act was passed recognising the legality of 'taking interest upon loans'; 10 per cent was permitted. This easing of the burden on the moneylender immediately led to an increase in commercial activity. However, seven years later Edward VI repealed the Act, and heavy sanctions were again imposed; but the severity of his statute defeated its own object, for instead of diminishing, usury greatly increased. This unexpected result was frankly admitted in a statute of Elizabeth in

1571 which confessed failure in a most unusual burst of political candour:

> It [the previous Act] hath not done so much good as we hoped it should ... rather the said vice of usury ... hath much more exceedingly abounded to the utter undoing of many gentlemen, merchants, occupiers and others.

The Act of Henry VIII was restored and once more 10 per cent was allowed. During the reign of James I the limit was reduced to eight per cent; in the reign of Charles II to six per cent; in Queen Anne's time to five per cent. Despite these later reductions the high water mark of legislation against usury had effectively passed in Henry's reign, and by the end of the sixteenth century moneylending was on the way to enjoying the legal security of a recognised and reputable profession. In the light of economic necessity it was finally emerging from the shadow of religious prohibition and state intervention. Notwithstanding hundreds of books written by ecclesiastics during the sixteenth and seventeenth centuries still urging that usury should be condemned, the bankers, growing stronger and more secure, with increasingly improving techniques at their disposal, were more confidently asserting that parsons knew nothing about business, and that it was 'not in simple divines to show what contract is lawful'. The bankers' view was that the whole controversy surrounding usury was nothing more than 'a clerical mare's nest constructed by pious rhetoricians'.

Those who favoured the abolition of laws against moneylending argued that history showed clearly that the borrower could not be protected by such laws. The richer the borrower, the better terms he can make; the poorer he is, the worse; but no laws will ever enable the poor man to borrow on the same terms as the rich. If a man can offer such security as would justify a loan at 10 per cent no law will enable him to borrow at 5 per cent. What the law can do, and will do, is force him to pay 10 per cent *plus* an amount sufficient to compensate the lender for the risk he runs in violating the law. In his essay *Of Usurie*, Bacon concluded that the advantages of usury outweighed its disadvantages. This contention was developed by Locke, Hume, Adam Smith, Jeremy Bentham and a whole school of political economists. In

1750 Lord Mansfield, in his usual blunt language, set out some of the arguments in the case of *Chesterfield* v. *Janssen:*

> A notion prevailed for many years, that it was not lawful to take any [interest] for money. This was adopted from the canon law, and even prevails today in many catholic countries. It is astonishing how prejudice should have kept common sense so long out of the world! Why, is not money a commodity as well as anything else?

He did not believe that to limit a man's freedom to borrow was in the public interest:

> Then what is this public good, this rule they so must insist on, that no man shall spend above his annual income? How can that be prevented? Is it in human nature? He will spend it; men of the best sense have done it; where will be the public utility? Where the encouragement to industry? Will the court consider every man a lunatic who exceeds his income?

Jeremy Bentham declared that the rate of interest, if left alone, would settle itself according to the laws of political economy, and he was the first to advocate the complete abolition of all restraints against moneylending. His proposition was:

> No man of ripe years and of sound mind, acting freely, and with his eyes open, ought to be hindered with a view to his advantage, from making such a bargain, in the way of obtaining money, as he thinks fit, nor (what is a necessary consequence) any body hindered from supplying him on any terms he thinks proper to accede to.

He said that it was impossible to fix any rate as a maximum which could be just, for there was no uniformity of opinion. He pointed out that permitted English rates had fluctuated between five per cent and 10 per cent:

> Even at present it is in Ireland at 6%, and in the West Indies at 8%; and in Hindistan, where there is no rate limited by law, the lowest customary rate is 10% or 12%. At Constantinople, in certain cases, as I have been well informed, 30% is a common rate. Now, of all

43

these widely differed rates, what one is there, that is intrinsically better than another?

He argued that if a man was of sane mind, and not a minor, or under duress, or a habitual drunkard (for all of which cases the law provided relief), he must know better than the legislature whether it would be to his advantage to borrow, at whatever rate he chose. In many commercial activities one man obtains a bargain at the expense of another, but it was only when money was the commodity involved that the church and state legislators thought they should intervene:

I question whether there ever was an instance that . . . a bargain was rescinded, merely because a man has sold too cheap, or bought too dear. Were I to take a fancy to give a hundred years' purchase instead of thirty, for a piece of land, rather than not have it, I don't think there is any court in England, or indeed any where else, that would interpose to hinder me . . . But in the case of borrowing money, it is the borrower always . . . who is on the safe side; any imprudence he may have committed with regard to the rate of interest, may be corrected at any time. Yet if I find I have given too high an interest to one man, I have no more to do than to borrow of another at a lower rate, and pay off the first. If I cannot find any body to lend me at a lower, there cannot be more certain proof that the first was not in reality too high.

Legislative restraints, it was contended, were not only useless, but pernicious, and worsened matters.

There was still considerable opposition to this view, and the contrary argument was well expressed by Richard Preston, a barrister Member of Parliament, who raised points which will be particularly relevant when we come to consider Sam's career. One of his concerns was that the removal of the usury laws would be ruinous to landed property:

All experience has proved that usury is committed by men of the most rapacious character; men who have no feeling for the distresses of others; and the law seems, by its policy, to have endeavoured to guard men against their own folly in borrowing money. It seems more particularly to have contemplated the situation of young men; just entering into life, the sons of men of large property, having expectancies; and also of men given to speculation by way of gambling, or to live in extravagance, beyond their means . . . Men of this description will borrow money on any terms; content to gratify the moment, without looking to the consequences. It would be very easy to recount instances drawn from actual practice, in which persons of this description have spent the whole value of their life estates, or of their expectancies, in the short period of three or four years . . . The mischief does not end with their ruin; it frequently implicates the whole family . . .

He was particularly concerned with the disparity of experience between the moneylender and the borrower:

It will also readily occur that the bargains of the most severity, respecting the rate of interest of money, will be negotiated on the one part by young men, extravagant tenants for life, or by persons having expectancies on the death of relations; and on the other part, with men whose system is that of rapacity . . . and when once a man . . . becomes liable to pay a high rate of interest of money it rarely ever happens that he extricates himself, but he goes on from year to year increasing the amount of his debts, and consequently the amount of his interest . . . in general, the party becomes a prey to those who dupe him of his expectations.

Preston was here touching upon the very complaints which were to be made against Sam. It was said, by Sir George Lewis in particular, that Sam was on the lookout for exactly such renegade youngsters, and that he was rapacious. There can be no doubt that some of Sam's clients fitted Preston's description exactly, but whether Sam was rapacious will be a matter for investigation.

Despite the opposition, the arguments in favour of permitting moneylenders to operate freely eventually won the day. A Select Committee of the House of Commons of 1818 recommended the immediate and total repeal of the usury laws, but it was not until 1854 that all such laws were repealed, and that remained the position until 1900. The Act of 1854 gave moneylenders a new freedom. Not only would they not be penalised if they charged high rates of interest, but the law would help to enforce their charges. If, therefore, you had decided to earn your living as a moneylender, and wished to engage in your profession untrammelled by legal restraints, the best period to have done so was between 1854 and 1900. Sam was able to engage in his calling free of any legislative limitations. Once again, the time and place were right.

As might have been expected, some moneylenders abused this new freedom, and in particular took unfair advantage of the growing class of small and often ignorant borrowers. Many harrowing stories were to unfold of the harassment of debtors. In the last quarter of the nineteenth century some of the admitted evils of moneylending became rampant, and this raised acute social problems for many of the lower and middle classes. The legislature acted to curb the iniquities. Following another Select Committee of the House of Commons in 1897–8 the Moneylending Act of 1900 was passed. This gave the courts powers to alter the rate of interest under contracts whose terms were considered 'harsh and unconscionable', and introduced the requirement of registration of moneylenders under their real names. After a third parliamentary committee, which sat in 1924 and 1925, the Moneylending Act of 1927 was passed. It repealed the 1900 Act, but provided that in cases where the rate exceeded 48 per cent the burden of proof was placed on the moneylender to show that it was reasonable in the circumstances.

Evidence was produced before the Select Committees that a money-lender whose average rate was 60 per cent made no more than a reasonable return on his loans. For a time the general rule of thumb was that out of every £3,000 payable in gross interest to the money-lender, £1,000 went on expenses, £1,000 went on bad debts, and £1,000 was net profit. However, each year that passed brought with it an increase of expenses and a resultant drop in net profit. One or two particularly bad debts could extinguish a goodly proportion of any profit remaining. The moneylenders found it difficult to persuade the Committee members of this, but in one case subsequent to the 1900 Act a court accepted the argument that on its particular facts 160 per cent per annum was not excessive. To some extent, very little had changed.

The current legislation in England is the Consumer Credit Act of 1974. Parliament has reintroduced the power of the courts to reopen moneylending agreements in cases where the rate is 'extortionate', which in this context means the same as 'harsh and unconscionable'. A credit agreement, including simple moneylending, is considered extortionate if it requires a debtor or a debtor's relative to make payments which are grossly exorbitant or grossly contravene ordinary principles of fair dealing. So far as the debtor is concerned, regard is paid to his or her age, experience, business capacity and state of health, and the degree to which he or she is under pressure and the nature of that pressure. So far as the creditor is concerned, regard is paid to the degree of risk, taking account of the security provided, or the lack of it, and his or her relation to the debtor.

But the 1974 Act also appears to have had little or no effect on interest rates, and is rarely used. A survey reported in the *Observer* newspaper in August 1988 showed that the bank base interest rate was then 11 per cent, and the mortgage rate 11½ per cent; the most popular credit card companies charged 25 per cent and 27 per cent; the in-house credit card of a national chain of shops carried 39.9 per cent; secured loans were at rates between 20 and 45 per cent; and unsecured loans from 100 to 5,000 per cent. As we have seen, each and every one of the above is a rate which in the past carried severe penalties, both temporal and spiritual. Some are in excess of the rates charged by the most important Victorian moneylenders for which they, Sam included, were heavily criticised and indeed despised and publicly berated. One can imagine the reaction of a modern High Street bank manager, arranging a personal loan for a customer at, say, 25 per cent, on being told that for this his soul would be damned for ever.

5 · The new moneylenders

What are the great bankers and financiers who are so
honoured by emperors, kings, and minor potentates,
else than moneylenders on a grand scale?
Letter to *Jewish Chronicle*, 31 May 1905

Between 1290, when the Jews were expelled from England, and 1656, when they returned, the whole concept of banking and moneylending had changed, and a more sophisticated system was emerging. The network of trading fairs in northern Europe at which the produce of the cloth industries of Flanders and France was sold came, over a period of time, to be used for the international settlement of debts. Italian merchants accepted credits at one fair and honoured them at another, and gradually grew into banking firms, operating from their home bases through overseas agents. In the early fourteenth century, for example, the city of Florence was in the forefront of public banking, and its Bardi banking house had more than 350 staff, with branches in London, Bruges, Spain, North Africa and the Levant. Though European trade and commerce were in the doldrums for most of the fourteenth and fifteenth centuries, the sixteenth century saw population growth and increased demand for coinage and bullion, both of which were in short supply. The Italian banks helped to fill the gap. The market fairs continued to flourish until they gave way to permanent institutions. Antwerp (1531) was followed by London in 1570, in which year Queen Elizabeth I opened the Royal Exchange in Cornhill as a meeting place for merchants, an early forerunner of the stock exchange.

The seventeenth century brought the issuing of cheques and the creation of state banks, the Bank of Sweden (1668) being the first. The Bank of England was founded by a Scotsman, William Patterson, in 1694. Some of the earliest banks in England first saw the light of day in the seventeenth century. Hoare's was founded 'at the sign of *The*

48

Golden Bottle' in 1673; Coutts' in 1692; and Child & Co. in 1693. By the end of the eighteenth century London had no fewer than 70 private banks. Martin's (1712) and Glyn's (1753) served the merchants in the City; Coutts', Child's, and Drummond's (1717) were in the West End to serve the aristocracy and the politicians in Westminster; and all the while the bankers were improving their techniques and expanding the area in which they provided their services.

Nations still required privately raised loans, and these were the province of the investment bankers, 'the mighty loan-mongers, on whose fiat the fate of kings and empires sometimes depends', as Disraeli described them. Pre-eminent among them were the Rothschilds whose London branch was established by Nathan Mayer Rothschild in 1804, and who maintained a perfectly distinct position of their own, despite fierce competition from such as the Barings, Hopes, Hambros, Kleinworts and Schroders. During the nineteenth century these merchant bankers were disproportionately Jewish, especially at the topmost levels, but there was no Jewish syndicate and they acted quite independently of each other.

Stockholder banks became a common feature in the first half of the nineteenth century and, most importantly, deposit lending arrived. Bankers borrowed from depositors and loaned out again, and this sounded the death knell of the old-style moneylender. The man who could loan only his own capital was at an obvious disadvantage when trying to compete with a banker who made loans out of his customers' deposits. Such a man could neither command adequate capital to finance large undertakings, nor could he do so as cheaply. The outcome was that loans which were left to him were comparative scraps from the banker's plate, either small loans or loans for which there was no adequate security to satisfy the banker. Thus the need for the sole trading moneylender no longer existed to the same degree. There was even less reason for Jews to become moneylenders, as the commercial restraints upon the types of occupation they could undertake were gradually lifted during the eighteenth and the first half of the nineteenth century, though not without a great struggle on the part of the Jewish community. The more prosperous engaged in wholesale commerce, brokerage, stock jobbing and trade in precious stones. There was a middle class of shopkeepers, silversmiths and watchmakers, and lower down on the social scale came pencilmakers, tailors, hatters, embroiderers, glass engravers, diamond polishers, traders in old clothes and, as we have seen, pedlars. That does not mean that there were no Jewish moneylenders, but it was no longer one of the primary Jewish occupations.

None the less, those Jews who did conduct a moneylending business seriously worried the Jewish community, who preferred that there should be none. In September 1883 this concern was well expressed in an editorial in the *Jewish Chronicle* (founded in 1841 and today the oldest extant Jewish newspaper in the world):

> But there are in England further reasons why usury is particularly unjustifiable on the part of an English Jew. By remaining or becoming a moneylender he is of his own act carrying on the Middle Ages and all their memories into the present day. And he is not alone doing this for himself, but he is preventing the community in general from rising out of the medieval trammels. He does this in two ways: he fails to rise himself, and brings upon the community the discredit of not rising. For the odium and hatred which he cannot help raising against himself, is transferred, in the case of Jews only, to the community of which he is often only nominally a member. Nay, even when he may have long ceased to be a Jew, all his discredited actions are quoted as typically Jewish.

After the abolition of the usury laws in 1854 there were four types of moneylender operating, two of whom had no money to lend. The first of these was the man who had no intention of making a loan, and who made his living out of charging preliminary fees. He advertised widely in the press, offering large loans without security, but first required a preliminary fee from the borrower, to cover his alleged paper work and other expenses, perhaps anything from half a guinea to three guineas. He then posed a series of questions which no one who needed such a loan could possibly answer satisfactorily, and thereupon rejected the application and kept the preliminary fee. It was outright fraud, but very difficult to prosecute if the criminal made even the occasional loan. Such forms of fraud have existed over the centuries, and still continue today in various guises and degrees of subtlety. The second type of moneyless moneylenders were men who purported to be moneylenders, and advertised themselves as such, but were in fact agents or touts for the genuine moneylenders. They earned their living by the commissions they obtained from introductions.

The third class were those who made small loans, up to about £300, to such as farmers, clergymen, servicemen, and government and local authority employees. Most were perfectly honest and ran a straightforward business but, because of the lack of security, charged an admittedly high rate of interest – usually between 40 and 60 per cent. They were fair and reasonable towards those of their clients who encountered difficulties in keeping up with their repayments. But there were also among them a minority who were devious, vicious, mean and in some cases completely merciless and even brutal when there was a default. These latter advertised widely in the London, provincial and religious press; made misleading statements as to their rates of interest, often implying a rate of five per cent per annum when it was five per cent per month; usually operated under names other than their own, often several different names in different locations, or gave themselves a title suggesting that they were not individuals but large established banks; and they engaged in all manner of underhand methods to hound their victims and squeeze them dry. They obtained signatures to documents which were not what they led the borrower to think they were, for example presenting a bill of sale over the goods of the borrower, who signed believing the document was simply a receipt for the money he had received. They used ruses to obtain court judgments by ensuring that the borrower had no real opportunity of even knowing about the action, or alternatively telling him that he need not do anything until the hearing, and then signing the judgment when no defence was filed. In the usual moneylending agreement the total interest payable over the whole period of the loan became immediately payable upon a single default. The mere threat of proceedings was often sufficient to persuade the borrower to enter into a fresh agreement in which the whole of the amount originally advanced, plus the whole of the interest, was capitalised, and interest then continued to be charged upon the new total. In this way the original debt could double and treble within just a few months. Only too often a County Court judge before whom the matter might come could do nothing but give judgment for the moneylender, because he came armed with *prima facie* legally binding documents, signed by the borrower. As one judge put it, 'It is frightful that men should be living amongst us doing this kind of work. It makes one's blood boil.' It was the unscrupulous behaviour of this type of moneylender which led to the establishment of the Select Committee of the House of Commons in 1897 to look into the abuse; this Committee, the witnesses called before it and the evidence they gave will be dealt with later.

The fourth class of moneylender was known as the 'West End Usurer'. Small in number, confined almost exclusively to London, they did business largely with society, with heirs to large estates not yet in possession of their inheritance and others who had expectations which might or might not come to fruition. Their loans could range from £50 to £25,000 or, in the exceptional case of the most successful moneylenders, even higher. Some of these private loans were the present-day equivalent of a million pounds or more.

There was also a hidden sub-class of moneylender. A solvent aristocrat or successful trader, jealous at the profits he saw money-lenders engendering, who wanted to engage in the trade but who did not wish his involvement to be known, secretly supplied funds for the moneylender's use. The normal arrangement made was that the provider of the funds and the 'front' man each received half the profit; the front man sometimes shared his portion with a tout or 'jackal' who brought in the business. It was the aristocrat or trader who was truly the usurer, but the front man accepted the infamy and, most importantly, held his tongue.

Apart from the preliminary fee fraudsmen, who were totally evil, there were good and bad among the other moneylenders as there are in all walks of life. The problem for the good, however high-minded and charitable they were in their business and private lives, was that they were almost invariably tarred with the brush of the bad.

6 · Sam in Cork Street

When Sam arrived in London he continued for a time in business as a jeweller. Inevitably he came into contact with the moneylending fraternity, because so many of them sold jewellery as a means of increasing their profit and decreasing their risk. If, for example, the retail price of a diamond ring was £50, the moneylender could probably purchase it for £25, or manufacture it himself for even less. A young man with expectations, but no money, might wish to buy a present for a girl friend and have sufficient cash to entertain her. He could borrow £100 from the moneylender, and part of the deal would be the purchase of the ring for £40, £10 cheaper than it could be bought in a shop. The moneylender would thereupon advance only the £60 balance in cash, and this, with the £25 the ring had cost him, meant that he had only £85 out on risk instead of £100; so both he and his customer obtained an advantage. Such moneylenders would have been customers of Sam in his capacity as a jeweller. He decided to join their ranks.

Sam had to choose which class of moneylender he would be. The preliminary fee men never became rich; they were fraudsmen operating on too small a scale for that. The agents earned only a moderate living, though some went on to become moneylenders. Those of the small-loan moneylenders who ran a reputable business could certainly attain a decent standard of living for themselves. But it was the moneylender who advanced the largest loans to the aristocratic borrower, and who took the highest risks, who could increase his capital most rapidly. Sam chose the aristocracy as his target clientele. It was a particularly difficult section of the business in which to succeed, and it required special qualities. His career had already shown that he was possessed of enterprise, determined will, good nature and pleasant manners. This work additionally called for a combination of confidence, ability, detailed research into the borrowers' backgrounds, a deep understanding of their minds and a close knowledge of their means, foibles, interests and weaknesses. Essential equipment included a gambling instinct and the capacity to speak on equal terms with those born into a higher class and maintain a friendly relationship to smooth over the inevitable rough passages when the client did not honour his commitments. It also required the aptitude to judge accurately whether a client's failure to pay was a deliberate attempt to avoid a liability freely undertaken, or whether the default was occasioned by a temporary setback in the client's finances which, when overcome, would lead to full repayment of the debt. When Sam concluded it was the latter, then he was considerate, and freely extended the time for repayment, and indeed he went further. If he thought that the debtor, through unfortunate, unforeseen and unforeseeable circumstances, was unlikely to be in a position to repay, or could do so only at the expense of great distress to himself or others, then he was ready to forgo the whole or part of the amount due. But where Sam concluded there was a deliberate evasion on the part of the borrower he was relentless in his pursuit of his rights under the contract, and was prepared, if necessary, to use the courts to the full extent.

The West End moneylenders whose principal clientele were the scions of Society congregated around Old Bond Street and its environs. Their offices were mainly to be found within a half mile west of Piccadilly Circus. In 1869 Sam acquired premises in Cork Street which runs parallel to and is sandwiched between Old Bond Street and Savile Row. It was then secluded and tree-lined, having been developed by the third earl of Burlington and Cork in the 1720s and 1730s, and contained fine houses. At the end of the century its character changed: the aristocratic residents moved out, the doctors moved in, and nearly every house became the home of an eminent physician. Later, from about 1845, the doctors drifted away to Harley Street, and by the time Sam arrived the main occupants were tailors. He took over No. 17 from Truefitt, the men's hairdressers who today operate just around the corner in Old Bond Street.

Sam was Cork Street's sole moneylender or, as he was listed in the *Post Office Directory* of 1870, 'financial agent'. This description would appear to be the reverse of the true position; far from being an agent he was a principal. He had sufficient capital to set up on his own account, either from his own savings, or from any *nedunya* (dowry) he might have received on his marriage, or possibly his father-in-law backed him in the initial stages. David Davis was not a wealthy man, certainly not according to the size of his estate at the date of his death, but he had always lived in some comfort in desirable districts and residences, ending his days in a substantial home in what is now the fashionable 'Little Venice' district of London. It is certainly possible that he supported Sam in some way.

What was crucial to Sam's success was that he obtained access to a further resource which other moneylenders could not acquire directly. Normally moneylenders were unable to obtain loan facilities from banks, which did not consider their custom to be desirable, not even if adequate security was offered. Most banks feared that the poor reputation of moneylenders among the general public might attach to themselves if they were seen to be associated in any way. Money-lenders therefore could not rely on the banks to help them to expand their capital base; but Sam was different, very, very different. The Bank of England, no less – the leader, the very bastion of sobriety and accepted distinction in the banking world – afforded him the most generous of facilities. He opened an account with their Burlington Gardens branch, just two minutes' walk from his office, in November 1871. It was a remarkable testament to his growing reputation that he should have been accepted so early in his career. From the outset, the manager of the branch was writing approving letters referring to the 'fair account' Sam kept there, and was urging the deputy governor of the Bank, under whose direct supervision the account was run, to allow him to advance moneys to Sam to the full extent of the securities deposited, and even beyond. For a considerable time these loans were well in excess of £100,000, and at the most favourable rates of interest. They enabled his business to accelerate at a phenomenal pace. Sam's bank ledgers show that his bankings increased from just over £100,000 in 1872 to more than £1,000,000 in 1894, and all the while his personal wealth, his investments in stocks and shares, was steadily increasing.

When the account was first opened, Samuel Lewis was described in the ledger as a jeweller, and this description was never altered, even though the Bank well knew his true profession. They shared many of the secrets of his business, because the cheques he issued revealed to them the names of his borrowers, names which would have astonished many in society had they become publicly known. Why the Bank favoured Sam alone is a matter for conjecture. Certainly he stood out from the others in his probity and reliability. The Bank knew from the manner in which he conducted the account that his business was sound, and his acumen great. The names of those he dealt with, and the families to which they belonged, were comforting guarantees of eventual repayment of his loans to them, and the Bank recognised that in Sam they had a client who was responsible and respectable, and likely to bring them good profits.

However, it was not only Sam who benefited from the Bank's loans. There was a great deal of cooperation and mutual dealing between the West End moneylenders. If one of them had a business opportunity, but not the readily available moneys to fund it, the moneylender would approach a colleague who was in funds. During the early years of Sam's practice, particularly during the first five or six years, he became known by his colleagues as the person who could help in this way. Sam used some of the facility provided by the Bank of England, at three, four, and five per cent, to take a share in deals which were earning up to 60 per cent. It can be said with confidence that the Bank of England funded not only Sam but a fair proportion of the most important West End moneylenders; and since they saw the names of well-known practitioners of the art on the cheques he issued, the Bank could not have been ignorant of what was happening.

Sam was well aware of the severe risks involved in this type of business, for heirs of the landed gentry were particularly protected by the law; but these could be overcome if the lender knew as much about his clients' affairs as they knew themselves. How could this be achieved? How could Sam come close enough to those in Society, his prospective clients, to learn about them?

He planned his strategy with care; laid out for himself four clearly defined objectives; and then set out to accomplish them one by one. Clients were the first essential. He never encountered any difficulty in attracting clients. For reasons which will be examined there was always a steady supply of willing borrowers available from among the aristocracy, and his clientele was to range from the innocent striplings to some of the most distinguished and respected figures in society. He also recognised the necessity for building up a reputation for being for being straightforward and fair in dealing with men who would not have come to him had they not been in difficulties. This came naturally to him, for he was an honest man. Shrewd, and cunning too, perhaps, but fundamentally very honest. Thirdly, he saw the need for living in the very midst of his prospective clientele, having the finest home he could afford in the finest district, and in this he succeeded three times over. Lastly, it was also a requirement that he should be able to move freely among his clients, sharing their leisure activities and interests, and patronising the same restaurants, theatres and shops as they.

All this was a daunting task for a Victorian Jew who had been born in poverty. It would have been a daunting task for any moneylender. For a Jewish moneylender it was doubly difficult; but within just a few years Sam had achieved all his aims.

Society imposed strict restraints; fences were erected to keep out interlopers, those who did not fit in. A Jewish moneylender would have been almost at the very top of the prohibited list. And yet Sam and Ada succeeded in passing through the barriers, something which could not have been achieved even 20 or 30 years earlier had it not been that he was assisted in his task by the attitude and influence of the Prince of Wales, later Edward VII. To the social aspirant noble birth was important, but wealth no less so. Whenever English aristocracy faced a financial crisis it refuelled itself in time, and thus retained its social sway, by permitting entry to its circle of those with money, whatever their origins. Edward encouraged this trend.

Queen Victoria was the constitutional monarch, but after the death of her beloved Albert she largely retired from social activities, and to fill the vacuum the Prince of Wales became the unchallenged king of the social scene. He saw no reason for depriving himself of vivacious companions merely because they lacked social credentials. At first his friendships were inclined towards the more raffish members of the titled classes, men such as Lord Charles Beresford, Lord Aylesford and Lord Randolph Churchill (the first two certainly, and the third possibly, clients of Sam), but later his fancy was directed towards the wealthy, whether their background was aristocractic, industrial or commercial. Those he favoured passed through the entrance door to Society. His approval was so vital that T. H. S. Escott, the editor of the *Fortnightly Review* and prolific writer on the social scene, defined

Society as the social area of which the Prince of Wales was personally cognisant, within the limits of which he visited, and every member of which was to some extent in touch with his ideas and wishes. To some of the old guard Edward was considered an 'utterly commonplace person' through whom 'the new vulgarians, those loud, extremely rich men for whom the Prince had an abiding taste', made their way into Society.

Those who wished nothing to change still observed the old rules of social behaviour. The novelist Elinor Glyn, having entered Society through marriage in 1890, was coached by Lady Warwick. She was taught that army or naval officers, diplomats or clergymen, might be invited to lunch or dinner; the vicar to Sunday lunch, or supper if he was a gentleman; doctors and solicitors to garden parties, 'though never of course to lunch or dinner'. Anyone engaged in the arts, the stage, trade or commerce, no matter how well connected, could not be asked to the house at all. But the prince broke this strict social pattern, and even a mere solicitor such as Sir George Lewis was invited to Sandringham. Miss Winifred Sturt, later Lady Hardinge, told her fiancé that while staying there as a guest she could hardly believe her eyes when she discovered Lewis was in the party. But there was absolutely nothing the old guard could do about it, and self-made men became fashionable and respectable within the prince's circle.

It has been said that the prince did not especially care whether a man's ancestors came over with the Normans, or whether he had begun his career as a Hamburg bank clerk, provided he deserved attention as a person, and particularly if he amused or informed the prince. Not only did the prince not object to the plutocracy, he showed a positive predilection for them. He enjoyed their company, their talk of worldwide commercial operations, and their financial advice which, according to some, occasionally amounted to financial support. And if they happened to be Jewish, their religion was no bar. 'His Royal Highness', said Escott, 'regards the best class of Hebrews with conspicuous favour.' Lady Paget noted that he was 'always surrounded by a bevy of Jews and a ring of racing people. He has the same luxurious taste as the Semites, the same love of pleasure and comfort.' But those to whom he opened Marlborough House could scarcely be snubbed and excluded by those who sought the privilege for themselves.

It was by this route that some Jews became members of the inner fraternity in the last quarter of the nineteenth century and joined those, such as the Rothschilds and the Sassoons, who had been members of the Marlborough House set almost from its inception. Two of the prince's closest friends were Jews. Baron de Hirsch, the main source of whose wealth came from financing railway development in the Balkans and Turkey, and who was richer even than the Rothschilds, was host to the prince at his estate in Hungary. When he was in turn warmly welcomed by the prince in England during the Season of 1887 obedient hostesses followed suit, albeit somewhat reluctantly. It was Hirsch who introduced Ernest Cassel to the prince, the beginning of the most intimate masculine friendship of the prince's life. Cassel was born in Cologne in 1852 into a comparatively insignificant Jewish family, and left a commercial school at 14 years of age to become a bank clerk. He arrived in Liverpool when he was 17, with just his clothes and a violin, and worked in a local bank for a year before being sent to its Paris branch. In 1870 he returned to England and joined the London merchant bank of Bischoffsheim and Goldschmidt. (He arrived in London at about the same time as Sam, and they were later to have at least one point of contact – they became neighbours in their Grosvenor Square mansions.) Cassel showed great flair, and by the age of 22 he was manager, and earning what at that time was an unheard-of salary for someone so young, £5,000 a year. He travelled the world acting as a 'company doctor', rescuing some of his employer's ailing subsidiaries. He also dealt on his own account, and when he married in 1878 was able to set aside capital of £150,000. After the death in 1881 of his wife, a Catholic, he devoted his life to international finance, to his daughter Maud (her daughter, Edwina, became Lady Mountbatten), to charitable work (he gave away at least two million pounds), and to his entry into high society.

Cassel's cosmopolitan character was in harmony with Edward's needs, and their friendship was genuine. So close was their relationship that he was known as 'Windsor Cassel'. When Edward went to see Oscar Wilde's play, *The Importance of Being Earnest*, and asked the Marquis de Soveral, the Portuguese minister in London who had become a court favourite, whether he had seen it, the reply was 'No Sir, but I have seen the importance of being Ernest Cassel.' Cassel took over from Hirsch the role of principal financial adviser to the prince, and remained so when Edward succeeded to the throne. He, together with Lord Esher, Lord Farquhar and Sir Dighton Probyn (all four of whom were to become closely acquainted with Sam and Ada), successfully masterminded the administration of the king's investments. Perversely, Lord Esher, while putting the king's finances in order, was unable to control his own. He became a regular and long-time client of Sam's.

The success of the likes of the Rothschilds, the Sassoons, Hirsch, Cassel, Louis Bischoffsheim and other Jews in gaining admission into the highest circles of Society, and the open attitude towards them of the prince, influenced others, and percolated through until it reached the level on which Sam operated. Though Sam found several of his clients among the prince's closest associates and advisers, Sam himself was not part of the emerging fusion between the landed aristocrats and the new industrialists. His profession precluded this. He was with them, but not quite of them. He lived in their midst, joined in some of their pastimes, was comfortable when with them in the gambling clubs, in the restaurants, at the races, and even taking part in the daily parade in Hyde Park, perhaps the most important social event of the day. But he could not aspire to honours or complete acceptance, though he could help make Ada acceptable, as was to prove the case after his death.

Miss Sturt was surprised to find Sir George Lewis at Sandringham; she would have been mortified to see Sam or Ada there. None the less the attitude of the prince facilitated Sam and Ada's acceptance within circles which otherwise might have been closed to them. If Sam and Ada had been born 30 years earlier the probability is that they could not have advanced as far into Society as they did.

With this advantage, and with the aid of *Burke* and *Debrett*, by keeping an ear close to the ground and picking up the current Society gossip, by becoming a regular at the racecourse, the theatre, the hotel or restaurant dining-room, and in the more raffish clubs which were open to every decently dressed customer with a sufficiently well-lined purse, and by taking an interest in politics, Sam was at least as well-informed as the leading Society hostesses. In this Ada was of great assistance, for she became an accepted figure in her own right among important sections of Society and was a valuable source of information as to what was happening in the social world.

According to the *Daily Telegraph*, Sam's clients became his friends, and were frequent visitors to his town house. On first nights, at race meetings, 'and even at certain *semi-official* functions' – perhaps the utmost limit he could reach – Sam was 'always surrounded by the best men in a certain sense of the word'. He equipped himself with detailed information about his potential client's financial status and that of his family, and so could gauge accurately the risk he would be running in making an advance. He made a remarkable impact on the profession in a short space of time. Very soon he was regarded as its major player and unrivalled leader, and his success must be partly attributed to the personal qualities which brought him from the slums of Birmingham to its surrounding districts as a pedlar and now to an office in Mayfair. Within ten years his fortune grew to the extent that in today's terms he was a sterling millionaire several times over.

Sam's mother did not live to see his full worldly success. She stayed on at Vyse Street until her death in 1871 at the age of 66. She was described in the death certificate as 'an annuitant' and the wife, not the widow, of Frederick Lewis. Sam inserted a notice of her death in the *Jewish Chronicle*: 'On Wednesday the 17th of January at 104 Vyse Street, Birmingham, beloved mother of Samuel Lewis of the above address and 113 Gower Street, Bedford Square, London.' Given his fondness for her, and his synagogue attendance, he probably observed the period of *shivvah*, the seven days' mourning following burial. During this period all ordinary work is prohibited, the mourners sit unshod on low stools, and visits by friends are made to the mourners' home for prayers and condolence.

Sam Lewis was the first man to come to mind when a large loan was being sought. The disadvantage this brought with it was that he became a main target of those who were outraged by what they considered the evil effects of the repeal of the Usury Acts, which they believed had led to an increase in gambling and crime. One man in particular, Sir George Lewis, believed Sam to be the greatest menace in the country, and stalked him for the whole of his moneylending career, relentless in his pursuit as the hounds on the fox; but Sam was to prove a wily fox.

Cork Street occupied a strategic position, being close to the clubs and restaurants popular with the men-about-town, prospective clients all. Sam would never have been invited as a guest at the clubs in St

James's, such as Boodle's or White's, but would be welcome in The Field in Park Place, where illegal gambling took place, or at The Pelican, a sporting club in Gerrard Street in Soho, where the fourth earl of Lonsdale was a regular, and the Prince of Wales an occasional visitor. The restaurants which were then 'favoured by those who had more money than sense were Limner's in St George Street, the Bristol in Berkeley Street, Simpson's and Romano's in the Strand, the Blue Post in Cork Street and Long's Hotel in Bond Street, the favourite resort of racing men. They also patronised a number of chop houses and foreign restaurants around Leicester Square. All were within easy reach of his business and his home.

At each of these venues were to be found young men of good family who had either inherited a fortune or had expectations of doing so. There they were surrounded by men determined to acquire part of their fortunes. Nothing more or less than confidence tricksters, using excessive flattery of their victims as their weapon, they included among their numbers 'professional gamblers of unsavoury reputations, ex-jockeys who had been warned off, boxers who preferred to act as hired bodyguards, and older men of experience who sought to pick them clean by selling them horses, introducing them to women or dubious clubs, or involving them in heavy drinking'. Some of the victims, without present funds but with great expectations, were introduced to moneylenders to engender an income which their 'friends' then sought to share.

So Sam was well placed and well prepared to embark on his profession. The moneylenders who acted solely as agents were happy to refer business to him. He was meticulously prompt in paying business debts, looked after his agents well, and from the beginning set the standards he was to follow throughout his career. His rates were no lower than the next man's – he generally sought the maximum he could achieve – but he was scrupulously open with the prospective borrower. If he thought a man had sufficient security to obtain a loan at a lower rate from a banker, or from his trustees, he would advise him to do so. Once a client had indicated he wished to proceed with Sam, then the terms were clearly set out and carefully explained, the loan quickly and informally agreed, and the money immediately forthcoming. This pleased both the client and the agent who had introduced him, making the agent keen to pass on further business. Sam never found it necessary to advertise. His clientele increased solely by word of mouth recommendation.

He was able and willing to make quick decisions. He employed a legal clerk on the premises who would prepare the necessary papers while the client enjoyed a cigar, and within half an hour of entering the office the borrower could walk away with a cheque for thousands of pounds. Speed of payment, together with secrecy, was a facility borrowers treasured above all; their needs and desires almost always required urgent attention. Further, his solicitor, Algernon Edward Sydney, was on call at short notice to deal with any particularly difficult legal point which might arise.

Sydney was four years older than Sam, and came from a family of lawyers. His father and two generations before him were solicitors, and two of his own sons followed him into the profession. His grandfather had been on the Board of Management of the New Synagogue, and his father was a warden there. His uncle, Professor David Woolf Marks, was the Chief Minister of the West London Reform Synagogue. Algernon followed in their communal footsteps. He too became a member of the Board of Management of the New, and was elected to the post of Overseer of the Poor. This stood him in good stead when, in 1859, he became the youngest founder member of the Board of Guardians for the Relief of the Jewish Poor, and their Honorary Solicitor, a position he held until his death in 1916. In 1870 he was one of the founders of the United Synagogue, and at its first meeting was elected Honorary Solicitor. Being also on the Council of the Anglo-Jewish Association meant that he was deeply immersed in every aspect of Jewish communal matters, and by his association with the Board of Guardians became well versed in the needs of the poor, Jewish or otherwise. Apart from his professional skills his outstanding attribute was sound common sense. He never rushed at a decision. Caution was his watchword, and he was very rarely tripped. Though not vain, he did boast of being a practical man who could see through any amount of verbiage. Sam, who was blunt and to the point, who dealt with matters in a concise and decisive way, appreciated these qualities. They became firm friends as well as business colleagues.

Sam was a true professional, and Ernest Benzon, one of his grateful clients, gave a revealing description of his methods – and also, incidentally, of the mentality of the borrower. Benzon was to inherit

63

a quarter of a million pounds when he reached the age of 21, but until then was kept on such a tight rein by his guardians that he resorted to borrowing on his expectancy. Horse racing, billiards, women and general high living accounted for his downfall, which was easy to predict. R. D. Blumenfeld, originally a journalist with the *New York Herald* who was to become the editor of the *Daily Express*, entered in his diary for 27 June 1887:

> Had the extreme felicity today of meeting a youth who is fast becoming world famous, young Mr. Benzon 'The Jubilee Plunger'. He has just reached his 21st year and has come into a fortune said to be £300,000, presumably all in cash, for he is throwing it about recklessly. At this rate it will not last many years. He is a decent youngster, with no experience and not much brain, and he seems to want to cut a dash – racing, four-in-hand, late suppers, cards and so on. Consequently he is always surrounded by a gang of harpies who are having a profitable season.

He lost £10,000 at billiards in a night's play at Long's Hotel and £16,000 playing cards at the Field Club. When his inheritance fell due one of his very first acts was to go to Coutts, the bankers to royalty who held his securities, and borrow £50,000. 'Of this sum I paid £33,600 to Mr. Sam Lewis for money obtained for me before I came of age. I have no desire to complain of the treatment I received from the lender; upon the contrary, I think he used me exceedingly well and always has been a great friend to me.' However, Benzon did complain bitterly about his guardians. They, he felt, had neglected their duty to him in that they had given him no training or education in the proper way to handle his inheritance. His autobiography, published in 1889 in the hope of recouping some of his fortune, was sadly entitled *How I Lost £250,000 in Two Years*. One of those of whom Benzon spoke kindly was Sir George Chetwynd 'who has certainly been all through the greatest friend to me that I ever had. If I had listened to him I should have had the greater part of £250,000 now, instead of being without it.' In this instance Benzon was not the best judge of character. Though rich to all outward appearances, Chetwynd was in fact constantly in debt to Sam, and far from being as knowledgeable about horses as people imagined, he was a losing gambler. Furthermore, there is every reason to think that he acted as a tout for Sam, and steered likely borrowers to him. We shall meet up with Sir George again.

Once he had run through his money in record time, young Benzon was to learn one of life's hard lessons:

> The worry of feeling the want of money was not the most unpleasant thing I had to encounter. Many men who had only a few weeks before ostensibly been my warmest friends, and who, if professions are to be taken as being worth anything at all, were always prepared to do anything for me, began to drop away from me. And it was indeed painful in the extreme to go into the various racing enclosures and see men, who within a short space of time had been my guests, and who had expressed the most cordial feelings of admiration for me, turn their backs on me, and to all intents and purposes cut me.

According to his testimony, 90 per cent of 'the men who are best known about town' – presumably he meant men best known in the circles in which he moved – had resorted to borrowing. He warned them against going to the family solicitor for a loan, particularly if they wanted money quickly, as so many of them did. Although the rate of interest would nominally be six or eight per cent it would have to be on good security, and the solicitor's charges would effectively add another 25 per cent to that. Not only were their costs outrageous, he said, but they delayed completion on the merest of trifles and technicalities, were forever consulting counsel, and charged more on security than a banker would.

The bankers were not recommended either, because they would lend only a fraction of the value of the security, and were slow to move:

> How very different is the treatment a borrower receives from the professional money lender . . . he will let you have the money you want quickly enough, and he does so without any of these little delays and petty quibblings that usually characterise the conduct of the man of law. At first sight a shilling a month for every pound one borrows seems plenty to pay for money and more specially so as the interest for three months is usually deducted from the

amount advanced, but in justice to the moneylender it must be remembered that all his transactions do not turn up trumps.

He explained that when they came of age some minors disclaimed liability for their debts, and others couldn't pay, so that the overall rate of interest the moneylender received was materially reduced.

As Benzon had considerable dealings with Sam it can be assumed that 1s per month per pound, 60 per cent, was Sam's rate in such circumstances. If the interest was deducted from the advance this increased the rate to more than 70 per cent per annum:

> Whatever their other failings might be, I can only say of the English usurers with whom I have had dealings, that they have upon the whole treated me fairly. I did not apply to them until I was in want of money, and they let me have it upon terms which, though high, were the only ones upon which it was to be had at all ...

Then, in a passage based on his experience, which reflected the arguments adduced by Jeremy Bentham nearly 100 years before – it was indeed almost a paraphrase of the passage already quoted above from Bentham's writing – he continued:

> Consequently both parties to the transaction got what they wanted – they their coveted interest, and I the ready money I was in want of. I cannot see, therefore, why outsiders should criticise such pieces of business in the way they so often do. They would not lend nine tenths of the men who go to the moneylenders a hundred pounds, or even part of it, upon the security the borrower has to offer. Why, then, blame the man who takes the risk for asking a high rate of interest? Of course, a large number of fellows who go to West End moneylenders come to grief soon afterwards, but it should be remembered that ninety per cent of those who do go broke, were to all intents and purposes on their last legs when they went to such sources for assistance. The usurer doubtless owes a great deal of his unpopularity to the fact that he is in at the financial death of so many victims, but this is generally owing to the fact that the distressed individual in question has mortgaged to the money-lender the last payment of his fortune, which no other capitalist

10 Grosvenor Square. Sam and Ada lived at no. 23 on the north-west corner of the Square from 1880. Ada moved to no. 16 after Sam's death

National Monuments Record

Drawn by W Westall A.R.A.

Engraved by Edwd Finden

Hulton

11 Brunswick Terrace, Brighton. Ada and Sam lived at no. 13

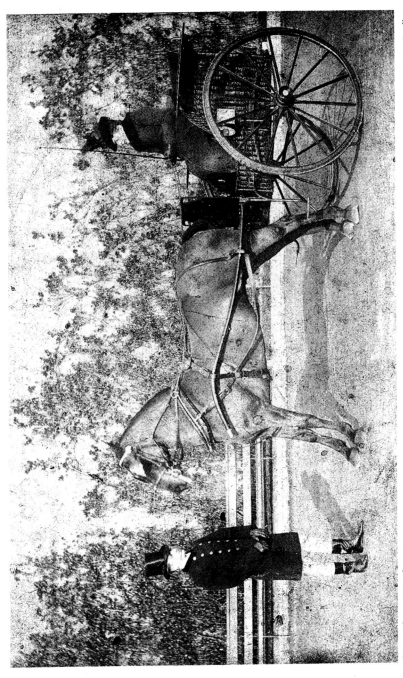

12   Ada at Brighton

Mrs J.B. Bradley

13 'Woodside', Maidenhead, near Boulter's Lock. Sam bought it from Lord William Nevill's sister, Lady Cowley, for £11,000 in 1895

R.A.C. Darmanin

14   Sir George Lewis, England's leading solicitor and Sam's greatest enemy

Hulton

15 Henry Labouchere,
Sir George's close friend, a
politician and investigative
journalist. At first criticised
Sam, but later came to admire
him   *Hulton*

16 The Prince of Wales, later
King Edward VII, in 1885.
Sam met him on the
racecourse and at the Pelican
Club   *Hulton*

17 The social scene in Hyde Park in the 1880s. Sam and Ada were part of the daily parade

18   Ascot on Gold Cup Day, 1882. Sam rarely missed a meeting

would accept as security. Rather reproach the fellow's friends who, to be consistent, should have lent him the money themselves upon the security at a lower rate.

To demonstrate that all moneylenders were not as black as they were painted, he told the story of a 'Welsh friend' who approached Sam:

'What can I do for you, Mr. "X"? asked the genial moneylender.
'I want to borrow some money.'
'How much do you want?'
'I want £500.' 'My dear fellow' said the moneylender 'do you take me for a pawnbroker? When you came along you said you were introduced by so-and-so, but I already knew all about you. When you are of age you will come into so much money. Your property is situated in a certain part of Wales, and is encumbered to the extent of so-and-so. *Moreover, I make it my business to know all about gentlemen and their affairs,* and when you came and said you wanted money I thought perhaps you wanted ten, fifteen or twenty thousand pounds; but when you ask me for such a bagatelle as £500, I have to say you really must be taking me for a pawnbroker.'

On the Welshman protesting that he wanted only £500, and there was no use his taking more than he wanted, and that he was prepared to give proper security, Sam said:

'Well, if you must have £500, here it is, but don't bother about security. Here you are (writing out a cheque and pushing it across the table). I don't, as a rule, lend money in dribs and drabs like this. You came to me, and you wanted £500. Here you are. I should have been much better pleased had it been £5,000.'
'But don't you want the security?'
'No, not a bit, when you come into your money you can pay me. I am very pleased in the meantime to have obliged you.'

Not a word was mentioned about interest. When he came of age the Welshman sent Sam a cheque for £1,000. Benzon added: 'In the meantime the reader may rest assured that the lender did not lose anything by advancing the money in this way, for the circumstances

67

were talked about all over the town.' Of course they were, doubtless exactly as Sam knew and intended they should. He had taken a calculated gamble. He obviously considered the borrower was an honourable person, as indeed the majority were, and even if he had defaulted, or died before reaching the age of 21, the resulting favourable publicity Sam had already gained was alone worth the £500. But, as the narrative shows, Sam had tried to encourage him to borrow more than he intended or needed.

A similar story was told by the Hon. George Lambton, fifth son of the second earl of Durham and younger brother of the third Earl of Durham. He described Sam as 'the best and straightest moneylender of all time'. Lambton decided at an early age that the turf would be the profession for him. His income from his family estates was less than £900 a year, and he soon realised that it would not go far to satisfy his passion for keeping race horses and a stud of hunters. The cost of keeping just one horse in training was a minimum of £300 a year. In consequence his visits to his family lawyers increased, and his capital and income steadily decreased, as he borrowed from them against the capital sum held in trust for him. Whenever he called at their office he was made to feel like a boy at school up before the headmaster, and so after one particularly disastrous week at the races at Manchester he found himself on Sam's doorstep in Cork Street the following Monday morning. By the time of his first call Sam was, according to Lambton, quite a personality in the fashionable world and already had an extensive business. He said he believed Sam was a man of minimum education who had started life in a small way. Little could he have guessed just how small a way that was, indeed how many of those who sat opposite Sam in his office could have envisaged Lower Hurst Street and the bailiffs?

Lambton described their first meeting:

When I was shown into his room I saw a little fat man with a bald head sitting at a desk smoking a big cigar. As I was proceeding to explain who I was he said, 'Never mind about that, I know all about you, young man; you have been betting very high and have got no money. I have been expecting you here for some time. What can I do for you?'

Here was the right sort of man for me. I no longer felt like a schoolboy, but was quite at my ease, so I did not beat about the bush but said, 'I want a thousand pounds this morning.' He asked me what security I had, to which I replied that I thought I had about £10,000 in the hands of my lawyer, giving his name. 'Well, why on earth don't you go to him and get the money instead of coming here?' was his question, so I frankly told him that I was really ashamed to show my face in the office. 'Don't be a fool,' said Lewis. 'Get into a cab, go to him at once, and you can get the money at five per cent'. But I was a fool, and an obstinate one, and eventually Sam wrote out a cheque for £1,000, and I signed a bill for three months: and so ended the first of many similar interviews between myself and Sam Lewis. But as I was going away his manner changed from that of the pleasant, easy-going man to the hard business one. 'Remember,' said he, 'I expect my bills to be met when they become due.' I walked out of his house treading upon air, thinking how splendid this was, that life would be quite simple, as I could get £1,000 as easily as picking a gooseberry off a bush.

This is a description of a first-rate moneylender practising his art.

Leon Poliakov, in *Jewish Bankers and the Holy See*, refers to an investigation carried out in 1950 by an institute of motivational research on behalf of an American loan company. In its report the institute said that moneylending differs from other commercial acts chiefly because of the borrower's feeling of embarrassment at the situation in which he finds himself, and his desire for secrecy. The investigators concluded that most borrowers had a 'guilt complex'. They advised the loan company that they could increase their business by putting their clients at ease; by treating them with discreet deference. Sam was doing just that, without the benefit of a doubtless expensive team of experts. He had made young Lambton feel at ease, and on at least an equal footing with himself. He had treated him as an adult; had brought the problem into the open and not dealt with it in a hushed voice as though it were a guilty secret; had indicated that the situation in which Lambton found himself was quite normal and frequent, and that he was doing the right and sensible thing by coming to him.

It is interesting that Lambton said Sam had started life in a small way. In London probably only Ada and Sydney knew his full story.

His manner must have betrayed something about his background, and one wonders whether his accent was revealing. Today a person born and bred in Birmingham is easily recognisable immediately he starts to speak, and if the accent was as strong then as it is now perhaps Sam never lost his.

Lambton added some further revealing comments about Sam:

> Sam had a merry, quick wit, and was a wonderful judge of character, and curious as it may seem, the majority of his clients were also his friends. Often when there was nothing to do in the afternoon we would say, 'Let's go and see old Sam,' and if he was not busy one would be certain to have an amusing half hour and hear all the news of the political, racing, and social world. He certainly was a great gossip, but when it was necessary he could be as silent as the grave, and I think he knew more secrets than any man in London.

Gossip was the currency of the times, one of Society's most sought-after commodities, and Sam had an immense store of it. Lambton had touched upon what was perhaps Sam's strongest characteristic, the ability to make friends of his clients at whatever level of life and achievement they had reached. He not only made young men such as Lambton feel good about coming to him, but he also accommodated such important and intelligent personages as the second Viscount Esher, the man considered to be a power behind the throne and the government, the adviser both to the monarch and to prime ministers; the twentieth earl of Shrewsbury, the premier earl of England; and Count Kinski, the handsome and talented son of a great Austrian landowner, who was Jennie Churchill's most ardent admirer – just three of the many who came to Cork Street.

In the following passage Lambton caught what was probably an accurate description of how Sam liked to think others saw him:

> His great pride was in being above all a man of his word, and when you dealt with him you knew exactly where you were. He naturally drove a hard bargain, otherwise he would not have been a successful moneylender, but in all his dealings he was as straight as a die, and he expected the same treatment from his clients. It was a bad day for anyone who tried the other game with Sam, for he could then be

a tiger. I could tell many stories of his good nature and kindness to men who were really down.

This view of Sam was later to be echoed by no less a personage than the Lord Chief Justice of England.

Lambton's memoirs were written many years after Sam's death and this was his measured appraisal of the man. He also considered that Sam changed the whole course of his life for the better. The time came when Lambton had run through all his available money. Lord Durham had helped until even his endurance of his younger brother's follies was exhausted, and after having saved him several times from his financial difficulties eventually decided that enough was enough. He arranged for Lambton to go to Canada and join their uncle, Lord Lansdowne, who was governor-general, while his financial affairs in England were settled, and there he hoped his brother could make an effort to lead a more useful life. On the afternoon of his departure for Liverpool to join the boat, Lambton was arrested and taken to Holloway Gaol at the instance of Sam, who was his principal creditor. He was released after 24 hours on giving his word that he would not leave England. Sam's action greatly surprised Lambton, who thought he had behaved badly, and it was not until two years later that Sam told him exactly what had happened:

> On hearing the rumour that I was being sent to Canada, he went to Marcus Beresford [Lord Marcus Beresford who acted as racing adviser to the Prince of Wales], who was a great friend of mine, and asked him if it was true, and also if I really wanted to go myself. Marcus said yes, I had to go, but that I hated the idea of leaving England, and that in his opinion I was quite unsuited to the life that I was intended to lead there, so Sam said, 'Well I shall stop him going, but it must be a secret between us two,' and until Sam told me himself, Marcus never breathed a word to me.

Marcus Beresford confirmed that Sam's account was accurate. Lambton overcame his financial problems and thereafter became the most respected, and successful, of the gentlemen trainers. An acknowledged first-rate judge of a horse, he became the twentieth earl of Derby's trainer in 1893. They established the most modern and lavish training establishment in Newmarket, and it became a dominant influence in racing. Lambton and the stables enjoyed unrivalled success for almost 40 years, and none of this might have happened had Sam not acted as he did.

Sam loved being involved in the personal intrigues and secret manoeuvrings of others, and became a trusted confidant of many. Margot Tennant, one of the shining young stars of the social scene, later to marry Herbert Asquith who served as prime minister from 1908 to 1916, had cause to be grateful to Sam, and tells the story in her autobiography. She had many admirers in her youth who fell for her looks, sparkling intelligence and madcap ways. One such was Peter Flower, Lord Battersea's son, a handsome horseman and boxer, with whom she had had an alliance for several years. He was yet another of the immature youths who fell into the gambling trap. 'Thoroughly inconsequent' about money, and consistently borrowing large sums from Sam over a period of ten years or more, he reached the point when he felt that his only chance of economising, and incidentally escaping from the physical presence of his creditors, was to sell his horses and go to India to shoot big game. But a writ followed him there from one pressing creditor (not Sam), and he was on the point of bankruptcy and, even worse, about to lose his membership of all his London clubs, when another friend of Margot, whom she coyly does not name, came to the rescue. He asked Sam to approach the creditor, come to terms with him, and pay him off, and when this was done he reimbursed Sam. It was only some time later that the friend told Margot, after making her swear on the Bible not to divulge the secret. She learned that the sum involved was £10,000, and asked her friend why he had paid the debt.

Margot: Is Peter Flower a friend of yours?
My Friend: I don't know him by sight, and have never spoken to him in my life, but he's the man you're in love with and that's enough for me ...

Surely greater love and sacrifice cannot be imagined! Some time later Peter Flower returned from India and proceeded to tell Margot how his debts had been paid by Sam through an unknown benefactor, and how he had begged Sam to reveal who it was, but that he had refused, having taken his oath never to reveal the name. Sam was reliable and discreet, and though many of his business transactions with the aristocracy of England became matters of common knowledge, and the subject of frequent speculation, such information and gossip never emanated from Sam.

For most who knew Sam, Lambton's description would have been considered accurate. A profile of him in *Town Topics* in June 1894 commented:

> There is no moneylender who has ever lived who is so popular, and, moreover, who is so much respected, as Mr. Lewis. He is a gentleman of refinement and education, and his clients say of him that he is just and liberal in his dealings. He is a millionaire and his fortune is of his own making – honourably and honestly made. No man about town can aver with truth that Mr. Lewis ever treated him shabbily, or even immoderately, while there are many poor devils who will talk with tears in their eyes of the many acts of thoughtful kindness. There is nothing of the moneylender of fiction about him, a spruce, well-dressed man, his house, his expenditure, his equipages, his whole life indeed, is one of generous and hearty expense, and his handsome wife does the honours of her beautiful home with the aid of the highest in the land. Money-lending has in these days ceased to be identified with cruelty and oppression. It's a business like any other financial undertaking, with its risks, and worries, and losses. And where should we all be, sometimes, but for men like dear Sam Lewis? Where indeed?

The remarkable thing about the article is not in what it said, and surely there was more than an element of exaggeration about it, but that it could be publicly printed at all without bringing howls of derision down upon the head of the author.

Despite the success of a few like Sam, moneylending was a precarious way to seek one's living, and for every moneylender who was successful several failed, often themselves appearing in the bankruptcy court. Not only were they left with the most risky lending, but even for that the competition was fierce. Further, not all borrowers were honest men down on their luck; many deliberately defected on their obligations, not because they were unable to repay, but because they had set out with, or subsequently acquired along the way, the intention of deceiving and defrauding the moneylender. Some moved address as soon as the loan was made; others falsely declared that they had security, which in the event proved not to belong to them; or denied the existence of other outstanding loans they had obtained; and yet others forged the signatures of guarantors. Some debtors, finding their backs against the wall, tried to avoid responsibility by making false accusations against the moneylender, claiming they had not understood the agreement, or that the signature upon it was not theirs. The reputation of the moneylenders in the eyes of the general public, and indeed of the courts, was so low that no allegation made against them was too outrageous to be believed. It was easy for a debtor's lawyer to attack the rate of interest charged by the money-lender and distract attention from his client's own shortcomings. One moneylender giving evidence to the 1897 House of Commons Select Committee on moneylending said:

> I lent a man £40 upon some horses and some sheep and some cows, and at the time he told me that he had only been in possession of that farm for one month. He did not pay me any money, and I took possession, and then I found that the horses and the sheep belonged to some other farmer in the neighbourhood, and the farmer came and gave his evidence to that effect, and instead of his having been in possession of the place for one month, he had been living there for some years and owed about two years' rent.
>
> And did you prosecute him? – I did.
>
> For false pretences? – Yes, and he was committed by the magis-trates.
>
> Then you were cross-examined? – I was.
>
> As to the interest you charged? – Yes.
>
> And did that get the acquittal of the prisoner? – Yes, and afterwards it was applauded in court.'

The activities of fraudulent borrowers, taken in conjunction with the losses sustained from clients who failed to pay for quite genuine reasons, made it inevitable that a high basic rate of interest had to be levied. One reputable moneylender who gave evidence to the 1897 Select Committee generally charged 60 per cent, and his books of account, which he produced for examination, showed clearly that his net return on the sums advanced was 11 per cent. He claimed that to charge much less than a basic 60 per cent would inevitably lead to a loss instead of a profit. Sam frequently charged 60 per cent or more. Sir George Lewis, in a letter to *The Times* written in April 1898, said that in 1884 a rich Australian had sent his son to England to be educated at Cambridge. He was just 20 years of age and had an allowance of £300 a year. He became acquainted with Sam following an introduction, and gave him three promissory notes totalling £1,500 against which Sam had advanced only £550. According to Sir George, the interest amounted to 800 per cent per annum, and Sam must have known that the undergraduate 'could only have required the £550 for evil purposes'. Directly the father learned his son was in the hands of a moneylender he telegraphed to the manager of one of the Australian banks in London requesting him to send his son back by the next boat. This was done, and the young man's university career was ruined. The manager then instructed Sir George on the young man's behalf. Sir George met Sam and offered to repay him the amount of the advance with 5 per cent interest. When this offer was refused Sir George said he told Sam that the undergraduate was under age and the claim could not be legally enforced against him. He alleged that Sam replied: 'I have his letter, in which he states that he is of age, and I can prosecute him for obtaining money by false pretences.' Sir George, though apparently admitting that the under-graduate had obtained the loan by deceiving Sam about his age, told him that prosecution was not a possibility as the young man was no longer in the country. Sir George sent Sam £550, together with £100 for interest, and Sam returned the promissory notes and the incriminating letter. Sam did not respond to the letter in *The Times*.

Assuming Sir George's recollection of the incident was accurate, and he was known for his remarkable memory for facts, the question must be asked whether this was a typical case for Sam. It must be said that it certainly was not an isolated one. But how far, if at all, did he transgress the barrier of honest dealing? Did he engage in policies which could be regarded as moral blackmail, by using litigation as a weapon to embarrass not only the debtor, but also his family or friends, into making payment? How far, if at all, did he deliberately set out to ensnare young inexperienced wastrels of noble birth into a web of debt? There were those who alleged he did both, and others who maintained that he did neither. However, before a full enquiry and judgment are made of his business ethics, we must turn our attention to the question of why on earth Englishmen of high birth, the landed aristocracy, needed to approach a man such as Sam Lewis for loans.

7 · Why borrow?

'Ah – it's no doubt a fine thing to be a Lord, and all that – but
I'll answer for it, some of 'em's as poor as a church mouse';
replied Titmouse.
> Samuel Warren, *Ten Thousand a Year* (1841)

You can have no conception of the increase in expense in
seeing company . . . now only just imagine what would be the
increase if we went into the London life – first we must have
either a house or what is worse to go to an hotel. Then I must
have another carriage, horses, and coachman. The people care
little for you and will not entertain you unless you entertain
them . . . and it must be kept up or it is of no use.
> Lord Monson writing to his son in 1854

If a moderate estate be left to a man now, there arises the
question whether he is not damaged unless an income also be
left with him wherewith to keep up the estate. Land is a
luxury, and of all luxuries is the most costly.
> Duchess of Stevenage in Anthony Trollope's
> *The Way We Live Now* (1875)

Let us be happy, and live within our means, even if we have to
borrer the money to do it with.
> Artemus Ward, *Science and Natural History*

Sam found his clientele not only among the renegade scalliwags, but
also from the ranks of the seemingly soundly financed landed gentry.
Despite their thousands of acres, many of the landed aristocracy were
short of ready cash and could not pay their way; their financial health
was deplorable. The cost of the lifestyle they adopted, either by
choice, or because Society foisted it upon them, pushed their expenditure to greater levels of extravagance. Ever-increasing spending
outstripped their large incomes, and there was no lack of attractions
on which to spend both the money they had and the money they
anticipated they would have. Borrowing filled the gap.

Aristocratic debt was not a new phenomenon; it did not suddenly arise in the nineteenth century, nor was it confined to England. We have outlined the position during the medieval period and in the centuries immediately following. From the seventeenth century debt was a predominant feature of the aristocrats' lives: a group of people who on paper were enormously wealthy had difficulty in making ends meet. Elizabethan and early Stuart aristocracy made such demands on the credit market that they brought about an increase in the interest rate, which in turn became a brake on economic growth. At the end of the sixteenth century the Earl of Leicester owed £59,000; Lord Vaux of Harrowden was forced to pawn his parliamentary robes; and the Earl of Cumberland could hardly raise £20. It was said of Shakespeare's patron, the Earl of Southampton, who had to surrender his estate to his creditors, that he 'scarce knows which course to take to live'.

Land was increasingly mortgaged to support payments of portions to widows, younger sons and particularly to daughters, so that their dowries could attract a good match. Many borrowers made payments only of the interest; the capital debt was left intact. Debts were frequently carried forward from generation to generation, sometimes for a century or more. When the sixth duke of Devonshire died in 1857 his nephew inherited no less than £1 million of debts, as did the heir of the fifth Earl Fitzwilliam. The possession of encumbered estates was the common lot of the landed gentry, and it was estimated that in the 1840s possibly two-thirds of English land was settled with debt. However, for all the apparent dissipation, comparatively few families went bankrupt; they called a halt just in time.

In this context it is right to refer to the 'landed aristocracy' because effectively 'aristocracy' was synonymous with the possession of vast estates. Far into the nineteenth century, perhaps as late as the 1890s, 90 per cent of the aristocracy came from landed origins. In the 1870s 80 per cent of the land in Great Britain was owned by a mere 7,000 individuals, and of the peers among them all but a small percentage held large estates.

This same landed aristocracy also dominated the group which was accepted as being 'Society'. Dukes, marquises, earls, viscounts and barons always figured prominently in the 300 or so families who could be counted as being in the topmost flight. Although Society was divided into sets, of greater or lesser exclusivity, the most cliquish of which were rigidly barred against the outside world, it was none the less cohesive. It resembled a club, and until the arrival of the plutocrats, the self-made men of trade and commerce, almost all its members had similar backgrounds, were educated at the same schools and universities, entered the same regiments, went to the same parties in London and at country houses, enjoyed the same pastimes – hunting, shooting, fishing and particularly the turf, and intermarried. Everyone within the circle knew, or knew of, everyone else.

The aristocrat needed money to provide for his family, the maintenance of the family mansion in the country, and for his country pursuits; for his house in 'town', and the wherewithal to fund his and his family's stay there during the Season; and, later in the nineteenth century, for his homes, owned or rented, at the fashionable resorts of 'London-by-the-Sea' – Brighton – and 'London-by-the-River' – Maidenhead. At all these venues he had to entertain other members of Society so that he might be invited by them in return. This expenditure, together with the cost of remodelling and modernising town and country houses (the old families sometimes had to build to keep up with the new), finance for his involvement in politics, legal battles, the upkeep of mistresses, and other self-indulgences in a variety of activities, created for some of them an almost insatiable demand for ever-increasing loans on whatever security they could offer.

Gambling was the greatest danger. In the casinos of the South of France a man could gamble only to the limit of the money he had in front of him, whereas in London a gentleman's credit was never in doubt. The great bookmakers of the day would take bets of thousands of pounds at the nod of the head from a man of good family, because they knew that default by the gambler would mean social ruin. A loser was expected to pay his debt by the following morning, even if it meant selling up or mortgaging his estate to do so, and such a man was particularly vulnerable to both the bookmaker and the moneylender.

If your background was right there was no difficulty in obtaining the services of both. The fifth earl of Rosslyn, who became a regular client of Sam, described in his autobiography, *My Gamble With Life*, just how simple it was. A friend of his at Balliol College, Oxford, was Sir Robert Peel, a descendant of the prime minister. Peel betted in hundreds of pounds which, even given his allowance of £2,500 a year, was insufficient to cover his losses. One day at Northampton races he lost £2,000 to a well-known bookmaker of the day, 'Chippy' Norton, so called because of the enormous diamond stud he wore. Rosslyn was aghast when he heard this, but Peel assured him it was all right, and that he could borrow £50,000 from moneylenders if he wanted to. In Rosslyn's words, 'Peel soon went smash.'

Rosslyn's own introduction to a bookmaker came through Sir George Chetwynd. As an undergraduate his allowance was very modest, and he told Sir George that he urgently needed £100. Sir George told him to 'go and lay £4,500 to £1,000 on *Donoval*, it's the biggest certainty racing', an ominous description of any racehorse. Rosslyn did not have £10 let alone £1,000 to lay out, and in any event did not know any bookmakers. Sir George then and there introduced him to R. H. Fry who took large odds from him, saying he knew Rosslyn's father well. Unsurprisingly, Donoval lost, and Rosslyn, at the instigation of Sir George (and he was neither the first nor the last to be put in this position by him), had entered upon the well-trodden path to financial ruin.

It had been estimated that for most of the nineteenth century an income of £10,000 a year was sufficient to maintain a country mansion and to participate in the London season. 'Ten thousand a year', said Mr Aubrey in Samuel Warren's novel of that name published in 1841, 'is far more than my necessities require – it affords me and my family every luxury that I can conceive of.' To exceed that figure a man needed to 'go into horse racing or illegitimate pleasures', and many, of course, did just that.

The London season extended from January to July, with May, June and July representing the peaks. Parliament opened in January, and from then to March, and again from the end of April to the beginning of July, the Court was in London. With the end of the hunting season and the beginning of spring, Society flocked back to its town mansions and took off the dust covers. The opera season started in March, which also saw the first royal levée, and no competition was as keen, or as expensive, as that to curry favour and recognition at Court. There was the Royal Academy exhibition to be visited, one's own portrait to be sat for, the Queen's Birthday to be celebrated. One went to the running of the Derby at Epsom, to Ascot in June and to Goodwood in

July, social occasions rather than sporting events. Weekends in June and July were spent on the river at Maidenhead and Marlow.

London was the fulcrum of fashion; the resort of art; the place on which the single of both sexes converged in search of a partner. All those considered worth knowing in Society were to be found there, in one convenient spot, and there they engaged in matchmaking, visited and were visited, danced and ate, rode in Hyde Park in the smartest carriages and on the best horses in the kingdom, and gossiped, above all gossiped. The small circle of Society engaged in one long party extending over several months, at levées, balls and soirées, held in the great Mayfair mansions. For most it was unthinkable not to be there, whatever the cost. Somehow the money had to be found, however much debt was incurred, even if it meant using the services of a West End moneylender.

Unfortunately for the landed aristocrats their income from their estates decreased dramatically during the last quarter of the nineteenth century. Land was believed to be safe. It could not burn down, or be blown up, or sink at sea, or run away. It was irremovable and reliable, and considered the most prestigious form of investment. For most of the nineteenth century estate duty was nonexistent or minimal, and land profitable. Lenders, who could be just as profligate in their lending as borrowers in their borrowing, felt confident about its security, not believing it would ever fall in value. They were wrong. A great depression in agriculture between 1873 and 1896 produced profound effects on land ownership. At the end of that period rents were on average 41 per cent lower than they were at the beginning.

The twin roots of this agricultural problem were bad weather and the flood of imported foodstuffs. Technical advances contributed to the latter. For example, railways in overseas countries could now bring goods to their ports more cheaply and efficiently. Allied with fast sea transport the cost of sending one ton of grain from Chicago to Liverpool was reduced from £3 7s in 1878 to £1 4s in 1884. Britain was hit harder by these developments than other European countries because so much of its agriculture was devoted to wheat and other grains. Between 1850 and 1880 imports of barley into Britain increased by 212 per cent; of wheat by 267 per cent; of oats by 324 per cent; and of maize by 560 per cent. Refrigeration techniques made the importation of cheap beef from the Argentine a practical proposition, and Danish eggs and bacon invaded the English market for the first time. One result was that tenant farmers on country estates had declining incomes, became increasingly in arrears with their rent, and many went bankrupt. Their difficulties were often exacerbated when they sought to retrieve their positions by obtaining loans from the minority type of moneylender previously described, the unscrupulous small-loan man who resorted to unfair and often illegal devices. Such moneylenders frequently targeted farmers, and borrowing from them often hastened the plunge into bankruptcy. The effect upon the landed aristocrats, particularly those with mainly arable estates, was immediate. They either had to allow their tenants' arrears to accrue, or write them off, or fix a lower rent, or be left with untenanted farms. Many an estate had its income and its capital value reduced by half. Receipts failed to keep pace with costs, and in the early 1880s landed property was being described as a quicksand which engulfed large fortunes.

The 1880s and 1890s were particularly difficult times for those whose wealth was founded on land. Many old-established families tried to sell at least portions of their estates. The Settled Land Act of 1882 gave the power of sale to tenants for life, and under it, wrote the Duke of Marlborough in 1885, 'were there any effective demand for the purchase of land, half the land of England would be on the market tomorrow'. When they were unable to sell, and found themselves pressed for funds, some turned to the moneylenders.

There was little change in general consumer prices in the latter years of the nineteenth century, indeed from time to time they decreased. For the aristocrat, however, the cost of the London season escalated, particularly the price of fashionable London housing. By then the plutocrats were well provided with hard cash. Agricultural profits might be declining, but the returns from commercial enterprises, the factories, railways, ships, mines, warehouses, banks and large-scale retailing were increasing. But of what avail was it to be an industrial or commercial millionaire if the world did not know of your wealth, and you were not accepted into the inner circle? The new plutocrats followed the example of the long-established brewers and first impinged upon, and then entered, Society. They penetrated this inbred community by using their wealth to buy a title or marry one.

They were prepared to pay handsomely for a home in Grosvenor Square or Belgrave Square, the most aristocratic of addresses, and thus inevitably caused prices to rise. This rise, together with higher servants' wages and the increasingly luxurious standards of housing and entertainment expected of those in Society, caused extensive cash problems for the landed aristocrat. The pressures were well expressed by one of Sam's clients, Sir John Astley:

> Then, again, it was imperatively necessary that we should have a house in London every now and again . . . well, you couldn't take a decent house for the season in London under £500, don't you know. Then you couldn't expect your young and lovely wife to drive about on fine days cooped up in a brougham; so she must have a park phaeton and a pair of nice-actioned horses to drive in it. Then, as she was such a perfect rider, she must of necessity do Rotten Row on as exquisite a hack as her doting hubby could find . . . Of course, I might have done as many rich husbands (I am ashamed to say) do – mount my lady on a forty pounder, warranted to hammer up and down the Row in the morning, and trail the brougham in the afternoon, and vice versa; but I was proud of my girl's equitation, and without doubt she and her hack were graceful ornaments to the Row. These almost necessary expenses played havoc with our limited income . . .

That arbiter of Society, Lady Dorothy Nevill, the daughter of the Earl of Orford, writing in 1906, complained that £10,000 a year was no longer a princely income, but sufficient only to have 'a little shooting, some hunting, a modest house in the country, and a small pied-à-terre in town'. Many aristocratic families could by then afford only an occasional day's shopping in London, staying with friends in the suburbs.

When Lady Dorothy was younger, London society was more like a large family than anything else. It was almost impossible for a stranger to find a place until his credentials were carefully examined, discussed and approved. Mere wealth was no passport. In the 1840s the industrial millionaires had not yet appeared. But how things had changed, as she agonisedly complained:

> . . . half a century ago a rich man – let us say a landed proprietor (the

wealthy of that day as a rule drew the greater part of their revenue from land) was quite content to live the greater part of the year on his estate, where he amused himself with the sport which satisfied the moderate taste of those days. If he had not a house in town, he hired one for three months or so, when he would bring up his wife and daughters for the season. Entertainments were certainly given – entertainments the comparative modesty of which would today provoke a contemptuous smile – and the season over, the family would once more return to the country, there to remain until the following year ... Country house parties were few, but lasted longer than at present, when people go hundreds of miles to stay a day. Life, in short, was slow, rather solemn, *inexpensive*, not undignified, but, according to modern ideas, dull.

What is the life of the rich man of today? ... His expenses are in all probability enormous – a wife whose extravagance he is too indolent to check (her expenditure seeming insignificant by the side of the immense sums which are daily at stake in the City); children who also spend largely; houses, hotels, horses, motors, pictures, and other works of art, and very likely, in addition to all of these, most costly of all – a yacht ... Such individuals have changed the whole standard of living, and imported the bustle of the Stock Exchange into the drawing-rooms of Mayfair ... The forties and fifties were aristocratic days, when the future conquerors of Society were still 'without the gate'. The vast increase of railways, however, ended all this exclusiveness, and very soon the old social privileges of birth and breeding were swept aside by the mob of plebeian wealth which surged into the drawing-rooms, the portals of which had up till then been so jealously guarded.

She was prepared to accept that the new plutocratic class deserved some praise. They were public-spirited, and often generous. They tempered the aristocratic vices with the more solid qualities of the industrious and enterprising tradesmen. But she had two major complaints; the new Society no longer engaged in conversation, only chatter; and they had pushed up the cost of the Season beyond belief, putting additional pressure on the already strained aristocratic incomes.

Those who approached the Season encumbered by debts accumulated by themselves or their predecessors were severely hampered and restricted. The extravagance which led to such situations was on an astonishingly high scale. To quote just one of many examples, in the 1820s the Cavendishes at Chatsworth entertained 40 people to dinner every day, and had about 150 servants to cater for their needs. One visitor reported that 'nothing could be more agreeable from the gaiety of members and the entire liberty which prevails; all the resources of the house, – horses, carriages, keepers etc. are placed at the disposal of the guests, and everybody does what he likes best.' Serious wealth was required to maintain these standards.

Personal extravagance was a factor in the bankruptcies of the Duke of Newcastle, the Earl of Winchilsea, and Lord de Manley. In the 1840s the Duke of Beaufort and the Earl of Mornington teetered on the edge; the second duke of Buckingham went over. After a profligate five years of reckless extravagance Buckingham had incurred a deficit of about £1 million, and his interest payments alone then exceeded his annual income by £26,000. He failed to abide by the biblical injunction, 'Do not beggar yourself by feasting on borrowed money' (Ecclesiastes xiii: 33), and was brought to such a pitch by the cost of entertaining at his Stowe mansion that in 1848, according to *The Times*, the British public was 'admitted to a spectacle of a painfully interesting and gravely historical import':

> One of the most splendid abodes of our almost regal aristocracy has thrown open the portals to an endless succession of visitors, who from morning to night have flowed in an uninterrupted stream from room to room, and floor to floor – not to enjoy the hospitality of the lord, or to congratulate him on his countless treasures of art, but to see an ancient family ruined, their palace marked for destruction, and its contents scattered to the four winds of Heaven ... the Most Noble and Puissant Prince ... is at this moment a destitute man ... and tomorrow the auctioneer will begin his work.

In the state dining room alone 60,000 oz of gold and silver plate were set out for inspection, and 'the heirlooms of many great families' were to go under the hammer. The tragedy of it all so overwhelmed *The Times* that it compared the unhappy event to 'the overthrow of a nation or a throne'. And it had all come about not by force of arms, or revolutionary dogma, but because 'in the midst of fertile lands and an industrious people, in the heart of a country where it is thought virtuous to work, to save, and to thrive, a man of the highest rank, and of a property not unequal to his title, has flung all away by extravagance and folly, and reduced his honours to the tinsel of a pauper and the baubles of a fool'.

It was no wonder that so many aristocrats needed to borrow.

8 · *The favoured eldest sons*

The right of primogeniture, however, still continues to be repeated, and as of all institutions it is the fittest to support the pride of family distinctions, it is still likely to endure for many centuries.
Adam Smith, *The Wealth of Nations* (1776)

The cash flow problems of the landed aristocracy were severely worsened by the steps they took to ensure that the eldest son was guaranteed succession to the family estates. Their efforts to achieve this, which they considered almost as a fundamental law of nature, were supported by the courts; and the more successful they were, the more the younger sons sought financial consolation from the moneylenders.

English law did not (and still does not) allow a man to provide for property to pass from eldest son to eldest son in perpetuity. The involvement of three generations was the maximum. A father could settle an estate only as far as a grandson. On achieving his majority the grandson would then, in theory, gain unfettered possession, and the power to deal with the family estate in any way he chose, including selling it to a stranger. In practice, however, it was not allowed to happen.

The eldest son was normally dependent on his father for his maintenance and spending money, and he might need additional funds either to improve his standard of living or to pay off his accumulated debts or because he wanted to marry. As soon as he reached 21 a new settlement was entered into between him and his father. In return for giving up his right to become the sole unfettered owner of the estate on his father's death, which might not occur for twenty or thirty years or more, and accepting instead a life interest only, the eldest son was given an immediate increased allowance, secured by way of charge on the estate. It gave him a measure of independence during the lifetime of his father, and enabled him to marry earlier than might otherwise have been possible. The father, too, was happy with the arrangement for he had followed the tradition of keeping the estate in the hands of the family for future generations. By repeating this procedure the rule against perpetuity was defeated.

When he inherited, the eldest son took over the benefit of the whole of the settled estate. The disparity of income between him and his brothers and sisters was invariably prodigious. There was, of course, nothing to prevent a father from providing for his other children out of property he owned in addition to the settled family estate, but such extra funds were more usually employed not to increase the comparative pittances provided for the younger children but on the principle of 'to him that hath shall be given'. There were many critics, including Adam Smith, who believed that nothing could be more contrary to the real interest of a numerous family than a system which, in order to enrich one, beggared the rest of the children.

It was claimed for primogeniture, this right of succession for the first-born son, that it produced an essential stability and security in society. It was better, it was said, for rural England to be governed by a comparatively limited hierarchy of eldest sons than for estates to become subject to division once in each generation, with the risk of their passing into the hands of new purchasers who had no previous connection with the ancestral land. It was argued that the ideal owner of an hereditary property, having been thoroughly instructed during his father's lifetime in all the duties which befell the owner of the family estates, and conscious that a large number of tenants and dependants would look to him for guidance and example, would enter into his duty of managing the estate in an altogether superior manner and spirit than one whose sole concern was commercial self-interest. It was said that a hereditary owner would build churches in neglected hamlets; spend more on drainage and farm buildings than he would receive in rent; erect model cottages and carry out sanitary improvements, patronise schools and help the most promising of the youths in the parishes of which he was lord. He would be actuated not by hope of pecuniary reward but by a sense of honour, public spirit and family pride. Not only that, he would be a 'rounded' person. He would have education enough to understand economics and the law, and leisure enough to follow events at home and abroad; refinement enough to appreciate art and literature; and energy enough for a social life embracing both the full range of country pursuits and the rigours of the London season. Such was the ideal, and doubtless some conformed to it. We shall look in detail at the careers of some of these eldest sons and, as will become apparent, the reality could be very different.

Primogeniture had many critics. Some considered it dangerous that so high a percentage of the total acreage of England was in so few hands, and that they were afforded so much power and social position. While metropolitan proprietors, such as the dukes of Westminster, Bedford and Portland, mostly exercised their powers with forbearance and discretion, what if such power passed into undesirable hands? While the head of the family, of mature age and feeling the weight of responsibility, might set a good example, could this be said of the eldest son on whom no such responsibility rested, whose right to succeed was guaranteed, whose current income was reserved out of the rental of the estate, and who had unlimited power to raise money on his expectation? It was this power which was grist to many a moneylender's mill.

George Brodrick, in his work *English Land and English Landlords* published in 1881, said it would not be difficult to cite a large number of instances where the heirs of ancestral estates had been spoiled and demoralised by their great expectations:

> Would not the senseless frivolities of the London season, the scandals of turf speculation, the restless passion for amusement, and the ignoble race of social competition, be sensibly checked by the withdrawal of this *jeunesse dorée* from English society, and specially from those circles in which match-making is the supreme end of human ambition? Would the army be less efficient if it should lose the services of a few officers in the Household Brigade and cavalry regiments who take up with military life as a gentlemanlike pastime, and have no intention of continuing it for more than a few years? Would the wisdom of Parliament be diminished if the number of young country members were lessened by the subtraction of those who owe their seats to mere acreage and family names?

Family settlements often set up in influential positions men of luxurious and idle habits, depraved tastes and corrupted morals.

89

In some measure the existence of a strict settlement was an encouragement for an eldest son to borrow. There was nothing to prevent his mortgaging his future life interest in the *income* of the estate. It was more expensive than borrowing on the security of a freehold, but this was no deterrent to the eldest son who, in his youth, could see only the Elysian fields, and not the reality of the damaging effect which incurring interest rates of 40, 50 or 60 per cent, would have on his income when he eventually took up the life interest on the death of his father. The value of the right to ultimate succession to the family estate naturally varied according to the ages of the father and the son at the date of the loan, and the income of the estate. The younger the father, the longer the lender was likely to wait before he would obtain a return on his loan, and the less the reversion was worth. It was estimated that if the father was 45 and the son 21, and the estate produced £10,000 a year, the value of the son's reversion was only £15,000. An advance to him of £5,000 would swallow up one-third of his prospective rental from the date of his father's death.

Primogeniture held out the assurance of wealth and power to the eldest son, irrespective of his ability or merit, and required nothing of him but that he should outlive his father. At the same time it frequently weakened the authority of parents, since some settlements contained provisions preventing a tenant for life from so much as cutting a tree without the consent of his son and heir. Fathers had to seek the permission of their eldest son for many of the things they wished to do. 'It is a hard thing for a father to have to confess and excuse his extravagance to a son, or to justify his desire for a second wife. It is a worse thing for a son to judge of his father's excuses, or to decide whether it is right that his father should be allowed to marry again.' It was also harmful because, it was said, it introduced a degree of inequality into the relations of the children of the family likely to mar what should have been a cordial relationship in their adulthood.

Adam Badeau, an American commentator on the English scene, who looked upon the system with the cool eye of a foreign resident, considered it inflicted immense wrongs upon the greater proportion of its own members, and he contrasted it with the system on the Continent where property descended for the most part to all the children. Entail and primogeniture had been abolished in France at the time of the Revolution, and in Spain fell into disuse in 1836. They were not outlawed in Russia and Prussia, but were very rarely used, and in Austria-Hungary the practice was less widespread than in England. Yet without their alleged benefits, Continental families still managed to continue noble for centuries. It was only the English who sought to maintain the importance of a family by the sacrifice of all its sons and daughters to the head. As Badeau pointed out, even the wife of a peer was sacrificed on the altar of family pride. A woman who had been a duchess abdicated when her son came to his title, handed over the family jewels to her successor, and was turned out of the mansion where she had once presided. Although she still retained the title of duchess, it was with the prefix 'dowager', which indicated her fallen state. The brothers and sisters, bred in luxury and splendour in their father's house, descended to comparative poverty and insignificance. The eldest son who inherited thought nothing of requiring them to leave to make way for his own wife and family, and they accepted their fate as inevitable. They knew it was coming, and were prepared for what was to happen.

Despite this the brothers and sisters of the peers did have a certain position in Society – powerful friends, prestige, and sometimes opportunities to marry well. As a rule, the younger sons were placed in the army or the church, or entered politics or diplomacy or possibly the law. They had another advantage, one that the less scrupulous among them were ready to use. So strong was the desire to maintain the family reputation that families would go to extreme lengths to avoid its being damaged. An extravagant wastrel could run up debts and be fairly confident that his family would pay rather than have its name dragged into the mire by his appearance in the bankruptcy court. Those prepared to lend to younger sons were also well aware of this.

Wealth from estates naturally varied widely. By the end of the eighteenth century grandees such as the dukes of Bedford, Devonshire and Northumberland already had incomes in excess of £50,000 a year; others, like the Earl of Clarendon, had an income from land of only £3,000. The estates could be vast, as revealed in John Bateman's *The Great Landowners of Great Britain and Ireland* published in 1876. To name just four landowners who will figure prominently in our story, the Earl of Shrewsbury and Talbot, premier earl of England and the hereditary Lord High Steward of Ireland, had 36,000 acres in

Stafford, Chester, Worcester, Shropshire and Derby producing £62,000 gross; the Marquis of Ailesbury, whose family had been landowners for almost 400 years, then had 55,000 acres in Wiltshire, Yorkshire and Berkshire, producing £60,000 a year; the Marquis of Abergavenny had 29,000 acres in Sussex, Kent, Warwick, Monmouth and Worcester, producing £30,000; and Colonel Owen Williams owned 14,000 acres in Co. Roscommon, Carnarvon, Anglesey and Buckinghamshire, producing £22,000. These figures were to some extent underestimates, because many families had other large sources of income, for example from industrial and urban development. When urban landed income was taken into account there were 17 landowners whose income from land exceeded £100,000 per annum, led by the Duke of Westminster with £300,000 or more.

However, the gradual accumulation of charges secured on estates meant that there could be a very considerable difference between gross and net income, and therefore a severe restriction of the money available for everyday living. A life tenant of a great estate might find it burdened with mortgages and payments, not only to his brothers and sisters, but also to his mother, aunts and uncles. If his father and grandfather died young, there could well be more than one dowager drawing a jointure. Badeau wrote of one such case where an earl had to pay the jointures of three countesses, the widows of his predecessors. The reigning countess told him she could not afford a house in London until the last of these ladies died; but they were long-lived, and while they were able to keep up their establishments near Grosvenor Square, she was forced to remain in the country, or to live for only a month or two of the Season at an hotel in town.

Sam's clients included expectant heirs. It was a potentially treacherous area. Anyone setting out to be a moneylender to the landed aristocracy had to cross a minefield, because the courts set out to booby-trap his movements in whatever way they could. It was a long-accepted establishment view that property rights were of the utmost, almost paramount, importance. The ruling classes were convinced that it was the existence of a paternal landed aristocracy that prevented unrest, and even revolution, among the populace, and this opinion was shared and supported by the courts. Anything that might upset the *status quo* was to be confronted. The expectant heir was given a specially protected position in law, a protection not afforded to others. The law laid down that where on the one side there was an expectant heir whose needs made him agree to any terms in order to obtain ready money and on the other a moneylender who took advantage of these needs to make a hard bargain, the law presumed the bargain was 'unconscionable', and put the onus of proving its fairness on the moneylender. If he failed to do so, the court would set the bargain aside, and order payment only of the amount advanced, plus interest usually at the rate of five per cent per annum.

The courts did not go so far as to say that there were no circumstances in which an heir or expectant could borrow on his expectancy. Some fathers were so tight with their money that an heir, if he was prevented altogether from borrowing, 'might starve in the desert within view of the land of Canaan'. But as the contracts for such loans could be set aside, they were risky in the extreme for the lender, a risk which could only be taken if the interest charged was sufficiently high to cover the cases in which losses occurred. If the borrower died before his father and so did not take up his inheritance, the lender lost his money. If the borrower did survive, then he might disclaim his agreement and rely on the law and be required to pay only five per cent. Either way the moneylender stood to lose, because five per cent was insufficient to cover the risk.

The strength of the moneylender's position was, as has been indicated, that most borrowers were hesitant to go to law for fear of the adverse publicity it would bring to themselves and their families. Sometimes, however, this fear was overcome by the encouragement of families who were prepared to face the inevitable embarrassment, either because they wished to put a brake upon the moneylenders' worst excesses, or because they were at the end of their tether so far as their wayward heirs were concerned. When this happened the moneylenders would argue in vain that there was no law against being extravagant. If there were, many of us would be condemned. If a young man bought racehorses or jewellery on credit at an enhanced purchase price, the law did not interfere to upset the agreement. No law compelled the seller to take back the goods and return the price. Why then, they protested, should the position be different simply because the moneylender loaned the money directly, so enabling the youth to make his purchases? With cash in hand the young man might well be able to make a better bargain for himself than if he had to seek credit. But the law feared that whole estates might be swallowed up, and the *status quo* of society upset, by attempts to repay the high interest rates of moneylenders. It was taken for granted that the moneylender had helped and encouraged the youth in his folly, even though there might be no fraud, no haste, no pressure put upon him.

The court's discretion to interfere in contracts of loan was further extended to include younger sons in the case of *Nevill v. Snelling* which took place in 1880, a case in which Sam was indirectly involved. Here the plaintiff, the young man in question, was the third son of the Marquis of Abergavenny, and this was not the only occasion on which the long-suffering marquis was called upon to come to the rescue of one of his children. Like most younger sons, he had no property of his own and no expectation of any, except such as might be founded on his father's position in life. The marquis allowed him £250 per annum, which was increased to £400 when he reached 21. He lost money betting, and felt too abashed to ask his father to help him out. Instead he became involved with a moneylender, one Snelling, and borrowed £900, but even after payments totalling £420 the accumulated interest left him with a debt of £1,235. Inevitably he defaulted, and Snelling issued a bankruptcy petition. Snelling also wrote to the marquis and informed him of the debt, and pointed out that his son's bankruptcy would follow if payment was not made within a week – a clear case of moral, if not criminal, blackmail.

The marquis stood firm and put the matter in the hands of his solicitors who offered to repay the £900, less the £420 already paid, plus interest at five per cent. This offer was declined. Snelling argued that young Nevill was a free agent in the transaction, perfectly willing to borrow from time to time, and until just before the action had never raised any objection to the terms. It was argued for Nevill that although he was not an expectant heir under a will, or a reversioner under a settlement, he was given credit on his expectation as the son of a marquis, and in the hope that rather than submit to the exposure attendant upon his being made bankrupt his father, whom Snelling knew to be a large landed proprietor, or some other member of Nevill's family, would pay the amount claimed.

Snelling's object, it was claimed, was that Nevill should come to ruin by indulging in betting and other extravagance, and that his father would pay. Nevill did in fact use the loans for buying a horse and paying his gambling losses. On one occasion he needed an advance because he had lost £300 in one day at Doncaster races, £50 more than his entire income for the year; another loan was because of 'rather a bad race at Newmarket', and yet another because 'I have played the fool at Newmarket again.' The court's decision was that Nevill was in the same position as the expectant heir, and needed to pay only the amount which had been offered by his father's solicitors. In the opinion of Mr Justice Denman, Snelling was 'a person looking out for young men to prey upon'. Judgment was given to Snelling only for the amount he had advanced, plus five per cent interest. He was also ordered to pay the costs of the action, and so at the end of the day was out of pocket. This decision made lending to the sons of the aristocracy even more of a hazardous adventure.

And what was the source of Snelling's funds? From 1875, if not before, he had been backed by Sam. In 1878 there were many transactions in each of which Sam advanced Snelling no less than £4,000 for his moneylending business. Was he using Snelling as a shield between himself and the debtor, Snelling taking the obloquy in return for a share of the profits? Was Sam the person seeking out young men to prey upon? There is absolutely no evidence connecting Sam to this particular transaction or to show that Sam ever wrote to a debtor's family in the way that Snelling had done, or that he knew of, or approved, the action Snelling had taken.

The cases in which expectant heirs disgraced illustrious family names were exceptions, but by no means rare. It is perhaps surprising that there were not more, since eldest sons were exposed to special temptations in the hands of moneylenders prepared to lend on the security of their expectations. To some extent their borrowing could be considered reasonable. They could anticipate their future income and spread it more evenly over their whole adult life. Taken to extremes, however, such borrowing posed a serious danger, because they sometimes saddled their own future inheritance with debts which, added to the portions for the other brothers and sisters, and jointures for widows, encumbered the estates to such an extent that net income might be reduced to nil.

9 · Sir George Lewis, the enemy

Inevitably the increased expenditure of aristocrats, coupled with reduced incomes, ensured that many members of Society eagerly sought the services of the moneylenders. But there were soon forces at work seeking to curb the undesirable moneylending elements whom they held responsible for a great deal of misery, gambling and crime. Two men who came to the fore early in the campaign were Henry du Pré Labouchere and Sir George Henry Lewis.

Labouchere, affectionately known as Labby, born in London of French Protestant stock in 1831, was a maverick. Educated at Eton, and then at Trinity College, Cambridge, he managed to run up debts amounting to £6,000 while still an undergraduate. At the age of 21 he was sent to South America, where his family had important commercial interests. He fell in love with a circus lady in Mexico, and joined the troupe; later he lived happily for six months in a camp of Chippaway Indians. He entered the diplomatic corps, and served extensively in America, Germany, Sweden, Russia and Turkey. By his own account he was insubordinate and indolent, and his passion for gambling coloured his life wherever he went. He was fortunately able to indulge this proclivity, for he inherited a great fortune from his uncle, Lord Taunton. He then turned his mind to a political career, but at first it did not flourish, and after being briefly in Parliament in 1865 and again in 1867/8, he lost his seat. It was to be another 13 years before he was a successful candidate again.

In the meantime he won fame as a journalist, and adopted a pithy and penetrating style. He wrote for, and became part owner of, the *Daily News*. In 1874 his friend Edmund Yates founded a new weekly paper called *The World*, with which he hoped to reform the world. Labby agreed to write for it, and from his first contribution on 13 July of that year provided his readers with a weekly exposure of swindling company promoters, newspaper puffers and others considered sufficiently wicked to incur his displeasure. He was one of the earliest of investigative journalists. In 1877 he started his own paper, *Truth*, which he described as 'another and a better *World*', and continued as before. *Truth* too won admiration and gratitude for its fearless exposure of fraudulent enterprises. It also brought upon him a series of libel actions, most of which he won. The publicity generated by each action led to such increased circulation that the lawsuits were effectively self-financing. Several newspapers and magazines have since followed his example.

In 1880 Labby began a 25-year representation as Member of Parliament for Northampton but did not obtain office owing, it was said, to the opposition of Queen Victoria. He welcomed the spotlight, and revelled in the personal publicity that his activities attracted. One observer believed that notoriety to him was as the breath of his nostrils, though he was supremely indifferent to the praise or blame of his fellow-creatures. His name became a household word. He associated with the Bohemian element, in whose company he was at his happiest. Yet the highest circles were open to him. His birth to social position, his fortune and his education were all eminently aristocratic, and he was favourably regarded by the Prince of Wales. It was said that although he regarded life, political and social, as a game, he knew its laws and did not break them; and that is why Society tolerated him.

The solicitor who represented him in his many lawsuits, and who became his lifelong friend, was George Henry Lewis. He was born on 21 April 1833 at 10 Ely Place, Holborn, in London where, according to the fashion of the day, his father lived over the offices in which he practised as a solicitor. His father, James Graham Lewis, belonged to a family of Sephardic Jews who settled in England in the eighteenth century, changing their name from Loew to Lewis. Being Jewish meant that George was effectively barred from attending a public school or Oxford or Cambridge, and he was educated first by a governess and afterwards at Henry Solomon's private Jewish boarding school in Edmonton. He graduated at University College, London. In 1851 he was articled to his father, and admitted as a solicitor in 1856, joining the firm of Lewis & Lewis which his father had founded. The practice dealt largely with criminal matters, insolvency and civil litigation arising out of fraud, and had a large theatrical clientele. He gained experience in advocacy by regular appearances at the police courts. He prepared for every trial with a thoroughness which left no opening for surprise, and possessed an intuition beside which, according to one admirer, 'the rather mechanical processes of Sherlock Holmes seemed the efforts of a beginner'. His deliberate speech and gesture, his intelligence, astuteness and photographic memory – he used few notes – made him the equal of the leading barristers of the day, and when, on occasion, he found himself pitted against them, he usually won.

By 1870 he had established a formidable reputation, and for more than a quarter of a century held the virtual monopoly of those cases in which the seamy side of life was unveiled, where the sins and follies of the wealthy classes and well-known public figures were threatened with exposure and disaster. Everyone wanted him to fight their battles for them, and those about to be embroiled in scandal literally raced each other to Ely Place to retain the services of this 'most sagacious, acute, and amiable of English solicitors' before the enemy did. Oscar Wilde's comment was, 'George Lewis? Brilliant. Concerned in every great case in England. Oh, he knows all about us, and he forgives us all.' According to another of his clients, Lillie Langtry, the actress mistress of the Prince of Wales (and many others), people 'who had compromised themselves one way or another, all flocked to his little office parlour in Ely Place, where often, over a cup of tea, he gave them shrewd advice, helped them over stiles, and suppressed scandal, mediated between and calmed down many ruffled couples.' She was not the only beautiful woman to sip tea in his office while pouring out her troubles. Ellen Terry, Lady Warwick, Mrs Patrick Campbell and Katherine O'Shea all sought his advice.

Thaddeus, the fashionable portrait painter, who numbered among his sitters Lady Byron, the Duke and Duchess of Teck, Gladstone, Pope Leo XIII and Pope Pius X as well as Sam and Ada and her parents Sarah and David, described the waiting room adjoining George Lewis's private office as 'dismal'. There was a bare table, three or four hard-backed horsehair chairs, 'well-worn carpet trodden out of all recognition by the feet of impenitent sinners', a few forbidding-looking law books on a dusty shelf, with a law calendar as the only ornament on the walls: 'It was enough to give anyone the blues.' Another client said that he was so depressed by the stern and uncompromising character of the surroundings that sitting there he felt he could believe himself guilty of the most deplorable crimes. The inner sanctum was also of calculated ordinariness, containing a wide mahogany desk, furniture upholstered in a dark sage green, and a round Chippendale table. However, in winter there would be a cheerful fire by the side of the desk at which the proffered tea could be drunk.

It was said that Lewis knew enough secrets to send half the City of London to penal servitude, and he once told an interviewer that 'no novel was ever written, no play ever produced, that has or could contain such incident as at the present moment are locked up in the archives of my memory, and which no man will ever discover.' He ensured this last by destroying all his notes, and refraining from writing his autobiography. The bulk of his successes lay in the cases in which, by adroit handling, he kept his clients out of court. He possessed an unequalled knowledge of the past records of criminals and adventurers of both sexes, in England, Europe and the United States, which was particularly serviceable to him and his clients in resisting attempts at blackmail. He built up an international information network – 'a spider's web of narks and informers' – of inestimable value in his work, and he was sometimes referred to as being more of a private detective than a solicitor. Those who traded on the belief that their prospective victims would be averse to having their monetary difficulties or peccadilloes revealed were often made forcibly aware that Sir George possessed information concerning their own behaviour which they would have found it very inconvenient to have drawn into the light of day. It was said of him that he often played the game in defiance of the rules, relying on his audacity to carry him through.

In two cases, the Aylesford adventure, about which more later, and the Tranby Croft case, which came to be known as the Baccarat Scandal and involved an allegation of cheating at cards made against a fellow house-guest of the Prince of Wales, the prince went to him for advice. Edward said that on these and other occasions, Lewis's advice enabled him to ride out a scandal and retain, sometimes even increase, his popularity with his subjects. These cases set the seal on Lewis's friendship with the future monarch and established his reputation and stature as London's leading Society solicitor beyond any doubt. And so it came about that if you were an aristocrat in need of legal representation in a delicate matter, you went to George Lewis. If you were an aristocrat who needed a large loan, you went to Sam Lewis.

George Lewis married his second wife, Elizabeth, the daughter of Mr F. Eberstadt of Mannheim, in 1867 (his first wife had died two years earlier), and they had a son and two daughters. In 1876 he moved his family to 88 Portland Place, which was to remain his home for the rest of his life. There Elizabeth established a salon which was thronged with many of the best painters, sculptors, musicians, actors, writers and politicians of the day. Rank, though not a bar, did not automatically entitle admission; talent was a requisite. Thus their parties were free from the obsession with rank that so often laid a dead hand on the gatherings of Society. At Portland Place there was the best of two worlds, Bohemia and talented Society, and Whistler and John Sargent, Thomas Hardy and Oscar Wilde, W. S. Gilbert and Sir Arthur Sullivan were among the regular guests. George Lewis was knighted by Queen Victoria in 1892; on the coronation of Edward VII in 1902 he obtained a baronetcy, and in 1905 was made a Companion of the Victorian Order.

George Lewis always exhibited a strong interest in law reform, and was vociferously in favour of the re-enactment of the Usury Laws to counteract the evils which he believed flowed from the freedom which had been given to moneylenders. His particular target was the West End moneylender. In 1898 he told the House of Commons Select Committee on Moneylending that in all his years of practice he had never known a person who was one shilling better off for having made use of the services of a moneylender. On the other hand he had seen the moneylenders grow rich. So far as he was concerned, they were a curse to the poor and to the younger sons of the rich, and were 'the vermin of the world'. He believed that if they were swept off the face of the earth, not only would the commercial industry of the country not suffer in the least degree, but it would actually improve, for the usurers would be compelled to leave their trade and carry on an honest business. He could not have been more embittered towards them, but he reserved his utmost venom for those among them who were Jewish.

He was not himself a particularly observant Jew nor a regular synagogue attender, though he was a member of the Great Synagogue in Aldgate and the Central Synagogue in Great Portland Street, and Elizabeth was on the Council of the Anglo-Jewish Association and active on its Ladies' Committee. But George Lewis was conspicuously proud of being Jewish; his innermost feelings were Jewish, and he had a deep sympathy with the aspirations and suffering of his brethren all over the world. 'So far from wishing to disguise my race,' he told the *Jewish Chronicle*, 'I always make a point of acknowledging it in all the relations of my life.' He was jealous of the Jewish community's good name, and did all he could to enhance it. He knew too much of the foibles of humanity not to be charitable in his judgments; but he made one exception to this rule. He told the *Jewish Chronicle* that he had watched 'the gentleman known as Mr Sam Lewis' from the very outset of his career, and his indignation was such that his ambition was to expose him. Not only was Sam, in his opinion, one of the moneylenders who were such a danger to all who dealt with them, but he tarnished the good name of the Jewish community in England. 'We cannot afford to court the denunciation which the proceedings of such people as Mr Sam Lewis bring upon us'.

He was a formidable enemy, particularly on his home ground, the courts. The trick was not to be tempted to issue proceedings when he deliberately set out to libel and provoke an action for damages against himself, for then you would lay yourself open to his relentless and merciless cross-examination. If you were a moneylender, you needed to be doubly cautious, because moneylenders were generally so unpopular that magistrates, judges or juries would find against you if they possibly could. He embarked upon what was to prove a persistent campaign, pursued over a period of 25 years, to bring about Sam's downfall. The case in which he most longed to appear was *Lewis v. Lewis*.

George Lewis gathered an impressive range of information about the main West End moneylenders and, with Labouchere, decided that the best way of putting an end to their activities was to publicise and expose their backgrounds. They used Labby's columns in *The World* for the purpose. In the issue of 9 December 1874 Labouchere wrote:

In spite of all that can be said to warn the young fool against the toil of moneylenders, he is no sooner in want of £50 than he hurries forth to put himself in the hands of Shylock ... We shall strip some of these worthies of their aliases, and give to their dupes the opportunity to know who and what their would-be benefactors really are. We have made our selections in no invidious spirit. They are samples of the class to which they belong, and, in order to allow the entire class to take issue with us, we distinctly express our opinion that any man who advances money to an officer, a clergyman, or any other person of small means at forty or sixty per cent, *should be treated as a dog by every respectable member of the community.*

There could scarcely have been a more open invitation to sue for libel given to the members of the nine firms Labouchere then set out to name.

The first had been a member of the College of Surgeons in Edinburgh, but had been struck off for indulging in quackery, and was twice fined by the Marlborough Street magistrate, Mr Knox, for unlawfully continuing to use his former qualification. In 1868, after unsuccessful business ventures, he executed a deed of assignment for the benefit of his creditors, and in 1869 a deed of composition by which his creditors were promised two shillings in the pound. Despite this he advertised that he loaned large sums of money 'on note of hand simply'. The second was the brother of the first, and traded under the grandiose title of the Reversionary and Mortgage Company. The third was his brother-in-law; the fourth a man who, according to his advertisements, loaned money to 'officers, noblemen and gentlemen on their simple note of hand'. The fifth had registered two deeds of composition with his creditors, and had recently been acquitted, much to Mr Knox's displeasure, because the main prosecution witness refused to continue with the charge of defrauding a lodging-house keeper. The sixth was brother of the fifth, and had registered a deed to pay his creditors one shilling in the pound. Despite this setback in his personal finances he offered money to the impecunious 'from' four per cent. The seventh was the son of a bankrupt who had been imprisoned for fraud, the son adopting as his trading title the name of well-known legitimate bankers; and the eighth was trading as 'Mr

Lester', a name not his own. Ninth in the list were Henry Beyfus and his brother-in-law Albert Boss, who traded as Albert Boss & Co.

From the above details it will be seen that, in almost all cases, the advertising moneylenders are ruined and disreputable adventurers, who have been bankrupts and insolvents, who trade under false names, and who are in the habit of occasionally visiting Mr. Knox. It would appear highly improbable that men who have failed in every other occupation, and who, if they have money, ought to hand it over to their creditors, should inspire confidence. But we believe, strange as it may appear, that many of them have numerous clients, and that they, in some cases, have become wealthy by their vile trade. When 60% is charged for money, capital accumulates quickly at compound interest ... We warn the impecunious that *no usurer can be an honourable man for his calling precludes it*; and a fly may as well go for aid and assistance to a spider as a lad in difficulties to a West End usurer.

The following week's issue carried a letter from 'A ruined mother' confirming all that they had warned against:

Sir, – I thank you heartily for your exposure of moneylenders. Not that I suppose you will do much good; young men will always be foolish, and necessarily become the prey of these villains. But perhaps some of the inexperienced may yet have a tenderness for their parents, or at all events for their mother, and to such my case may act as a warning. My only son, a lieutenant in a marching regiment, got into the hands of one of the men whose antecedents and present condition were described in your issue this week; the usurer came upon me, and to avoid seeing my son disgraced among his comrades, I sacrificed all my savings, broke up my suburban home, where I was surrounded by pleasant friends, and came away to end my days in this quasi-cheap retreat, where I know scarcely anyone, and where I am debarred from any intercourse with congenial acquaintance.

Yours faithfully,

A RUINED MOTHER   St. Colomb, Cornwall

The World said that judging from the above, and numerous other letters they had received from the relatives of the victims who had been ruined by the Shylocks of the West End, their course in publishing the real names and antecedents of 'these harpies' had met with general satisfaction, and they declared themselves 'absolutely indifferent to the indignation which this exposure had called forth from the tribe of usurers'. They promised to continue the series. The use of the expressions 'Shylocks of the West End' and 'tribe of usurers' carried obvious overtones. Two of the moneylenders wrote letters of complaint, which were published, but there was no retraction.

In the issue of 30 December there was a second list, which included Sam, and on 13 January 1875 a third list. Sam was described as 'a large discounter', confirming his rapidly appreciating wealth and importance in the business. It did not allege that he traded under any name other than his own, or that he advertised or circularised.

In all, in the three lists, there were 41 firms or individual traders named. Two were solicitors in partnership who charged between 60 and 80 per cent; another was a former solicitor who had been struck off; one usurer who was 'almost penniless and whose large-hearted offers of assistance are probably dictated more by his generous sympathies than by any real power to assist the embarrassed'. There was one who was in the habit of making advances in the form of cigars, jewellery and just a little money, and who was insolvent, and not for the first time; two were simply moneylenders' touts; yet another had 'made the acquaintance of Mr. Knox' and was a bankrupt; and one had been convicted of obtaining money by false pretences for which he had been sentenced at Middlesex Sessions to five years' penal servitude. There was no attempt to make any distinction between the various individuals concerned, or to suggest that possibly some were straightforward, and perfectly honest, moneylenders – such a thought clearly did not commend itself to Labby or George Lewis.

Half of those mentioned were Jewish, and this set alarm bells ringing among the community. It was used to facing attacks which implied that if one Jew, or a few Jews, were guilty of some particular misbehaviour, then all Jews, indeed Judaism itself, were responsible for the miscreants. There had been just such an accusation only ten years previously, in April 1865, arising out of a pamphlet written by one Captain Colborne. The community fortunately had its own respected bodies which could counter such accusations. The Jewish Board of Deputies (founded in 1760) and the *Jewish Chronicle* could be relied upon to put such allegations into perspective, and individual leaders of the community such as Sir Moses Montefiore, Lord Rothschild and the Chief Rabbi would add their voices. The *Jewish Chronicle* of 21 April 1865 put the argument thus:

It is quite possible that in comparison to the rest of the population there may still be among the Jews more moneylenders than is due to their proportion. But this would give the detractors of the Jews as little right to stigmatise a whole community for the faults of individuals as the preponderance of certain crimes amongst the Christian population would justify the Jews to charge all Christian-dom with them. Take, for instances, drunkenness, adultery, and the crimes of murder, rape, burglary, and, in fact, all acts of violence. Statistics throughout Europe, and more so still in those countries in which the Jewish population is densest, have proved the comparative freedom of Jews from atrocities of this kind. The criminals in these cases are nearly always Christians, while a very large proportion of their victims are Jews. Would it not be easy for a Jew to pen paragraphs in the spirit of the reviewers of Captain Colborne's pamphlet insinuating that all Christians, or at least the mass of them, are ruffians, drunkards, and murderers, lying in wait for unfortunate Jews whom they lure, despoil and kill? The malignity of such an insinuation would be self-evident. We cannot sufficiently repeat, a man is not a burglar, a drunkard, an adulterer or murderer because of, but despite his Christianity ... By holding up a whole community to public reprobation for the faults of a few of its members, these libellers lay themselves open to the just suspicion that it is less a regard for the general good by which they are actuated than an unworthy feeling of revenge on a whole race for a real or imagined injury received from a member of this body; or, worse, that they are prompted in their attacks by hateful religious fanaticism.

The World received a letter in similar vein from a Jewish reader, which they published in their edition of 21 December:

As a Jew I thank you for your attempt to break up the trade of the

West-End usurers, for many of them being of that religion, their proceedings tend to keep alive the feelings of antipathy and prejudice against the community still entertained by the illiberal and unthinking portion of the public. But by no one are they more despised than by their co-religionists; they are looked upon as swindlers, and avoided like the plague. Let them amass any amount of wealth, they are not admitted into any but their own circle, and among their guests ... cannot be found a single Jew of the least consideration. It is therefore with regret that I notice in your recent number the word 'Shylock' in your article, and 'crucifying' in one of the letters you publish, as applied to these men, thus tending to stigmatise all those who profess the faith to which some of them unfortunately belong. I appeal to your sense of justice, and that of your correspondents, not to give to the castigation which these men so well deserve a religious or sectarian colouring.

The World said they printed the letter with pleasure; and to show their opinion of the Jews as a nation, they begged leave to refer their correspondent to an article on the Rothschild family which they had printed in an earlier edition, in which the following passage had appeared:

The greatest philosophers, the greatest musicians, and the greatest statesmen of modern days have been Jews. In every walk of science, art, and literature, this people have excelled. They were great and powerful when this country was inhabited by savages, or by wild beasts, and today our Prime Minister is a Jew ... The only cavalry commander who distinguished himself during the Siege of Paris was a Hebrew, and he died bravely fighting at the head of his horsemen. Search the world over, and no race will be found which contains so many distinguished men or so many beautiful women.

What their correspondent had not known or appreciated, however, was that at least two of those mentioned in the articles, Albert Boss and his father-in-law Solomon Beyfus, were members of the General Council of the United Synagogue, the federation of London Ashkenazi synagogues formed in 1870 by Act of Parliament. Boss was in partnership with Solomon's son Henry. (Solomon was not alleged to be a practising moneylender.) The articles put Boss into a most invidious situation. Whichever course he took would be wrong. If he allowed the articles to pass without comment, then it might be construed that he accepted the strictures contained in them. If he took legal proceedings, then the risks involved could be greater than doing nothing, for he might lose, and the consequences, and the costs, would be even more damaging. Even if he won, people might still be inclined to the view that there was no smoke without fire. In the event his hand was forced. Someone wrote a letter to the *Jewish Chronicle* which it did not print, and he then sent a copy to *The World*, which referred to it in their 13 January edition. The correspondent had suggested that if Boss did not clear his reputation in court then the United Synagogue should purge itself of his presence, because he was a communal representative and as such reflected dishonour and discredit upon the entire Jewish community. This was, of course, just the reaction which Labouchere and Lewis had hoped for. *The World* commented that the writer's advice was sound and should be followed. Usury, they declared, was not a matter of race or religion: '*the usurer should be ejected from church, chapel, and synagogue*'.

Albert Boss could contain himself no longer. At Guildhall Magistrates' Court he and his partner Henry were granted a summons for criminal libel against one Freeman, the nominal publisher of *The World*. The information laid before the magistrate had originally sought to include Edmund Yates and Labouchere, whom Boss knew were respectively the editor and author of the articles, but as he could not provide any direct evidence against them, they were not made defendants.

The proceedings started before Alderman Sir Thomas Gabriel on Friday, 29 January 1875, and were to prove of importance to Sam. He was not directly involved in the case, but his bank account shows that he had business dealings with Boss and at least another seven of the 41 persons named in the articles. George Lewis suspected that this was so, and brought it out in his cross-examination of Boss. He used the proceedings to raise doubts about the propriety of Sam's dealings, and also to link him with the worst abuses perpetrated by some of the other West End moneylenders.

Two members of the Bar, Mr Montagu Williams and Mr Douglas Straight, appeared for Albert Boss and Henry Beyfus; George Lewis

107

appeared alone for the defendant. In his opening statement Williams contended that because of the selections made by *The World*, and the order in which they were printed, his clients were stamped, by association, as being insolvent, bankrupt, trading without capital or sufficient capital, as persons who had been brought before magistrates of the metropolis, and as associates of a man who had been made the subject of a criminal trial. Beyond that it had been alleged that Boss was unfit to enter the place of worship of the Council of which he was a member. Williams said that there had to be some bridle on what the press could say. He said that as a very humble member of the Bar he had always, when called upon to do so, been proud to act in the defence of one of the greatest institutions of this country – namely that of a free press; but *The World* had grossly abused this liberty. He asked the magistrate to send the case to the Central Criminal Court, the Old Bailey, so that a jury could adjudicate on the criminal libel.

Albert Boss, who was a close neighbour of Sam in Gower Street, was called to the witness box. He told the court that he was in the business, in partnership with Henry Beyfus, of lending money and discounting bills of exchange. They were also diamond merchants, in which business their turnover exceeded £100,000 a year. He had never been insolvent or bankrupt; had always traded with sufficient capital; had never been charged with, let alone been convicted of, a criminal offence; and had not done anything which entitled anyone to stigmatise him as odious or contemptible. He had always traded in his own name, and charged only such rate of interest as was compatible with the risk involved.

George Lewis then rose to cross-examine him. Boss told him that he had been a moneylender for about 12 years, and in addition to being a diamond merchant and bill discounter, he also had a business in the City of London as an umbrella manufacturer, and was a dealer in house property. When he first went into partnership with Beyfus he was 25 years old and Beyfus just 20. He admitted he made loans to youngsters at college, and then immediately revealed a gap which existed between the moneylender and the general public. Most moneylenders considered they were entitled to charge whatever rate they could achieve, and simply did not appreciate that an admission of levying a high rate on youngsters would be met with general disapproval:

Tell me at what rate you charge a boy of twenty. Is it 100%? – No.

Is it 80%, 70% or 60%? – It all depends who he is.

Have you charged any boy of twenty years of age 100%? – No.

Or 80%? – I should think not.

Or 70%? – I might. [*Sensation.*]

Have you written to their fathers before you have done the transaction? – No.

Why not? – I do not think it reasonable. I assume that he had asked his father before he came to me.

You assume that he had asked his father, and that his father had referred him to you? – Certainly not. [*Laughter.*]

Once laughter enters a courtroom during the presentation of the prosecution case it augurs badly for the prosecution and presages well for the defence. It means the prosecution evidence is not being taken as seriously as they would wish.

Commissions in the army could be bought and sold, and Boss made loans to army officers on their capital value. He agreed that he and Beyfus described themselves as 'Army Agents' even though no regiment of the British Army had appointed them.

Now, I ask you this: did you not describe yourself as an Army Agent . . . to give yourself an air of respectability, that young men might come to you to borrow money from you as an army agent? – Young men who came to us would know we were not regular army agents.

Did you do it with that object? – I cannot say what was the object we did it with.

Lewis then took him in turn through his business relations with others on *The World*'s lists, and Boss admitted that he had entered into transactions with at least six of them, including some who had been insolvent and had appeared before the criminal courts. He was asked about Sam:

Have you had any transactions with Sam Lewis who carries on the trade of usury under his own name? You see no Lewis is ashamed of his name? [George Lewis seems to have overlooked that his own family name had been changed from Loew to Lewis] – I have.

Have you discounted bills for him? – No.

Has he discounted bills for you? – No.

Have you had any discount transactions together on bills? – Yes.

Then Samuel Lewis and you discount on joint accounts? – Yes.

At 60%? – I forget.

Through his cross-examination George Lewis succeeded in establishing that many of those named in the articles dealt with each other, and that if one became bankrupt, or otherwise lacked capital, he could still continue in business. He simply changed his name and address and passed such business as he obtained from his circulars and newspaper advertisments to another of the West End moneylenders, who would then accept the bill and pay him a commission for the introduction.

After Boss had suffered further humiliating cross-examination, the prosecution chose not to put Henry Beyfus on the witness stand. This was doubtless a wise decision, but it was a bonus for George Lewis, on which he could capitalise in his final submission. He delivered a powerful address. The trial was not a dispute between *The World* newspaper and Messrs Boss and Beyfus, he said; it was a question between Messrs Boss and Beyfus and society at large [*great applause, which was instantly checked*]. *The Times*, the *Pall Mall Gazette* and other newspapers had from time to time, when one young nobleman after another had been forced into the Court of Bankruptcy by the odious effects of the trade of usury, drawn attention to it, with a view to preventing its continuance. The fundamental question raised by the case, he claimed, was whether advertising in public newspapers by 'a parcel of bankrupts and dishonourable men' who sought to lend money to young men under age, over age, at college, in the army, belonging to the nobility, or whatever their position or rank in life might be, was to be allowed to be continued by persons advertising under false and fictitious names to delude and ensnare the unwary into borrowing money at 60, 70, 80 and 100 per cent; or whether it was within the province of a public newspaper to call attention to a great social grievance such as that was, and whether if it did call attention to it the newspaper was liable to be charged with libel. That really was the question before the court, and he denied that any libel had been published. He was particularly concerned about the effect of the circulars they distributed:

> For eleven years they have sent out circulars unasked to young men just starting in life. 'Come to me, and borrow money at 70% and 80%.' What for? Are these circulars sent out to enrich or benefit the young man? By what right have they got the impertinence to come into my home with their horrid circulars, and to say 'Come and borrow money of me'? Not that they would put on their circulars 70% and 80%. Many a young man would never dream of borrowing money, or have been led into the excesses which the borrowing of money has brought upon him, except by these odious circulars sent by those people . . .

> Many young men in this country who might have held proud positions in society, who might have succeeded in professions, who might have held high rank in the army, have been ruined by Messrs. Beyfus and Boss; many families have been disgraced. [No evidence whatsoever was brought before the court to establish that Beyfus & Boss had ruined anybody, and it is surprising that it was allowed to be said unchallenged either by prosecution counsel or the magistrate.]

> Having wrung every shilling and 70% and 80% out of their victims, they drive them into the Court of Bankruptcy; so that their fathers, or their mothers, or their sisters, should come forward and try and prevent disgrace to the family by means of their connection with Messrs. Boss & Beyfus.

At an early stage during his speech, Lewis dealt with the allegation that the paper had made reference to the United Synagogue in a sneering way. He denied it, but added:

111

Let me say this, in the hearing of the public and a great number of people, probably many of whom are of the same religion as Messrs. Boss & Beyfus, that by no persons in the whole of this community is the trade of usury, and those who follow it, more despised and loathed than by the Jews of this country. [*Great applause.*] *The World* newspaper has said this is not a question of sect; it is not a question of whether a Jew should be on the committee of a synagogue ... There are bad Jews as well as bad Protestants and bad Catholics, and I am surprised that Mr. Williams should have introduced this subject.

Mr. Montagu Williams: Really the subject is introduced by the newspaper.

Lewis: You have observed upon it to enable your client to cling on to the skirt of one of the most respectable communities in this country.

He then turned his attention to Henry Beyfus. Where was Mr Henry Beyfus? He would not meet *The World* face to face. Mr Henry Beyfus was the person who swore the information on which the summons was issued, and swore that there was no truth in the allegations made against him, that they were utterly and wholly without foundation. That being so, why didn't he appear in the witness box? The answer was clear – he was ashamed to submit his transgressions to the public gaze.

Lewis thanked the magistrate for having granted the summons, because this had enabled the matter to be brought under the searchlight of the legal process. What *The World* had done was done for the public interest, for the public good [*great applause*]. The resultant publicity would have a tendency to drive Boss and Beyfus out of this odious trade, and compel them to restrict their activities to their umbrella manufacturing factory or their diamond business. He moved to his peroration:

The question is between this list of people and society. They are waging war upon society: they are enriching themselves by their horrid and odious trade; and what I ask you is this: to say that what has been written about them comes within the privilege of public journalism – that it is the duty of *The World* to expose this matter, as other journals have from time to time exposed it; that in exposing it the journal has not gone beyond what is the truth, and what is the honest, fair, and temperate history of each one of these men; and therefore that you have no other alternative than to dismiss this summons. [*Applause which was with difficulty suppressed.*]

Sir Thomas Gabriel dismissed the summons on the ground that it had not been proved before him that the libel was published with malicious motive but, on the contrary, good and ample grounds for its publication had been proved on the basis of public interest.

According to the following edition of *The World*, the decision was greeted by uproarious applause in the court, which had been densely crowded during the whole of the proceedings. Those who attended the hearings, the paper claimed, consisted to a large extent of private gentlemen, army officers and clergymen, who had specially come to town 'from all parts of the three kingdoms', prepared with evidence which had either been brought to their knowledge, or was within their own personal experience, of the extortion which had been practised by Boss and Beyfus.

It had been a bravura performance by George Lewis, and he deserved the result and acclaim he received. *The World* was naturally delighted, and justifiably praised themselves in their edition of 10 February.

The manner in which the proceedings instituted by Messrs. Boss and Beyfus against *The World* have terminated is, we venture to think, matter of congratulation, not merely for ourselves, but for society at large ... The irrepressible and ringing cheers which interrupted Mr. Lewis from time to time in his masterly address, and which greeted Sir Thomas Gabriel's final words, showed conclusively the extent to which the public mind is with us.

Although usury was, they said, the blight of many a once-promising career, the curse which had descended on and destroyed many a happy home, the law had probably gone as far as it could. Unlike George Lewis, Labby and Yates thought Parliament was sensible not to re-enact the repealed usury laws. For them experience had proved that

113

repeal would not lead to a cessation of moneylending at high rates. None the less, they considered that the press had a role to play where the law stopped:

> ... when a social mischief and nuisance is rife, with which the law can only imperfectly deal ... it becomes the duty and the privilege of the Press to interfere – to speak on behalf of the community with a voice whose influence is proportionate to its publicity. That is exactly what we have done in the present instance, and this is the ground on which our action has been taken.

Their only complaint against counsel appearing for Boss and Beyfus was the allegation which they considered Montagu Williams had made, that 'we intended in any remarks of ours to cast opprobrium on the Hebrew race'. Echoing medieval comments, they added: 'There are Teutonic extortioners as well as Semitic; and we do not know that the former are more merciful than the latter.'

The case had been a salutary lesson for all moneylenders, whether or not they were in the same category as Boss and Beyfus. Doubtless Sam took it to heart, and became even more resolved never to allow himself to fall into the same trap. If faced with a provocative press, and incited to issue proceedings, the clear message was that the moneylender should sit tight, bow his head, and let the storm pass over him. And although a more convincing denunciation of the activities of the West End moneylenders can hardly be imagined, what were the lasting consequences of *The World's* resounding success? The answer to the question is, none whatsoever.

George Lewis's aim had been not only to secure the acquittal of his client, but to strike a severe blow at the moneylenders named in the articles. *The World* claimed, rather half-heartedly, and without mentioning names, that within a few months three of them had left the business, though they did not claim that such leaving was permanent, and they did not seek to say that Beyfus and Boss had ceased trading. Other newspapers complimented *The World* on its stance, but still accepted advertisements from moneylenders. Moneylending continued exactly as before, as though the case had never been. More than 20 years later, when he was giving evidence to the House of Commons Select Committee on Moneylending, Sir George, as he by then was, had to admit that not only was this so, but that

114

some of the people he had attacked in 1875, including Sam, were still prospering in 1897.

There was just one immediate effect. On 2 March the United Synagogue accepted Boss's letter of resignation from his membership of the Council. He regretted the adverse publicity the case had brought upon them, but was bitter that his resignation had been called for in an anonymous circular sent to other members of the Council. He concluded his letter defiantly:

I was known to be a bill discounter and a lender of money at high rates of interest when elected to your Board. I therefore need not enter upon a defence of an avocation which so many follow privately, but which public opinion now so vehemently deprecates. I will only add that I have always conducted my business with the strictest integrity, and I hope, for the credit of the community, that every member of the Board has been actuated through life by the same sentiments of honour and probity as I have been.

The whole episode illustrated a lesson history can teach us. What is believed to be adverse, even fatal, publicity, against a person or institution, can pass completely unheeded, or misunderstood, by the general public to whom it is addressed. There have even been cases in which an organisation attacked for its alleged ill practices enjoys enhanced business following the attack, the public remembering its name, but not the criticism.

Sir George never wavered in his views on Sam, and continued whenever he could to attack him, taunt him, and try to inveigle him into court. Labouchere, on the other hand, mellowed towards him. In the obituary he wrote of Sam he acknowledged that he was a most remarkable man who had occupied a unique position in London for many years. He said he had not often found occasion to speak in favour of a moneylender, but Sam was in most ways unlike all others of his class. He had never heard any suggestion that Sam had dealt other than fairly and properly with his clients. 'He did not seek to get impecunious idiots under his thumb for the purpose of squeezing them dry and chucking them aside, ruined.' He then added a sentence which clearly indicated that the two of them had met socially quite frequently – probably in clubs, or on the racecourse, or at casinos. 'He

115

was always the best of good company, and will be truly missed in all those haunts which he frequented.'

Sam could hold his own with the brightest and the best. He continued with his business completely unruffled by the fuss occasioned by the trial.

10 · London, Brighton and Maidenhead

Mid pleasures and palaces though we may roam,
Be it ever so humble, there's no place like home.
John Howard Payne (1791–1852)

As Sam's career progressed, so his fortune grew, and by 1880 his annual income exceeded £100,000. He and Ada set about acquiring houses in areas which were plainly selected for a particular purpose. Each one provided them not only with a home, but also a place amidst Sam's clientele, and each was of a scale and luxury which elevated Sam and Ada closer to his clients' level, making socialising and acceptance easier. They both had an unerring instinct for the rewarding location. In 1880 they moved from Gower Street to Grosvenor Square, which represented the pinnacle of London living. In 1892 he acquired a second home at Brunswick Terrace, Hove, and in 1895 a third, 'Woodside', by Boulter's Lock at Maidenhead. Each was a prime example of its kind.

The first move, to Grosvenor Square in the heart of Mayfair, was the important one. Sam and Ada went to live among an elite, a privileged few, in what had become an historic area. Grosvenor Square was not London's oldest square – that title belonged to Covent Garden – nor its largest, for Lincoln's Inn Fields was larger, but it was the most fashionable, rivalled in Society's affection only by Belgrave Square. It was the most aristocratic of addresses, and at the time it was built surpassed all others in the size of its mansions and the social eminence of its inhabitants. The ownership of a home in Grosvenor Square was considered a peak of achievement for the most superior members of Society, let alone for a boy from a Birmingham slum, and it is difficult to exaggerate what a social triumph this move

117

represented. It had the added advantage for Sam and Ada of being within ten minutes' walk of the West London Synagogue.

For centuries the land on which the Square was built formed part of the Manor of Ebury, broad agricultural land belonging to the abbots of Westminster, and so continued until the spoliation of the monasteries by Henry VIII, after which much of it passed into lay hands. Most appositely for our story, it came into the possession of the Grosvenor family through Hugh Audley, a well-known money-lender to the nobility, who was born in 1577. According to the *Dictionary of National Biography* he was a 'heartless bloodsucker'. Isaac Disraeli said half-ruined prodigals were fleeced by him, and described him as 'this genius of 30%'. According to F. S. Merry-weather in his *Lives and Anecdotes of Misers*, Audley's whole life was one of trickery and disreputable craft. 'His schemes of villainy were so intricate, and his deceptions so subtle, that few could discover their purpose, or tread the labyrinth of his plot ... there was never one so disreputable as Audley; there was never usurer so usurious, never a creditor so unrelenting; and there never was one whose craft wrought the ruin of so many unfortunate, but honest, men.'

However, Arthur Dasent, who in 1935 chronicled the detailed story of the Square, accepted evidence that much of Audley's money was loaned out at six per cent. His comment was: 'I am sure that the late Samuel Lewis, himself a sometime resident of Grosvenor Square, would have regarded him as being out of his mind to treat his clients so leniently.' He added that at the date of Audley's death his creditors were not young spendthrifts or gambling ne'er-do-wells, but men of responsible standing and distinction, a description which would fit many of those who were debtors of Sam at the time of his death.

When, in 1656, Audley bought the Manor of Ebury from the Earl of Middlesex for £9,400, its only inhabitants were a few shepherds and tenant farmers, and its lanes were infested with thieves. But Audley was a shrewd judge, and he appears to have forseen its enormous potential value although its development as a building estate did not take place until three-quarters of a century after his death in 1662. The estate eventually passed to his great-great-niece, Mary Davies, who was just six months old when her father died intestate. Under the then existing law his fortune was divided as to one-third to his widow and two-thirds to her.

As an heiress she was an investment, something guardians sold for a price, and parents purchased for a son. When Mary was eight her mother and stepfather, John Tregonwell, began negotiations with Lord Berkeley of Stratton. He was then busily acquiring building plots around a Piccadilly mansion he had just completed. Berkeley Square and Stratton Street remain today as reminders of his presence in the area. Mary's land, just to the north of his, would have greatly enhanced his estate. He put down a £5,000 deposit with the Tregonwells to bind Mary to become betrothed to his ten-year-old son, Charles. Part of the contract involved an additional payment of £3,000, but when the time came Lord Berkeley was unable to meet this obligation. He had been expecting a substantial financial reward from Charles II for his long and faithful service to him, but there were more pressing demands made upon the King from the surviving mothers of his 13 bastards. After his mistresses had been financially satisfied there was nothing left for veteran loyalists like Berkeley.

So the match fell through, and Berkeley requested to be relieved of his liability. He claimed that as it was the King's fault, not his, that he could not proceed, the £5,000 deposit he had paid should be returned to him plus interest. If the marriage had taken place it would have made the Berkeley family the wealthiest of London's landlords; instead that honour was to pass elsewhere. The Tregonwells, who had already spent the £5,000 on themselves, sought another suitor. According to Mrs Tregonwell there was no problem about that; it was a question of deciding among the many offers which had been made. The choice fell upon Sir Thomas Grosvenor, ten years older than Mary, whose 'circumstances, familie, and character, appear'd to bee most suitable'. It was a happy selection. Sir Thomas was well-bred (though his family were then mere baronets), well educated and wealthy, his income being double that of his bride. When they married in 1671 (she was just 12 years old), the 100 acres she brought with her were of much less value than her husband's rich Cheshire property.

It was the apparently inexhaustible demand for new London houses for the rich which soon reversed the position, and from the early 1700s until today Mary Davies's meadows have steadily increased in value. They were in a superb position, on the plateau south of the Oxford Road, now Oxford Street. Mary's eldest son, Richard, the fourth baronet, embarked on a building scheme for the area. Londoners had never lived so high up – Hampstead and Highgate were not then part of London – and it had the benefit of being in open country. Healthy surroundings were an important consideration, and flower beds and fruit trees could flourish in the pure air. It became a small rural suburb of smoky London.

Sir Richard's aim was to attract the fashionable world to his estate, and in Grosvenor Square he built, or granted building leases for, terrace houses which were larger and more handsomely equipped than any previously seen in London. They had gardens at the back and cottages in the mews for coachmen and the upper servants. The scheme was brilliantly successful. From its earliest days the Square and the surrounding streets of the estate, including North and South Audley Streets, named after Hugh Audley, and Davies Street, named after Mary, attracted residents of high social status. By 1751 there were 39 peers of the realm living there. Until well into the twentieth century over half the residents were people of title. Not only was it mainly occupied by the highest of the aristocracy, but until very late in the day there was not a plebeian professional among them.

The Square remained a centre of fashion, and did not deteriorate socially until it had to change its position somewhat with the arrival of the late nineteenth-century plutocrats; then blue blood mixed with the red blood of the commercial millionaires. Its standing was made secure partly by its favourable position just two or three minutes' walk from Hyde Park, one of Society's favourite meeting places. There were no guardians at the gates of the park to keep out 'socially inferior' visitors, but in the structured Victorian society everyone knew whether they were acceptable or not, and it is significant that both Sam and Ada formed a regular and prominent part of the parade.

A home in the Square provided an unrivalled window during the Season from which to observe the flirtations, intrigues, assignations and manoeuvrings among Mayfair society during their daily rides and drives. Lady Augusta Fane described the scene:

In the 1880's and before, Rotten Row was packed with riders on weekdays (no one rode on Sunday), the fashionable hours being 11–1. Everybody who was anybody had a hack and turned out dressed to the nines. Men wore dark cloth frock coats, very tight trousers, collar and tie, and a silk top hat. Ladies had habit-bodices buttoned to the neck, surmounted by a white collar, and white cuffs on the sleeves. These bodices had little coat tails at the back which reached to the saddle. A long skirt, rather full, varnished boots and a silk hat like a man's, completed the costume. The ladies who did not ride, drove pony phaetons; and the men 'buggies' with hoods, drawn by a high-stepping horse ... the rest of the world sat under the trees and gossiped.

The lady riders were accompanied by grooms. Ada was a first-rate horsewoman, and her horses and carriages were acknowledged to be among the finest in the parade which was the focus of social attention, as Sam well understood. George Lambton told a story which illustrates this, and which he said was typical of Sam's good nature and shrewdness. There was a certain, unnamed, great lady noted for her beauty who had the best-turned-out carriage in London. Being rather extravagant she was often in need of money, and on one occasion, being especially hard up, and knowing that Lambton often had dealings with Sam, asked him if he thought Sam would give her £600 for her pair of horses, because she had heard that he was looking out for some for Ada. Lambton went to Sam who immediately said that the price was fair, and that he would buy them. The next morning, however, after Lambton had relayed the good news back to the lady, Sam told him that he had changed his mind. 'It is impossible, for I have found out that she is head over ears in debt, and if Mrs. Lewis is seen driving her horses every tradesman in London will be down on her, and there will be a crash, but you can tell her that, although I will not have her horses, I will lend her £600 on her note of hand.' No question of interest was raised. The lady in question sent him her most grateful thanks, but did not accept the generous offer. It is worth noting that Sam had uncovered her exact financial position within hours.

The absence of any squalid surrounding areas, and careful management by the Grosvenor family, helped the Square to maintain its supremacy. By the rack rents they charged, and the premiums they required when the original building leases expired, the family ensured that potential residents were limited to the very wealthy. Once the new occupants acquired leases they tended to spend lavishly on the upkeep of their houses, and the best architects of the day worked in the Square, including Sir William Chambers, Sir John Soane, Robert Adam and James and Samuel Wyatt.

The Square kept the outside world at bay for longer than anywhere else. It retained oil lamps for lighting until 1842, long after gas had been in general use, for its introduction was opposed by diehard residents of the older generation who, proud of their flambeaux, lamps and candles, refused to accept the new invention, considering it vulgar and unsuitable for their aristocratic square. They also kept their cobbled stones, and until well into the 1880s the Square was still full of carriages during the Season, with a dignified butler and two footmen standing ready at almost every door to receive visitors.

Within the first 75 years of its existence, the Square boasted the presence of four prime ministers: the Duke of Grafton, the Marquis of Rockingham, Lord North and Henry Addington. In its first 200 years there were twice as many dukes, dowager duchesses, and Knights of the Thistle and St Patrick as there were individual houses. George Frederick Handel took a small house in Brook Street, and composed *The Messiah* there. William Beckford, the owner of Fonthill Abbey, author of *Vathek*, and twice Lord Mayor of London, lived at No. 2 between 1797 and 1801. He rented it out for a short time to his friends Sir William and Lady Emma Hamilton, and it is no surprise that in December 1800 Lord Nelson stayed with them after the Battle of the Nile. Lord Shaftesbury, the philanthropist, lived at No. 27 from 1851 to 1885, and the house had then been in the uninterrupted occupation of his family from the time of the fourth earl in 1732.

The 1871 census, the last before Sam and Ada moved in, revealed that no fewer than 840 of the residents on the Grosvenor Estate belonged to the titled and 'leisured' class, including 25 peers, 14 baronets and 109 other persons of title. It was a close-knit community, very much inbred, a coterie which it was difficult to enter.

During the latter part of the century more than one-third of all employed women between the ages of 15 and 25 were in domestic service, so that for their masters and mistresses life could be very comfortable. On the day of the census in 1881 there were 440 servants in the 29 houses of the Square which were in normal occupation. These included housemaids, ladies' maids, kitchen maids, scullery maids, stillroom maids, children's maids, schoolroom maids, undermaids, butlers, under-butlers, valets, footmen, porters, hall porters, ushers of the hall, hall boys, housekeepers, needlewomen, nurses, cooks, governesses, laundresses, coachmen, grooms, stablemen, stewards' room boys, house carpenters and some described simply as attendants. At No. 16, a house subsequently purchased by Ada, Lady Charteris and her two sons and two daughters were attended upon by no fewer than 17 servants. Sam and Ada moved into No. 23 in 1880, and contented themselves with a butler, coachman, cook, and three domestic servants. Thirty-six of their neighbours were titled.

Number 23 (until the Square was renumbered in 1888 it was No. 20) was on the corner of Upper Brook Street and North Audley Street. The house was built under a lease dated 1727 granted to Robert Andrews. In 1731 he assigned it to a building tradesman, John Warrington, but the first tenant noted by Dasent did not take up residence until 1780. Owners prior to Sam included, prophetically, Caroline (Campbell), the Dowager Countess of Ailesbury (1796–1803); the seventh earl of Newburgh (1829–1833); the Earl of Faversham (1862–1868); and Lady Charlotte Wentworth Fitzwilliam, who lived there in 1879. It was from her that Sam presumably acquired the lease, which had another 26 years to run. The ground rent was £400 per annum, and the price was probably between £30,000 and £40,000.

It was a gigantic and impressive leap forward for Sam, then just 42 years old – a very far cry indeed from 1 Lower Hurst Street, Birmingham. Gower Street had been a desirable address, but Grosvenor Square was the summit, the culminating glory. What was the motivation for the move? It was certainly more convenient for Sam to reach his office, but that was unlikely to have been a main reason. To show the world that he could afford it? He was not an ostentatious man. To prove that he had arrived? Quite possibly. What it did do was to set him firmly in position within the neighbourhood of the wealthiest and most influential in the land. During the time they were there, their neighbours included the sixth duke of Portland (at No. 3), the sixth Earl Fitzwilliam (No. 4), the twelfth earl of Home (No. 6), Viscount Farquhar (No. 8), the fourth Earl Grey (No. 11), Henry Spender Clay (No. 16), the eighth Lord Howard de Walden (No. 19), the third marquis of Donegal (No. 25), the seventh earl of

123

Shaftesbury, the sixth earl of Albermarle (No. 34), the second earl of Harrowby (No. 44), the fifth earl of Dartmouth (No. 45), Sir Ernest Cassel (No. 48), and the Dowager Duchess of Marlborough, Lord Randolph Churchill and his wife Jennie, all at No. 50.

The house afforded Ada, who undoubtedly harboured social aspirations, a fitting home in which to entertain the growing number of Sam's clients and acquaintances who were prepared to accept his invitations and offers of hospitality. Business apart, they had a very wide circle of friends, and of course the family were frequent visitors. It was also ideal for Ada so far as her love of horses and riding was concerned, because the Park and Rotten Row were so close, and Sam later acquired a house at the rear, at No. 3 Lees Place, which was rebuilt as a coachhouse and stables with a coachman's quarters above.

Sam was the first Jew to live in the Square, and the first money-lender to be connected with it since Hugh Audley owned the land on which it was built. Many of his highly placed neighbours pulled wry faces at his coming, and indeed there was some protest, partly on account of his religion and partly because of his occupation and social standing, but as the *Daily Express* was later to remark, when this happened 'Mr. Lewis only smiled the more when he met their friends and relations in his private office in Cork Street'. It must have taken considerable courage, or a dose of Jewish *chutzpah*, to move in among such distinguished company knowing that the welcome might be less than warm. Sam, however, was wrapped in the security of his fortune, and his intimate knowledge of what many of the aristocracy were really like, which to some extent inured him against any possible indifference or even snubs, and neither Sam nor Ada felt in any way inferior. Sam was certainly wealthier, and Ada more cultured and artistically talented, than most others in the Square. They lived there for more than 20 years, and were eventually accepted as belonging.

Living in Grosvenor Square, they were well serviced by their local shops, being so close to Bond Street, Regent Street and Oxford Street; and there was no shortage of provision for the horses, all within easy distance of the Square. When in Brighton and Maidenhead, Sam and Ada similarly patronised the local suppliers.

Sam's next venture into house purchase took place in 1892. Brighton and Hove had a threefold attraction for Sam. It formed part and parcel of the extended London season; it had its own attractive racecourse (and was close to those at Lewes and Goodwood); and it had a small Jewish community which met for prayer in its beautiful synagogue in Middle Street. Brighton's modern prosperity had been laid in the middle of the eighteenth century by Dr Richard Russell. He had strongly recommended its bracing air and sea bathing to his patients as the cure for many illnesses, particularly diseases of the glands. Many distinguished visitors followed. Dr Johnson was one of the few who were unimpressed by the town, and he told his friend Mrs Thrale that he found it 'so truly desolate, that if one had a mind to hang oneself for desperation at being obliged to live there, it would be difficult to find a tree on which to fasten the rope'. George III's brother, the Duke of Cumberland, rented a house in 1779, and became leader of the hunting, racing and gambling set in the town. But it was the arrival – to the accompaniment of the ringing of bells and a royal salute of guns – of the King's son, the Prince of Wales, later George IV, that led to the growth of a town of splendour and some size. He placed it firmly on the social map from the time of his first visit in 1783, when Brighton was little more than a mere fishing village. He returned the following year, having been advised by his physician that sea-bathing was essential 'to perfect the re-establishment of his health', and took a lease on the house on the Steine which, when later enlarged, was to become his summer residence, the still famous and recently restored Royal Pavilion. Queen Victoria also used it for the same purpose for a few years before she came to prefer Osborne on the Isle of Wight.

The prince's arrival in the town set off a boom in house building. Brighton was transformed into a fashionable, bow-windowed town by the sea. The ten years after his accession to the throne saw the creation of Kemp Town and Brunswick Town, and the large and small squares, crescents and terraces which give Brighton and Hove their present distinction. It was to Brunswick Terrace (the form of which was largely inspired by the terraces in Regent's Park in London) that Sam and Ada were to look for their south coast home. Sam acquired No. 13.

The previous occupier had been Lady Emily Williams. It was the centre house of the second block of the terrace, facing the sea and overlooking the lawns and promenade, and considered to be one of the most favoured and fashionable parts of the town. Sam spent heavily on decorating and improving its 14 bedrooms, dressing room, two bathrooms, handsome double drawing room, and the dining room and inner hall which was used as a library. As befitted the former Lower Hurst Street resident, there was a separate butler's pantry, sitting room and bedroom. Ada's love of horses and riding was catered for by stabling in the rear comprising four stalls, a loose box, a double coach house, harness room, and three living rooms and a loft over. The whole was expensively and handsomely furnished. It made an ideal home entirely suitable for entertaining friends, particularly during the racing season. It was not a poor neighbourhood. Harry Barnato, Barney Barnato's brother, was at No. 1; His Honour Judge Holl at No. 6; Baroness Horatia de Teissier at No. 7; the Dowager Lady Duke at No. 24; and Princess Betzold-Soutzo at No. 25.

Royal patronage inevitably attracted London Society, and the opening of the London to Brighton Railway in 1841 gave the town an added boost. The *beau monde* came and paraded along four and a half miles of uninterrupted drive, with the sea in front and a glorious backcloth of wealth and fashion. For them it was not the beach, with its boats and bathing machines, which was the main allurement; it was to see and be seen. According to Richard Jefferies, writing in 1875, 'the beach is ignored ... No one rows, very few sail; the sea is not "the thing" in Brighton, which is the least nautical of seaside places. There is more talk of horses.' A 'Tourist's Guide to Brighton' of 1886 referred to the wonderful backdrop Brighton provided for the horses and their riders:

> Rotten Row, on an afternoon in the height of the season, or even Bond Street, Regent Street, or the 'Drive' and 'The Lady's Mile' by the Serpentine, presents a most agreeable spectacle; but to understand Brighton you must suppose that Rotten Row, Bond Street, Regent Street and 'The Lady's Mile' have been bodily transferred to the sea side; that they have been prolonged eastwards to the ascent of the magnificent Downs; that before them expands a glorious breadth of many coloured waters; that in the distance the radiant cliffs lift up their walls of pearly chalk to a formidable elevation.

Brighton too had its seasons, and one's position in Society was set by the time of year of one's visit. It effectively provided an extension of the London season for those not going abroad: 'the crème-de-la-crème frequent it from the beginning of November until Christmas. The middle class season commences about Whitsuntide, and lasts to the close of October. Persons of moderate means, and robust health, affect it from February until June.'

C. B. Cochrane, the impresario, grew up in Brighton. He said that in the 1880s and 1890s the front displayed, particularly on Sundays, a cross-section of English society. The peerage, the Bar, the turf, the stage, literature, were all represented in 'the crowd of saunterers'. At weekends in the season the Brighton front was 'thick with celebrities' – including Sir George Lewis. As for the aristocracy, 'they were there by the dozens'.

In later years Edward VII might be seen walking on Kingsway, and he frequently stayed with Arthur Sassoon at his house in King's Gardens. For many years it was the custom of several of the leading pictorial papers to publish a full-plate representation of Brighton front during the Season. 'Among the personages who would be identified there would always be the fashionable lawyer, the fashionable doctor, the fashionable actor, and the fashionable moneylender. In this latter respect . . . Sam Lewis of Cork Street fame was very much in evidence.' The *Brighton Gazette* suggested that 'Uncle Sam' was there presumably to keep an eye on some of his clients 'for he believed in looking after his sheep without any inquisitive feelings'. There may well have been some truth in this. His presence in Grosvenor Square, in Brighton, and in Maidenhead, where so many of his clients gathered at the appropriate times of the year, would not appear in any way false or sinister while he had homes there. The racecourse naturally held a particular attraction for Sam. His new home was no more than 10 or 15 minutes' drive from the track, nor more than an hour from Goodwood or Lewes, the facilities were excellent, and Ada could help him entertain his cronies after the meetings.

A Jewish community had been established in Brighton by the end of the eighteenth century. It fell into temporary decline, but was formally reconstituted in 1821 and played its full part in local affairs. In the 1840s there was a Jewish Chief Constable of the town, Henry Solomon. He was murdered in sensational circumstances, being attacked with a poker by a deranged youth who had been brought to the police station in connection with a charge of robbery. Queen Victoria donated £50 to the appeal fund set up for his widow and nine children. Solomon's brother-in-law, Hyam Lewis, was a Town Commissioner and a member of the first Police Committee, and another brother-in-law was Levi Emmanuel Cohen, the editor of the *Brighton Guardian*, and twice president of the Newspaper Society. Sir Isaac Lyon Goldsmid purchased the Wick Estate in 1830, and became the first Chairman and Life Commissioner of the Board of Commissioners of Brunswick Square. He developed Palmeira Square and Adelaide Crescent, and his son, Sir Francis Goldsmith, the one who had stood unsuccessfully in the parliamentary election in Great Yarmouth, was responsible for the development of a considerable part of Hove.

The Middle Street Synagogue, which is still in use, was founded in 1874 and was conducted on traditional orthodox lines, in contrast to the reform services Sam attended at West London Synagogue. Middle Street benefited considerably from the generosity of the Sassoon family; Baroness Rothschild and Hannah Rothschild presented a magnificent pair of candlesticks, and Sir Moses Montefiore donated a Sefer Torah (scroll of the law). It also boasts two stained-glass windows dedicated to the memory of the Jewish wife of an English prime minister, Hannah Rothschild who married Lord Rosebery. By the time Sam purchased his house the congregation consisted of about 70 families, enlarged on the Sabbath by a constant stream of short-stay visitors. He was a regular attender whenever he was in residence at Brunswick Terrace, and became a good friend of the minister, the Reverend C. Jacobs.

The town was very popular with Jews as a holiday resort, and in the summer months well-known families, such as the Rothschilds, took up temporary residence. The Sassoons acquired ornate villas, and Labouchere described Brighton as 'a sea-coast town, three miles long and three yards broad, with a Sassoon at each end and one in the middle'. The Chief Rabbi, Dr Nathan Adler, moved to Hove in 1880 and remained there until his death in 1890. In its heyday in the 1890s, the London Brighton & South Coast Railway had engines named Goldsmid, Rothschild and Jonas Levy. Most of the hawkers and pedlars on the beach were also Jewish.

Maidenhead, also known in the latter part of the nineteenth

century as *London-by-the-River* or *Mayfair-by-the-River*, came into its own in June and July of each year. Society's members occupied houses on the river in Maidenhead itself or on the banksides of the pretty villages close by in either direction. Cookham is just 2 miles distant, Bray 2½, Marlow 6, Windsor 8, and Henley only 14 miles away. This stretch is ideal for boating, its current gentle and its varied scenery possessing a quiet, typically English beauty: low hills and wooded cliffs, luxuriant meadows, handsome country houses and pretty bungalows with gardens and lawns sloping down to the river. Along the riverside, by the double arched bridge designed by Sir Isambard Brunel, the greatest span ever accomplished in brick, are well-built houses with lovely gardens and shrubbery, green lanes brightened with beds of flowers, groups of shady trees and pleasing villa residences. At the end of the nineteenth century householders and riparian owners let their houses for the season, and vicars were enabled to take continental holidays on the proceeds of renting out their vicarages.

At its northern extremity is Boulter's Lock, with the beautiful hanging woods of Taplow in the background. At the height of the Season more than a thousand boats passed through daily: steam and electric launches, punts and every other kind of river craft jostled with each other. On fine summer days it was the rendezvous for representatives of the smartest society – a social event no one could afford to miss. Sunday evening, between four and eight o'clock, was the climax of the week. Society congregated at Boulter's and socialised there, many coming from the grand mansions such as Cliveden, less than a mile away and owned by Mr William Waldorf Astor, and from Mr and Mrs Grenfell's Taplow Court. At these two mansions house parties were entertained in Ascot Week, and at weekends during the river season. Over the years their guests included kings, queens, dukes of the royal blood, ambassadors, prime ministers, generals, writers, leading actors and other distinguished personages. The Prince of Wales was a guest at Taplow in June 1896, and when he passed through Boulter's on the steam launch *Duchess* the crowd waved, but because it was a Sunday forbore to cheer. Other members of Society came from smaller houses such as the Jacobean Braywick Grove. The Duke and Duchess of Newcastle were frequently at Ditton Park, and the Duke and Duchess of Westminster at Runnymede.

Earl Russell was close to the lock at Hanbury Cottage; Lord Stanley and Lady Alice Stanley stayed at Cowarth Park; Lord Burnham at Hall Barn; and Colonel Ricardo at Cookham.

All classes gathered in Maidenhead on Sundays. According to the *West End Review* of August 1897:

> It is the day par excellence to study the masses and the classes ... In the narrow shelters of Boulter's Lock the luxurious launch, with its luncheon spread out ostentatiously, will have as near neighbour a perky canoe, filled perhaps with men, who take their refreshment up in a carpet-bag, while on the other side a merry party of ladies are being propelled in a smart business-like punt by a trim girl who steers her way forward to be out first. Possibly a large launch with boisterous crowd on board will enliven the scene with music and song, or those afoot will cause some merriment by being humorous over the frantic efforts of the novice to avoid bumping. Ah! it is a merry, irresponsible, throng, and the constant *va et vient* quite kaleidoscopic.

From 1880 onwards the town developed with remarkable rapidity, due not only to its charming surroundings but also because of its ease of access to and from London by rail. Many trains took less than half an hour to cover the 24 miles, and the weekend rate for a first class ticket was just five shillings and six pence.

Lord and Lady Cowley, the sister of Lord William Nevill, had a beautiful home, called 'Woodside', immediately on the river, in what could justifiably be called the prime, the most desirable position, just a few hundred yards north of Boulter's. From it there were no other buildings at all fronting the river on either bank right the way up to Cliveden; just trees and bushes overhanging the water providing many shady corners where boats and punts could hide discreetly, with sheltered nooks for lovers to sit in peace and seclusion. The house stood in two and a half acres, and had a frontage to the river of more than 200 feet. (It still exists, and is now divided into three large homes.) There was a wonderful view of all the passing parade from any of its three balconies, and most importantly one could be seen from them as well as see. In 1895 Sam purchased the house and grounds for Ada for just over £11,000. He also bought a yacht, the *Isis Hathor*, and they made frequent use of it. They became familiar

130

figures on the Thames during the summer months. When the Prince of Wales paid another visit in July 1898, Sam and Ada joined the throng at Boulter's aboard their own yacht. The house and yacht were invaluable investments.

In London, Brighton and Maidenhead Sam was relaxed and at ease, and the fondness he felt for each town was later to be demonstrated by the munificence of the legacies he bequeathed to local charities. By the acquisition of their three homes Sam and Ada had completed Society's circle. They were not only enabled to be wherever the Season demanded, but they were well placed to offer hospitality to their friends and Sam's clients. In No. 23 Grosvenor Square, No. 13 Brunswick Terrace and 'Woodside', Sam had a trio which could be equalled by very few.

11 · The Turf

One area in which Sam became deeply involved was the Turf.
Horse racing was of supreme importance in late nineteenth-century
Society. According to Escott, writing in 1885, the principal bond
uniting London Society was not the similarity of background, or
politics, or even family relationships, but sport in its various branches
– shooting, hunting, the card table – and, above all, the Turf. An
Englishman did not need to profess any high opinion of art or
literature. He could affect an attitude of indifference towards politics.
But in sport Society provided itself with a centre around which the
social atoms revolved. All Englishmen, and a good many Englishwomen, even if they had no vested interest in horses, bet or gambled
in some way:

> It is the ruling passion, and in virtue of its predominance it does in
> effect group society around itself. The Prince of Wales, as Society's
> king, is a patron of the Turf; seldom misses an important race
> meeting, and is reported to have a share in the proprietorship of
> some racehorses. The Duke of Richmond celebrates the Goodwood
> meeting, held in his park, with a brilliant country house party, of
> no less than thirty or forty in number, containing the cream of
> London Society, and every one of them interested, or making a
> show of being interested, in racing. Many other mansions in the
> neighbourhood are filled in the same fashion, though on a less
> splendid scale. What takes place in and about Goodwood in August
> has been previously witnessed in the neighbourhood of Ascot in
> June. A fortnight before Ascot the Derby has been run at Epsom,
> and the week between Epsom and Ascot traditionally marks the
> zenith and the apogee of the London Season ... Rightly, therefore
> will you learn to look upon the Turf as one of the great rallying

centres of London Society – as the embodiment of the principle which unites Society the most.

The prince's patronage supplied the sport with its supreme accolade even though his mother, Queen Victoria, strongly disapproved. She advised him, advice he steadfastly ignored, to keep his distance from the 'fast racing set'. She considered their manners had worsened to such an extent, and their faults had become so widely known, that her son ought to mark his disapproval by 'not asking them to dinner nor down to Sandringham – and, above all, not going to their houses'. His position as the acknowledged head of Society made racing socially *de rigueur*, and because of this owning racehorses was an accompaniment not just of wealth but also of social standing. This proved irresistible to the plutocrats. If they became owners, not only would the world see their names on the racecards, but meetings in the paddock might lead to invitations elsewhere.

It was a highly expensive pastime, but Society found the glamour and excitement irresistible. It was pursued with vigour, and huge fortunes were spent, whether they could be afforded or not, on buying and breeding horses, building studs and training stables, on lavish house parties for race meetings and, of course, on gambling. At Lowther the Lonsdales had an established stud in the 1690s, imported Arabian stock being highly favoured. By the latter part of the eighteenth century Lord Grosvenor was lavishing £7,000 a year on the sport. However, it was gambling rather than ownership which increased the cost. Without gambling the sport would not have survived then, nor would it now. The breeding of gambling debts rivalled the breeding of bloodstock.

Betting on horses does not alter in any fundamental way through the centuries. The bookmakers win, the punters lose, even though individual backers may buck the trend for short periods. Inevitably there were those who bet beyond their immediate means, and had to borrow to repay their losses. Society gamblers considered it *infra dig* not to pay gambling debts within 24 hours, and gave them priority over worthier objects. Default could bring social ruin. In times of emergency they turned to the moneylender, and the best known, the most trusted, the man who was to be seen regularly at all the tracks, was Sam, who was himself fond of a bet. He became accepted as 'the punters' friend', though perhaps a more accurate description would have been 'the bookmakers' friend'.

By the time Sam became involved in the Turf, in the 1870s, horse racing had undergone a social transformation without which he could not have operated as he did. The sport was being made more accessible by the coming of the railways which provided transport for the racehorses, jockeys, trainers, owners and punters, but it had two main problems. It was unable to provide safe and comfortable facilities for those frequenting the track, particularly for the ladies, and it was beset with corruption among jockeys, trainers, stable staff, officials and owners.

The responsible regulatory organisation was the oligarchically exclusive Jockey Club, founded in about 1750, whose membership from the outset was predominantly aristocratic. At the end of the nineteenth century it still remained very much an association of peers and squires, largely limited to a select circle of landed gentry whose positions were founded on old-established estates. In 1898, for example, 41 of its 54 members were titled or closely related to those who were, and eight were members of the British and continental royal families, headed by the Prince of Wales. Baron Meyer de Rothschild managed to break into the tightly knit group – he was the first Jewish member elected – but generally the doors were closed to outsiders. One disappointed industrialist complained: 'to become a member of the Jockey Club, you have to be a relative of God, and a close one at that.'

The Club's original aims were simply to promote good fellowship between horse-breeding and horse-racing gentlemen throughout the country, and to attempt to exclude the pickpockets, ruffians and other undesirable elements who had been attracted to the sport from its earliest days. As one successful owner remarked, 'I do not say that all those who go racing are rogues and vagabonds, but I do say that all rogues and vagabonds seem to go racing.' Although the Club quickly acquired prestige, its authority was undermined because it had no effective means of control over the type of person attending the meetings, which were open and free. The remedy was the introduction of the enclosed course with turnstiles, and the imposition of an entrance fee. Access to certain stands was restricted to members, who had to be properly proposed and seconded by existing members, and acceptable to the trustees. Sam had no difficulty in finding proposers and seconders – several members of the Jockey Club were his clients! He became a member at Sandown Park, Lingfield Park, Hurst Park, Gatwick, Alexandra Park and Kempton, and at most, if not all, of the other enclosed courses. He rarely missed a meeting at Newmarket, and was a familiar figure on nearly every course in England. Gambling was in Sam's blood. Apart from his family, racing and playing the tables at Monte Carlo were his principal pleasures and relaxation. They were also important venues for the ambitious moneylender, if he could gain admission to the members' stands, for there he could be seen in a setting in which his clients, or prospective clients, were relaxed.

The increased security at the courses helped make them pleasurable resorts for the wealthier supporters of the Turf and their female companions. The races, luncheon, the musical accompaniment, strolling round the lawns and flower beds, and meeting and conversing with one's peers, could now be enjoyed in comfort. The first enclosed course in England was at Sandown Park, and the man who opened it in 1875, the year in which he succeeded to his family estates, was General Owen Lewis Cope Williams, one of the most popular soldiers and sportsmen in London Society. He knew Sam well and they had doubtless first met as a result of their shared interest in racing. General Williams was representative of a group of men, all exercising influence at a high social and political level, whose trust and friendship Sam earned.

The general was a descendant of an old Welsh family, long settled in Craig-y-Don in Anglesey, which had also acquired considerable property in Ireland, Wales and Buckinghamshire. Born in 1836, he was educated at Eton, entered the Royal Horse Guards in 1854, and eventually rose to the rank of Lieutenant-General in 1887. He joined the smartest clubs – the Carlton, White's, the Turf, the Gun, Boodle's, the Four-in-Hand and the Marlborough – and gave his recreations as hunting, shooting, fishing, yachting and racing. He represented Marlow in Parliament from 1880 to 1885, following in the footsteps of his great-grandfather, grandfather and father, and was elected to the Jockey Club in 1881.

He was an intimate of the Prince of Wales, whose equerry he had been during the prince's tour of India in 1875–6, and he was one of the house party at Tranby Croft who was closely involved in the attempts made to extricate the prince from the so-called Baccarat Scandal. It was he and Lord Coventry who broke the story to the prince, and who confronted Sir William Cumming, the man accused of cheating. A great favourite in all sections of society, the general was most genial of manner, a bright conversationalist, and considered a man of the world, full of shrewd common sense. Because of this he was frequently consulted in all manner of social affairs. As a breeder, owner and rider, he was ever-present at the course, and his weekend hospitality in June and July each year at Temple House, a beautiful home on the Thames at Marlow which had been purchased by his great-grandfather in the eighteenth century, was a notable feature of the London season between Whitsun and the end of July. He also had a town house in Hill Street, just off Berkeley Square.

We have already noted that General Williams's family estate consisted of more than 14,000 acres producing £22,000 per annum gross; but he, like so many of his class, particularly those with racing interests, was deeply in debt. He regularly went to Cork Street for help throughout the 1880s and 1890s, and by 1901 owed Sam £145,141. He was one of Sam's longest-standing clients. Relationships between moneylender and client can obviously become strained, particularly if there are arrears. Sam's aptitude for making friends of his clients, and behaving in a reasonable manner at all times, greatly helped the client in difficulties. A borrower could repay such support, and also ingratiate himself with Sam, by doing him a favour if he could. There were certain barriers beyond which the likes of Sam could not pass, but the support of the general and of men like him would ensure that at least he could go to the very limit of the permitted boundaries; and should attacks be made upon him, Sam could rely on the backing of many who operated at the highest levels of influence. They provided him with a protective coating.

To know Owen Williams, and be known by him, carried with it a distinct social advantage, because he had access to, and the confidence of, those at the very top of the social tree. To be the friend of a friend of the Prince of Wales was as much as most men and women could aspire to. The general could use such influence as he had to promote or demote you within these circles; ease your way, or bar your entry.

Simply by being at the course, and constantly meeting old and possibly new clients there, Sam oiled the wheels of his own and his clients' businesses. This was something which, for the reasons described above, could not have been done prior to the 1870s with any degree of success, and once more Sam was to be found in the right place at the right time.

From the moneylender's point of view, matters were considerably improved by the growing involvement of the plutocrats in the sport. To successful men in industry and commerce such as Blundell Maple, the furnishing magnate, and Jack Joel, who made his fortune in South Africa's mineral fields, spending part of their fortunes on racing offered them an opportunity to be accepted by the prince. Ownership of thoroughbred bloodstock was predominantly a possibility only for the very rich, for the great Turf magnates such as the Duke of Westminster, the Duke of Portland and the Earl of Rosebery, who dominated the racing scene during the last 20 years of the century. The plutocrats could afford to pay for immediate success. They engaged in chequebook breeding, and their presence and activity at the sales, and rivalry with each other, inevitably increased the cost of engaging in the sport, making matters even more difficult for the hard-pressed aristocrats. For those who could not afford the expense, heavy betting appeared to offer the way of bridging the gap between their resources and their needs. But not even those who were reputed to be winning gamblers actually were; whenever a close examination of their accounts could be made, it always revealed a loss, no matter how successfully they concealed this truth from others or themselves. A number of owners were constantly in debt and on the verge of bankruptcy.

The Jockey Club made determined efforts to deal with its other main problem – corruption. Horses were frequently 'pulled' or 'nobbled', and deliberately made to run below their true form in order to defeat the handicapper who decided upon the weights the horses carried. It was mainly through the efforts of the Hon. Admiral Henry Rous, a younger son of the Earl of Stradbroke, that effective handicapping was introduced. Fresh rules were issued in 1870, and redrafted and tightened in 1876. Horses had to be registered at Weatherby's, as, from 1883, were all partnerships in the ownership of horses. This system was introduced because in the event of any infraction of the rules it was important for the authorities to know who the responsible party was. Some owners could not be traced because racing under assumed names was common. Young bloods anxious that their parents or trustees should not know their degree of involvement in the Turf, gamblers who felt that anonymity would secure better odds, and others who for various reasons preferred that their interest should not be known, all broke the rules by adopting pseudonyms or failing to register an interest. In 1889 Sam was to be accused of just this when one of the most publicised of racing scandals came to court – the libel action brought by Sir George Chetwynd against the Earl of Durham.

Both men were not only members of the Jockey Club but had also acted as stewards at meetings, and the fact that their differences involved airing a great number of the worst aspects of the sport in open court naturally caused a considerable degree of concern among all those connected with the Turf. Sir George Chetwynd was never as wealthy as people believed. He was a particular friend of Sam, and borrowed heavily from him for almost 30 years. He was a sportsman, pure and simple. Having been educated at both Eton and Harrow he had the unusual distinction of playing cricket against his old school at Lords. Beyond his stables, horses and attendance at race meetings, he had no occupation, and was commonly believed to be successful. A tall, slight, handsome, distinguished-looking man, he was charming when he chose to be, but inclined to be rather overbearing when enjoying a run of success. He was described as being more talked of, more envied, and in some quarters more disliked, than any man of the fashionable world. As a landowner with an income mainly dependent on his agricultural land, he was particularly vulnerable. Though never rich, he was, according to Lambton, determined to live as though money was no object and, in Lambton's view, was the most extravagant man he had ever met. He played the tables at Monte Carlo, enjoyed life exceedingly, and was to be found in smart company. Despite this, he was at the same time a familiar of some of the more disreputable types who frequented the track.

Chetwynd indulged himself with mistresses, and during the 1880s competed with Hugh Lowther, the fifth earl of Lonsdale (of Lonsdale Belt fame), for the favours of the ubiquitous Lillie Langtry. On one occasion when she was riding with Hugh in Hyde Park she stopped to speak to Sir George, and the two men confronted each other. Sir

George demanded that Hugh should 'stop meddling with my Lily', and struck out at him with his whip. Hugh, who was six foot five inches tall, of strapping physique, and one of the leading amateur boxers of the day, responded, and both men dismounted and continued the fight with their fists. Given Hugh's superior strength and experience, it was a brave, or foolhardy, thing for Sir George to do. Eventually, rolling in the dirt, and spattered with blood, they were pulled apart by the Duke of Portland and Sir William Cumming. So Chetwynd was a man prepared to fight his corner.

His interest in racing began even before he came of age, and he sought to support his style of living from gambling. He was not the first, nor was he the last, to discover that ownership of racehorses carries with it no guarantee of successful betting, not even on one's own horses. His trainer was 'Buck' Sherrard and his jockey Charlie Wood. The stables at Newmarket, though called Chetwynd House, were owned by Wood, and became popular with other owners who were heavy gamblers, such as Ernest Benzon, of whom we have already heard, and Lord Lurgan. Sherrard was a simple man who loved his horses and thought of nothing else but ensuring that they were always well turned out. Sir George had about a dozen horses in training with him; Lurgan had six; General Owen Williams 20; and Benzon 36. In common with Chetwynd and General Owen Williams, Sherrard, Benzon and Lord Lurgan all borrowed regularly from Sam.

Wood, in contrast, though undoubtedly a highly skilful jockey, concentrated his thoughts on the acquisition of money. Backed by such an ostensibly respectable figure as Sir George, he was rumoured to have breached the rules of the Jockey Club with impunity. A rule was introduced forbidding jockeys to own horses, but it was believed that many of the animals officially owned by Sir George, and registered in his name at Weatherby's, were Wood's property. Speculation also grew that Wood was 'pulling' horses and 'squaring' other jockeys to ensure that Sir George's bets, made on his own behalf and on behalf of Wood, were winning bets. When *The Licensed Victuallers' Gazette* went so far as to say that Wood had nearly pulled a horse's head off to stop him winning, he sued for libel. He won, but the jury awarded him only one farthing damages.

The Earl of Durham then entered the controversy and fanned the rumours into flames. After the death of Admiral Rous he had become the leading figure in the administration of racing. At the annual Gimcrack Club Dinner in York in December 1887 he made a speech in the course of which he said:

There is a well known, and what the sporting press calls a fashionable and aristocratic racing stable, that has been conspicuous throughout the racing season for the constant and inexplicable in-and-out running of its horses. Their running has surprised and disgusted the public besides losing them money, it has driven the handicapper to his wits end to discover the true form of the horses he apportions weights to, and it has scandalised all true lovers of the sport of horseracing.

But the darkest part of the matter is this – that the owners, or *nominal* owners, of the horses to which I am alluding win large stakes when their horses are successful, but do not lose much when they are beaten.

If you wish to purify the Turf you must go to the fountain head.

The accusations pointed directly at Sir George. Any ambiguity that he might be the target was removed when Lord Durham, in reply to a direct question, stated that the stable he had in mind was Wood's and that he had no intention of implicating any of the stable's patrons other than Sir George. Chetwynd's first reaction, as it had been with Hugh Lowther, was to inflict personal violence upon his opponent. He suggested a duel. Then, his temper cooling, he sued for libel instead, claiming damages of up to £20,000.

He must have approached Sam for support, for the solicitor who acted on his behalf was Algernon Sydney, Sam's own solicitor and closest friend. Given Chetwynd's financial position, it seems reasonable to assume that Sam guaranteed payment of the costs. Lord Durham's solicitor was none other than Sir George Lewis, and the evidence suggests that because of his hostility towards Sam he may have abused his position by gratuitously dragging him into the case when there was absolutely no evidence to justify such a course.

Lord Durham contended that everything he said was true. He alleged in his written pleadings that Wood 'pulled' horses; that the running of horses trained at the stables was deliberately inconsistent to deceive the handicapper; that Sir George bet heavily on his horses when they won, but did not bet when they lost because, it was implied, he knew when they were being 'stopped' or 'pulled' and when they were genuinely being ridden to win. There was then included a further allegation that in 1885, 1886 and 1887 no less than 44 horses which Sir George registered at Weatherby's as owned by him were in fact owned jointly by him, Wood and Sam. If this had been proved to be true, and Sam shown to be a party to such deception, the effects could have been catastrophic for him in the world of racing which he loved so much. His reputation for honest, plain, open dealing would have been in tatters, and the Jockey Club would have had no alternative but to warn him off, thus depriving him of his most pleasurable hobby. It would have kept him apart from his friends, hindered his advancement in Society, caused great distress to Ada and the rest of his family, and doubtless also directly affected his business activities. The mere making of the allegation was disturbing enough.

The court, which sat at the High Court of Justice in the Strand, and which by agreement between the parties consisted of the three stewards of the Jockey Club, the Rt Hon. J. Lowther MP, the Earl of March and Prince Soltykoff (the last two were occasional clients of Sam), listened to the evidence for several days spread over nearly three weeks, including an adjournment for a week so that all those involved could attend the Ascot meeting. Alexander Baird, known as 'the Squire', against whom it was also alleged that he secretly co-owned horses with Chetwynd, gave evidence and did not leave the witness box until 12.30, but still managed to ride a loser in the 2.30 at Sandown that afternoon. Sam, Lord Lurgan and Ernest Benzon attended the hearing almost every day. The remarkable Lady Tatton Sykes, yet another client of Sam's, and her husband did not miss a session. Indeed, almost all the spectators during the hearing were connected one way or another with Sam. They were all supporters of Chetwynd, as were the Duke of Beaufort (another client) and General Owen Williams. Only Lord Marcus Beresford openly stood by Durham's side despite pressure to join the opposite camp; many who thoroughly agreed with what Durham had said at the Gimcrack Dinner withheld their public support for him.

Sir George Chetwynd, Sherrard and Wood all denied that Sam had any interest of any kind in the horses which had been specified as being part-owned by him. George Lewis was called to give evidence

141

and said that this allegation contained in the pleadings had been drafted by him 'on information received', but he produced no evidence whatsoever to back it up. In cross-examination he admitted that he had based the allegation partly on inquiries one of his clerks had made, but in answer to the crucial question about Sam's involvement he said: 'I don't think my clerk made inquiries as to Mr. Samuel Lewis's ownership.' When Lord Durham came to give evidence he said, 'I make no charges against Mr. Sam Lewis.' He simply withdrew the accusation, and made no attempt whatsoever to justify its having been made.

So Sam was cleared of any involvement. Why then had the suggestion been made in the first place? Was it simply a 'fishing expedition' – an allegation based on rumour or suspicion in the hope that some evidence might emerge in the course of the proceedings to warrant it? Was it made, knowing there was no admissible evidence available to support it, just to cause Sam problems, and some degree of anguish? Did George Lewis in this instance feel justified in abusing his position as an officer of the Supreme Court in order to attack a man he considered such a danger to society? There must remain a strong suspicion, but no proof, that he did just that.

Chetwynd produced his betting records, which showed beyond any doubt that he had plunged heavily on his horses both when they won and when they lost, and that overall he was a loser. (Goodness knows how much more he lost backing horses he did not own.) A very short judgment was delivered on Saturday 29 June which was so equivocal that both sides were able to claim victory. The court cleared Chetwynd of instructing Wood to 'pull' horses and 'square' other jockeys, but found that he had connived at other, unspecified, infringements of the rules of racing. Presumably they were here referring to unregistered partnerships with Wood. They ruled there had been a libel on Chetwynd, in respect of which they awarded him one farthing damages, and ordered each side to pay its own costs, which must have been considerable as Queen's Counsel and two junior counsel appeared on each side.

The Times interpreted the award as meaning that Durham had failed in establishing the serious accusation of swindling, and succeeded only in proving a breach of certain Club rules which did not necessarily imply any dishonesty on Chetwynd's part. It used the opportunity to moralise about the sport:

> The Turf is full of pitfalls for him who has to make his living out of it. . . . The inordinately rich man, to whom a few thousands won or lost are a matter of indifference, can afford to treat the Turf as a plaything and a pastime. It is very different with the man who, possessing a large income, cannot live within it. For such a man the Turf has a poisonous atmosphere in which it is little short of a miracle if he preserves his moral health unimpaired. Living by the Turf is, in truth, an ignoble pursuit even when the rules of fair play are strictly observed.
>
> It is to be hoped . . . that the glimpse which has been permitted behind the scenes of a racing stable will cause some foolish people to hesitate before they stake money on horses about which they know so little.

It was a forlorn hope. Most of their strictures about gambling, written more than a hundred years ago, would be equally applicable today.

On 8 July 1889, Sir George Chetwynd offered his resignation to the Jockey Club, and it was accepted. At least four of Sam's clients were present at this meeting of the Club: the Duke of Beaufort, Lord Gerard, General Owen Williams and W. J. Legh. Sam had moved heaven and earth to avert this outcome, but the pressures on Chetwynd were just too great for him to withstand. It was the end of his career as an owner. Many thought that Lord Durham too should have resigned, but he did not. The case split the racing fraternity in half, and it was to be several years before the two men were finally reconciled at the instigation of Leopold de Rothschild. At least Chetwynd died – in Monte Carlo in the winter of 1917 – a contented man. In his will he proclaimed: 'I die in the firm belief of God and with the conviction that he will pardon my sins, for which I am truly repentant.'

Sam's role in the world of racing was a significant one. Always involved, always there, he was an important source of the availability of money to oil the wheels of its functioning. He helped with the purchase of horses (Chetwynd and many others); possibly the building of racecourses (Owen Williams at Sandown Park); and of course with money for gambling. This last was one of the main reasons why George Lewis claimed that the existence of the West End usurers led to a life of gambling, which in turn sometimes led to crime and ruin.

12 · Hugh Lowther and the prairies of Wyoming

One who came to Sam with a proposition based on a genuine business investment was Hugh Lowther, although it must be said that he exemplified the typical spendthrift younger son of a landed aristocrat, quite unable to live within his means. Sam exhibited his usual percipience and astuteness in dealing with him. Hugh was an extraordinary extrovert character with some equally extraordinary friends. He blossomed in the limelight, and was one of that small band who become legends in their lifetime. An aristocrat, he became an idol of the working classes. When he was born, in 1857, his great-uncle the second earl of Lonsdale held the family title and estates. Hugh's father, Henry Lowther, was next in line, and Hugh's brother, St George, just two years older than Hugh, would then succeed. If St George should marry and have a son, Hugh's prospects of an inheritance would pass for ever.

From an early age Hugh showed great prowess as a sportsman. He rode to hounds when he was only nine years old, and proved more adept than most of his elders. At the same age Sam had probably never seen a field, let alone a hound, a hunter or a fox. When Hugh left Eton, after just two years there, his father was more concerned with St George, who was being groomed for a gilded future, and made no effort to further Hugh's education. His mother did try, and sent him to a finishing school for young gentlemen in Switzerland, a ploy with faint chance of success. Within a month he had left and, like Labouchere before him, joined a travelling circus, and spent a blissfully happy year with its artistes and animals.

He returned to England on his eighteenth birthday and learned that his father, who had by now become the third earl of Lonsdale, was prepared to make him a private allowance of £1,000 a year. For a young man of his tastes, particularly his fondness for gambling – he was a card-playing aquaintance of Ernest Benzon and a frequent guest of General Owen Williams during race weeks – it was woefully inadequate. Then, quite unexpectedly, his father died in 1875, and St George became the fourth earl. The difference in their fortunes was startling. St George received the income from the vast family agricultural estates, 50,000 acres in Cumberland and Westmorland, and another 50,000 of common land over which he owned the sporting and mineral rights. Lakes Windermere and Grasmere came within their ambit as, in West Cumberland, did the whole town of Whitehaven, whose rich coalfields stretched out under the Irish Sea. In addition to Lowther Castle, which was one of the largest houses in the country, and in which Mary Queen of Scots had stayed as a guest of Sir Richard Lowther, and another family seat, Whitehaven Castle, which had been built by the first earl, there was a London house in Carlton House Terrace (two great mansions knocked into one), a house at Newmarket, yachts lying at anchor at Cowes, and ownership of superior hunting country in Rutland. In all, the coalfields, iron mines and agricultural land provided St George with an income of £4,000 a week, after tax, more than Hugh and his younger brothers together received in a year. This was a prime example of the effects of the operation of primogeniture and the use of strict settlements.

Hugh's resentment of his rich brother became a dominating passion in his life. When St George married, Hugh resigned himself to having to make his own way, and he desperately sought to prove to the world that he was the better man of the two. His efforts to do so led him into a series of scandals which caused much of Society to close its doors in his face. At first, gambling seemed to afford the easy path to success. When he was just 21 he lost £18,000 in a single evening's play at écarte and was bailed out by a friend who extracted a promise from him, which he kept, never again to play cards for money or bet on a horse. (As Hugh told this story many years later, it was he who had helped a friend and extracted such a promise, but it is the earlier version which appears to be the correct one.) He married Lady Grace Gordon, the daughter of the tenth marquis of Huntly. The marquis was a substantial client of Sam's, and it may be that he introduced Hugh to Sam. The marriage was much against the wishes of his mother-in-law, who did not relish the thought of her daughter having to rely upon a husband already heavily saddled with debt. There appeared to be no possibility that his financial position would alter for the better when, out of the blue, what appeared to him to be the answer to all his problems suddenly presented itself.

Hugh had a close friend, the remarkable, resilient Moreton Frewen, known by some as 'Mortal Ruin'. A cascade of ideas flowed from his fecund mind, all of which held out the prospect of riches. Shane Leslie, in his *Studies in Sublime Failure*, described him as 'a first class mind untroubled by second thoughts ... he had a lightning range over the world of theory and a certain arrogance towards the facts ... companions of an hour were brought into companies which might prove illusory for a lifetime.' Whatever he undertook, his friends underwrote. Many of those who appear in our story had their financial fingers burned by investing in his schemes. He said being thought rich was the next best thing to being rich. By 1885, few thought him rich. His debts totalled more than £30,000, and the rest of his life was a spectacular effort to catch up.

Moreton's father was a solid squire of comfortable means who gave portions to his sons, but Moreton and his brother Richard soon exceeded their allowances. In 1877, having almost exhausted their funds. they left the shires of England for the prairies of Wyoming, where Moreton was certain he had detected a way to make their fortunes. It was the time of the great cattle boom in the American Middle West, and the talk in the clubs of London and Edinburgh was of the riches which could be made, why almost overnight! There was, it was believed, limitless free grazing available. Once bull calves had been purchased from the American trail drivers at £3 a head, they could be fed on the abundant grass at the cost of just a few shillings, and then sold for £12. There could be no simpler nor, Moreton believed, more certain way of making a fortune. He estimated, and in his mind it was a cautious estimate, that during the ten years or so before he and Richard arrived, cattle owners using the public domain country west of Missouri had not only drawn handsome incomes every year by selling just a small proportion of their herd, but that the herd doubled its numbers by natural increase every three years, just like a herd of deer in a park. Further, there was, in his view, little risk. The hygienic conditions in Wyoming were such that pleuropneumonia of the lungs, the most frequent cattle disease, was unknown. There was very little rustling, because each state or territory had a powerful central Stock Association with efficient inspectors and detectives who kept a careful watch on the railway stations and other points at which rustlers might try to sell what they had stolen. It was as though the land was growing not grass but money, and all one needed to do was to select the right spot to build a ranch house and then simply gather the money into one's arms.

The Frewen brothers set up their headquarters just north of Cheyenne, and expanded their 76 Ranch in Johnstone County along the banks of the North Powder River by the Crazy Woman, close to the site of General Custer's last stand. They also had land at Rawhide in Laramie County. They erected a vast wooden building to serve as their home and business base, and there, to the astonishment of the tough cowboys bringing their herds up country from the south, they installed internal sanitation, used silver knives and forks at table, and had fresh flowers delivered by rail and road. In the summer of 1879 they invited Hugh and his new wife, Grace, and some other well-known young English aristocrats, to join them for a few months' big game shooting, mainly buffalo. Hugh was immediately attracted by the vast open spaces and the sport, but most of all he was captivated by Moreton's enthusiasm and glowing financial forecasts. When Moreton described his grandiose plans for the Powder River Cattle Company, which had been incorporated to take over 76 Ranch, Hugh was hooked.

The Frewens' rapid expansion had left them short of working capital, and burdened with debts they could not immediately pay. Moreton accompanied Hugh and Grace when they returned to London because, as he explained, he needed to raise an additional quarter of a million pounds, and it became clear that he was generously prepared to allow his friends the first opportunity of investing with him.

Hugh imagined that he was being presented with the ideal opportunity to remedy his fortunes, free himself from reliance upon St George, and become a prosperous and independent man able to keep his wife in the appropriate manner, and he, all the while, would be able to indulge in his sporting pastimes. What was more, it would all be so easy. The Frewen brothers would be generating the income, and

148

he would be receiving the unquestionably high dividends that would flow from the Powder River to England, and his capital, in the safe hands of his friends, would double every three years. The only element missing in the scheme of things was that Hugh had no capital to invest, not a penny.

On arrival in London Moreton went directly to his club and, foolish fellow, pinpointed Sir George Chetwynd, among others, as a prospective investor, wrongly believing him wealthy, and quite unaware that he was one of those deeply in debt to Sam. He also tackled Lord Rosslyn (a friend of the Prince of Wales), who was similarly involved with Sam. Rosslyn did back Frewen, indeed he became chairman of the company, but as at Sam's death Rosslyn owed him nearly £80,000 it may well be that any funds he invested came from Sam. Hugh meanwhile was champing at the bit and desperately keen to raise as much as he could in order to obtain as large a slice of the action as possible. He was following in the footsteps of one of his predecessors, Lord Lonsdale, who in 1720 had borrowed £20,000 to speculate in the South Sea Company. No bank, of course, would contemplate a proposition from Hugh, so he too turned to Sam.

He had no need to spell out what the Lowther estate was worth or what his interest in it was. Sam was well aware that the value of the estate was probably as high as £4,000,000, or even more. The difficulty was that although Hugh was at that moment next in line of succession, St George was still in his early twenties and had only recently married a young wife. Hugh could well die before his brother, and in any event there was a strong possibility that St George's wife would give birth to at least one son, thus signalling the end of Hugh's interest. So he had almost nothing to offer as security. According to Allen Andrews, Frewen's biographer, Hugh told Sam that as a gambler he rated his chances of succession at 100–1 against, and offered to sell his reversion at those odds, i.e. for one hundredth of £4,000,000. Sam agreed, and paid Hugh £40,000, almost every penny of which Hugh then handed over to Moreton for him to use to make both their fortunes in Wyoming. It was a remarkably high sum for Sam to be able to provide for an individual client, just ten years after he started his business of moneylending. It proved conclusively, if further proof was needed, that by 1879 Sam was the doyen of the West End moneylenders.

From Hugh's point of view it was an exceptionally good deal. Even if St George died first without an heir, that might not be for another 30 or 40 years. Instead of waiting, he could now enjoy the fruits of his investment. From Sam's point of view it would, on the face of it, appear to have been a reckless decision to have laid out an enormous sum on such precarious security; but events were to prove him right. St George learned of the transaction, presumably when Sam, as he had to, notified his newly acquired interest to the trustees of the settled land. The thought that a moneylender might at some future date, however remote that possibility was, have a dominant interest in the centuries-old family estate, filled St George with distaste, and doubtless horror. He instructed the trustees to buy back the reversion. It was a comparatively small amount for them to find. This must have been exactly what Sam thought would happen, indeed the advance he made is explicable only on the supposition that he took the view that the family would act as they did. Sam was by now sufficiently wise and experienced in the ways of the world to be able to anticipate events. So he quickly recovered his £40,000 outlay, and doubtless made a satisfactory profit on the resale. He was probably the only one to emerge from the whole venture with his finances intact.

There were many who later made fortunes from dealing in cattle in the Mid-West, but Frewen and his friends, and the English and Scottish speculators who were also then heavily involved, were out of time. Cattle ranching for profit on a large scale was a much more difficult long-term proposition than Moreton and the other Europeans had anticipated and optimistically proclaimed. The early success of the first Scottish ranch venture, the Prairie Cattle Company, helped spread enthusiasm, and at the height of the initial boom a total of more than $15,000,000 capital, subscribed by English and Scottish financiers, was invested in Wyoming, Dakota and Montana. In 1882 alone ten major British-American ranch companies were incorporated. The fever for speculation in cattle spread, and when Lord Tweedsworth founded The Rocking Chair in Texas it was said that the capital had been provided by none other than Queen Victoria, on whose behalf he was running it – not for profit of course, nothing as common as that. The neighbouring ranch hands referred to it as 'Queenie's Cow Outfit'. British capital controlled well over 20 million acres of cattle lands. High profits were announced, and in some cases high dividends were declared and paid, but things soon started to go terribly wrong.

There was criticism in Congress against the extensive acreage held by foreign speculators. Then inquiring journalists began to question the validity of the figures produced by the cattle companies. The *Economist* thought it unwise to suppose that all the declared dividends came from actual profits, because these were inflated by the value put on the stock. The counting of many thousand head of cattle was notoriously difficult to achieve accurately. Indeed, the story went the rounds that Frewen paid three times the value for his first herd of cattle; they had been driven in a circle round and round the hill from which he was viewing them. The book value was calculated by the directors who, not necessarily with any dishonest intent, based their estimates not only on head counts but also on the generally accepted assumption that Frewen had made as to the doubling of the herds every three years by natural increase. Then a correspondent of the *Scottish Banking and Insurance Magazine* wrote what few had any intention of mentioning: that most of the stockmen were merely squatters, and usually owned only narrow strips along the waterways. They used the range on *suffrance* of the United States government, and the time was to come when the government required the ranchers to give up their 'rights'. The *Laramie Boomerang* reported that the Secretary of the Interior had begun to move against all fencing enclosing government land. Frewen had indicated to his investors that he had 20 years at least on the land around 76 Ranch, but this proved not to be so.

Large herds were driven north to Wyoming by newcomers who sought the higher prices being fetched there, but the increased competition then forced prices down. Additionally the Leghorns the newcomers brought with them carried a threat of fever, and their blood was inferior to the northern cows and pure-blood herd sires. But it was the increasingly overcrowded ranges which were the main problem. The movement of stock grew, with cattle arriving in Wyoming from as far away as Ohio and New York State, even from Florida. Sagebrush sprang up where previously good grass had grown, and in any event it had never been consistently 'belly high to a horse', as Moreton had so often declared. Whereas at one time 40 acres of good grazing land fed ten cattle, 100 acres were needed to achieve the same end after the grass had been thinned by overstocking and the usual invasion of mesquite, cactus and other thorn had occurred. If the spring rains failed, grazing on the upper range was almost nonexistent. Old cowhands crossed their arms over the saddle horn, chewed their tobacco and opined, 'Them bulls sure are going to raise a fine chorus come winter, bawling around the corrals for somebody to come shovel out the feed. Hell they'll want to get inside. Look at them soft bellies sticking out. Ain't built to cut the wind like the Longhorns.'

The large cattle companies, particularly the foreign ones, were faced with the problem of falling dividends. To show a paper profit some sold off too much stock before the cattle's peak age, which helped the grass to grow but reduced the number of saleable stock for the following years. Moreton could also see that the reducing summer feed for his herds was at a point where his cattle were failing to build up enough flesh to carry them through even a mild winter. A hard winter could destroy all the profit, and indeed the business.

In the winter of 1880, thousands of Frewen's cattle died on the frozen prairies, and with them died Hugh's hope of a fortune from the venture, though he did not know this at the time. The figures Frewen produced for 1882 appeared to show a healthy position, but the reality was different. After facing further vicissitudes, Frewen headed with his herds to the shores of Lake Superior and made a final effort to escape the closing net. He attempted to cut out all the middlemen, obtain his own transport, and sell the cattle direct to English farmers, but it all came to nothing. His position was rendered untenable, and wriggle as he might he could not avoid disaster. The price of the company's shares began to decline, but unfortunately for him he could not sell his own shares because his contract of service forbade him to do so until 1887, and the company collapsed well before then. When its affairs were settled, and all its debts paid, the shares he still owned in his own right and those he held on behalf of his relatives and friends, including Hugh Lowther, were completely valueless.

The whole sad story was described as 'an example of Moreton's brilliant imagination, and even prophetic vision, aborted by a fatal inability to face inconvenient facts'. Many wondered whether he was fraudulent or just unlucky. Lord Rosslyn had no doubts. 'I fearlessly challenge anybody', he wrote, 'to prove that you have not always been right in your actions, your prophecies, your suggestions for escape from a most difficult crisis. Your only fault latterly has been that you could not raise money fast enough.' It was a fault which remained with him to the rest of his life. His active mind soon produced other schemes, but he was constantly pursued by his creditors. The most persistent was one Richardson, who drove him almost to distraction. Frewen wrote to his wife Clara, a sister of Jennie Churchill, 'It would have been wiser to have accepted the position five years ago instead of being bled to death by the moneylenders all these years past. *Compared with Richardson Sam Lewis is a gentleman and a Christian.*' Coming from a man who had said, 'I don't like all these vulgar people, and I would sooner break stones than have any dealings with Nathaniel Rothschild. His co-religionists are worse', it was a backhanded compliment indeed.

What of Hugh the while? The completely unexpected happened. In 1882 St George died at the young age of 27 and left no heir; Hugh became the fifth earl of Lonsdale. His succession had arrived just in time, for it was as he was being hounded by his creditors to the verge of bankruptcy, and being spurned by most of Society, that overnight he became one of the richest men in England. He did not press Moreton for the repayment of the £40,000, and he did not mention him or the ill-fated venture again, but he suffered for the rest of his life from his involvement in the scheme. For the Lonsdale trustees who had bought Hugh's reversion back from Sam now controlled the purse strings, and it was they who had the management of the settled land at Whitehaven and Lowther. Instead of enjoying direct access to the income of the estate, he had to obtain it through them. He could, initially, rely upon an income of about £80,000 a year, but for the 62 years that he was the earl, he constantly fought them tooth and nail to extract every penny he could to keep up his fantastic lifestyle. To tide him over the periods when he was waiting for the trustees to make payments, he sought advances from Sam. Even as late as 1896 he was borrowing several thousands of pounds at a time.

It became an obsession with him that he had to have the best and the most of everything. His entertainment for the Kaiser and other European royalty was lavish. He had a private orchestra, and poured money into equipping a private battalion to fight both in the Boer War and the First World War. He had an extensive stable of horses, though the only classic he won was the St Leger in 1922. It became the tradition that during Ascot week he rode down the course in his yellow carriage immediately after the royal coach. With his side-whiskers, the ever-present six-inch custom-made 'Lonsdale' cigar jutting out of his mouth, he looked the part of the sporting grandee. All the world of sport, hunting, racing, coursing (he won the Waterloo Cup), shooting, fishing, yachting, and a special interest of his, boxing, was open to him. But this all cost a greater fortune than even he possessed. During the period of agricultural depression the greatest grandees found the cost of hunting more than they could bear. Lonsdale was obliged to resign as Master of the Quorn because his trustees effectively ordered him to do so. In 1902 they sent him on an extended visit to India and the Far East in an attempt to curb his expenditure. Gradually, one by one, his assets were sold off or closed – the horses, Whitehaven Castle, Carlton House Terrace, and finally Lowther. Lonsdale's view of Sam can be gauged by the comments of his official biographer, Lionel Dawson. He compiled the book (published 1946) while Hugh was still alive, and with his help, and referring to the time of Hugh's youth, described it as 'the age ... of spending too, with the benevolent presence – *and sometimes it really was benevolent* – of Sam Lewis, the famous moneylender, in the background to provide the ammunition for those whose supply was finished, or temporarily checked'.

13 · The clubs

Hugh Lonsdale got on well with Sam, and never had cause to complain of the business they did together, and Sam was a popular member, and regular attender, at a club of which Hugh was president. This was important to Sam, since there were clubs to which he could never hope to be elected, either because of his religion, or his profession, or the combination of both. If he could have gained admission to a club such as Boodle's or White's in St James's Street it would have been of inestimable value to him, as a high percentage of those with whom he conducted business were members of such West End clubs. It was said of Boodle's that if anyone called out for 'Sir John' he would immediately have been surrounded by a crowd. At White's there was heavy gambling at the tables, and the Prince of Wales was a member. One of its earlier managers made a fortune from the counters he recovered from the floor when he swept up after gaming had finished for the night.

The majority of devoted club men had no occupation and, so far as they were concerned, the club was the focal point of their lives, the pivot of the universe. They got up late, lounged about until lunch time, and stayed at the club until early evening, perhaps indulging in a leisurely stroll in the afternoon. About seven they would return to their rooms, change, go back to the club to dine, after which, except when they went to a theatre or a party, they would sit till the small hours of the morning with congenial sprits drinking and gambling. Clubmen were much addicted to gossip. Who was marrying whom, and what the financial arrangements were; who was being brought before the courts and who was being expertly extricated from such a fate; proposed divorces and hushed-up scandals; great wins and losses at the course or the gambling tables. Such up-to-date information was meat and drink to the dedicated moneylender, but friendly as Sam was with so many of his clients, they knew as well as he that he would have been out of place in such clubs, and even if proposed, would have been blackballed. He could not have been invited even as a guest for lunch or dinner.

Sam never strayed into areas where he knew he would be rebuffed or feel ill at ease. He made no pretence of culture. According to Lady Randolph Churchill, after a fortnight's stay in Rome which he had been recommended to visit, he was asked how he liked it. 'You can 'ave Rome' was his laconic answer, and he did not return. The Kursaal at Ostend or the tables at Monte Carlo were more to his liking. He did not join those of the newly rich who sought to purchase respectability and acceptance by acquiring a country estate, learning to ride to hounds, and generally engaging in country pastimes to which they came late in life, for which they were often ill-equipped, and frequently in the process becoming the laughing stock of those they sought to impress. Sam could easily have afforded to purchase an estate, but instead restricted himself to areas in which he felt comfortable. It was at the casino and the racecourse, where membership was more easily obtained, that the atmosphere was to his liking. He preferred a luxury motorised yacht gliding sedately on the Thames to an ocean-going boat under sail. His idea of exercise was a walk to the paddock at Goodwood or Ascot, not jumping fences in country fields. He was relaxed in the houses he acquired in Grosvenor Square, Brighton and Maidenhead; he would have been a fish out of water in the shires, and knew it. He never became an integral part of Society. He knew he could not aspire to complete acceptance in their circle, but he none the less lived in their midst. He shared many of their pastimes, and was with them, but not of them.

There was, however, a half-way club. Those who found the West End clubs too sedate, restricting and solemn, sought escape and pleasure in rather more bohemian, more raffish, outlets. Many such opened and failed, but one of the most successful for a time was a club which was the forerunner of the present-day National Sporting Club. It originated in 1887 in Denman Street behind Piccadilly Circus, under the name Star Club. Its owner was an occasional tipster for the *Sporting Times*, William Goldberg, known as 'the Shifter', who had managed to find a financial backer. Quite why one club, or restaurant, succeeds and another fails, though their location and facilities are as identical as may be, is to an extent a matter of chance, however professional the management. Sometimes, somehow, in some inexplicable way, the elements gel, and the club becomes the in-place. This happened to the Star Club, which soon moved to larger premises in Gerrard Street, and was rechristened The Pelican in honour of a large stuffed pelican which shared a glass case with a stuffed flamingo in the club's smoking room. Its object was to provide a rendezvous for supper and other nocturnal recreation for young men about town of sporting inclinations. It attracted as colourful and diversified a group as could be expected to gather under one roof.

The chairman was one of Sam's clients, Sir John Astley. Known as 'the Mate', and compulsively generous, he was one of the most popular, and poorest, characters on the Turf. An unmistakable figure, with a thick shock of white hair and beard, his career was a constant struggle against the threat of financial disaster, though this did not prevent his being a steward of the Jockey Club in the 1870s. At the end of one year he recorded in his betting book: 'am dead broke, shall have to live at Elsham like a blooming maggot in a nut. Shall I ever bet a monkey [£500] on a race again?' He ran a few horses from time to time, but the best of them he inevitably had to sell to meet his debts before he could enjoy the fruits of their success.

Almost at once, The Pelican became the meeting place for some of the most extraordinary characters it would seem possible to gather under one roof. 'A conglomeration of mixed spirits' was Astley's description. Exclusiveness was not one of its attractions. Even journalists and Jews were admitted, and Astley was an ideal person to preside over a club with an aristocratic committee, and a membership catholic enough to embrace on the one hand the Marquis of Queensberry (whose rules for boxing, including the introduction of gloves, had given some respectability to boxing's tarnished name), the Duke of Hamilton (one of the wealthiest landowners in the country), the Duke of Manchester, Lord Rossmore and Lord Marcus Beresford, the Prince of Wales's racing manager; and on the other Billy Harris, the sausage king, George Edwardes, the impresario, and Sam Lewis.

In addition to Edwardes there were several other members of the theatrical profession, including the impresario Littler and several actors. Sam had a wide circle of theatrical friends. It was later noted that many of them attended his funeral, and he seems to have been a theatrical 'angel'. He made several payments to both Edwardes and Littler and it may well be that these were investments in their productions and not moneylending transactions. After Sam's death Edwardes put on a season at the Apollo Theatre in Shaftesbury Avenue which included a production of *Véronique*, the operetta written by André Messager who had married Ada's youngest sister Dotie.

The Prince of Wales dropped in to the club from time to time, and apart from the racecourse this was probably as close as Sam got to him, though Ada, as we shall see, formed a much closer friendship. The stage, the press, the law, the city, the officers of the Brigade of Guards and the nobility were all well represented. There was an admirable restaurant, a champagne bar and a cocktail bar (an innovation from the United States), a grand piano, a billiard room and a boxing saloon. Cards and strangers were taboo, but that apart there were few restrictions.

Most evenings Hugh Lonsdale strolled from his home in Carlton House Terrace to The Pelican's cigar-laden rooms, because he knew that there he could participate in constant chatter about two subjects which fascinated him, horses and boxing. It was reported, chiefly by himself, that in his youth he fought and beat John J. Sullivan, the heavyweight champion of the world. He was made chairman of the boxing committee and took his duties extremely seriously. He organised contests which were the first to be held in conditions of comparative comfort for the spectators, and he tried to eliminate some of the more glaring evils then prevalent in the sport. By law the contests were illegal, but the high percentage of nobility in the audience was normally sufficient protection against police interference, though on one occasion the club was raided because the police thought that baccarat was being played. Barney Barnato became a patron, and was a regular whenever he was in London. He was always the first to shower the ring with 'nobbins', a fistful of sovereigns to reward boxers who had put on a particularly good fight. Sam was in his element in such a club.

Stories told about the club and its members were legion, and one which went the rounds concerned Sam. It appears that a young subaltern, stationed in Dublin, was urgently in need of £500, and he sent Sam a very fine diamond ring in the post with a note: 'I realize you would not *lend* me £500 on the ring, but I need the money very badly and am willing to sell the ring, although it is a valuable family heirloom. Only it is five hundred or nothing. Please don't waste time in haggling.' The ring was worth the money, but it went against the grain for Sam to pay a first asking price. He sent a long letter explaining why he could not pay more than £400. A telegram arrived: 'Five hundred pounds or return the ring.' Sam was not easily beaten. 'Dear Friend', he wrote, 'Your troubles have caused me a great deal of worry. I hate to disappoint a client in need, but what am I to do if the ring will not fetch more than I am offering? I know that I am running a terrible risk, but for old time's sake I will give you four hundred and fifty for it. If you accept, don't even bother to open the box but send it back by return of post.' The officer was sorely tempted, but in the end decided to stick to his original price, and he opened the jewel box. Inside there was no ring, just a piece of paper on which Sam had written 'All right. Five hundred.'

Some clubs were gambling clubs, pure and simple, and no pretence was made that they were otherwise. The main qualification for membership lay in being possessed of ample funds and a tendency to part with them while still young. They operated illegally, but were normally left alone by the police who felt they had more important work to do than keep watch on and then raid them, because they knew full well that the fines imposed would be minimal and the whole operation would start up again, usually on the same premises but under a different name. It was only when matters went so far as to become a public scandal that the police intervened. At two o'clock in the morning of Sunday, 12 May 1889, the police raided the Field Club in Park Place, St James's. There they found that baccarat was being played, with chips on the table and a pool totalling more than £5,000. The players were a few gentlemen of no particular occupation, one Baron Farrao, a barrister or two, four of Sam's clients – Lord Lurgan, Ernest Benzon, the Earl of Dudley and Lord Henry Paulet – and Sam, described as a 'financial agent', himself.

George Lewis appeared for the Earl of Dudley, Lord Lurgan and Lord Henry Paulet when the matter came before the magistrate sitting at Marlborough Street. All three appeared before him resplendent in 'the correctest morning costume with flowers in their buttonholes'. The maximum penalty he could impose on these wealthy

159

defendants, Sam included, was to compel them to enter into their own recognisances not to enter such houses in the future, or a fine of 6s 8d a day if they refused. As he pointed out, it was less than one-sixth of the penalty he could impose on any urchin who played pitch and toss in the streets. To the delight of the large number of spectators, mostly lady friends of the defendants, the magistrate took the view that it was pointless to impose any penalties, and the charge was not proceeded with against the players. The keeper of the club and the croupiers were heavily fined.

What was the 51-year-old Sam doing there at two o'clock in the morning, gaming with men of wealth, or expectations of wealth, who were just in their twenties? A shared interest in gaming? Keeping an eye on his money? Or was he there to encourage them to bet, just as Sir George alleged he did? Sam could, of course, afford to lose on such occasions. He would still make a profit on the evening if the others lost too, and borrowed from him at 40 per cent.

14 · Sam and the fourth marquis of Ailesbury

Usurers live by the fall of heirs, as swine by the dropping of acorns.
G. Wilkins, 1607

I can get no remedy against this corruption of the purse; borrowing only lingers it out, but the disease is incurable.
Falstaff, in Shakespeare's *Henry IV, Part II*

A young man of low tastes, bad character, and brutal manner.
The Complete Peerage, of the fourth marquis of Ailesbury

There were some who, on the death of a relative, would become masters of large estates producing high incomes, but who had impoverished themselves long before that event occurred. When they eventually succeeded they had little or no income with which to maintain themselves or the estate. Others, whether heirs or not, driven to desperation by existing debts, often brought about by gambling, resorted to crime in an attempt to extradite themselves from their plight. The stories of the fourth marquis of Ailesbury and of Lord William Nevill, in both of which Sam was heavily involved, provide an example of each and also the opportunity to consider whether the young men concerned were authors of their own misfortune, or whether Sam was also a guilty party.

A conspicuous example of an encumbered estate was Savernake, in Wiltshire, the home of the Ailesbury family. Its history illustrates perfectly the effects of a combination of extravagance, fecklessness and prodigality, which brought the estate to the verge of collapse. The Ailesburys can trace their ancestry back to the time of Robert Bruce, and have held land in England in unbroken male line at least since the reign of Henry VII (1485–1509). In 1675 they established their principal residence at Savernake, near Marlborough. The estate was

161

acquired by the family on the marriage of the then earl with Lady Elizabeth Seymour, sole heiress of her brother William, third duke of Somerset. He had inherited it from the first duke of Somerset, the Protector. Two hundred years later it was still in the hands of the Ailesbury family – the family whose acquaintance Sam, the boy from the Birmingham slum, was about to make.

The estate consisted of about 40,000 acres, the greater part arable, but with some pasture. There were 95 separate farms, and over a thousand cottages. The family's mansion, Tottenham House, and its immediately adjoining park, covered nearly 8,000 acres, including Savernake Forest, a beautiful tract of oaks and beeches 16 miles in circumference. It produced £40,000 a year gross, and the Ailesburys also owned 15,000 acres in Yorkshire engendering a gross income of £18,000. Yet by the 1880s their finances were almost in ruin.

The rot had started to set in 60 years earlier. Charles Brudenell-Bruce, the Earl of Ailesbury, had long harboured the ambition to be a marquis. In the nineteenth century earls were comparatively numerous, but marquises rare, and Charles achieved his goal in George IV's coronation honours, becoming the first marquis of Ailesbury (from 1821 to 1856). Society's conventions demanded that a marquis lived and behaved in almost princely style, so he set about improving Tottenham House to rival the grandeur of the greatest mansions. He engaged Thomas Cundy as architect, and exceeded the limit of his funds by spending £250,000 in creating and furnishing a residence designed for large-scale entertainments, with a whole series of reception rooms running one into another. The house required the attention of 20 servants, and the gardens of 20 gardeners. This expenditure forced him to sell two other houses he owned, and in 1832 his financial pressures were so great that he was compelled to put his property in the hands of trustees. It was not until they took restraining action that his exuberant spending was temporarily halted. In 1845 his income from the estate was £25,000 a year, but repayment of his debts absorbed £23,000 of that. There followed a period of retrenchment during which the debts were gradually, very gradually, reduced, and no further land needed to be sold.

The second marquis, George Brudenell-Bruce (1856–1878), did nothing to revive the family fortunes, quite the contrary. He kept a stable of racehorses and, though he made several laudable improvements to the house, lacked the foresight to see where his spending was leading him. He continued the lavish entertainment – his guests included the Prince and Princess of Wales – despite the reduction in the family's fortunes due to his father's expenditure. When he died in 1878, the third marquis, Ernest Brudenell-Bruce (1878–1886), inherited even less than George had. In order to continue to live at Tottenham House he had to tread very carefully. There was just a hint of stability about him. Born in 1811, he was a Lord of the Bedchamber to William IV and Vice-Chamberlain to Queen Victoria. He sat in Parliament as member for Marlborough from 1832 until 1878, though without ever once making a speech in the House and, being deaf in his later years, scarcely ever hearing one. He was described as having 'a power of tuneful sleep' which was the wonder and delight of the members. He had a genuine love of, and pride in, the estate. Within eight years, however, entirely because of the depredations of the man who was to be his successor, his grandson Willie, he was compelled to sell the family's Yorkshire estate and its principal mansion, Jervaulx Abbey.

Ernest died in October 1886. He was succeeded by the fourth marquis, George William Thomas Brudenell-Bruce, till then Viscount Savernake, but better known to his family as 'dear Willie' and to his friends as 'Billy Stomachache' or 'Ducks'. Willie's father was George, Ernest's eldest son, a kindly and generous man, and in the normal course of events it was he who would have inherited the title. Known as 'the Duffer', he unfortunately adopted a thoroughly dissolute and reckless mode of life, and devoted so much of his time to the pleasures of the flesh and the bottle that he soon undermined his health. He died in Corsica at the age of 29. Ominously, to obtain immediate cash he at one time discounted bills with a Mr James Davis, a moneylender of Clifford Street, who lost a great deal of money because George did not live long enough to succeed to the title. His widow, a daughter of the second earl of Craven, showed no interest in bringing up their two children, and Willie and his sister were cared for at Savernake by their grandparents and thoroughly spoiled. Willie followed his father's example.

Willie was born on 8 June 1863, and proved to be the perfect example of a man with a myriad of superb opportunities in life who wasted and misused them all. He was soon in trouble at Eton, and ran away after refusing to take a beating which had been ordered for his impertinence to the headmaster and 'for other enormities'. According to Lord Curzon, Willie was taken in hand at Cambridge by an amiable man named Bull who 'found the only possible method of discipline was to knock the young ruffian down about once a week'. The treatment was unsuccessful. Willie was allowed to go out in the world with a generous allowance, but no serious occupation. He continued to behave in a pathetic and ridiculous manner, and soon proved that he would be more of an embarrassment to his family than ever his father was. Variously described as a young blackguard and a stupid, boorish oaf (and those were just the kindest remarks), he surrounded himself with the most dissolute of friends. A good many undesirables, men and women, surrounded this young heir to a peerage whose generous disposition was matched only by his unworldliness and lack of common sense. Addicted to the Turf, and extravagant in his purchase of horses, he was 'warned off' by the Jockey Club when still in his early twenties for having his horses 'pulled', thus creating the only record he ever held, being the youngest person to be so punished by that august body. When he applied for membership of White's Club his grandfather recorded the event in his diary: 'Poor little master Willie blackballed at White's. Nineteen members in room. Fifteen white balls. Four black.'

He was unwelcome in superior Society circles and so had to seek the company of those who were not to be found in reputable London drawing rooms, and most of his female acquaintances were engaged on the variety stage. In 1884, just before Willie's 21st birthday, his grandfather came to London to see him. His diary shows that he called three times at Willie's lodgings and left messages for him to call, but there was no response. In May he repeated the exercise, and Willie promised to call, but the marquis waited all day in vain. On 6 May without a word said to his grandfather or any other member of his family, he married Julia Haseley, best known by her stage name, Dolly Tester, an actress of no great talent. Society has seen several young ladies who crossed the footlights into the peerage. Gertie Millar became the Countess of Dudley, Merrie Crawford the Countess of Suffolk, Oriel Ross the Countess Poulet, Tilly Losch the Countess of Carnarvon, and May Etheridge the Countess of Leicester. They all enjoyed more professional success than Dolly, though she had appeared on the London stage. One of the peaks of her career seems to have been an appearance at the Theatre Royal, Brighton, in its 1879 Christmas pantomime, *Sinbad the Sailor*, in which she played the important role of Jinbad the Jailor.

It was not until four days after the marriage that his grandfather was told, by a third party, that it had taken place. He could not believe 'the dreadful news'. On 12 May he wrote in his diary 'Alas! Alas! it is all true ... overwhelmed with grief.' But Dolly came of a respectable hard-working Brighton family, was dainty and attractive, and much more intelligent than her husband. The general opinion, including that of Willie's relations, was that he had found a better wife than he deserved.

She had married into a heap of trouble, and their early years were far from easy. He was short, overweight, with a heavy jowl, and frequently dressed like a costermonger, or wore a box coat of the type worn by coachmen at the beginning of the century, which he embellished with buttons as huge as saucers. He favoured a hard black hat with a low flat crown. His language was vulgar and common in the extreme, and the unattractive set of young men with whom he cavorted were disagreeable, crude and brutal. When Blumenfeld looked in at Romano's one Boat Race night, he saw Willie, with Dolly 'the Brighton barmaid', Charlie Mitchell the pugilist, Abingdon Baird the 'gentleman' jockey, and several 'convivial spirits dispensing vociferous hospitality to all who entered'. Those who refused to drink were 'playfully tripped up on the sawdust covered floor'.

After his marriage, and before he inherited the marquisate, Willie, actively aided and abetted by Dolly and slow racehorses, continued to spend at an assiduously immoderate rate. It was inevitable that he would, sooner rather than later, have recourse to a moneylender. The Savernake estate was entailed, but the entail was due to end with him. On the death of his grandfather this excessively foolish young man would become the possessor of very extensive estates. In the meantime, however, he was seriously in debt and needed a generous transfusion of funds. There was only one man in London who could handle matters on so grand a scale. Dear Willie paid a visit to Cork Street and saw Sam.

They were ill-matched in experience, intelligence and temperament. Sam's knowledge of the world, what he had been through to achieve his position and the street sharpness he had acquired from his days on the road all made for an uneven contest. It was an adult dealing with a child, and a backward child at that. Sam probably foresaw at the very first meeting what the eventual outcome of Willie's behaviour was likely to be. By July of 1885 Willie had borrowed £112,000 from Sam on the security of his expectations, most probably at between 40 and 60 per cent interest, and had other debts of £60,000. He was exactly the type of reckless, thoughtless, foolish, prodigal, squandering wastrel a moneylender dreamed about. He was young, and was in line to inherit from his grandfather who was by now in his mid-seventies. Sam could cover the minor risk that Willie might not survive his grandfather by taking out a policy on his life.

Should Sam, or indeed any man, have pandered to such a person's requirements, to benefit from his weaknesses with money? Should a person like Willie be given the means to indulge in such immoderate behaviour? Sam was not engaging in any illegal activity, but was it morally right? Should the lender be criticised, or is it, as Jeremy Bentham (and Ernest Benzon) contended, entirely a matter which concerns only the lender and the borrower? An experienced casino owner can probably judge within five minutes whether a man sitting down at the tables is a compulsive gambler or not; whether he is likely to continue betting until he is financially ruined; indeed, whether he is likely to go further and steal to support his craving. Should the casino owner refuse him admittance at the outset to save him from ruin? Or what of the arms dealer who supplies weapons to those he suspects might use them for unlawful purposes, or governments who supply corrupt regimes with tools which could be used to suppress their population by force? The answer often heard from the money-lender, casino owner and arms seller is that if they do not provide their services others, less scrupulous, will. If this was a problem which concerned Sam's conscience at all, he would probably have given the same answer.

Before Willie succeeded to the title, word of his indulgences had reached his grandfather, who feared what would happen when Willie became the unfettered lord and master of the family estate. On hearing rumours of Willie's wild behaviour he asked his lawyer to investigate, and thus learned the whole sorry story of debauchery and debt. For the aged marquis it was unthinkable that Savernake should fall into the hands of Willie's creditors. He saw only one way out – to sell the Yorkshire land, which was free from settlement, and pay off Willie's debts, but only on condition that Willie entered into a fresh settlement renewing the entail on Savernake so that, for another three lives at least, the old estate would be saved. Willie consented, and the settlement, entered into in 1885, provided that Savernake would go to Willie for his life and thereafter to his son if he had one, or failing that to Willie's Uncle Henry.

It broke Ernest's heart to part with the properties at Jervaulx, Tanfield and elsewhere. Each year he visited Yorkshire, and all these places held memories for him of happier times. The land had been given to Lord Bruce of Kinloss by James I, and had been held by the Bruces and Brudenells for almost 300 years. But hard as it was to dispose of Jervaulx, Savernake had to be preserved at all costs. One of his friends, Sir Reginald Graham, said that when he and Ernest sat together for nearly an hour in Wath Church, on part of the Ailesbury estate in Yorkshire, Ernest confided his misgivings. Speaking with much feeling and emotion he told Sir Reginald that the Yorkshire estates were to be sold, and that he had agreed to do this 'on the strict understanding with my grandson that the Wiltshire property is to be entailed. Whatever happens after my life thank God Savernake must remain in the family.' Sir Reginald later testified in court that he had no doubt that the third marquis believed that he had made a binding agreement with Willie for the preservation of the Savernake estates within the family, though this was denied by Willie.

The Yorkshire estate was sold to Samuel Cunliffe-Lister for £310,000, but the proceeds were not received until shortly after Ernest's death. They were immediately applied in payment of several, but by no means all, of the encumbrances on the Wiltshire estate, and in payment of large sums to Willie, his mortgagees and other creditors. This enabled Savernake to be saved, but only just, and still left Willie with heavy debts. The financial position of the estate when Willie succeeded was that the net annual rental, after paying outgoings in respect of rates, taxes, tithes, insurance, repairs and general estate charges, was about £11,600. From this another £10,700 had to be paid out for jointures in favour of the three still living widows of Willie's great-uncle, grandfather and great-grandfather, and for interest payable on two mortgages which had been entered into in 1863 at four per cent. This left Willie with only £900 per annum. Although this sum would increase as the widows died and the jointures fell in, any such increase was likely to be at least partly matched by the prospect of still further diminution as a result of the prevailing agricultural depression.

It was obvious that Willie's position as tenant for life of this estate, which was to be described in future court proceedings as 'the biggest white elephant ever known', could only be sustained, if at all, by the exercise of the utmost care and self-denial, both foreign to his nature. He continued to behave as though there were no obligations accompanying his titular nobility, and led his life of spending and general debauchery at an ever-increasing pace. With patience and planning the estate could have been made to pay its way, and even become once more a source of prosperity to the whole locality, but it was not in Willie's nature to act with such caution. His friends helped him along the road to ruin. A typical acquaintance, and an important influence on his life and lifestyle, was George Alexander Baird, known as 'the Squire' or 'Mr Abingdon' (the name he used on the course). The Squire was typical of Willie's friends, not in his wealth, for few inherit £3 million at the age of ten as he did, but in his inordinate expenditure and his uncouth behaviour. He wasted his time at Cambridge, and left not only uneducated but also unsophisticated.

Though Willie had an aristocratic background whereas Baird's father was a plutocrat, a Scottish ironmaster, he and Willie were made for each other. They were of similar age, Willie being just 18 months the younger; they had both been left fatherless at a tender age; and both got caught up with the parasites who frequented the West End and with the racecourse riff-raff. Baird had also been 'warned off' by the Jockey Club and, perhaps surprisingly, despite his great capital and income, also borrowed heavily from Sam. Sam advanced him individual amounts ranging from £500 to £21,000. Presumably he needed to borrow from time to time when his trustees were unable, or unwilling, to act as fast as he wished, and doubtless the loans would have been at 40 per cent or more. Every foolish step these two renegades took seemed destined to enrich Sam. Baird and Willie became close drinking cronies, and for a while they even shared the same woman, Dolly.

At first, Willie had been loving and attentive to Dolly, and jealous. He was quickly offended if anyone paid her too close attention. One evening when they were dining in a Cork Street restaurant with Sam, a young captain became over-generous in his compliments. Willie poured the contents of a soup tureen down his back. But in time his ardour waned as his drinking increased, his general behaviour became more monstrous, and she looked elsewhere for affection. She could scarcely have chosen worse; she started an affair with the Squire. She acted as his hostess at his house parties, and at least with him enjoyed the advantage of having a benefactor who was wealthy and generous, unlike Willie, who was becoming increasingly dependent on Sam for his weekly living expenses. In Ascot week of 1887 or 1888 the Squire rented a house in the neighbourhood of the course, and to show his appreciation of her services he instructed a West End jeweller to send a selection of his best pieces to the house the following day so that she could take her pick. That evening, however, the Squire and Dolly quarrelled violently – a frequent occurrence between him and his women – and Dolly took her revenge. When the jeweller arrived the Squire was out. She chose the most expensive piece for herself, distributed the remainder of the trinkets among the other ladies in the party, packed her bag and ran, leaving behind only a jeweller's bill for £10,000, and not even a note of explanation.

The Squire waited patiently to repay the score. In May 1889 Dolly and Willie were staying at a house in Maidenhead. One of the Squire's unsavoury associates secured an invitation, and a day or two after his arrival, on the pretext of taking her for a drive, forcibly carried her off and kept her incarcerated in rooms at Southsea. She was kept isolated from the outside world, but after a fortnight managed to persuade her keeper that there would be no harm in his taking her to the races at nearby Grange Port, and somehow or other word reached Willie. He came galloping to the rescue, had a half-hearted bout of fisticuffs with his opponent, who was no braver than he, and drove Dolly triumphantly away. It was probably his finest hour.

The Squire took Lillie Langtry as his mistress in Dolly's stead. Many of Lillie's lovers and admirers, including the Prince of Wales, Sir George Chetwynd, and the fifth earl of Lonsdale, were connected with the Turf, and the last two were also clients of Sam. Baird was brutal to all his mistresses, but particularly rough with Lillie. He proved to be the most turbulent lover she ever had. She none the less allowed their relationship to continue despite the terrible bruising he inflicted because, as she frankly stated, 'I detest him, but every time he does it he gives me a cheque for £5,000'; and Lillie, although she had many wealthy and highly placed lovers, and enjoyed some success on the stage, was frequently short of funds. Indeed, at one time some of her friends had suggested she visit Sam, recommending him as 'an honourable shark', but she did not become a client. She found it impossible to refuse Baird. In a jealous rage he once pursued her to Paris where she had gone with another man. The humiliating beating he gave her was this time followed by a cheque for £50,000 and a yacht for which he had paid £20,000. Though named 'White Ladye', the yacht became commonly known as 'The Black Eye'.

A compulsive womaniser, and for ever surrounded by a crowd of disreputable cronies who battened upon him for his money, the Squire was almost totally taboo in Society. At the age of 32 he died in America, in squalid circumstances, surrounded by thugs and hangers-on, having gone through two-thirds of his inheritance. Such a man was typical of the friends with whom the fourth marquis of Ailesbury consorted, and both were typical, to some extent at least, of some of Sam's clients. They were hardly men of whose company one could feel proud.

Willie continued to spend at an alarming rate. He casually remarked one day that he thought a quarter of a million had passed through his hands since his coming of age, but, except that he fancied he had paid double price for everything, he had no idea how it had gone. He was rarely at Savernake. He went back to the moneylenders, Sam included, and borrowed even more heavily. He consolidated his debts to Sam, including the whole of the accumulated interest, by executing a mortgage on his life interest in the estate for £173,000 at five per cent. Sam thus converted a high-interest unsecured debt into a secured debt at a reasonable rate of interest. By now an interest charge of only five per cent, either equal to or just half or one per cent above that then being charged by the banks and insurance companies, was not unusual for Sam. There was an increasing number of substantial landowners who preferred to pay him five per cent rather than borrow from banks at four per cent. The banking and insurance world was comparatively small, and many of its directors were part of the same social circle as the borrowing landowner. Despite supposed banking privacy, word soon spread as to who was in financial difficulties. Sam, on the other hand, was the absolute soul of discretion. Further, although he had to employ lawyers just as bankers and insurance companies did, his business was conducted more informally and expeditiously. He had no need to consult district managers or head office directors, and he was prepared to advance a greater proportion of the equity in the property. All this meant that at the same time as Sam continued to deal with expectant heirs at 40 to 60 per cent, he was balancing and improving, it could be said was legitimising, his 'book', by attracting business from some of the more sedate, sober and substantial members of the aristocracy. At the date of Sam's death 90 per cent of his loans were secured.

Although Sam now had a first mortgage on Willie's life interest in Savernake, it was to prove less secure than it seemed. With the consolidated mortgage at a low rate of interest Willie had once more been given the chance, if he would only use it, to reorganise his finances, reduce his annual outgoings, and have sufficient surplus to enable him to live modestly; but, true to the fashion of his life, he spurned the opportunity. His excesses were not to be curbed. The number of his creditors continued to increase and he could no longer afford to reside on the estate at all. The moneylenders who had been so accommodating began to make unwelcome demands. He paid no interest to Sam, who allowed him to default for almost three years before taking action. Eventually even Sam's patience was exhausted, and in April 1890 he went to court and obtained the appointment of a Receiver to administer the estate and receive the rents and profits. Independently of this, and simultaneously, other creditors for a total of £30,000 were pressing forward with bankruptcy proceedings. Willie was able to subsist on a day-to-day basis only because Sam, alone of all his creditors, continued to advance him small sums of money, £20 or £30 at a time.

His creditors suggested that, rather than be made bankrupt, he should raise money by selling Savernake. When he explained that he was only tenant for life, which they knew quite well, they pointed out that that did not, of itself, prevent him from selling; it merely compelled him to pass the sale proceeds to his trustees. If he obtained a

171

good price they would have enough to pay his creditors in full, and by investing the balance could produce for him an income greater than he was currently receiving.

It was at this late juncture, well past the eleventh hour, that the undeserving Ailesbury was presented with yet another escape route. A white knight appeared on the horizon who made such a generous offer for Tottenham House and the Savernake estate that, if accepted and completed, it would have relieved Ailesbury of all his debts and left enough for him to live in an adequate but more modest way. Sam convened a meeting of the other creditors, who by now had obtained a receiving order in bankruptcy against Willie, and persuaded them to hold their hand to enable the sale of the estate to proceed. As was increasingly the situation in the second half of the nineteenth century, the would-be rescuer of the aristocrat in distress was a member of the plutocracy.

The houses in the fashionable parts of London were objects of great luxury and magnificence, and to some extent supplanted the country mansions in beauty and expenditure. But many of the new rich, once they had acquired their Mayfair or Belgravia abodes, hankered after the respectability and substance which a country mansion house, set in a spectacular estate, with country pursuits available, would bring them. As Marc Girouard has said, the mystique of land was exploded by the depression, but not the mystique of the country house. There they could dispense hospitality and mix with the older landed aristocracy on their own territory, and claim hunting, shooting and fishing as their hobbies. The merchant princes longed to become country gentlemen. For them, the country was a place where money was spent, not made, and the possession of such an estate brought the ultimate social respectability to men such as Edward Cecil Guinness, whose family company had been brewing beer for the working classes since 1759.

Guinness was born in Dublin in 1847, the youngest of the three sons of Sir Benjamin Guinness. He played an active role both in the family brewery business and in Dublin municipal life, and was sufficiently wealthy to retire at the age of 42. To mark his retirement he put £250,000 in trust, to be used as to £200,000 in London, and £50,000 in Dublin, for the purpose of erecting housing accommodation which could be let at rents within the reach of the poorest of the labouring population, exactly the type of housing which Sam's parents Frederick and Sarah would have coveted. As we shall see, this magnificent charitable gesture made a deep impression on Sam. In 1885 Guinness was created a knight, and in 1891 he was raised to the peerage as Baron Iveagh of Iveagh, Co. Down. In anticipation of this latter honour he sought a suitable country estate befitting his forthcoming elevation, and his eye fell upon Savernake, which had been favourably mentioned to him by no less a person than the Prince of Wales, who had been a guest there in happier times. The attraction for Guinness was the whole estate, that is the mansion house, the forests, the parkland and the farms. He wanted it all or nothing, and Willie was a willing and anxious seller. So keen was Guinness that his offer of £750,000 was well above the market valuation. It was agreed that £250,000 was to be paid on completion, and the balance of £500,000 left on mortgage for five years at four per cent. It would have been enough to enable Willie to pay off Sam and all his other creditors, who were naturally eager that the transaction should be rapidly completed. The surplus capital in the hands of the trustees would have provided Willie with a higher income than he was then enjoying.

On 23 June 1891 a contract of sale was signed, but Willie was immediately beset by two problems. The first, which could have been contained, was that Dolly, his by now estranged wife, let it be known that she meant to be well recompensed out of the proceeds. More importantly, the law allowed one exception to the general right of a tenant for life to sell. It was provided in the Settled Land Act of 1890 that in the case of a family's principal mansion house and its immediately surrounding park, there could be no sale unless the trustees of the estate consented or, failing that, the court made an order for sale. One of the trustees, an uncle of Willie, objected, and so Willie had to go to court and petition for leave to sell the entire Savernake estate.

The matter came before Mr Justice Stirling in August. Two land agents and surveyors of great experience told him that £750,000 was in excess of their own valuation, but it was essential to sell the whole estate together. The forest, parks, farms and other lands without the mansion house would fetch a comparatively small sum, while if the mansion house and its immediate surroundings were sold without the rest of the estate, the former would lose the characteristic of being the centre of a great landed estate. No other suitable offer had been received and they considered it was highly unlikely that anyone would improve on Guinness's price. Further, in the depressed state of agriculture the demand for the labour of the rural population was small, and the presence of a resident wealthy proprietor, ready to keep the estate in good condition, and to employ the labour at hand, would make all the difference between hardship and comfort to a very large number of inhabitants, of whom there were said to be 4–5,000 on the estate.

Against this it was argued on behalf of Willie's uncle, Lord Henry Bruce, the next to succeed if Willie did not produce an heir, that having regard to the receiving order in bankruptcy made against Willie, and his mortgage to Sam, he no longer had any beneficial interest whatever left in the estate, and his wishes should therefore not be paramount. In any event, it was said, the contract of sale had been entered into by Willie under pressure from Sam and his other creditors, under threat of making him bankrupt if he declined to concur in the sale, and for this reason should be set aside.

Willie denied this. He said he had been trying to sell the estate long before any receiving order had been made against him. Because of his embarrassed circumstances it was not being kept up as it should be, and many of the trees in the forest were in a decaying state. He could neither pay his debts nor maintain the estate. He said everyone would benefit from the sale – the tenants because they would have a very wealthy man in residence; he and all those who would succeed him would possess a largely improved income; and his uncle, the next tenant for life, would then be in a much better financial position to support the dignity of the Ailesbury title.

When he gave evidence Willie showed scant regard for the seriousness of the occasion, and appeared to treat the proceedings with casual levity. Under cross-examination he was asked:

Is it not a fact that Mr. Lewis makes you an allowance? – No, if I want money I go and ask Mr. Lewis for some . . . If he likes to lend it me, he does.

And he usually does like, you have what you want? – Well, he does not refuse me; but he does not let me have what I want.

Perhaps you want a good deal more than he will let you have? – Quite right.

Lord Ailesbury, is it not the fact that you are living now on moneys supplied by Mr. Lewis? – Yes.

Are you dependent on Mr. Lewis for your daily maintenance? – Well not exactly, but partly, certainly.

Mainly, will you say mainly? – Yes, I will.

The questioning then turned to the contract with Lord Iveagh.

Is not Mr. Lewis very anxious that this contract for the sale of Savernake should be carried into effect? – Well, I do not want to be hard, but wouldn't you naturally be very anxious if you had all —

There is not the least necessity for that remark. You can answer my question? – I will answer it.

He is very anxious? – He is very anxious.

But Willie added: 'Mr. Lewis did not request me to sign this contract. I did so because I want to pay my creditors; it is a matter of great regret to me that the Savernake estate should be sold.' The fifth marquis later commented on this: 'This is untrue. Lord Ail. wanted an annuity to live on from Samuel Lewis who is under agreement to pay him £2,500.'

Mr Justice Stirling had no difficulty in coming to his decision. Willie, he said, was hopelessly insolvent, and had squandered a large sum which would have gone far to enable him to maintain his position and dignity as the head of a great family. There was no reasonable probability of his ever retrieving his finances. He came to the conclusion that the proposed sale, however desirable it might be for the creditors of the petitioner, was not one in which due regard had been paid to the interests of all the other parties entitled under the settlement. He refused to sanction the proposed sale.

The decision came hard on Willie, Sam, the other creditors, and of course on Lord Iveagh. *The Times* considered the judgment at length in a leader column and showed a touching concern for both Willie and Sam:

There remains the difficult question how Lord Ailesbury is to escape bankruptcy, and how Mr. Samuel Lewis is going to get back his money: It is easy to say that he can get it back if Lord Ailesbury borrows £250,000 at 7½%, including premiums, on the security of his life interest and his life policies. But his life interest, as was proved in the trial, is only worth a net £900 a year, so long as the present charges on the estate remain payable; and the life policies of a man of twenty-eight are not very good security. It will be interesting to see whether any insurance office or other corporation or individual is anxious to come forward out of regard for Lord Ailesbury and Mr. Lewis. If this is done it would be remarkable indeed; if it is not done, we fear that we shall see a bankrupt Marquis, and that Mr. Samuel Lewis will have to reconcile himself to what is doubtless to him the unusual experience of a bad debt.

They were wrong on this last point. Bad debts were not that unusual for Sam. His bank account reveals several cheques which came bouncing back, and more than a few of his debtors eventually became bankrupt. There were also the many cases in which Sam, out of kindness, did not pursue the debt because of the borrower's distressed condition brought about by circumstances beyond his control.

So Willie and his creditors were back to square one. Iveagh was becoming restless, but agreed to wait until the matter was heard by the Court of Appeal. This took place four months later, and the Appeal Judges adopted a more practical and robust view. They said that as lawyers, but also as men appreciative of business necessities, they knew what misery resulted from handing over an estate to a receiver who could be involved for as long as 50 years, and every other interest would be sacrificed to getting in the debt. In all probability everybody connected with the estate would be ruined unless it was sold as one entity. Those considerations, they felt, overpowered all others on the other side. Lord Justice Lindley said that although sympathy was with Lord Henry Bruce and the family, sympathy could not be allowed to determine the case. Lord Justice Bowen said that unless the opportunity was given for the house to enjoy a better and brighter future it might well become the home of owls and rats. The appeal was allowed.

This delighted the *Marlborough Times*. It pointed out that although the £750,000 which Lord Iveagh was to hand over was very large in relation to the financial yield of the estate, it was reasonable when taking into account its great historic interest, the wild beauty of

'the most magnificent forest in Europe', the great stretches of Wiltshire downs, farm upon farm, parish upon parish, the patronage of
nine livings, a vast influence in many towns and villages, and a
glorious mansion with unrivalled surroundings. There were nearly a
million trees on the estate – if they were worth only one pound each it
would make the purchase a bargain:

> ... we look forward with hope to a speedy transition to a vastly
> improved state of things when the Savernake Estates come into the
> hands of Lord Iveagh. It has been bad enough for some years now,
> the ancient glories of the Forest have been much impaired, towns
> and villages which prospered under the aegis of the Bruces have felt
> all the evil of enforced absenteeism; society has been without a
> leader; village charities and institutions founded and fostered by
> charitable ladies and others of the great family in bye-gone years
> have been kept going with difficulty by a body of clergy whose
> sacrifices have been great, having no landlord or squire to apply to
> on the one hand, and only an impoverished tenantry on the other;
> cottages, in an improving age, have only deteriorated for lack of
> funds; and a blight has seemed to settle on the neighbourhood. But
> this gloom would only have been deepened had the estate gone into
> the hands of a mortgagee, whose only aim would probably have
> been to wring out the last penny therefrom, until its resources were
> exhausted. He could have cut down the timber, ruined the loveliest
> and most picturesque parts of the noble Forest, rack-rented the
> tenants, withheld all assistance to charity, diverted the whole of the
> revenues from local expenditure.

What is more, they said, the patronage of nine important livings of
the Church of England might virtually have been in the hands of a
Jewish moneylender! If that had happened, one wonders, to whom
would Sam have turned for advice about the appointments of vicars –
the Archbishop of Canterbury or the Chief Rabbi?

This, however, was still not the end of the matter. Though Willie
was anxious to sell, his Uncle Henry was even more determined that
Savernake should remain in the family and out of the hands of 'the
mere upstart merchant, a *nouveau riche* Irishman', who had been 'so
presumptuous as to suppose that an inheritance of centuries could be
bought for cash'. Henry was a formidable foe. In his earlier days he

177

had a career in the army, and performed the remarkable feat of translating the *Infantry Drill Book* into Japanese; by comparison the complications of the Chancery Division of the High Court were simplicity itself. Lord Iveagh desperately sought a country estate, but as time passed his purpose in regard to Savernake was beginning to weaken. Henry rallied his troops, by exhortation and persuasion, and the late marquis's sons besought the House of Lords to set aside the decision of the Court of Appeal. This caused a further delay until August of 1892.

Before that appeal was concluded Lord Henry, sensing that the Lords would probably dismiss it, tried another tack. He studied all the documents in the case carefully, and came to the conclusion that there had been fraud in the arrangements made for the sale of Savernake, and he and his brothers brought yet another action, to have the sale set aside. They alleged that Willie had privately admitted that if and when Savernake was sold he would receive £2,500 a year from Sam as a reward for his subservience, and Sam had agreed to provide for this in his will. It was said that if it had not been for this 'bribe' Willie would not have signed the contract. There had indeed been a provisional agreement for Sam to make an allowance to Willie, as part and parcel of an overall agreement, but that had been openly discussed by the solicitors acting for Willie and Sam, and had been made known not only to the other creditors but also to Henry's advisers. In an affidavit he swore in support of his claim Lord Henry alleged:

On or about the 12th day of October, 1891, a Mr. Scott Saunders called upon me by his own appointment at my house, 36, Eaton Place, and said that he came from Mr. Samuel Lewis, the mortgagee of the life estate of the Marquis of Ailesbury, with a view to induce me to withdraw my opposition to the sale of the Savernake estates. The said Scott Saunders informed me that Mr. S. Lewis was prepared to give me, in the event of my withdrawing my opposition to the sale, the sum of £50,000, and that he (Mr. Scott Saunders) was to receive the sum of £5,000 for his trouble in carrying the matter through. I was subsequently, and after the trial in the Court of Appeal, approached by a member of the House of Commons, and was informed that Mr. Lewis was still prepared to offer me a sum of money, and on my declining to be a party to anything of the sort I was pressed to think the matter over. I replied that I did not intend to sell my birthright to any one, or, words to that effect.

This would have been a remarkable story for Lord Henry to invent, and there is no reason to disbelieve his account. If Scott Saunders was telling the truth, then Sam was, at the very least, behaving deviously, though not in any way dishonestly or illegally. But Sam denied that he had sent Scott Saunders to Lord Henry. Where therefore did the truth lie? The most likely interpretation is that Scott Saunders was a lone agent trying to drum up business. This happens all the time. It is something some estate agents do today. They write to an owner and say that they have a client interested in buying the owner's property, which they do not, and ask whether the owner would be willing to sell. If they obtain a positive reply they then ascertain a price at which the owner will sell, and then set about approaching a possible buyer and tell him that they can obtain the property for him at such and such a price. Similar tactics are adopted by sportsmen's agents. They approach a club which has a star player and say that they are acting on behalf of another club, which they claim to have been sworn to confidentiality not to name, which is prepared to offer £X million for a transfer of the star. If a positive response is received they then approach one or two clubs they think might be interested and say that they can procure the services of the star for them at £X million, provided, of course, that they are suitably rewarded for their part in the transaction.

Lord Frederick Bruce swore an affidavit in which he said:

(1) On July 24th last I had a conversation with Mr. Samuel Lewis, the mortgagee of the life interest of the Marquis of Ailesbury, and in the course of that conversation I informed Mr. Lewis that Lord Henry Bruce had been offered a sum of £50,000 if he would withdraw his opposition to the sale of the Savernake estate, and I said to Mr. Lewis, 'I am under the impression that this offer came from you' to which he replied 'Nothing of the kind; you can take my word for it that the offer did not proceed from me'; and I thereupon said 'Then if it did not come from you, it must have come from Lord Iveagh' to which he replied that 'he did not think that was so'. (2) I subsequently asked Mr. Lewis whether it was a

fact, as I had been informed, that he, Mr. Lewis, pulled the strings. He said that was so, but that in doing so he did not intend to act in an unfair manner towards Lord Iveagh, and he led me to believe that he was in a position to put an end to the contract with Lord Iveagh if he chose to do so.

Once again there is no reason to doubt the truth of this account. Sam was the largest creditor, was still supporting Willie, and quite naturally had the greatest say in the steps being taken to secure the best result not only for himself and the other creditors, but what would have been the best result, financially, for the Ailesbury family. But finance was not the principal consideration of the family.

Lord Iveagh strongly denied that he was in any way involved in such matters, and told Lord Frederick so when they met. But the action was not withdrawn, and so both Iveagh and Willie applied to have it struck out as 'vexatious'. The matter came once again before Mr. Justice Stirling. Iveagh gave evidence, but no one sought to call Sam. The judge held there was no evidence to support a charge of fraud:

> I can only explain ... [some aspects of this case] by supposing that the bitterness of the plaintiffs' disappointment at the result of the former proceedings has deprived them of the power of judging calmly the matters connected with the sale of the Savernake estate ... Looking at the whole history of the case, and without attributing to the plaintiffs any want of good faith, I come to the conclusion ... that they have no reasonable ground for action ...

The Law Lords had no doubts in the matter either. They did not even call upon Willie's lawyers to argue the case. It was not for the good of the state, the Lords said, that an encumbered proprietor should be compelled to continue in a position in which he could do no good to himself or anybody else. They dismissed the appeal.

But though he lost the battle, Bruce had won the war. Lord Iveagh, wearied by the constant bickerings and court proceedings, set aside the contract and purchased the Elvedon estate in Suffolk where he spent most of the rest of his life.

Although the net income of the estate had by now increased to £4,990 per annum because certain jointures and annuities had fallen in, this still left Willie without any money, and Sam with his action against him still outstanding. Beyond Sam there was a second charge in favour of Hoare's Bank, which had been lending to the Ailesbury family for more than 50 years, and a third in favour of Dolly for £3,000 a year. The Receiver continued to collect the rents, but this was barely sufficient to cover the interest payments and the jointures, let alone reduce the capital debt, and Sam, of course, had good security only for so long as Willie was alive.

A premium of £13,000 a year was payable to cover Willie's life to the full extent of the outstanding debt, but Sam did not effect full insurance. Presumably so long as the sale seemed imminent he did not consider it money well spent, and perhaps in any event it proved impossible to obtain total cover. Willie's lifestyle was now so licentious that there was no way of knowing, young though he was, how long he would survive. At the age of 30 he was to all intents and purposes an old man, and himself said that the insurance company doctor had thought him ten years older than he was.

Sam pressed ahead with his action and asked the court to certify the amount still due to him and, once this was established, to foreclose on the estate if the sum was not paid. Foreclosure was a most unusual step for Sam to take, one he avoided if at all possible, but Willie's extravagance had produced an impossible situation. In August 1893 the court fixed the amount which Willie owed Sam at £256,000. The judge ordered foreclosure, but deferred enforcement for nine months to allow Hoare's and Dolly to pay off Sam if they wished and thus become first and second mortgagees instead of second and third. Willie then appealed against the decision on the grounds that there had been improper conduct on the part of Sam's solicitors and his own solicitors, and that the judgment had been obtained following collusion between them. Though Willie was the nominal appellant, it appears that the guiding force behind it was his uncle. Moneylenders were easy prey to such accusations, but the appeal court held that the 'evidence' which Willie presented entirely failed to substantiate the allegation, and this appeal was dismissed.

Lord Justice Smith said that nothing in the affidavits impeached Sam's conduct. None the less the appeal had caused problems for him. His name had been maligned, and as the *Estates Gazette* commented, 'it looks as if the Ailesbury case could be finally settled at about the

181

same time as the Irish question. We should like to know the amount up to now of Mr. Lewis's little lawyer's bill. Certainly he who puts his head in chancery never knows when he is going to get it out again.'

Willie's condition deteriorated rapidly. He went to live at 121 Leander Road, Brixton, dressed permanently like a costermonger, offered drinks to everybody, and was prepared to fight anyone who declined his hospitality. On 10 April 1894, at the age of 31, he died. Dolly and Lord Henry had been summoned to his bedside but arrived just too late to comfort him in his last moments. Lord Henry placed a wreath of flowers on the body, saying, 'I have never had a cross word with my nephew.' He was buried at St Katherine's Church, Savernake Forest.

Scarcely a one could be found to say a good word of him. The *News of the World* commented:

> It is hardly possible, going over the facts of the life of the late Marquis of Ailesbury to find among them a single one that redounds to his credit ... A man is known by his friends, and the chosen intimates of the late Lord Ailesbury were the scum of those who frequented the turf ... One can almost fancy the shades of his ancestors revisiting the halls of Savernake, and as they gazed upon the 'noble' who so disgraced his name and station, muttered sadly their own family motto, 'FUIMUS', we have been.

Lord Curzon said only the Radical Party mourned his death, grieved to lose so deplorable an example of a hereditary legislator. To be fair to Willie he never sought to take his seat in the House of Lords. When he succeeded to the title he had told local tradesmen that the day he took the oath they could all go to the best London tailor and order a suit at his expense. The thought that he might take his seat almost caused the fifteenth earl of Derby to have a fit. He confided to his diary, when Willie was 'warned off' by the Jockey Club, that Willie was a disreputable youth married to a woman of bad character, and unfit for decent society from which he would be excluded; but the awkward fact remained that 'though he will probably be voted out of every club of which he is a member, he cannot be voted out of the House of Lords, and the scandal of his possible presence there will remain the same, whether he attends or not.' He wanted a law to be passed to overcome this dreadful situation. The *Complete Peerage* summed him up succinctly: 'a young man of low tastes, bad character, and brutal manners'. The *Marlborough Times* struggled to find a kind word to say:

And so ends the sad story, enlivened only by the reflection that Lord Ailesbury was nobody's enemy but his own – he was generous to a fault, and his geniality was proverbial . . . We must leave him, and to those who are fond of moralising upon poor erring human nature, we can only point to the stern command – 'Judge not, that ye be not judged.'

Lord Henry Augustus Brudenell-Bruce succeeded to the title as the fifth marquis. At the audit dinner following his succession he told his tenants:

It is true that I have gone through a period of great worry. But, gentlemen, I was fighting your battle, as much as I was fighting for my birthright. I fought, and fought successfully too, against your being handed over body and soul to an Irish merchant who was hand in glove with Shylock. I say you are known by the society you keep [applause], and I feel quite sure that in the action I was performing I was doing an honest act, not only by those who came after the late Marquis, but by your own selves [hear hear].

He gained little more than honour for his victory over the 'upstart' Guinness. His agent calculated that if Guinness's offer had been accepted the fifth marquis would have been 17 times richer than he was. He worked hard to improve the farms. At first he lived in a small house on the estate; the game and deer in the forest were made self-supporting by greatly expanded sales of birds and venison, and by widespread letting of shooting rights; and the estate was kept going on a bank overdraft until 1911, yielding no personal income to the marquis. He was eventually able to move back into one wing of the great house, but there he led the life of a modest country gentleman and made no attempt to resume the proud manner of aristocratic living. By the 1970s the 40,000 acres of the estate had been reduced to 6,000.

Dolly did well for herself. She was the beneficiary of a settlement of £100,000 made in 1889, though the source of the fund is not clear, and she had a jointure on the Ailesbury estate of £3,000 a year. She married David Waddle Webster in March 1901, by which time she had already given birth to a son and a daughter, and lived a comfortable life in Scotland. When she died in 1917 she left an estate of £35,000.

Sam and the other creditors were heavy losers. On Willie's death Sam had no further claim on the estate, and he was only partly reimbursed by the policies he had effected on Willie's life, said to total only £100,000. Were the creditors hard done by, or were they themselves to blame for this sad tale? Sam probably took the view that he had taken a calculated risk and lost, then shrugged his shoulders and looked to the next prospective client. It is difficult to avoid the conclusion that by lending such large sums Sam directly contributed to Willie's downfall. But Ailesbury's fate was sealed by his own nature, and he would have found a source of funds even if Sam had not been there. He would inevitably have come to the same end.

15 · Sam and Lord William Nevill

'He is a young brute, though he don't look it.'
Lord William Nevill of his friend, Mr Spender Clay

The moneylender knows the man is pledging his character and his position and that, in the last resource, he probably is pledging the benevolence and friendship of those to whom he belongs, his family or friends.
Mr Justice Matthew, witness before Select Committee, 1897

Sir George Lewis was vehemently wedded to the view that money-lending led to crime and there were many who agreed with him. He argued that if it were not for the facilities that usurers gave and the way that debtors were deliberately entangled in their webs, many crimes would not have been committed. This conviction, and his strongly voiced contention that Sam was a menace to society, were to be reinforced when, in 1897, Sir George acted on behalf of Lord William Nevill, the fourth son of the Marquis of Abergavenny.

Lord William was a member of the historic house of Nevill, whose family had been peers of England since 1295. Before the end of the Middle Ages various branches of the family had held the dukedom of Bedford, the earldoms of Westmorland, Salisbury, Warwick, Kent and Northumberland, and the baronies of Nevill, Latymer and Abergavenny. The Nevills have provided the country with a Marshal of England, more than one Lord Chancellor and Lord High Admiral, two Archbishops of York, ten Knights of the Garter and a Queen of England. Lord William Nevill proved himself an unworthy descendant.

His father, the marquis, was one of the great landowners, holding nearly 30,000 acres of profitable land, a kingmaker in the

Conservative Party, and well thought of; but he did not enjoy unalloyed pleasure from all his children's activities. As we have already seen, in discussing *Nevill* v. *Snelling*, his third son, George, became embroiled with moneylenders when still in his early twenties, and the marquis had had to rescue him. His daughter Violet, Lady Cowley, from whom Sam had purchased his house in Maidenhead, also went to court at the beginning of 1897 – the divorce court. After a distressing, widely publicised case, she obtained a decree against her husband, the Rt Hon. Henry Mornington Wellesley, Earl Cowley. Her solicitor in the proceedings was Sir George.

William Nevill was born in 1860. He served for a short period as a lieutenant in the 3rd battalion of the Royal West Kent Regiment, and held a minor position in an insurance office in Charles Street, but his work produced little by way of remuneration. He married Mademoiselle Louisa Carmen de Murrietta, the daughter of the Marquis and Marquise de Sauturec, at Brompton Oratory in 1889 and the wedding guests included the Prince and Princess of Wales, the Duke of Teck, M. de Staal, the Russian Ambassador, Señor Albarado the Spanish Ambassador, Mr Alfred de Rothschild, several earls, and Lord Dudley, a client of Sam and a close friend of Sir George Chetwynd. William was an extravagant man of slender means. Not being an eldest son he was yet another victim of the rule of primogeniture. By 1896 he was a frequent visitor to Cork Street and heavily indebted to Sam. Upwards of £100,000, much of it interest, had passed between them over a period of five or six years. Perhaps, but only perhaps, if he had received a fairer share of the family wealth, he would not have been such a spendthrift. If families such as his had either been more ready to make loans to their offspring themselves, or if they had encouraged honest work, or if they had done more to curb the excesses of their young and imposed more discipline, many of the problems involving younger sons would not have occurred.

When William's brother George had dealt with Snelling he said that 'getting a friend to back a bill is a thing I don't like doing ... asking any one to go shares in a bill is a thing I shall never do.' William had no such scruples and when Sam, quite naturally, required a guarantor for his bills, he always managed to find a friend who was prepared to sign. On one occasion the parents of a co-signatory paid Sam £40,000 when Nevill defaulted and their son could not meet his commitment. Sam was later asked about that particular transaction and he replied that 'they paid without a complaint'.

In June 1896 two of Nevill's bills became due for payment and he had run out of amenable friends. A few days before Ascot week he called to see Sam and suggested that his then outstanding bills should be satisfied by a fresh loan of £11,000 and asked him to accept as surety a Mr Spender Clay of whom Sam had heard, but not met. Nevill told him, which was true, that Clay, a subaltern in the Life Guards, was a gentleman of position and fortune. His father was dead, and his stepfather was a Member of Parliament with a home at No. 16 Grosvenor Square, just a few yards from Sam and Ada's house. According to Sir George Lewis, Clay had 'just come into a very, very, large fortune'. He was acceptable to Sam and two bills were drawn, one for £3,000 at 30 per cent and the other for £8,000 at 40 per cent. Nevill gave Sam a cheque for £20 signed by Clay. He endorsed it and told Sam to present it at the bank on which it was drawn in order that Sam could verify the signature, but Sam handed it back and said that he trusted him. Nevill took the bills away and when he returned with them, duly signed by Clay, Sam gave him the £11,000.

When the bills matured Nevill asked that they should be extended and also sought an additional advance of £17,000, again with Clay as surety. Sam was inclined to agree, but wanted to see Clay in his office before doing so. Nevill said that Clay was so busy with his military duties that he could not come to Cork Street, and had asked Nevill to bring any documents requiring his signature to the barracks (still there) in Albany Street, by Regent's Park. Sam consented and Nevill returned with the signed bills. There was, however, a minor irregularity in the signatures which had to be rectified, and Sam would not part with the £17,000 until this had been attended to. Nevill said that he was in urgent need of the money (probably to settle a gambling debt), so Sam suggested he contact Clay and ask him to come to Cork Street at once. Sam's clerk made a telephone call to the barracks and handed the telephone to Nevill who spoke to Clay. Sam, of course, heard only Nevill's part of the conversation. When it ended Nevill told Sam that Clay had said he was just going on duty, but that if Nevill went to the barracks immediately, with all the documents, he would somehow find time to sign them. Once again Sam agreed.

This would appear to have been rather slapdash behaviour on Sam's part. He was the most experienced moneylender in England, and he should surely have had some reservations about the explanations being given to him for Clay's repeated non-appearance. On the other hand he knew Clay's signature from the £20 cheque and he had had numerous dealings with Nevill, all honoured and satisfactorily profitable. In the event, Nevill did not return with the bills and the further advance was not made. He later told Sam that he had managed to do without the money, and had returned the signed bills to Clay so that he could destroy them. That, however, still left the two original bills totalling £11,000 outstanding. In December Sam presented them, but Nevill did not pay. He had had an accident which was to necessitate several operations, and was confined to bed. He told Sam that he had intended to make arrangements for payment, but his injuries had prevented this and he gave Sam a 'cheque-is-in-the-post' promise. But no money was forthcoming and so after a while Sam wrote to Spender Clay and called upon him to honour the debt. A reply came from his solicitors stating baldly, without any accompanying explanation, that Clay was not liable upon the bills.

Sam at once sent his secretary to Nevill to make enquiries. Nevill wrote to Sam:

> Clay has repented and wants to back out of it, so it is as well to be rid of such people. I have sent them [the overdue bills] to my father's solicitors and they are getting the money together. If I had not asked him about three weeks ago about that other thing [the proposed further loan of £17,000], and given the documents back to him, none of this would have occurred. He knew quite well that he would not be called upon to pay. He never thought of being disagreeable until three weeks ago when he mentioned the matter to others who induced him to force my hand. If it were not for the sake of others it would serve him right to make him pay up, then he could have a go at me and make me bankrupt. *He is a young brute and just as sharp, though he don't look it, as possible.*

Sam went to see Nevill, who told him he was very angry with Clay for suggesting there was anything wrong with the bills. He again called him a brute and added that when he recovered sufficiently he would issue a writ for slander against him for spreading the false report that in some way he was not liable upon bills which he had signed. As nothing further resulted, Sam issued proceedings against both Clay and Nevill. He obtained judgment against Nevill, but although he put the bailiffs in, no money was forthcoming. In March 1897 Nevill left for the Continent and did not return until, in circumstances which will be described, ten months later.

So Sam proceeded against Clay and the case of *Lewis* v. *Clay* came to court before Lord Russell of Killowen, the Lord Chief Justice, and a jury, in November 1897. The *Abergavenny Echo* reported the case as though it were a stage production:

LORD ABERGAVENNY'S SON
AND THE MONEYLENDER

A SENSATIONAL DRAMA IN HIGH LIFE

Dramatis Personae

SAM LEWIS .... A Well-Known Moneylender
LORD WILLIAM NEVILL .... One of His Clients
SPENDER CLAY .... An Officer in the Guards

In his pleadings Clay alleged that his signature had been obtained by means of a fraudulent trick, and that when Sam accepted the bills he knew of the fraud. This allegation, if true, would have meant that Sam was guilty of aiding and abetting a criminal offence.

Clay's version of the events leading to the signing of the bills was presented for the first time, and it revealed an entirely different picture. Clay, a well-built fellow who looked more than 22, said that on 4 June 1896 he came of age, and was thus able to sign legally binding contracts. He had known Nevill for many years and regarded him as a good friend, although Nevill was 15 years older. Nevill suggested that it would be a splendid idea to arrange a house party for Ascot week, which was two weeks ahead, and this was done. Nevill arrived on the Monday, having previously seen Sam and obtained the two bills for £11,000 which Clay would have to sign, and Clay followed on the Wednesday. At that time Clay knew nothing of the bills. They attended the races and greatly enjoyed themselves. On the Sunday, Nevill came to Clay's bedroom about lunch time, and had with him what Clay described as a wrapper composed of blotting

189

paper, in which a document – for it appeared to Clay to be just one document – had been inserted. Four holes had been cut out of the blotting paper, leaving blanks beneath. Lord William told him the document was a power of attorney dealing with his sister's marriage settlement which he wished Clay to sign as a witness, and, he added darkly, 'you know what is going on'. Clay knew that Lady Cowley had instituted divorce proceedings, and replied that he did. When Clay asked the exact nature of the document, William replied that if he insisted upon it, he would show it to him, but he thought that in such a delicate matter Clay might trust him after having known him so long. Appealed to in that way, Clay signed what he thought was one document without seeing its contents. He was, of course, signing the bills of exchange as guarantor.

Quite what Nevill would have done if Clay had called his bluff is not certain, but he would most likely, in a voluble show of disappointment, have said that he would rather not proceed with someone who showed so little faith in him, leaving Clay feeling guilty and Nevill to find some other way of securing a further advance.

Six months later, on 2 December, Nevill visited Clay at Regent's Park Barracks armed with a document similar in appearance to the first. It was the same sort of wrapper on the same kind of paper, with four slits, and Clay was again invited to sign. When Clay inquired as to its contents, Nevill replied that it was a power of attorney relating to a gift of money that a certain Catholic gentleman wished to distribute secretly to a Protestant charity. When Clay asked why such a document needed to be signed by him, Nevill replied 'You remember that document you witnessed in June? If I can get the same witnesses to this it will save the matter of a £20 stamp and that is why I have come again.' Again Clay signed. He had now, of course, signed the bills for £17,000. It makes one wonder whether the Army insisted on any minimum intelligence qualification for holding a commission in the Guards.

It was only after Nevill had left that Clay remembered that this story was not the same as Nevill had given six months before, the one about Lady Cowley's divorce. Nevill, caught up in complex inventions, had forgotten what he had previously told Clay, and had been caught out. He was to have cause to reflect upon Sir Walter Scott's lines:

O what a tangled web we weave,
When first we practise to deceive.

Clay immediately contacted his solicitor and was given appropriate advice. Just a few hours later he received the telephone call previously mentioned that Nevill made from Sam's office and in Sam's presence. Nevill, who was doubtless congratulating himself on the apparent success of his guile, must have been shaken to the roots when Clay told him that his solicitor insisted that the documents should be returned for examination so that the solicitor could satisfy himself that Clay had not been compromised. Nevill must have had considerable difficulty in disguising from Sam the shock he must have felt at what Clay had said. He none the less managed to keep up a bold front and had immediately thought what to tell Sam in order to give himself a chance to deal with this unfortunate turn of events.

He contacted Clay later and arranged a meeting, but Clay wrote to say that he was bringing his solicitor with him. Nevill replied: 'My dear Bertie, It is not in the least necessary for you to bring your solicitor, as I am going to return your four signatures as I don't require them. You can cancel them. I will cut them off and you can burn them.' But then he wrote again: 'You must trust me. You don't know what trouble I am in. Believe me I can get out of it all right. I am fairly in a fix . . . All I ask of you is that you hold your tongue. If you talk you will ruin me for life, but I know you won't.' According to Clay they met a few days later, and Nevill said 'Don't look at me. I have a confession to make to you.' He made a full admission of the deceit he had practised, and promised that Clay would not be troubled further in the matter, as he would meet the debt himself as indeed, he said, he had always intended. At the end of a painful, stormy, scene they parted, their friendship, not unnaturally, completely broken.

It was essential for Sam's reputation, and indeed his liberty, that he should convince the jury that he had no part in Nevill's fraud and that he was at all times completely unaware of it. After Sam had given evidence, the Lord Chief Justice put certain questions to the jury, having indicated fairly clearly throughout the hearing and in his summing-up the answers he expected them to give. The questions and answers were:

(i) Did the plaintiff, Mr. Lewis, take the notes in good faith? – Yes.

191

(ii) Was the account which the defendant, Lieutenant Clay, gave of the way in which the notes were signed substantially true? – Yes.

(iii) Was the defendant in signing the documents recklessly careless and did he thereby enable Lord William Nevill to commit a fraud? – No, under the circumstances.

(iv) Were the signatures to the documents given in misplaced confidence in Lord William Nevill as to their nature? – Yes.

(v)   Did the defendant sign his name to be used by Lord William Nevill for any purpose he chose? – No.

After further legal argument another question was added for the jury:

(vi) Did the defendant sign the documents without due care? – No, not under the circumstances.

Although Clay had enabled Nevill to perpetrate the fraud, the jury crucially concluded that he had not, *in the circumstances*, acted either recklessly or even carelessly.

This meant that there were two innocent parties, Sam and Clay. Which one was to suffer the loss? Sam's counsel contended that if Clay trusted Nevill, and was fool enough to sign documents he did not read, then he was the victim of his own credulity. He should pay Sam, and look to Nevill for reimbursement. Clay's counsel severely criticised Sam for not at any time during the transactions insisting on seeing Clay, for if he had the fraud would have been thwarted. The Lord Chief Justice said that the case was 'one in a million'. He found, as a matter of law, that on the jury's answers judgment had to be given for Clay, and so Sam lost his £11,000. But he had one consolation, and he cherished it for the remainder of his life. During the course of his summing-up Lord Chief Justice Russell said of him:

> His business of bill discounting and money lending is not a very popular one, but at least be just to those who carry it on. The plaintiff has been for thirty years at the same address in Cork Street, and there has been no attempt to show that he deserved other than the name of a man who was honourably engaged. He has conducted his affairs in an honest and straightforward manner, and his word is as much to be credited as that of any other man of business.

Sam, so jealous of his reputation for fair dealing, would sometimes quote this, and claimed that never in English legal history had such a thing been said in a court of justice about a member of his profession.

There was a strong public reaction to the decision, and several letters to *The Times*. Many considered Sam was hard done by, and that it would render all business dealing with bills impossible, if loans could not be advanced against signatures recognised as genuine. There were merchants in the City of London whose business life revolved around the giving and acceptance of bills of exchange. Thousands of cheques were handled daily, and if businessmen had to make searching enquiries into each and every one to ascertain the exact circumstances in which the signatures had been affixed, trade would come to a halt. Others expressed the view that moneylenders were astute in keeping just the right side of the law of fraud, and although a moneylender did not always have to ascertain the circumstances under which signatures were presented to him, 'if a bill drawn up by a known scamp comes endorsed by a greenhorn just come into a fortune, the moneylender is not so green himself as to be without suspicion, or even knowledge, of the risk under which he accepts it'. One correspondent suggested that Sam had no one but himself to blame for his loss, because he chose to depart from the custom of satisfying himself of the genuineness of the transaction by personal communication with the surety.

Sam appealed against the decision, but before it was heard Nevill reappeared on the scene. Sir George Lewis was retained to act on his behalf. Nevill was taken to Bow Street Magistrates' Court and there charged with obtaining signatures to documents by false pretences. He was also charged with the graver offence of forgery, which was legally possible even though he had not personally penned the signatures. He was remanded for a week on bail of two sureties of £2,000 each, provided by his brother Lord Henry Nevill and his brother-in-law Colonel the Hon. Charles Gathorne-Hardy.

It was obvious that he was still suffering the effects of recent illness, but it was reported that at the resumed hearing the following week he looked somewhat brighter and smarter, though pale and careworn. A six-feet-tall, slightly built man, clean shaven and dressed in a dark suit, he stepped into the dock with a firm, quick step, held himself very erect, took a commanding view of the court and appeared in no way unnerved by his position. Mr Horace Avory (later to be appointed a judge) appeared for the prosecution and Sir George for Nevill. Algernon Sydney was in attendance to look after Sam's interests. Spender Clay gave evidence in the same terms as he had done in the civil action. Well groomed, looking very fresh and debonair and bearing all the signs of contented prosperity, he presented a striking contrast to Nevill. Now and then Nevill looked at his accuser steadily and keenly, but Clay never returned the glance. Indeed, throughout the hearing Nevill listened calmly to the evidence and arguments, his head on one hand, as if he were simply a spectator.

Sir George indicated that as it was a case which obviously would have to go for trial he would not be cross-examining Clay at that stage, and Nevill would be reserving his defence without in any way making any admissions. At this the magistrate, Sir John Bridge, indicated that this could affect his mind when the question of bail was raised. 'This is not a mere question of fact. A man's honour is at stake as well as his honesty, and, therefore, I should have thought he would come and say "These are the facts". If he does not I shall draw my own conclusions.' Nevill later described Sir John as a very old, irritable, infirm man, harbouring a strange animosity against him, who did not seem to hear much of what was going on, and was too feeble in body and mind to be made to understand what had really happened.

Sam was next to be called to the witness box, and all the papers reported that he was sworn in 'in the Jewish fashion'. For almost 25 years Sir George had been manoeuvring for just this moment, the opportunity to cross-examine, and thereby expose, the activities of the man he considered responsible, more than anyone else, for the continuance of the despised and evil trade of lending money to impecunious aristocrats; the man responsible for bringing others such as Lord Nevill before the criminal courts; the man who in his opinion brought the good name of the Jewish community into disrepute. But for Sir George the occasion was untimely. Much as he would have liked to cross-examine Sam about his dealings with Nevill, the interest he charged, the profits he had made, and the depths to which Nevill had been brought, his first priority was to obtain bail for his client. He needed Sam's assistance at this stage, not his antagonism, and he therefore had to treat Sam gingerly, not in a hostile manner. He also had to consider whether Sam, who had almost certainly lost all hope of recovering the £11,000, might not be embittered towards Nevill, and seek some sort of revenge. He decided that whatever other reservations he might have about Sam, he did not think he would indulge in recrimination, though given Lewis's behaviour in the Chetwynd case Sam might have been forgiven if he had done so.

Since Nevill had once left England for the Continent, out of reach of Sam and the courts, Sir George knew that if the magistrate entertained the thought that he might do the same again, bail would certainly be refused. He sought to establish that Nevill had made no secret of his trip to the Continent, did not hide his address abroad, and had even volunteered to come back and give evidence for Sam in the Clay case – though just what help he could have been is difficult to see.

Sir George Lewis – You are aware that immediately after the bills became due Lord William Nevill underwent several operations. His jaw was broken, and he was seriously ill? – Sam Lewis – Yes.

When he left England, did his departure appear in the newspapers? – I think so.

So he did not leave secretly? – I think not.

You have spoken of him being in Spain, but lest misapprehension should occur, did he not marry a Spanish lady? – I believe he did.

You do not suppose he went to get out of your way? – Oh no!

Then he came to Paris, and resided there for some time? – Yes, there was no secret about it.

You know that Lord William Nevill repudiated the charge that he had acted unfairly? – Certainly I did.

I think on one occasion during his illness you saw him in his bedroom in Brechin Place? – Yes and very ill he looked. He told me that he had not acted dishonestly.

You had innumerable transactions with him with other names to the notes dealt in? – Yes.

And the notes had been met? – Yes.

In this matter you are the loser of the money as well as loser of the action? – Quite true Sir.

Did Lord William intimate his desire to you to come to London and be examined as witness in the action against Mr Clay? – Yes, several times, but I left it to my legal adviser. He was not called as a witness by either side.

An experienced advocate, as Sir George was, would not have risked asking such questions if he had not been fairly certain in advance of the answers he would receive; it would have been too dangerous. This raises the suspicion that Sam must have indicated in advance to Sir George, probably through the medium of one of Lord Nevill's relatives or friends, that he could safely ask such questions. This would appear to be confirmed by the reporter of the *Daily News* who wrote that from the very beginning of his evidence Sam was benevolent and that the onlooker never lost that impression. He seemed rather to enjoy confessing that by putting the bailiff into Nevill's premises he got less than nothing, being out of pocket on the costs. It was almost with warmth that he expressed the conviction that Lord William had not gone on the Continent to avoid inquiry about the promissory notes. And Sam's amiable manner did not change even when it was brought out that his charges were 40 per cent.

Detective Inspector Hare confirmed that when charged, Nevill had replied, 'I am innocent'; but despite strenuous efforts by Sir George to convince the magistrate that there was no danger at all that Nevill would not attend his trial, Sir John was not impressed. He took the view that the alleged offences were of the greatest possible gravity, carried out in a manner which suggested an older, experienced, man using these advantages to take money from one who was practically a boy. Nevill was committed in custody to stand his trial at the Old Bailey. The only remark he made was when he stood up to his full height in the dock and, speaking with emphasis, said 'I am innocent.' He was taken to Holloway prison where he occupied a furnished cell, and it was reported that he was relaxed and frequently declared his innocence. All his meals were sent in from outside, and he saw his friends and Sir George every day.

Criminal justice was then processed more expeditiously than is the case today. In just a fortnight Nevill was brought from Holloway to stand his trial at the Old Bailey. It had been very many years since a person of his social distinction had appeared there on such serious charges and no *cause célèbre* within the memory of the oldest official of the court had attracted such a fashionable crowd. Broughams blocked the street outside. The reserved enclosure was full of ladies 'in the smartest frocks', and men in 'gorgeous raiment', who looked unfamiliar and incongruous in the surroundings. It was clearly an occasion when Society considered it should look its best to uphold the dignity of its status, even in such distressing circumstances.

Many of the general public who had come early in the hope of securing admission found the doors closed against them. It was to be a Society event. Lady Nevill, dressed in deep mourning, and looking pale, sat still and quiet. Spender Clay, 'the picture of a healthy, prosperous, young Guardsman, with fresh complexion, clear skin, blue eyes, regular features and well-groomed appearance', was accompanied by a number of friends who sat beside him in the middle of the court behind the seats of counsel. Also present, and seated in a prominent position, was Sam. Sir George, fur-coated as usual, arrived with Mr Lawson Walton QC (who had appeared for Sam in his civil case against Clay), leading a team of three barristers instructed on behalf of Nevill.

A day or two before the trial Nevill had struck up a conversation with another prisoner, whom he later described as 'decidedly gentlemanly-looking', a man who had seen better days. The man asked who was to be Nevill's trial judge, to which Nevill replied that he did not know. 'Well, for your own sake, I hope you won't be tried by Mr. Justice Lawrance, for he is about the worst man on the bench for anyone like you to come before. If you were plain Bill Sykes he would make it much lighter for you. He will punish you more for who you are than for what you have done.' The prophecy was to prove strikingly accurate. Mr Justice Lawrance did preside at the trial, and Nevill was brought up from below to answer to the charges. Though outwardly in control of himself, he appeared to be labouring under considerable distress which he endeavoured to hide. He was fault-lessly shaven and dressed in a black morning coat with a high turned-down collar and black tie. He leaned forward over the dock to speak to Sir George and, after casting one general glance around the court, thereafter looked straight ahead and preserved an absolutely impas-sive demeanour almost throughout the entire proceedings. In answer to the more serious charge of forgery he pleaded, in clipped tones, 'not guilty'; but to that of 'with intent to defraud, causing and inducing Herbert Henry Spender Clay to write and affix his name upon certain papers in order that the same might be afterwards used and dealt with as valuable securities' he pleaded 'guilty'. The prosecution offered no evidence on the forgery charge, which was a felony, and accepted the plea of guilty to the second, which was a misdemeanour, and upon which the maximum sentence was five years' imprisonment. It was the general opinion prior to the trial that there was no possibility of Nevill escaping a custodial sentence, but that if the forgery charges were dropped he would receive a punishment of 12–18 months' imprisonment.

After the prosecution had outlined the facts of the case, Mr Walton had the difficult task of addressing the court in mitigation of his client's offence. What could possibly be put forward in his favour? What would the reader have said? Walton began by saying that he hoped the judge, when considering sentence, would bear in mind that although Nevill had undoubtedly obtained the signature of Clay by misrepresentation and deception, he had fully acknowledged this error, this great indiscretion, immediately he was challenged, and had not sought to retract this confession. (Walton seems to have conveniently overlooked that Nevill's original response was to call Clay a brute whom he would sue for making a false report about him, and it remained to be seen whether the judge considered that what Nevill had done could properly be described as mere 'error' or 'indiscretion'.) At the time Nevill committed these acts, continued Walton, he knew that they were wrong and that he was taking advantage of a friendship, but he had not the slightest idea that he was committing a criminal offence, for he had at all times intended that he, not Clay, would pay the debt to Sam, just as he had met all the other bills which had been backed by his friends. Again, Walton seems to have overlooked, or had not been instructed about, the occasion when the family of one of Nevill's guarantors had had to find £40,000 to pay Sam.

Walton said there was only one cause which had prevented Nevill dealing with the matter himself, as he had always intended, and that was his serious illness which had intervened. He had been in the hands of several doctors, and was under the influence of morphia and other drugs for weeks together. It was thus impossible for him to complete the arrangements which were then in hand. He had been in touch with friends in Egypt on whose assistance he relied and had those arrangements been effected, Clay would have had no cause to complain. It was the misfortune of Nevill's illness which had led to the misfortune of the trial. He added that in June 1896 Nevill was indebted to Sam in the total sum of £70,000, and he understood that the whole of that sum had been paid. (In a letter to *The Times* a day or two after the trial Algernon Sydney, writing on behalf of Sam, denied that this was so.) Nevill realised, Walton continued, that the punishment in such cases had to be a period of imprisonment, but the court could justly remember that Lord William Nevill had already been very heavily punished. He was a member of a family universally respected in all ranks of English life. The suffering that his conduct had brought upon his family and friends must have caused very severe suffering to Lord William Nevill himself. The ruin which must attend that injury was terrible for a man holding the position which Lord William did. He invited Mr Justice Lawrance to bear in mind that no punishment could ever seriously add to the terrible penalty which in any case must attend these proceedings which had involved Lord William in such a humiliating position. This was, perhaps, his best point. The judge could appreciate just how much hurt, both physical and to their pride, the family and Nevill must have suffered. Walton appealed for a lenient sentence.

Nevill then rose and stood before the judge, steadying himself by placing his hands on the rail of the dock and looked straight before him with a rigidly expressionless face. Speaking with much feeling, Mr Justice Lawrance said that the offence to which the prisoner had pleaded guilty was extremely serious, and it had been committed against a friend who relied upon his good faith and honour:

> In my judgment, morally speaking, the crime was as great as if you had abstracted the money from Mr. Clay's pocket, or broken into Mr. Lewis's office and taken the money from his desk. I mention this because I wish you clearly to understand that the result of the crime was to put £11,000 into your hand, leaving somebody – I am afraid you did not care who – to bear the loss.
>
> I have listened with great care and attention to the eloquent appeal made by your counsel, and I desire to give the fullest effect

to it. It is said on your behalf that you were suffering from pecuniary pressure: but Mr. Walton has said that that is no excuse. If this had been the case of some wretched City clerk, with a family of seven children, who, under heavy loss, helped himself from his master's till, there would have been nobody to speak for him in the circumstances; he would have been left to his fate.

It is said that to a man in your position any punishment passed on you would be felt more keenly by you than by an ordinary person: but I wish to point out to you and others that the higher the position persons hold the greater are their responsibilities. Then it is said and this most touches and goes nearest to my heart, that what you have done will bring sorrow to those connected with you. That also happens in every case. In the case of the clerk whom I have mentioned the blow falls with the greatest severity on his wife and children. I have looked, and I am sorry to say that I have looked in vain, for any extenuating circumstances. It seems to me to be about as bad a case of fraud as it is possible to conceive.

... by your conduct you have brought disgrace and dishonour upon an ancient and a noble name, you have brought sorrow and suffering and shame to those who are near and dear to you, you have forfeited the position which you held and which should have been a guarantee for your honesty at least, if not for your honour. Your crime has been great and your sentence must be severe. The sentence is that you be sent to penal servitude for five years.

The deathly silence in court was at once broken. Only once was Nevill moved during the hearing, when the judge referred to the shame he had brought upon his family. His lips then were compressed, and he appeared to clutch the dock more tightly, but he quickly recovered and received his sentence with calmness. He said nothing. He was removed from the dock and within five minutes the court had emptied. His wife had an interview with him in the cells before he was taken to Wormwood Scrubs in the custody of two warders. No one had said a word against Sam.

Nevill said later that he felt the judge was activated by class prejudice, and had given him double or treble the sentence a non-aristocratic prisoner would have received. But Nevill had broken two sacrosanct rules of Society. He had taken advantage of a friend; he had let down his class. By failing to set an example to his social inferiors, he had diminished his peers. Society believed that its existence was the cement which kept the country stable, kept revolution at bay. Any crumbling spelt danger and that was exactly what Nevill had caused. He could expect, and received, little sympathy. The comment of the *Daily Telegraph* on 'this sordid tragedy' was typical:

> There was some astonishment yesterday in London when the news of the sentence was disseminated; but we will undertake to say that there was a still greater horror and disgust, a more painful sense of indignation and dismay, at the dishonour which had been done, not only to those ranks from which Lord William Nevill himself sprang, but to the ordered polity and commonwealth in which we all have to move. The circumstances of the case were simple enough and peculiarly odious. Even in the most corrupt aristocracy which history has known, if there be no lingering respect for the motto *'noblesse oblige'* there is, as a rule, enough honour to prevent a man from defrauding a friend.

As to the guileless and gulled Clay, they considered he seemed to know even less about business than was usual with 'our military *jeunesse dorée'*. But he was not the main target and they made a wider point:

> When amusement takes the form of reckless expenditure, of display for its own sake, of inordinate gambling, of the thousand and one inventions whereby youth at the prow and pleasure at the helm squander money, fame, regulation, as the only serious business in life – then here and there we reach a crisis: the greed for wealth has impecuniosity for its shadow, and the footsteps of debt are always dogged by crime.
>
> ... There have been too many unsavoury cases of peculation and fraud ... If the punishment of Lord William Nevill helps to cure the wounds which social honour has lately endured, even his lamentable career and memorable ruin will not have been wholly in vain.

The following week Sam's appeal in his civil action against Clay came before the court. On his behalf it was said that as a result of the Nevill case he felt that he ought not to proceed against Clay, even though the appeal might be decided in his favour, and he was allowed to withdraw.

On the issue of Clay's behaviour in signing the documents in the way he did, perhaps Labouchere should be given the last word. Writing in *Truth* he said:

... without in any way extenuating Lord William's offence, I must say that some measure of blame for his downfall seems to me to rest on Mr. Spender Clay. It is a noble thing, no doubt, to have perfect confidence in your friend, up to a point, but beyond that certain point confidence degenerates into culpable simplicity ... I must confess that had I been on the jury which tried the civil action against Mr. Clay, I should not have acquitted that gentleman of negligence. To sign a document without knowing its contents is *prima facie* an act of supreme folly; and the flimsy excuse given by Lord William in this case for concealing the contents scarcely makes Mr. Clay's act the wiser. At any rate, it can hardly be a pleasant reflection for the gentleman now that if he had shown a trifle less confidence in his friend he would have saved him from five years' penal servitude – to say nothing of saving Mr. Sam Lewis from the loss of £11,000 ... The next confiding youth who signs a document through a hole in a sheet of blotting paper will deserve to bear the consequences himself.

Unlike Ailesbury, Nevill was not an innocent at large. Old enough to know better, his subsequent behaviour indicated that amid many good qualities which he undoubtedly possessed, there was a criminal streak in his make-up. He served the first seven weeks of his sentence at Wormwood Scrubs, 'and it seemed like seven years', and was then sent to Parkhurst Prison on the Isle of Wight. He was a model prisoner and received full remission. When he was released in November 1901 his weight had dropped from 12 stone to 9 stone 10 pounds. He then had to bear what he considered to be the toughest part of his punishment – the loss of friends, and the cold contempt of those who had been his closest acquaintances. He made up his mind to face the world with eyes straight to the front, looking neither to the left nor to the right, 'but leaving it to everyone who might wish to recognise me to make the first advance'. He expressed his gratitude to those who did not desert him, including his wife and family, which more than compensated for the loss of some of his friends who made it clear that as far as they were concerned they had no wish that their paths should cross again.

Under the *nom-de-plume* 'W. B. N.', he wrote a book entitled *Penal Servitude* about his experiences in prison, and made several well-argued proposals for reform of the system. He said, 'I shall not soon forget that morning [on the day of his release]. I got up at 5.10 a.m. as usual, and had my last – at least I hope it will be my last – prison breakfast.' Alas, there were more to come. He pledged a great deal of jewellery with a pawnbroker called Fitch, and one day asked him to bring all the jewellery to his house as he wished to consolidate his debts into one transaction, and said he wished to examine the condition of the pledged articles. While examining the jewellery Nevill distracted Fitch's attention, and switched the jewellery, which had been wrapped in tissue, for two pieces of coal also wrapped in tissue, which Fitch then took away. Presumably Nevill then either sold the jewellery or pledged it again. Or perhaps it had not belonged to him in the first place and he restored it to the true owner before the loss was uncovered. Fitch eventually discovered what had happened and he informed the police. When they arrived Nevill said, 'Don't lock me up, it will mean twenty years' penal servitude for me. I can get the money by tomorrow'; and when told he would be charged said, 'For God's sake don't do that, for the sake of my wife.'

Before the case came to court all the moneys due to Fitch were repaid. Lady Nevill gave evidence and said that the house in Eaton Place in which they lived had been left her by her mother. She had a separate and considerable income, and had several times redeemed pledges made by her husband, who had no income. It was she who had provided the money for Fitch. In April 1907 Nevill was sentenced to 12 months' imprisonment. Once more his family took him back into the fold, and he lived, seemingly happily, until his death in 1939 when in his 78th year.

The similarity between this and the Clay case was that in both Nevill convinced himself that he was not involved in any criminal act, because he intended to meet the debts before his deceit was discovered, so that neither Clay nor Fitch would be a loser. Unfortunately he deceived himself as well, for there was never any likelihood that he could pay. In his book he referred to Sam and Clay. He had thought he would not be prosecuted because neither of them, according to him, had really suffered. 'It was true that Mr. Lewis had lost his action against Captain Spender Clay, and with it his security, for those particular bills. But upon the whole account between us, from first to last, which extended over a period of nearly six years, he was a very large gainer ... Mr. Lewis's attitude towards me, in fact, all the way through, was straightforward. He was compelled to take the course he took and certainly I have never blamed him.'

16 · The Select Committee

A banker lends other people's money, and a moneylender lends his
own.
> Abraham Moore, witness before the 1897 Select Committee

You, Gentlemen, praise your winemaker and your tailor and your
bootmaker, but which of you ever praises your moneylender?
> John Kirkwood, witness before the Select Committee

I sell my money; I do not lend it at all.
> Isaac Gordon, witness before the Select Committee

I consider that I had to pay very large interest, but I also say that I
got the money on security that neither bankers nor anybody else
would have lent on, and if people go to moneylenders they know
that they must pay more interest than they would otherwise.
> Isabael Russell, witness before the Select Committee

Public disquiet about moneylenders was increasing, and had been for
some time, not so much about the Sam Lewis, aristocratic-lending
type, though Sir George never relented in his pursuit, but about the
activities of those who advanced only comparatively small loans. A
National Anti-Usury League was formed to coordinate opposition to
the malpractitioners. Mr Robert Yarburgh, the Member of Parliament for Chester, raised the question in the House in 1894, and in
July of that year Thomas Farrow, the secretary of a cooperative
lending society, the Agricultural Bank Association, who had been
investigating the subject in depth for more than a year, called for a
government inquiry, either by a Select Committee of the House of
Commons or a Royal Commission.

Farrow visited moneylenders' clients and obtained their answers to
a lengthy questionnaire. In 1895 he published an exposure entitled
The Moneylender Unmasked. The front cover was illustrated by
drawings of a spider in his web, and a shark. In his introduction he

quoted the remark of a county court judge: 'the absolute repeal of the
Usury laws has brought into existence those swarms of moneylenders
who, like parasites bred on animals, injure their vital power, and
impair the health of the commercial body.' Farrow then set out what
the book contained:

> The reader will be invited to view the subtleties of this financial
> snare in successive stages. His attention will first be drawn to the
> tempting baits offered by the moneylender to entrap his victim,
> whom, having allured, he persuades to part with an entrance fee –
> at length secured, and the door closed upon him, the trapper
> proceeds by various devices to prevent escape. The reader will then
> be asked to view the victim in his captivity, to hear his cries, and
> witness his struggles for freedom, often unavailing, sometimes, at
> great cost, effective. Finally, he will be made aware of the extent
> and profits of the process.

Though clearly accepting that there were some *bona fide* moneylenders who acted respectably and honourably, he argued that these
were in a minority. He admitted that a high rate of interest was not
incompatible with honesty. Some moneylenders stated their true rate
openly, and the prospective borrower either took it or left it, but he
none the less believed that even these men charged rates which were
unjustifiably high. The behaviour of moneylenders was such, he
claimed, that they could not rely on goodwill, and so they approached
their prospective victims in the guise of philanthropists. Individual
letters were addressed to nobility, clergy, medical men, officers, civil
servants and farmers whose names and addresses were taken from
Dodd's Parliamentary Companion, the *Army and Navy List*, *Crock-
ford's Clerical Directory*, *Court and Civil Service Guides* and *Stubbs'
Gazette* (for the addresses of borrowers who had given bills of sale
over their goods). They were sent on embossed or tinted notepaper
and envelopes, and sometimes even carried a quasi-religious motto –
in one case *'deus mihi providebit'* (God Will Provide). They advertised everywhere, in specialised religious, political, scientific and
arts magazines, at theatres, and in local and national newspapers.
Advertisements appeared on hoardings, buses, trains and costermongers' barrows. Two newsapers, the *Daily Telegraph* and the

London Standard, carried between them 18,000 such adverts during one year.

To test the market Farrow inserted an advertisement in four London papers, posing as a philanthropist prepared to loan at 10 per cent. He received 283 replies from bank clerks, civil servants, small tradesmen and the working classes. He did not, however, further the experiment by undertaking what would have been the only true test, namely making loans at that rate to ascertain whether it was feasible to carry on business on such terms.

Farrow then dealt with the various trickery of which moneylenders were capable, ranging from the preliminary fee frauds (obtaining a fee to cover 'expenses' with no intention of making a loan), to false statements as to the true rate of interest; trading under false names and guises; obtaining judgments without any forewarning; to eternal interest loans – providing a loan on terms where the monthly repayments equalled or were less than the accruing interest; and even blackmail. He spread his gospel to a much wider public by publishing *In the Moneylender's Clutches,* pamphlets at one penny each.

After persistent pressure from Farrow, Yarburgh and their supporters, a Select Committee of the House of Commons was set up in 1897 to '*inquire into the alleged evils attending moneylending transactions at high rates of interest, or under oppressive conditions as to repayment, between the poorer classes and professional money-lenders and to report thereon*'. On the face of it this remit did not include Sam, nor did the strictures, for no one ever alleged that Sam had misled a client, and indeed most of his business came from the recommendation of existing clients. He never had lent to the smaller borrower – by this time his minimum loans were measured in thousands of pounds – but this did not prevent his activities being referred to, particularly by Sir George when he came to give evidence, which he did shortly after the Nevill case had finished and when he was full of rancour towards Sam. Nor, of course, did it prevent the Committee making recommendations, some of which were eventually acted upon, which affected all moneylenders, whatever the nature of their business. And although Sam was not called before the Committee, details were given by other witnesses of bargains which he was alleged to have entered into which showed him in a poor light. The main problem for Sam was that most people did not distinguish

207

between the different classes of moneylenders, and all were tarnished by the misbehaviour of the worst.

In his book Farrow made a particular attack on a non-Jewish practitioner, John Kirkwood, a Scotsman, who had started business as a bill discounter in Lincoln in 1875. Farrow singled him out as the 'King of Moneylenders', a man who:

> loves extortion, he rejoices at the sight of his vast army of victims; he gloats over the success of his cunningly devised schemes; he prides himself on having among his plucked ones the Government itself. He has robbed it of large sums for many years by the deliberate manufacture of bad debts, and by the presentation of false and fraudulent returns to the Income Tax authorities ... he has become immensely wealthy ... his palatial establishment by Heene Terrace, Worthing could only be maintained by one who is justly described as the King of Moneylenders ... I hold him up to my readers as a deceiver, extortioner, and unprincipled scoundrel, and I do not hesitate to ask the press of this country to assist in the exposure of one of the most obnoxious blood-sucking leeches that ever battened on human misery.

It could scarcely have been spelled out any more clearly, but Kirkwood chose not to sue for libel. Kirkwood caused immeasurable harm to the reputation of his moneylending colleagues, but he was matched in this by one other – the notorious Isaac Gordon.

Gordon was born in Neustadt on the German/Russian border in about 1863 and emigrated to Scotland as a young boy. He was slim, wiry, and full of nervous energy and tension. He started in business as a moneylender when he was about 20 years of age, with no or little capital. Before the Select Committee was appointed he had been sentenced to 20 months' hard labour for fraud; had had his subscriptions to the synagogues in Glasgow, and then Birmingham, refused because of his outrageous behaviour towards his clients; and had made a fortune. It was said of him that he had wrecked more homes by his usurious practices than anyone else in the country, and that he was impervious to reproach from judge, jury and public press. It was recorded in the minutes of the Birmingham Hebrew Congregation of 5 January 1896, that is to say some 15 months before the Select

Committee first met, that it was unanimously resolved by the Council of the members that the synagogue's collector should no longer call on 'Mr. Isaac Gordon, Livery Street, and that any money sent by him shall be returned forthwith'. Gordon, a persuasive and flowing writer, bombarded them with letters asking them to reconsider. 'If I sin against the laws of the land', he wrote, 'the law will deal with me; if I sin against the law of man, I am responsible to my Maker. You have no right to sit in judgement upon me.' On 26 July the Secretary was instructed to reply that the Council had not in any way interfered with the seat he occupied, or his membership – they simply refused to take his money. He wrote yet again, requesting the Council to rescind its previous resolution, and threatened to take legal action if they did not. This would have caused them a serious problem, for they would not wish to have their internal matters discussed in public courts. Despite this they kept their resolve, and the Secretary wrote to him that the Council, having received his communications, begged to inform him that he must consider the previous resolutions conclusive of the matter. And so it remained; but the affair revealed the depth of Gordon's craving for acceptance within the community, and the community's disgust at his business ethics.

Everything Gordon did, he justified by a basic philosophy which, expressed simply, was that he was entitled to do whatever he liked with his own money. Anything he and a consenting adult agreed as to the terms of a loan was the business of nobody but the two of them. Sympathy for, or mercy to, his clients was not a consideration for him. He was asked about a loan of £100 for three months on which he charged £100 interest, a rate of 400 per cent:

You think it is fair business? – Yes, perfectly fair. I risked my money. I risked my money and I have the right to make the best bargain I can for myself. I know more about it than the Committee does, and if you will allow me I will give you one or two good hints that will put a different light on the affair altogether. I do not call it interest at all. I sell my money; I do not lend it at all.

No uncertainty, no doubts, no complications – a simple funda- mentalist philosophy which covered all his dealings. To be open and plain about his charges; extract the highest possible rate; and then be ruthless in pursuing the debt in the event of a default. As will be seen, the criminal courts had not always agreed that he was so open and fair.

The appearance of this infamous pair before the Select Committee was eagerly awaited by its members and the public, but feared by their fellow professionals, and by the Jewish community, many of whom cowered in embarrassment at the thought of the further indignities which Gordon would inflict upon them when he was subjected to a searching cross-examination.

Farrow was the first witness to appear before the Committee and in his opening statement catalogued his complaints in detail. The typical advertisement and circular, he said, contained misleading statements as to the terms on which loans were granted, and hid the identity and status of the lender. They often included tables showing five per cent interest rates, a rate which was never charged. Most moneylenders used the word 'Bank' in their titles, or concealed their identity behind terms such as 'Finance Corporation' or 'Advance Corporation'. One man traded in 11 offices under 11 different names, including the guise of a widow, by name Mrs Vincent, who wished to make loans to deserving cases at five per cent out of her inheritance from her 'late husband'.

One of the important advantages these moneylenders seemingly offered was strict confidentiality, a particular attraction to many borrowers who wished to hide their difficulties from relatives, friends and neighbours. Yet immediately an application was made it was registered by the moneylender with *Perry's Gazette Office*, an organisation which provided moneylenders with information of any other applications which had been made by borrowers. Farrow admitted that *Perry's* was a perfectly legitimate operation, but his complaint was that use of it breached the promise of confidentiality on which so much emphasis was placed in the circulars and advertise-ments, and which so many borrowers desperately sought. Further, some moneylenders sent clerks, with cash in hand, who persuaded the borrower to sign a bill of sale, often misleading the borrower into believing that the document was a receipt or promissory note. The bill was then immediately registered with the court, and once again confidentiality was breached, because the registers were available for public inspection.

Farrow told the Committee that 60 per cent was the normal rate, but there were many loans made far in excess of that. In most promissory note cases a clause was included to the effect that if one instalment was in arrears then the whole amount outstanding would become immediately due with interest at the rate of one halfpenny in the shilling per week, an annual rate of 216 per cent. No rebate was given for early repayment which, if made, effectively increased the interest rate. And under the law there was no compulsion on money-lenders to file a notice of satisfaction, a written acknowledgement that the debt had been repaid and the bill of sale discharged. The borrower either had to pay solicitors to register such a notice or the money-lender would charge an additional two or three guineas for doing so. All these devices increased the true rate of interest. Farrow also spelled out the various ruses used to obtain judgment without the borrower receiving notice, for example by telling him he need not bother to enter an appearance to a writ, and then levying execution. Some bailiffs were the moneylenders' own employees, and in some cases furniture was 'auctioned' and sold at knock-down prices by the moneylenders' own companies to purchasers who were also employed by them. Often the borrower was not allowed to read the document he was asked to sign or, shades of Nevill, the effective parts were covered up with blotting paper. Sometimes to the expressed rate of five per cent they added, after the signing, 'per month', or altered six per cent to 60 per cent. Some moneylenders required the borrower to swear a declaration as to his exact income and liabilities before a commissioner for oaths, and if there was even a day's delay in repayment, and the slightest error in the declaration, would then demand immediate payment of the whole balance due, backed by threats of prosecution for obtaining a loan by false pretences or perjury.

Farrow's conclusion was that most moneylending activities were fraudulent. There was practically no money lent under 30 per cent, and he considered that the evils to which he referred would perhaps not be so great if they were accompanied by a lower rate of interest; but accompanied by a minimum of 60 per cent they became evils. Pawnbrokers were limited by law to 25 per cent interest, and he urged a similar restriction on moneylenders.

Gordon followed him into the witness stand. Something of his turbulent career had already appeared in the press, and before he came to the House of Commons to give his evidence many newspapers printed articles about his business life. In 1889 Gordon's head office was at 6 Livery Street, Birmingham, where he traded under the name of G. Gordon. He advertised in the *Worcestershire Advertiser*:

> Cash immediately advanced from £5 to £500, at lower interest than charged by others – To farmers, gardeners, fruiterers, dairymen, carriers, clerks, tradesmen, shopkeepers, lodging house keepers, private householders and others, on their own security without bondsmen, on note of hand alone. Repayable by easy instalments to suit applicants. All communications are received in strict confidence. No genuine application refused, and honourable and straightforward transactions guaranteed. Intending borrowers are invited (before applying elsewhere) to apply to Mr. G. Gordon. Town or country, distance no object. Letters immediately attended to. Established 1851.

It is noteworthy that he claimed to have been in business for some 11 or 12 years before he was born. His target clientele was clearly defined, and like so many others he held out the prospect of a cheap, unsecured loan, dealt with in strict confidence, and repayable by easy instalments, with a guarantee of honourable and straightforward dealing. A Mrs Brown, a farmer's wife, was soon to discover just what such terms meant. In response to the advertisement she called on Gordon one Saturday on behalf of her husband. Gordon told her he charged five per cent interest, not deducted from the advance. He said he would advance her £100 the following Wednesday, subject to an inspection of the farm by one of his staff. Mrs Brown paid 10s 6d to cover the travelling expenses involved, a not unreasonable sum. Gordon's man duly arrived, and *after* the documents were signed deducted £40 from the advance for interest, proffered only £60, and refused to pay any more. The Browns, urgently requiring the money, reluctantly accepted. Gordon well knew that the temptation of cash in hand would overcome most doubts that a borrower in desperate need might have about terms. The following day the Browns regretted what they had done, but when Mrs Brown tried to return the £60 it was refused – she was told that she and her husband were bound by the contract they had signed.

Upon complaint being made to the police, Gordon was charged at Worcester with obtaining a benefit by false pretences. The jury found him guilty, but sentence was deferred until his appeal on a point of law was heard in the High Court of Justice. The appeal was dismissed, it being held that Gordon had falsely represented to Mrs Brown that he had £100 which he would give her husband when they both signed a promissory note for that sum. The case was then referred back to Worcester Assizes for sentence to be passed. In mitigation it was said on Gordon's behalf that he was a foreigner, only 26 years of age, and ignorant of the laws of this country. He had been in prison for most of February, and since that time had suffered great anguish of mind and had not been able to conduct his business. He had been deprived of his livelihood, and his defence had cost him £325 (lawyers apparently being as expensive to employ then as they are now). He had never previously been convicted of any offence, and had gained no pecuniary advantage for himself from this particular transaction, nor had Mr or Mrs Brown suffered any loss. There was, it was said, no doubt that his business had been completely destroyed. None of this impressed the judge, Mr Baron Pollock, who said that he thought it had been a very clever device on Gordon's part, and sentenced him to imprisonment for 20 months with hard labour.

No sooner had the prison gates closed behind him than Gordon set about pressing for his release. He was genuinely in poor health, and persuaded the Hebrew Minister at Worcester to join with Gordon's cousin in presenting a petition to the Home Office. After he had served only eight months he was released, solely because it was considered that further imprisonment would endanger his life.

The experience had taught Gordon a lesson; not the lesson that he should desist from making loans on outrageous terms, or that he should not engage in such trickery, but that he should never again put himself in a position in which he could be accused of criminal behaviour. As he was to tell the Committee, he thereafter ensured that he could always prove his case up to the hilt:

> ... when I lend money to a borrower, not only am I not content with his signature to the promissory note but I take a letter from them in their own handwriting ... 'I have this day borrowed and received from Mr. I. Gordon, Birmingham, the sum of £80 for which I have promised and agreed to pay back £100, that is 25 per cent in three months from date [equivalent to 100 per cent per

annum] as set forth on the note which I read over signed and clearly understood. I received the £80 in Bank of England notes'. He must give me a holograph letter written by himself, otherwise I shall not deal with him.

He said that he gave strict instructions to his managers not to deal with people unless they could write out such a letter:

> ... for the simple reason that my money is at stake and my liberty as well, because in the case of an ignorant man, he is always glad of the advantage of saying that he did not understand the contract. If I was to do business with a man, if he did not really understand, not only would the judge, and the jury, be too glad to release him of his liability to me, but I would go to a court and I should get convicted, although all the time I was innocent, as I was in that Worcester case. They will swear the life out of me, you understand, and any judge and jury would be only too glad to let them off their liability, and I should lose my money, as well as my liberty being at stake. Let me tell you ...

Here he was stopped and told 'not to run on'.

There was intense public interest even before 6 July 1897, when Gordon appeared before the Committee. In May *Truth* carried a story about 'the bloodsucker, Isaac Gordon'. Apparently he had refused to pay rates on two branch offices which he had had in Glasgow: 'The usurer's refusal to pay was characterised by his usual insolence, shiftiness, and prevarication.' At first he denied that he was anything to do with 'William Robertson', his alias at one of the offices. Then he tried a blustering letter of the type he sent to unfortunates in his clutches:

> I shall not pay you one copper, and you are perfectly welcome to take any steps or proceedings you think fit, which I shall defend to the bitter end. Please oblige me and do not trouble me with any more letters, as I have something else to do than to keep up a correspondence with you to no purpose, and for which I shall not get one penny.

Eventually a warrant to distrain his goods at 6 Livery Street was obtained. He then played his last card: the police who attended to

214

execute the warrant were gravely assured by him that Isaac Gordon had been dead for some time, and that a Mr B. Edwards carried on the business. The police were not deceived, and he paid up. Commenting on his 'death' the *Birmingham Daily Gazette* said:

> His friends will be glad to know that the time for writing his elegy has not yet come, and Spring poets need not at present devote the midnight oil to the composition of passionate threnodies. Isaac is alive, and considering the slight pecuniary reverse he has sustained, is as well as the cares of a busy philanthropist's business will permit him to be.

Truth also gave full details of his confrontation with the Assize Court in 1889 and his term of imprisonment. If they thought that giving him such prominent and adverse publicity before he gave his evidence might chasten Gordon and modify his usual blustering, attacking, attitude to those who confronted him, or that perhaps the solemn surroundings of a Committee Room in the Palace of Westminster and a formidable array of members ready to cross-examine him might daunt him, then they were wrong. He was never on the defensive, not for a moment. On the contrary he was keen, aggressive and voluble.

All 13 members of the Committee, including Mr David Lloyd George, the future prime minister, took the trouble to attend. Gordon told the Committee that he carried on business in Birmingham, Bristol, Bath, Manchester, Liverpool, London and Oxford, trading under a different name in each of the seven offices, and all chosen, he said, because they were easy to pronounce. His books were kept in Birmingham and from there he controlled business in each of his branches. He explained why he used so many aliases:

> Suppose a man comes and borrows money of me in London, and in due course, as some of them do sometimes, they skedaddle, they run away, forgetting to leave their name and address behind them; they very likely go to Manchester or Liverpool, and in due course they after a little time may apply to those places, and by trading in different names I have sometimes a chance to find them, whereas if I trade in the same name *they are not likely to walk into the same trap again.*

215

Perhaps the use of the word 'trap' was an unconscious slip on his part.

When he was asked about his conviction at Worcester he said, untruthfully, that after serving eight months he was *pardoned* by the Home Secretary, although he did not know why. 'The Home Secretary does not tell me his business.' Eventually an official from the Home Office was called to set the record straight.

The Committee found it difficult to believe some of the methods he adopted. In one case he offered a lady a loan of £100, repayable with £100 interest after three months, that is at 400 per cent per annum. The transaction was conducted by post, and in making his offer he enclosed a promissory note for her to sign, and then added a post-script:

> That will be charging you £100 interest for the loan of £100 for three months, which is the very best, easiest, lowest, and only way I can do it at, and is considerably less than anyone else would have it at, and I question and doubt very much whether you would be able to get it elsewhere upon better or even as good terms with as little trouble, and so much privacy and secrecy, although you may see advertisements in the papers offering to lend money at five per cent, and other ridiculously low terms, which are only frauds and swindles done to obtain fees, and seldom if ever advance any money: and in order to save time and delay I enclose you £100 in Bank of England notes herewith, and if these terms are satisfactory please sign and return me the enclosed promissory note and keep and acknowledge the £100 per return of post. If, on the other hand, these terms do not suit, please return me the same £100 registered, together with the promissory note unsigned per return of post. You must please not fail to let me have one or the other per return and oblige; and if at the expiration of the three months it should not be quite convenient for you to meet it, we can then make some other satisfactory arrangements, and if at any time when the bill falls due you should be prepared to pay part of the capital off, interest will only be charged on the part of the capital remaining in proportion to the above terms, which I think is very fair and honourable; but please note I cannot undertake to repeat this offer again should you once reject it, and you must please either accept it or reject it precisely as it stands, as I cannot write to you again on

the subject, and I hope this will meet with your entire satisfaction and approval, and that you will now be perfectly satisfied.

Now that is a pretty long postscript? – It is, sir.

Perhaps it is rather longer than the letter? – Perhaps it is.

I think probably the sting of the letter is in the postscript? – Very likely it is, sir.

Now are you in the habit of sending to people £100 in a letter in Bank of England notes without having the promissory note or the security beforehand? – Yes sir, I do it every day; I place every confidence in them.

Did you know, sir, before you did this, that this lady had an annuity of £600 a year? – She told me something of it. Yes I did.

You did? – Well, sir, excuse me. You do not expect me to send a hundred pounds to a tramp or a person I am not likely to get my money from? If I did not think she was a right person I should certainly not send her any money, of course I should not.

No. If you will allow me to say so, I think it an extraordinary thing for you to send £100 in banknotes to anybody? – Oh, my dear sir, I do it every day, I place every confidence in borrowers in a little loan.

In the event Gordon lost his money in this particular case, and strongly resented any suggestion by the chairman that he was to blame for the borrower's ensuing bankruptcy. 'She has done me for a good many hundreds, this very lady, annuity and all. It is all very well for you to pitch into the moneylender about this. He gets done too. What about this lady? She went and deceived tradesmen, money-lenders and everybody else, and when it came to the paying point she went to Scotland.' He complained that the Committee were not giving him a proper opportunity of presenting his case:

The Committee is not enquiring into what this lady did or did not do? – But if you are going to pitch into moneylenders you ought to

217

be fair, sir, to them; you have to be fair in regard to the borrowers' position as well. You know, sir, the Committee do not seem to take into consideration the conduct of some of the borrowers and their doings, which are absolutely inexplicable, some of them are right down rogues and robbers; therefore *the moneylender must take care of himself.*

The Committee is not here to inquire into what Mrs. Claremont did, or whether she became bankrupt or not; they are here to inquire into the system of moneylending. – If you are going to abuse me give me a chance to explain myself, and have the thing out fair and square. It is no use to be all one side.

He was making a justifiable point. It was noticeable that when professional witnesses were called they were allowed to make a full statement before they were questioned; not so the moneylenders. Kirkwood was an exception; he forced a statement on the Committee.

From very early on in the proceedings the Committee had made up their minds that there were evils in the system, and no longer considered they were investigating 'alleged' evils. They did treat the moneylenders unfairly, and did not give them a reasonable opportunity of presenting their case. Although the chairman denied that he was trying, as Gordon frequently complained, to paint Gordon as black as he could, and despite the chairman's assurance that Gordon would have a full opportunity 'to state all the beauties of your case in due course', in fact he was never allowed to do so. This is not to say that Gordon, and indeed most of the other moneylenders who appeared, were blameless and lily white, indeed the opposite was true, but none the less it is impossible to conclude that they received an impartial hearing before the Committee.

Gordon told the Committee that he dealt mostly with the middle class, mainly tradesmen:

Do you do much business with the professional class, professional men, clergymen, and lawyers? – Clergymen! I have dropped them, they are an awful lot. Excuse me. It is only three months ago that I lent to a clergyman £300, and never got a copper. That is an example of them.

As to how much money he had out, he had no idea.

Have you not really? – No: I have no partners, and I do not trouble about taking stock.

You cannot give me any idea? – Approximately, perhaps, £15,000 or £16,000: perhaps it may be £20,000, but it is rather a big order to tell straight off.

About £20,000 is the amount you have out at any one time, is it? – Yes, perhaps it is a bit more.

He explained later in his evidence that he had an additional £25,000 cash available, a total capital of about £45,000. He did not have any arrangement for banking facilities because, he said, bankers did not as a rule like to assist moneylenders. As we have seen, Sam was an exception to this rule. Nor did he resort to bills of sale, charge preliminary fees other than for genuine travelling expenses, or obtain security: 'When people have got security they know better than to come to me.' He took a simple promissory note, and very rarely was it backed by a surety because those who borrowed from him came chiefly for privacy, and did not want anyone else to know of their predicament.

He was then questioned about his basic philosophy with regard to lending:

You consider that so long as you are not guilty of any breach of the law, you have a perfect right to carry on that business to the greatest advantage to yourself? – Yes, sir, I do.

And may I also assume that you consider that you have a right to use every legal document you possibly can to secure yourself, and also to make use of every Court of Law to repay you the money that you have lent with the interest accrued? – Yes, any legitimate purpose.

Then your view is that so long as the law does not fix any limit to interest you may make a bargain for 5,000%, or any other per cent that the borrower agrees to pay? – Quite so.

And I suppose you have lent at 5,000%, or greater, percentages, where the borrower has been willing to pay it? – Well, I do not know that, but I have charged a good rate of interest: I do not know whether it would be 5,000%.

4,000%? – Say so, approximately.

Call it 3,000%? – Yes.

It makes no difference to you whether the interest is too high or too low; you get as much as you can, and as much as you think the man can pay? – Quite so.

May I take it that so long as you carry on the business of a moneylender, you intend to make as great a profit as you possibly can out of that business? – Yes sir, so does every business man.

He told the Committee that he made about 500 loans a year, of which about one-third would come to court, some 20 cases, that is four per cent of the total, leading to the bankruptcy of the borrower. The loans ranged from £10 to £2,000, but they averaged £150. When he did go to court he recovered all, or a portion, of his money in less than half of the cases. He said that for all the trouble and worry involved in the business it was really not worth carrying on. Though it was profitable, the risks were high and moneylenders were subject to a great many unpleasant remarks.

The Committee, like the courts, and society in general, were very concerned that married women's property interests should be protected from outside exploitation. Widespread marital infidelity might cause few heartaches; harsh treatment of a wife by her husband raised no eyebrows; but let a third party involve a wife in financial matters, then the full weight of judicial and society's displeasure and power were brought to bear on the miscreant. Sir George Lewis's view was that it was bad enough that men were the victims of usury, but when this abuse had grown to such proportions that married women became the prey of the moneylender, then the time had surely arrived when the strong arm of the law was needed to put it down. Normally any suggestion made to a moneylender that he was engaged in such business was denied, but Gordon was quite frank about his attitude:

Do you ever deal with ladies without the knowledge of their husbands? – Yes, I do, if I think that I will get my money back.

Do you ever use the secrecy that they are so anxious for as a screw to make them pay? – I never have done, but I might.

You would see no objection I suppose then to threaten a lady that you would let her husband know if she did not pay? – I should write to her if she did not pay me that I should certainly write to her husband about it, which I think I would be within my rights to do.

Do you remember having a transaction with a Mrs. Smith, who lived in Kensington? – Yes, the wife of a doctor, and I have lost my money with her. Fancy, a doctor's wife, lady and all!

Was she a surety for some other lady? – No. I believe she borrowed the money entirely herself; but thinking she was a doctor's wife and respectable, I sent her the money, and she has done me out of it ... I have been told that this was a trick between the husband and the wife upon moneylenders – a trick and a dodge. The husband was informed that they could not recover against him, and he has been sending her all over the shop, and very likely defrauded dozens of moneylenders, from what I have heard.

At a very early stage the Committee had it in mind to recommend that courts should once again be given the power to alter the terms of agreements made between moneylenders and borrowers:

Do you see any objection to giving the court power when any moneylending transaction comes before it, to inquire into the way in which the moneylender has treated the borrower? – To give the court power to deal with the moneylenders as they think fit, irrespective of the contract, is that what you mean? [Gordon was not prepared to allow his questioner to disguise the intent behind the question by the use of euphemistic language.]

No, to deal fairly with the moneylender, but still to take into consideration the way in which the moneylender has treated the borrower? – To give the judge and the court permission to revise the contract if they like?

Do you see any objection to it? – Of course I do. If you leave the moneylender to the tender mercy of the county court judge, he would not get much.

You would object to that power being given? – Of course I should, because it would be illogical. You make a contract with a man and the judge goes behind that ... If I did not have a free hand I would give up the business tomorrow.

221

Unless you have a free hand? – The same as every other trader, to make contracts ... I should give it up for the simple reason that it would not pay ... Another thing you have to bear in mind, if you are going to give a county court judge jurisdiction to revise in the case of heavy charges, he would only interfere with that contract. He would not take into consideration that you have to make a profit where another man has done you elsewhere.

He would not take into consideration that you are making up out of the so-called victim for the losses that you have sustained on other transactions? – Yes, other transactions elsewhere. It would practically take your profits off in addition to the other losses. You could not possibly make both ends meet ... I have to make up other losses, and I cannot do business and make a profit unless I make up the gaps of the losses.

When he was asked if his policy was only to advance money where he considered it was safe, his reply was that this was not always possible; he loaned money where he did not run too much risk, where he considered that there was a fair chance of getting his money back. There was a great difference between that and loaning only where it was definitely safe. All their business carried an element of risk because borrowers who came to them rarely, if ever, had any proper security.

Throughout his evidence Gordon showed a remarkable command of the English language, and had an extensive vocabulary, particularly when it was a matter of legal terminology. He even quoted case law to the Committee, and obviously knew his business, and the law affecting it, through and through. Yet he also knew, and accepted from the outset, that he would have a hostile reception, and that the Committee would be quite unable to accept his basic tenets of business. After he had completed his evidence he had a few words with a reporter for the *Star*. 'I suppose they are determined to corner me one way or the other,' he said, 'but at least they might be fair. They put their interpretation on my conduct fast enough, but they won't let me give my version. You know there are two sides to every question.'

The banks used, and today still use, the same techniques as Gordon. They make a charge for negotiating an overdraft or loan, the equivalent of asking for money to cover their expenses. The sum so

222

charged is deducted at the time the loan is made or the overdraft granted, effectively increasing the rate of interest. If moneys due remain unpaid the banks take court proceedings against their clients, including levying execution by putting in the bailiffs, and they are prepared to forfeit mortgages on clients' homes. The difference between the banks and such as Gordon lies in the manner and spirit, not in the substance, of the use of the methods of enforcing payment of loans.

For Labouchere, Gordon's evidence furnished remarkable proof of 'the brazen effrontery, insatiable rapacity, and utter unscrupulousness of this champion bloodsucker'. The *Jewish Chronicle* was also not impressed with what he had to say. They had thought that a man who apparently attached such importance to membership of a synagogue would pay more heed to the community's condemnation of his behaviour and that of others like him –

> But Mr. Gordon continues his nefarious methods unabashed and undeterred. It is impossible to deny that the trade of lending money may be practised in such a way as to do good to the country in which it is pursued, to give useful and remunerative accommodation to the borrower, and a legitimate profit to the lender. It is equally impossible to deny that such a business as Mr. Gordon's is detrimental to the community at large and disgraceful to the individual who carries it on. For a man of thirty-two there is still time to enter into a more reputable calling; and the result of the deliberations of the Committee will, we hope, be to make the evil kind of moneylending as unattractive to the most sordid minds as it is at present to all except the lowest and least scrupulous class of commercial gamblers.

They expressed the hope that by religious influences he might yet be brought to recognise the true character of his dealings, and to desist from further offending against Jewish morality, or bringing ill-fame to the Jewish community in England. It was a fond hope. He not only continued as before, but expressed his bitterness, wrought his revenge, and showed his contempt for the Select Committee, and all those who opposed him, by behaving in an even more outrageous manner. His circulars were sent out in increasing numbers, and under several different names; he attracted business by continuing to claim

223

that he was a private gentleman who advanced money 'without moneylenders' formalities of any kind'. He revelled and exulted in the notoriety his appearance before the Committee had brought, and referred to himself as 'the most usurious moneylender in the kingdom'. He even circularised members of the House of Lords just a few months after he had given his evidence! Labouchere could only exclaim that 'this scoundrel's impudence is scarcely less phenomenal than his rapacity'.

A year or so after he gave his evidence, a Mr Street responded to one of his advertisements, inserted by Gordon under the name George James Addison of 3 Holles Street, Cavendish Square, and it was only after he had defaulted on a payment that Mr Street learned that he had contracted with Isaac Gordon. He immediately tried to repudiate the agreement, offering to repay the capital advanced with 10 per cent interest. Gordon refused and replied:

> Your not paying your debts may do very well elsewhere, but not for Isaac Gordon, the extortionate and usurious moneylender, with about a gross of aliases, who is pretty well used to gentlemen of your sort and their bouncing ways, and who knows only too well how to treat them. I hope to teach you and to let you see that the many aliased Isaac Gordon is the hottest and one of the bitterest creditors you have ever had. I treat your epistles as though they were from an impecunious dog, and hope to have you through the bankruptcy court as well as your wife.

His language had become vicious and shrill to the point of being neurotic, even psychotic. He sued, and the case eventually came before the Court of Appeal. Lord Justice Smith expressed the issue in this way:

> ... to enter into a contract for a loan with a creditor such as Isaac Gordon so that, when the day of payment arrives, the borrower can have no possible chance of a day's or even an hour's grace, but on the contrary has the certainty of being pestered with writs and threats of writs and bailiffs and bankruptcy notices, whereby life is rendered unbearable, and health is often injured, is by no means, in my opinion, the same thing as entering into a contract for a loan with a man who, when the day of payment arrives, does none of

these things, but, on the contrary, deals in a fair and non-oppressive manner [an accurate description of Sam?] ... I would point out that amongst moneylenders, as in other ranks of life, there are many given to fair dealing and others given to the most rapacious tyranny known to mankind; and if a moneylender of the first kind honestly trades in an assumed name, that is one case, and clearly not this case; but if a moneylender of the second kind secretes his own name and uses another name for the express purpose of fraudulently inducing a man to trade with him and to get that man in his clutches, that is altogether another and a different case, and the two are entirely distinct.

The contract was set aside.

Gordon harboured a deep feeling of resentment at what he considered his harsh and unfair treatment by the Committee. He let it be known that he contemplated writing a book about his experience, and putting forward an elaborate defence of moneylenders. The *Birmingham Daily Gazette* welcomed this, and hastened to assure him that his book would be most eagerly expected, and most enthusiastically welcomed, because there was no one better acquainted with all the dodges and tricks of the trade, no one who knew better how to take the fullest advantage of the weakness of those who sought his aid. Further, it said, a list of his many aliases would by itself be good reading, and if his book were to be written with but half the virile force of his many epistles it would be a literary success. He never did publish. The synagogue and the community in Birmingham shunned him, and he attended only on the Day of Atonement. An angry husband of one of his clients threatened to horsewhip him at his Livery Street office, and someone who appealed to him on behalf of a wretched debtor, and was refused, threatened to throw him out of his office window, adding that he was sure that no jury in the land would convict him of either manslaughter or murder.

Gordon soon found it necessary to have a bodyguard, and to move from hotel to hotel. As soon as he was identified by other guests they would complain to the manager who would approach Gordon and politely request him to leave. He became an outcast, practically alone in the world. He had contracted tuberculosis, and begged the only friend he had to call to see him: 'I wish to pour out to you the bitterness of my heart.' He told him that he had decided to give up his business, but winding up his affairs would take at least a couple of years, and he doubted whether he would live so long. He was right. On 6 March 1900, at the age of 37, he died at Pitman's Hotel, Birmingham, a low-class establishment in Corporation Street. According to his friend, his end was undoubtedly hastened by the loathing directed at him by Jew and Gentile alike. He was buried, with scant ceremony, in the Jewish portion of Witton Cemetery. 'In the presence of a small crowd, several shabbily-dressed men carried out of the hotel a rough, unpolished, wooden coffin – partly covered with a black pall. The shabby-looking men placed the shabby-looking coffin into a shabby van, and thus all that was left of the moneylending millionaire went from the place which last knew him alive.' He was buried in an unmarked grave, and the Jewish Burial Society Committee refused to accept any of his ill-gotten gains for the ceremony.

In an obituary the *Daily Telegraph* wrote of him:

> His hide was proof against all hostile reflections on his conduct ... he unblushingly admitted all the charges of usury brought against him; returning gibe for sneer, and answering appeals for mercy with a bitter diatribe against the thievery of the debtor, and was not one to show shame because honourable men regarded him with undisguised, unmitigated contempt. No; he invariably assumed the offensive, never accepted the defensive attitude. He prided himself on being a man who met knavery with a relentless ferocity, which nothing could temper, or subdue, or withstand.

The estimate that he had left an estate of £1 million was wide of the mark. He left no will, and administration was granted to his brother, Leopold Gordon, who calculated the estate totalled just £34,000. Something was amiss, because two years later there was an amended grant to a chartered accountant who proved for £148,218, which probably more accurately represented the total of Gordon's assets, including all the moneys due to him from his debtors. However, most debtors must have denied liability and sought to have the contracts set aside. Collection proved too difficult or expensive, for there was yet a third grant in 1904 to Gitel Livenstein, a widow, and this time his effects were calculated at £35,453.

It was a great relief to the Jewish community when the spotlight of the Select Committee fell upon John Kirkwood. Kirkwood was a stocky, bald, but bearded man, with strong features and an imposing, even overwhelming personality. He had been engaged in the money-lending business for more than 25 years and the Committee held no terrors for him. He did not take the oath, but affirmed, and was to prove an even more doughty, abrasive, aggressive and forceful witness than Gordon. He refused to be stopped in mid-sentence, and once flowing proved difficult for the chairman to rein in. Unlike Gordon he was given, or ensured for himself, every opportunity to make his points. For him, attack was the best means of defence, and he constantly expressed doubts as to the validity of the actions of the Committee, and tried to lay down the ground rules for his questioning. Farrow sat in the room while he gave evidence, and was a frequent victim of his barbs – 'I have looked upon Farrow as beneath contempt, Sir; he is a scoundrel, an infamous scoundrel!'

Kirkwood was anxious to assure the Committee that his clientele included the holders of the most prestigious positions in the land, and, as he described it, it was as though his business was conducted by a philanthropist in charge of a charitable or benevolent society:

What kind of people do you do business with? – Members of Parliament, barons, metropolitan police court magistrates ...

These are the kind of people you do business with? – Pardon me, Sir, I have not finished.

Members of Parliament? – Barristers, solicitors, clergymen, medical men, naval and military officers, postmasters, government officials, merchants, ladies and gentlemen of private means, farmers, tradesmen and others, many of whom we have repeated business with, and who have been on our books for many years, and are perfectly content and satisfied with the treatment they receive as can be proved by the hundreds of letters in our possession (in this bag) from our customers expressing their gratitude for our kindness, our courtesy, our forbearance, and our leniency.

The chairman, Mr T. W. Russell, attempted to bring him to a halt with a jolt:

Have you come into collision with the law at all in carrying out

227

your business? – The law has come into collision with me, Sir, through unprincipled solicitors who listen to what their clients say. It is well known that clients often tell the greatest falsehoods to their solicitors.

Have you ever been fined by the courts? – I have been infamously fined.

But you have been fined? – I have, and that is enough without raking it up here; this is an inquiry into moneylending.

I must ask you to treat the Committee with some decency. – With the greatest possible respect, Sir, but I am not a dog: I am not come here to be treated like a dog. You take up things for which people have been fined and punished most innocently. I must protest against it, Sir.

He was asked about some alleged wrongdoing which had occurred 12 years earlier, and said he could not recall the incident:

This is a matter of memory? – It was in 1885. It is a wonder the Committee do not go back to my cradle and find my iniquity in the nursery.

He advertised that he had £250,000 to lend.

Is that so? – Yes, and far more when it is wanted; far more at my command when it is wanted. I have not got a quarter of a million pounds in my pocket now.

Should you have to apply for financial aid from other sources? – Well Sir, I do not think that has anything to do with this inquiry.

He was allowed to read a statement commenting upon the evidence of Farrow, and also a letter from a satisfied customer, a clergyman of the Church of England, who referred to dealings with Kirkwood's staff in Bristol, and who had spoken of them as 'the salt of the commercial world'. Farrow, Kirkwood asserted, had not obtained his information from such satisfied customers, but from discharged moneylenders' clerks and blackmailers. The only persons who had replied to Farrow and his questionnaires, he said, were defaulting borrowers who wished to be considered as victims. He alleged that Farrow had throughout magnified and exaggerated their stories, and had never sought information from the moneylenders themselves. Although he had 'thought good to describe me as the "King of Moneylenders" he has not come to the "King" for information'. He made no complaint about this appellation, but modestly thought that one of the Rothschilds would have a greater claim to the title. In his statement he said:

> Farrow has described borrowers as being 'as a rule straightforward and honourable people'. This is really too absurd ... Farrow, in his long incoherent harangue to the Committee, studiously avoided saying a single word about the fabulous losses of moneylenders. Frauds are often ingeniously committed by swindlers ... lenders' losses are incalculable owing to people becoming bankrupt and absconding, often going to foreign countries; in fact, we lose hundreds and thousands every year through people absconding; and grantors of bills of sale fraudulently and clandestinely dispose of their stock, furniture, goods, chattels, and effects which often cannot be traced. Then there are the necessary expenses for rent, rates and taxes, salaries, advertisements, law costs, commissions, travelling, hotel and incidental working expenses, all of which come out of whatever interest is obtained ...

Moneylending, he averred, was a most unprofitable business, and if he did not make more in 1897 than he had done in 1895 and 1896 then he was going out of it. Compared with many other businesses the net profits were very small, very small indeed. And as to Farrow's suggestion that the rate of interest of moneylenders should be limited to 25 per cent per annum, the same as that allowed to pawnbrokers, that completely overlooked the all-important fact that pawnbrokers were in possession of security, and that made their 25 per cent more than equal to 200 per cent per annum to a moneylender who lends on the borrower's note of hand. In his opinion all of Farrow's suggestions were untenable. There was also a personal problem that moneylenders faced, he added. A moneylender was a man who lived without the praise of anyone, and 'You, gentlemen, praise your wine merchant and your tailor and your bootmaker, but which of you ever praises your moneylender?' He was not afforded an answer then and there; the Committee's Final Report was to give their verdict on Kirkwood and others of his ilk.

Kirkwood disassociated himself from the preliminary fee men, and said he was always delighted when bogus moneylenders were convicted and punished. He often found that some of his applicants had been shamefully robbed by these penniless so-called moneylenders whose only object in advertising was to obtain the fees: 'We rejoice that the law has always proved itself more than equal to such scoundrels.' He was rarely at a loss for an explanation for anything the Committee chose to tax him with. Why, he was asked, had he not sued Farrow and the *Pall Mall Gazette* when they libelled him? Because, he replied, 'one of the highest firms of solicitors in England' advised him that although he would get the verdict, the damages awarded, on account of prejudice against moneylenders, would probably be a farthing, and his costs would be £1,500 or £1,600. He would also be tackling a millionaire, Mr Astor, the owner of the paper. The whole affair was so grossly libellous that it was beneath contempt, but everyone who knew him personally, friends or customers, knew 'it was lies, scurrilous lies, abominable lies'. Everyone knew that *Pall Mall* lived on libel, and there was therefore no point in taking expensive action against it. What of Farrow's allegations that he had defrauded the Income Tax authorities, that he had told them he had made a profit of £300 when the true figure was £4,000? That, he said, was based on the so-called evidence of dismissed clerks and blackmailers who 'ought now to be on the treadmill'. Would they believe the word of a dismissed clerk? Asked whether he had not been driven out of business from Sheffield, he replied that he had never been driven from anywhere, 'I come of a race that never flinches!' Was there any rate of interest which he considered unconscionable?

That is a very difficult thing to define, Sir; the conscience is trained differently in different countries. You know, Sir, in Turkey they would think a proper thing to do, what would be a disgraceful thing to do in this country; but it is quite in the conscience of a Turk.

Had he not made his own children, one of them just three years old, the shareholders of one of his so-called banks?

... Yes, if you want to hurt the child. Hurt me as much as you like, Sir, but keep your hands off my wife and children. My wife and children are sacred.

That has nothing at all to do with the question? – Abuse me as much as you like; I have got broad shoulders. This is simply ridicule, nothing else.

Why do you live in France if you have all those businesses in England? – For the education of my children.

Nothing to do with business? – No: and I do not think it has anything to do with you.

Nothing to do with business? – No, nothing: it is a happy country to live in. There are none of these inquisitions, and there are no society papers there at all, no *Truth*, no *Pall Mall*; it is a happy country ... I carry on no business there; and why should you invade my domestic hearth?

On two specific issues the Committee acted grossly unfairly towards him, and in doing so indicated just how low their opinion of money-lenders was. They obviously based their questioning very largely on the information provided by Farrow. Kirkwood was asked by Mr Ascroft if he had any idea of the number of his customers who had committed suicide while he had been taking proceedings against them. He refused to answer such a question, and said it implied a vile and unfounded accusation, an accusation he laid at the door of 'that scoundrel Farrow, your jackal ... a living proof of the Darwinian theory he is; look at him!'

Two cases were cited against Kirkwood. In one, which had occurred just two weeks previously, a customer called Thomas Mitchell, against whom he had issued a writ, committed suicide. Mr Ascroft suggested it was because of his harsh treatment by Kirkwood that this had occurred, and indeed the coroner's jury at the inquest considered that the facts should be brought before the Committee. Kirkwood had anticipated the matter would be raised, and came armed with details of the account, and of the correspondence that had passed. It was not until five months after Mitchell had stopped his payments that Kirkwood wrote and pointed out that because of his default the whole amount was now due and payable – 'Please let us hear from you by return of post what you propose to do, or we shall be reluctantly compelled to put the matter into the hands of our solicitor.' Mitchell replied saying that he had had a bad run in business, and asked what

231

was the minimum amount Kirkwood would accept in reduction of the account, and to this Kirkwood had requested fuller details of his position 'that I may see what can be done'. He had certainly not bombarded him with Gordon-type letters and, as he rightly said, he could not be held responsible because just one or two of his thousands of customers over the many years he had been in business committed suicide. There was absolutely no evidence to suggest his behaviour was the direct cause of it.

> Have you a book called the 'suicide book'? – The 'suicide book'! Do not insult me.

> Have you a book, Sir, called the suicide book; yes or no? – I never heard of such a book.

It really was a most outrageous question to ask if the Committee did not have a witness who was prepared to testify that such a book ever existed. The Committee was not sitting as a court of law, but it had a duty to act in a judicial manner. This was a case of guilt implied by simple accusation.

The other case, which had occurred in 1881, that is 16 years before the Select Committee was convened, involved a Mr and Mrs Osborne whose deaths, it was alleged, had been brought about by the cruel behaviour of Kirkwood's staff, acting on his instructions, in his Sheffield office, the Sheffield Deposit Bank. It was all over the sum of five pounds. The husband and wife had given a bill of sale on their goods, and it was said that when the bailiffs were put in the wife had died under the strain, whereupon within hours her husband had died at the shock of her passing. When this allegation was put to him Kirkwood denied any knowledge of the matter, and said he had never heard of it. Because he could not recall the incident he could only deny it, not refute it, and the Committee obviously believed he had been directly responsible for the two deaths.

During a break of some days in his evidence Kirkwood had time to undertake research, and came up with conclusive proof that the Committee was wrong. However, he did not present them with his evidence at once, or in a simple manner, but intended to shame them for having based themselves on an insecure foundation, and he gently baited them to ensure that he achieved a dramatic effect. He produced a copy of the *Sheffield Daily Telegraph* of 10 December 1881 which carried a full report of the inquest under the heading 'Usurers and their Victims – Sad Deaths of an Aged Couple, near Sheffield', and he insisted on reading from it. The Osbornes' doctor said that though the elderly couple could not have lived much longer, their troubles had hastened Mrs Osborne's death.

The Committee must have wondered why Kirkwood was giving such publicity to the report, but he had an ace up his sleeve and wanted to lead them on. He continued reading:

The deputy coroner, in summing up, commented in very strong terms upon the doings of the moneylenders of the district, and especially of those holding the bill of sale upon the effects of the couple who had died so unhappily, and on the same day. If the moneylenders were so cruel and heartless to people so old and in such great poverty, to people of whom it might be said they were on the brink of the grave, how much more cruel and heartless would they be to younger people? It behoved the people of Norton, and in fact of all places where these moneylenders carried on their shameful business, to beware of them, and to avoid, if possible, falling into their clutches. They showed these poor and aged people no leniency or mercy. The jury, while strongly condemning the conduct of the moneylenders, felt that they could do nothing beyond returning a verdict to the effect that both of the old people died by the 'visitation of God'. The utmost indignation is felt throughout the whole district, and especially in Chesterfield, at the doings of the moneylender, and it is believed the revelations which have during the present week been made in the Chesterfield County Court, and the timely and strong remarks of the judge, will have a very wholesome effect.

Mr Ascroft, the member who had made the original accusation against Kirkwood, could not resist the temptation any longer, and fell into the trap which had been laid. He asked: 'Do you call that a testimonial?' – only to receive the devastating, and truthful, reply that the article did not refer to Kirkwood or his company.

Oh, doesn't it? – If you will listen, and have a little patience, you will see your unfounded charge, Sir, against me.

233

This was your bank, was it not?

But it was not. He had nothing to do with the bank referred to in the report. The *Sheffield Daily Telegraph* had made that clear in its immediately following edition. Their report had referred to a society with a similar name to Kirkwood's company, but one which was quite unconnected with him. The *Telegraph* completely exonerated Kirkwood's company from being implicated in the matter in any way. The Select Committee had not done its homework properly. But no apology was forthcoming from Ascroft or the chairman, though one was truly called for.

This was the peak of his success before the Committee. For the rest he was defending an impossible position. There was clear evidence that the allegations Farrow had made in *The Moneylender Unmasked* were substantially true. Kirkwood made full use of bills of sale, and had lost almost every case taken to court by borrowers who alleged fraud against him or his staff.

Do you find there are many complaints that you get people to sign bills of sale when they do not know that they are bills of sale? – Everyone who wants to wriggle out of his contract says so.

Do you find that improper allegations of that kind are made by people against you? – That is a usual thing against every money lender.

When questioned in detail about such cases he could give no satisfactory answers. Instead he resorted to abuse of the plaintiffs in the cases and their lawyers. One plaintiff was 'a great scoundrel', others were 'thieves', and all the proceedings were instituted on their behalf by 'unscrupulous and infamous solicitors ... who go in for fees and costs; those men that get struck off the rolls sometimes'. Not even the judges were immune from his scorn:

Do you remember a gentleman of the name of Van Hoboken? Did he bring an action against you which came before Mr. Justice Grantham? – Oh, yes; Grantham! oh, yes.

And did he claim you had obtained a bill of sale from him by means of fraud? – One of the most eminent Queen's Counsel said that if

234

we had been before Mr. Justice Charles, in whose list the action was the day before, we should have won, but going before Grantham it was a foregone conclusion.

If you do not treat the Committee with respect, I must ask you to treat Her Majesty's judges with respect at all events? – I do those that command my respect, he does not.

Here, at all events, you will treat them with respect? – Well sir, I think you must leave me to answer in my own way.

No, not in that matter. A Member in the House of Commons would not be allowed to use that language towards Her Majesty's Judges? – I am a privileged person here; you told me I could say what I liked.

Even when it was brought to his attention that he had been convicted for using the title of an incorporated company after he had been refused registration under that name, it was, he said, of such a technical nature as to be 'an offence under the Companies Act, but not an offence in the sight of Heaven'. He was incapable of making any admissions of wrongdoing, even when the evidence against him was overwhelming, and thus completely detracted from any credibility he might have had with the Committee and the public. Between them, he and Gordon had ensured that the Committee would find that there were serious abuses by moneylenders, and would recommend important changes to the law.

Several other moneylenders attended before the Committee. Two who were called on the same day were Abraham Moore of Air Street, Piccadilly, and Daniel Jay of Jermyn Street. Sir George Lewis, accompanied by Labouchere, was among the spectators because he had been involved in legal proceedings with both men. According to the *Star* the Committee played with them 'like a cat with mice – or like Isaac Gordon with a defaulting borrower. The Sages of Palace Yard and Ely Place – Mr Henry Labouchere, M.P. who has pilloried the usurers in *Truth* these many years, and Sir George Lewis, who has pursued them in the courts and challenged them in the columns of *The Star* – kept keen eyes on the shuffling Shylocks.' The use of the term 'Shylocks' was clearly emotive and prejudicial.

Moore, who gave his evidence in a manner described as 'between sullenness and impudence', said he had started in the moneylending business ten years before with a capital of £8,000 to £10,000, and he loaned to noblemen at an average charge of 40 per cent. He gave as good a definition as anybody of the distinction between a banker and a moneylender. 'A banker', he said, 'lends other people's money, and a moneylender lends his own.'

Moore too was a victim of hypocritical questioning. His failure to recollect exact details of loans made several years before was cynically received, yet one of the members who examined him was completely wrong about an answer given to the Committee less than an hour earlier. And when members of the Committee were clearly proved to have been wrong in suggesting that he had made a particular borrower bankrupt, they neither retracted nor apologised. To some extent this justified his belligerent attitude towards them. When the chairman said he would have thought that a particular incident would have 'burnt itself' in Moore's memory, his reply was that he could not be answerable for the chairman's thoughts. When the chairman indicated that he had anticipated a particular answer that Moore gave, Moore replied that if they knew what he was going to say there was no need for him to give evidence.

In many ways, the forum itself was unsatisfactory, because serious allegations, many tantamount to allegations of criminal behaviour, were being put to the moneylender witnesses. These allegations were based on newspaper reports, or written statements made to the Committee, or on the evidence given by other witnesses who had appeared before them, but the moneylenders were not allowed a direct challenge to those making the charges. The Committee had to choose between the conflicting stories simply by deciding which evidence impressed them the most, without the benefit of cross-examination. In Moore's case allegations were put to him based on an affidavit made by one of Sir George Lewis's clerks in a bankruptcy hearing. The clerk was not a witness before the Committee, and indeed the Committee did not read out or even refer to the affidavits which had been filed in the case by Moore and others which countered the clerk's affidavit, despite repeated pleas by Moore that they should do so. Yet they clearly intimated that they accepted the contents of the clerk's affidavit.

Daniel Jay had been in business on his own account since about

The Select Committee

1883, and he too had prospered, and said he had an annual turnover of more than £100,000. He had been severely criticised in a recent court case, and was again censured by the committee for being instrumental in the making of a loan of £20,000 at 60 per cent to a lady who provided a bill apparently signed by the very wealthy Lord Burton, who alleged that the signature was a forgery. Jay admitted that he did not know Lord Burton, had not previously seen his signature, and had not communicated with him in any way. He simply assumed, as Sam had done with Clay's signature, that it was genuine because the person who handed it to him was well known to him. He had discounted the bill with another moneylender and had guaranteed to him that the signature was genuine. There appeared to be little doubt that the signature was, in fact, a forgery. As part of an overall settlement of the debt, which was paid for the most part by the lady's friends, Jay had to make a contribution.

Jay then admitted that in his early years he acted as an agent for Sam, for perhaps four or five years, passing on business which he could not handle himself. So Sam was tied in with a man whose business practices had been considered unethical by a court, and which were obviously looked upon with disfavour by the Committee. What the Committee did not know, and were not told, was that Sam was still in the habit of making large payments to Jay. In May 1898 there was one for £14,000, and it is clear that they were heavily involved in joint adventures. What is more, there were other bonds between them. They attended the same synagogue, and Jay was a very good friend of Ada's sister Clara and her husband Augustus Jacobs who was related to him. They were close enough for Augustus to have nominated Jay as executor to his will. As Clara and Augustus lived in Clifton Gardens, Maida Vale, just two minutes' walk from Ada's parents' home in Little Venice, it is reasonable to assume that Jay and his family would have been frequent visitors to both houses.

It quickly became apparent that there was a great divide between the Committee and the moneylenders over the basic nature of the moneylending business. The Committee was very concerned with the annual rate of interest charged, and thought it was desirable to make provision for a third party, that is a judge, to have the power of deciding what was equitable in any particular transaction. One witness complained:

237

We sell £5 for £6.15., and then that is calculated at interest per annum. Now if a butcher sold five shillings worth of meat and it cost him four shillings, that would be a shilling on the transaction ... If that was multiplied as you multiply moneylenders' interest, that would be 7,000% per annum. ... When I was working the business myself, a tradesman came to me whom I knew well, and said he wanted £30 on the following day; he had a bill that was coming due at the bank and could not meet it; he had not sufficient funds. I lent it to him for a week for a sovereign with which to meet the bill instead of having the bill returned dishonoured, or any process of law taken against him. If you calculate that sovereign at per centum per annum it amounts to a frightful sum; still I only received a sovereign in the transaction.

He was voicing an opinion shared by many borrowers who are not concerned with the rate of interest, but only whether they can afford the repayments.

The Committee having made up its mind at an early stage that there were evils which needed to be remedied, called before them those who were experienced in moneylending matters, and sought their suggestions as to what legislation might be needed. After Farrow, the most important witness was Sir George Lewis. He gave his evidence just three weeks after Nevill's conviction, and according to the *Star* he 'drove two or three big long nails into the coffin of the usurious moneylender ... and out of his forty-two years experience as a solicitor, and his absolutely unique knowledge of the financial and other difficulties of the people, he spoke with authority.' He also, in contemplating the evidence he was to give, had the *Boss* v. *The World* case of 1875 and its aftermath very much in his mind. He urged that High Court judges, judges of the County Court and registrars of the Bankruptcy Court should be given the unrestricted power to fix a fair rate of interest according to the circumstances of the case brought before them.

... I believe that the effect of this vicious system of moneylending at usurious interest by people of no character and no respectability tends to increase betting and gambling and crime; it induces people to go to moneylenders, to make false statements for the purpose of obtaining money; it induces them sometimes to commit forgery and other crimes, which would never be committed except for the inducements that are held out by these moneylenders.

With the exception of interference with the law in the Court of Equity on behalf of an heir, do you think that this country has ever yet adopted the plan of protecting any class of the community against extravagance, where they are of a contracting mind and in full possession of their faculties? – No, certainly not. There is no law to prevent a man spending his fortune in a week if he likes. His father may leave him a million of money and he may spend his fortune in a week if he likes.

As far as the general public are concerned that is no disadvantage to them, the money goes into circulation? – I am all in favour of money not being hoarded up but going into circulation, but instead of going into circulation a great deal of it goes into the moneylenders' pockets.

Unfortunately this interesting line of questioning was not followed up, for Sir George's reasoning was hardly convincing. Moneylenders were as much a part of the general public as anyone else. Certainly Sam, if not the others, circulated the money he earned by his lavish expenditure during his lifetime and by the way he disposed of it after his death, and it will be a matter for further discussion whether what he did with the profit he made was more to the general advantage than if the capital sum involved had remained locked in family trusts and settlements.

As to the West End usurers, Sir George referred to the exposures made by Labouchere and himself in *The World* almost 25 years before:

... The exposure of the true names of these moneylenders had the effect of putting an end for a time to the usurious practices of these West End moneylenders – men who had no means of their own – bankrupts, impecunious, disreputable, dishonourable people, who obtained their money from either Mr Sam Lewis or some other usurer with capital.

They were, as a matter of fact, mere touts? – They were touts and thieves; I can only call them that. Now there has been no exposure of them for some time and they are just as bad, or almost as bad, as they were at that day.

He had to admit that some of those exposed in 1875 were still practising their 'nefarious arts', and flourishing. He then turned his attention to Sam in particular, to the way he conducted his business 20 years before, and to his part in the Nevill case:

Then your opinion is that the West End usurers are worse than the country usurers? – I do think so from the cases which come before me. I will take the case of Mr. Sam Lewis, who is one of the greatest usurers in London. Twenty years ago there came before me cases where Mr. Lewis lent money or discounted bills for young men, giving part money, part jewellery at 60% or more; the meaning of which was, that if he discounted a bill (for his transactions then were not large) say for £500 and he charged 60% and gave the half in cash, and £250 in jewellery (which I need hardly say he charged at 50% profit), that gave him a profit of about 110%. After Mr. Lewis became rich at that sort of business he gave it up, and I believe for the last twenty years he has lent money on a large scale up to 40%. To these men it makes no difference whose security comes into their hands.

Sir George's arithmetic might not have been accurate, but he was certainly correct in alleging that in his early days Sam charged a higher rate of interest than he did in the latter part of his career. Sir George, however, appeared to be completely unaware of the large loans Sam was by now handling at rates competitive with the banks.

There was a case the other day [Nevill's] – a notorious case – I do not wish to mention the name, but of course it is known to the Committee – and I venture to think that, if it had not been for the facilities which usurers give and the way the debtor becomes entangled so that he cannot escape from their fangs, I think the crime for which a young man is now suffering would never have been committed. Mr. Lewis and these other persons do not lend money simply to the young men who come to them; the first thing they do is see who is the father, who are their relations, what is the chance of screwing it out of them; and the money is lent in the knowledge that the chances are the father will have to pay, because

240

a man who has any security can go to this bank and get money at 5%. . . .

It came out in that trial that upwards of £100,000 of transactions had passed between that young nobleman and Mr. Samuel Lewis. Fancy what that means at the rate of 40% for whatever period each of the transactions may have been running! It is impossible for any man to be otherwise than ruined by such transactions. . . .

The effect of this moneylending by all these people in London is that young men are encouraged to bet, because they know that they can go to the moneylender next morning and probably raise the money. . . .

I entirely deny that the community or society require the existence of these moneylenders; they have all amassed and do amass considerable fortunes out of the public. I have never seen one instance in forty-two years of practice where the borrower has gained any advantage by borrowing money. I have seen these moneylenders become rich. Take a few like Mr. Isaac Gordon, who came over here from Poland or Russia, or wherever it was, without a shilling, and tells this committee that after a few years he is lending £45,000 of his own money. What does this mean? Where did he get it from?

He was referred to the evidence which Kirkwood had given:

We have had these usurious moneylenders describing themselves as the salt of the commercial world. That is far from your view I think? – It is, yes.

You look upon them . . . ? – I look upon them as the vermin of the world.

As a curse to the poor and the younger sons of the rich? – I do.

There can be no doubt that the one moneylender he had in mind more than any other was Sam Lewis.

And may I take it your view is that the commercial industry of the country would not suffer in the least degree if the whole of these usurious moneylenders were swept off the face of the earth? – Not only 'would not suffer', but I think would be a great improvement;

and the moment these men were forced to leave their trade of usury, they would go into business like other men and carry on honest businesses no doubt.

Then am I right in understanding this, that judging from your whole forty-two years' experience you are not able to say you have discovered any uses, as apart from abuses, of moneylenders? – Never; I never found anybody who was one shilling the better for it, always a great deal worse.

It was a cause of great anxiety to Sir George, just as it had been in the Boss case, that so many of the moneylenders who had appeared before the Committee, with the conspicuous exception of Kirkwood and one or two others, were Jewish. And just as in the Boss case he wished to dispel any ill-feeling this might arouse against Jewry generally:

... The names of these men I have read to you, as you will very easily see, are the names of Jews ... There are Christians engaged in this business. May I be allowed to say one thing to this Committee, that is that I know that the Jewish community despise and loathe these men and their trade; they are not allowed to hold any public position in the community; they are utterly ignored; the Jewish clergy preach against them and against their usury in the synagogues; and I may be allowed to say this because I know it of my own knowledge. I am myself a Jew.

Does that apply to the country generally? – It does.

I think it only fair to say that in Mr. Isaac Gordon's case – after his evidence here – action was taken by the synagogue in Birmingham precisely as you, Sir George, point out here? [As has been seen, the action was taken well before the Committee was even appointed] – They are absolutely loathed; but it is impossible that the community can do anything with these men ... but they would be only too glad to see them put down and abolished altogether and imprisoned.

It was a courageous statement by one who had no need to identify himself in this way. It doubtless had its effect of showing, as he

242

intended, that not all Jews could or should be sullied by the activities of a few who shared their origins.

It had another effect, too. For the first time in their running battle, which had continued for more than 20 years, he enticed Sam into a dialogue, though Sam made sure it was kept at arm's length. Sam was abroad, enjoying the delights of the casino in Monte Carlo, but kept in touch with events by newspaper and probably also through Algernon Sydney. He obviously felt sufficient pressure to respond to the allegations made against him by Sir George, and agreed to give an interview to the *Star* correspondent. Unfortunately he was injured in a bicycle accident, and could not receive the correspondent, but instead sent him a letter, the gist of which was contained in a report in the paper on 22 March. He said that there had to be some cause for Sir George's hostility against him, quite apart from any antipathy he had for moneylenders generally. Exactly what the cause was Sam said he did not know, but he hinted it might be the reverse which Sir George had suffered in the Nevill case. Sam indicated that he did not intend to take any further steps. 'Those who know me are aware that the statements are false, and will not like me any better for tackling my accuser, and those that don't know me can think what they like.' He seemed to have convinced the reporter, for his comment was: 'I have been at considerable pains to find out the different opinions respecting the now famous evidence, and in fairness I am bound to say that Englishmen generally think there was more temper than justice in Sir George Lewis's remarks.' Sam's carefully built friendships with his clients and others in Society appear to have stood him in good stead in this instance.

There was an immediate response from Sir George, and once again he tried to lure Sam into litigation. A letter appeared in the *Star* of the following day under the headline 'A Strongly Outspoken Letter About the Moneylender with a Past':

Ely-Place 22 March, 1898

Sir,

I observe in this evening's *Star* that your correspondent at Monte Carlo reports an interview with Mr. Samuel Lewis, in which he states that my evidence before the Committee on Moneylending is false. This is an impertinence to which I will not submit. I am prepared to meet – in fact I should welcome – an action in a court of law in which I can plead the truth of every statement I have made before the Committee. I challenge Mr. Samuel Lewis to bring an action against me, and I undertake not to plead my privilege as a witness but to meet him 'in the open'.

Mr. Samuel Lewis more than thirty years ago began his career in Dublin by selling little bits of jewelry to officers stationed in the barracks there. He carried his shop in his pockets. He has lived for many years in Grosvenor Square surrounded by every luxury, and I assert that the fortune which has enabled him to live in this splendor has been wrung out of his victims by the shocking trade of usury.

I repeat (as I told the Committee) that when he honoured London with his presence thirty years ago he commenced his career by discounting bills for youths and undergraduates at 60% – part cash, part pieces of jewelry.

I feel strongly upon this subject of usury because for years I have been a witness of the evils attendant upon it, and I hope the time is not far distant when legislation will terminate this loathsome trade of usury, carried on by Mr. Samuel Lewis and the other West-end usurers. Yours etc.

GEORGE H. LEWIS

There was no further reply from Sam, but on 28 March, reference was made in the *Star* to a letter received from someone calling himself 'A Magistrate'. The contents point directly to Algernon Sydney as being its author:

'A Magistrate' writes to us to say that Mr. Sam Lewis is a straight-forward honourable gentleman with a large mind, a generous disposition, and a kind heart. I have known him (he adds) to do many kind and generous actions towards clients, and to lose large sums of money by his generosity, when he knew the clients were honestly inclined but were unable to fulfil their engagements through unforeseen circumstances over which they had no control. Mr. Sam Lewis is noted for straightforward dealings; he has had large business dealings with some of the greatest men in Europe, and he is not the bloodsucker that your correspondent's letter might suggest. He has been anxious for some time to retire and I know has lately refused pressing requests from solvent persons to extensive business for very large amounts. 'A Magistrate' nevertheless agrees with the necessity of the present moneylending inquiry for the rectification of gross extortion, and that very stringent new laws are urgently required for the protection of the public.

As we shall see, Sam had in fact been engaged in 'extensive business for very large amounts', and indeed at that very moment was negotiating the largest loan of his career with one of Society's leading figures.

The *Star* and the *Morning Leader* announced that they would refuse to to carry any more advertisements from moneylenders. This brought a heartfelt letter of thanks from Thomas Farrow, who complimented them for taking a stand which would prove 'a blow to the fraternity from which they will not easily recover'. He hoped their example would be followed, particularly by the religious press.

The time is happily fast approaching when my heart's desire in this direction will be fully realised. I have, as you and your readers know, for years done my best to expose the iniquitous practices of moneylenders, and to save the working and industrial classes from oppression and extortion. ... It required, however, such revelations as have been made before the Select Committee on Moneylending to show that my crusade was a justifiable one, and to convince the Government and the Press of the country that this monster usury needed to be grasped by the throat and its power destroyed for ever. ... All hail! then to *The Star* and *Morning Leader* who, for the future prefer to suffer financial loss rather than allow their readers to be deceived by the plausible advertisements of these modern vampires and drawn into a vortex from which escape is impossible. You deserve, as you will receive, the gratitude of every right thinking man and woman in the country.

Sir George's evidence also sparked off widespread discussion among the Jewish community and lengthy correspondence in the *Jewish Chronicle*. Oswald John Simon, who was a member of the Board of Deputies of British Jews, and on the Council of the West London Synagogue at Upper Berkeley Street which Sam and Daniel Jay attended, almost started an internecine war among the congregation when he commented on Sir George's remarks:

> Who will not commend his words as an effort to strike a blow at an evil which is not merely pregnant with untold mischief in itself, but which has been the means of casting injustice and misfortune upon the Jewish people? There is no more striking instance of the reaction upon an entire body of the misdeeds of individuals, than that which has afflicted the Jews in consequence of this nefarious trade being practised by individual members of the race. ... No person who is known to be pursuing this detestable trade ought to be admitted as a member of a Jewish congregation. His subscriptions should not be accepted ... he should be treated as though he were not a member of the community. The idea that any portion of the income of a synagogue is derived from the offerings or the payments of a person who is the undisguised enemy of Judaism is repulsive. The ministers and all those who are engaged in the conduct of the administration of the Jewish community should take a decided resolution on this point. It is simply a question of self-defence. ... It is easy to foresee the objections which may be urged to such a course. It may be said that the executive of a synagogue cannot exercise inquisitorial functions. But that cannot apply to cases in which the person seeking membership is a notorious money-lender and usurer ... It is a good time that the Jewish community should rid itself of the imputation that the spread of usury is in any way countenanced by them. This can only be done by showing that there is not the name of a single usurer upon our congregational rolls, or among the subscribers to our various institutions.

As the writer had anticipated, there were objections. One correspondent replied:

> I am not prepared to deny that moneylending is not a nice trade (though I doubt that it is worse than, for instance, importing opium into China, a trade for the sake of which England has twice gone to war) ... What I do protest against is the tone of Mr. Simon's letter. Is it right to hold up to scorn, in the manner he and others do, this, which is only one among many evils? It is

done, obviously, because it has come so prominently before the eyes of the English public. That is, no doubt, sufficient reason why we should try to stop or reduce the evil . . . but we should do so in a calm and judicial spirit, without letting our feelings get the better of us . . . A religious body must act on the principles of love and forgiveness, virtues inculcated both by Judaism and Christianity . . . Perhaps we ought not to make a moneylender an officer and leader of our congregations . . . but to say that he should not be admitted to membership of a synagogue . . . never! I do not stand on such a high plane of virtue as Mr. Simon. I think membership of a synagogue should be open to all who wish to join. It is for God to reject the undeserving, not for us. As for their offerings and payments, it is the destination, and not the source which concerns us. It may, indeed, be said that the true object of the money given in such a case is not the service of God, but the gratification of the giver. But if we are prepared to accept this argument, we must be prepared to accept a large reduction in the incomes of our synagogues and charities. It is not only moneylenders who give that the world may think them charitable and religious.

Another wrote: 'To loathe a man, even a moneylender, is not wise; mere hatred does not improve him. Is the synagogue – was even the Holy Temple – constituted for the righteous only? Assuredly not, for of what avail then is prayer for atonement? To shut out the sinner is not the way to eradicate sin.'

One correspondent calling himself 'J. A. P. G.' made a defence of Sam and Jay:

By all means exclude all questionable characters – rich or poor – from all communal distinctions, but do it in a dignified and unostentatious manner . . . We must be just even to moneylenders, who, in the West End at all events, are absolutely necessary, however much we may deplore that there are some Jews amongst them. Of Mr. Daniel Jay I know nothing, nor do I know Mr. Samuel Lewis personally, but in the West End and elsewhere, where he has long been well known, the general opinion seems to be that, though he charges high interest, he is a man of his word, and has often been known to advise and refuse desirable but youthful and inexperienced applicants for a loan, besides being generous and charitable in his private capacity ... I hold no brief for Mr. Samuel Lewis, but I consider it unjust and unwise to heap on an individual and a fellow-Jew the abuse which the trade as a whole may merit.

When the same topic was raised a few years later, another correspondent of the *Jewish Chronicle*, signing himself 'A Hater of Hypocrisy', pointed out that moneylending was a lawful occupation:

I know I shall be told that it offers opportunities for abuse, but what occupation does not? We all know that the greatest curse to this country is drink, but does that debar brewers and distillers from occupying the highest positions in the land? No vice has ruined as many homes in England as betting and horse-racing, and yet no one has ever suggested that some of the foremost men in the country should be excluded from public office because they are owners of race horses ...

No person is entitled to assume that every moneylender is dishonest simply because his merchandise happens to be money instead of boots. For after all moneylending is to the moneylender no more than law is to the lawyer, medicine to the doctor, knowledge to the professor, and religion to the clergyman, namely a means of earning a living. Conducted honourably, they each play their useful parts – applied to evil purposes, they are equally liable to become a curse to the fellow-man.

Sir George made one further effort to tempt Sam and Jay into court. In a further letter to *The Times* he wrote:

Mr. Justice Mathew has said that the transactions of these men approach blackmail; Judge Snagge has denounced these moneylenders as vermin; they appear to defend themselves by a conspiracy of silence, thinking by this means to escape further criticism and inquiry; but in order to afford the public a means of gauging their true character I offer Mr. Daniel Jay and Mr. Samuel Lewis the opportunity of bringing an action against me, and of going into the witness-box; in which event, I am convinced the consequent disclosures would awaken the public conscience to a sense of the real necessity for early legislation.

In my judgment they are a curse to society and a danger to the community.

But he failed in this attempt to evoke a response, either from Sam or from Jay. The memory of the Boss case still weighed heavily with them, and they were not to be tempted.

Sam and Ada continued their life openly in public. When Ada entertained, her invitations were accepted. Sam still visited his clubs, and the racecourse, and the theatre. Sir George must have known by now that there was nothing he could do to pierce Sam's rhinoceros hide and placid temperament and entice him into the witness box. There was to be no repetition of the Boss case. We can only speculate as to what might have been had Sir George had the opportunity to cross-examine Sam, and who would have emerged victorious. One thing is certain; Sam would have had such a torrid time in the witness box that even his aplomb was likely to have frayed at the edges.

The Select Committee issued its report on 29 June 1898. Its members had exceeded their original remit and had investigated the whole range of loans, not simply small loans to the very poor. They concluded that moneylending transactions frequently owed their inception to misrepresentation of a fraudulent nature. In many cases it was inevitable that the borrower would default, and the circumstances were generally such as to force him to obtain renewal after renewal at increasingly extortionate rates until he was utterly ruined. They 'unhesitatingly' came to the conclusion that the system of moneylending by professional moneylenders at high rates of interest was productive of crime, bankruptcy, unfair advantage over other creditors of the borrower, extortion from the borrower's family and friends 'and other serious injuries to the community'. Although they were satisfied that the system was sometimes honestly conducted, they were of the opinion that only in rare cases was a person benefited by a loan obtained from a professional moneylender, and that the evil attendant upon the system far outweighed the good. They had very largely accepted the evidence of Sir George Lewis and Thomas Farrow and others who supported their line of argument.

The fundamental proposal put before them for remedying the evil was that a maximum rate should be fixed, and any sum above that should be irrecoverable. The Committee were against this. They took the view that a high rate of interest was not in itself incompatible with fair dealing, and no limit of interest could be prescribed which would be adapted to the widely different conditions under which loans were contracted. Further, if a maximum rate were fixed in statute, the interest would tend to rise to that maximum in all cases. They were sure that, as had happened over the centuries, the greatest possible ingenuity would be exercised in circumventing any such provision, and they believed that any such hard and fast rule would be evaded. That was currently happening in the United States where most of the individual states had maximum rates which were regularly circumvented. They therefore did not recommend any statutory limitation of interest.

Their conclusion was that the only effective remedy was to give the courts absolute and unfettered discretion in dealing with moneylending transactions; that all such transactions should be open to complete judicial review; and that power should be given to the courts to reopen any account, and to fix what they considered to be a reasonable rate in all the circumstances. They were also particularly keen that all persons carrying on the business of moneylending should be registered, and that no one should be allowed to trade individually otherwise than in his own name. They also recommended that as many of the borrowers dreaded any publicity of their predicament the courts should, if they considered it desirable, have power to hear moneylending cases in private, but this was not taken up by Parliament.

The Moneylending Bill, incorporating most of their recommendations, was presented to Parliament in February 1899. It and the Report were generally welcomed, though there was some dissent. The three main assumptions of the Report and Bill – that judges were qualified to fix rates in moneylending transactions; that rates could be determined in individual cases solely on the merits of that case and without reference to other cases of the like nature in which the moneylender might be engaged; and that the proposed legislation would have the effect of lowering the rates of interest charged by moneylenders – were all challenged. Views were expressed that judges were no more qualified to fix the rate of interest on a loan than they were to fix the price of corn or the rate of discount for the Bank of

England. Indeed, the last two, it was said, involved far less complex problems than the first. It was certain that judges would differ very much among themselves as to the interpretation of the word 'reasonable', and there would be a great number of judgments which would be irreconcilable. As to the second assumption, critics of the Bill argued that usury was a peculiarly risky business, and by far the largest component part of the rate of interest charged was insurance against loss, and not interest on capital. This insurance would be spread over every transaction of the same class in which the usurer engaged, and in order to discover the rate of interest which the usurer obtained on the capital invested in any particular class of business, and in order that fairness should be displayed towards the moneylender as well as to the borrower, an average would have to be taken of his net gains in that class over a number of years. This would impose an impossible burden on the courts. On the question of lowering rates, it was urged that this had never previously happened throughout the whole history of moneylending, and nothing in the proposed legislation would make it likely now.

In the House of Commons the second reading of the Bill was moved by the chairman of the Select Committee, Mr T. W. Russell, the member for Tyrone South. He said that when he agreed to take the chair his views were that of a free-trader in money, and in answer to all the grievances which were alleged there arose in his mind the reply that if a man chose to be a fool it was impossible to protect him from his folly. But two sessions of exciting work had, he said, cured him entirely of these heresies, and he found that what he had imagined to represent free trade in money often represented free trade in rascality and fraud. Referring to complaints that the Committee had not heard cases of legitimate moneylending, he said that was because they were only commissioned to inquire into the causes of hardship.

Mr Lawson Walton QC, who had appeared for the moneylender Sam Lewis in his case against Clay, and for the borrower Nevill in his unfortunate brush with the criminal law, was also a Member of Parliament, and he opposed the Bill. He argued that the setting aside of a bargain by an appeal to the realm of ethics would introduce a principle absolutely unknown to English jurisprudence. The proposed measure would bring untold confusion into the administration of the law, and it would drive the moneylender into underground subterfuges. It was impossible, while there were people prepared to lend money and take the risk of its never being repaid, to prevent transactions of the kind which were then occurring.

There were others who also voiced some support for the money-lenders. One said that many respectable persons concerned in the business complained that they had not had a fair hearing before the Committee. The Bill was vindictive and seemed to have been founded on the misdeeds of just two men, the notorious Isaac Gordon and John Kirkwood. Another member of Parliament considered that the poor who wanted a small loan without security and without sureties would lose what was to them the inestimable privilege of repaying the money in driblets: 'One half of the world does not know how the other half lives, and it will be an act of great cruelty to a great number of poor people in this country, if you place such an obstacle as this in the way of their obtaining loans.' He too thought that often the fault was with the borrower and not the moneylender, and that the preamble to the Bill could with every justification be reversed, and should read:

> Whereas certain persons trading as, and known by, the name of money-borrowers, carry on their business of borrowing money by deceptive practices and inflict by harsh and unconscionable bargains great injury on those who lend money to them ...

Mr MacLean, who represented Cardiff, had met 'a great many gentlemen' connected with the moneylending business, and was perfectly astonished to find what a large body of respectable people they were. Isaac Gordon had so much prejudice raised against him throughout the country that MacLean's view was that any money-lender would have less chance of justice in the hands of a British jury than he would have had at the time of the Plantagenets. Mr Gibbs, the member for St Albans, said it was a mistake to think that all the rogues were lenders and all the honest men were borrowers. His experience had led him rather to the opposite conclusion. These contracts were entered into by grown-up men who were on equal terms – that is to say each was trying to cheat the other. The effect of the proposed reform would be that moneylenders would have to calculate the risk of their interest being reduced; and they would inevitably 'take it out' on the men who did not come to court. Another said that to allow the law to interfere in bargains in which no fraud was alleged was to return to the Dark Ages.

Mr Balfour, who was in charge of the Bill (and later to become prime minister), said that there was no desire to revive the usury laws in any way whatsoever. The desire was to prevent acts of tyranny against a small and very helpless class. They were not injuring the legitimate moneylender who performed a useful and important function in the social organism. They sought only to interfere with the extravagant exercise of power which, in every age, and in every country, had brought the profession into disrepute, and which in some countries had actually threatened the social and public order of the community.

Those who spoke against the Bill were minority voices. The Bill, with some amendments, was passed into law by a large majority, and took effect at the end of 1900, nine months after Gordon had died. The 1900 Act essentially inaugurated only two changes: it required registration of lenders in their own names; and it allowed the courts to go behind the bargains to protect the borrowers against undue hardship. For various reasons the first failed to attain its purpose and was much avoided. The second succeeded only in part, and many abuses continued. Circulars and newspaper advertisements were still used in large numbers by the London moneylenders, and the agent system remained in being.

Although Sam was not called to appear before the Committee we have some record of his views. R. D. Blumenfeld wrote in his diary for 10 November 1900:

> As I stood in the doorway [of a shop in Burlington Gardens] talking to the proprietor, Sam Lewis, the famous moneylender came along. His office is close by. He stopped and I asked him about the new Moneylending Act. Was it satisfactory and workable? 'Certainly', he said. 'There will be less fraud now that moneylenders have to register and disclose their real names. It is not easy business either. Moneylenders are more sinned against than sinners, but I am dead against Shylocks. No one ever accused me of being a Shylock, and I have about a million out on loan throughout the year. I never foreclose on a really honest person if I can help it.'

In 1925 Mr Barry Cohen, a solicitor in the City of London, who followed in Sir George's footsteps and acted for many of the young men who became involved with moneylenders, gave evidence before a Joint Select Committee of the House of Lords and the House of Commons. In answer to the question whether he could make any suggestion to prevent young men entering into moneylending transactions he replied, 'It is impossible to prevent the folly of mankind.' Perhaps the last word on the 1900 Act should be given to the man who drafted it, Sir Mackenzie Chalmers. He told the 1925 Committee: 'the usury laws have always been a failure, and an acute moneylender will always be able to circumvent them.'

17 · Other clients

Sam's clients were many and varied, a mixed bag not confined solely to wastrels such as the fourth marquis of Ailesbury, George Alexander Baird, and their ilk, though many such, including the fifth earl of Rosslyn and the seventh earl of Aylesford, contributed largely to his profits. There were some who would not merit the description wastrel, but none the less spent extravagantly, such as Lord Charles Beresford and Count Kinski. But his clientele also, perhaps unexpectedly, included some of the grandees who enjoyed high standing in politics and at court, men such as the eighth duke of Beaufort, the eighth earl of Wemyss, the fourth earl of Cholmondeley, the twentieth earl of Shrewsbury and Talbot, and Viscount Esher, who was adviser to kings and prime ministers. For their own reasons such men preferred to deal with Sam rather than the banks or insurance companies. The result was that he was constantly in contact with a wide range of upper society, and because of this was most knowledgeable about the events of the day. When particularly disreputable or dishonourable behaviour occurred, or blameless but important events unfolded, it was frequently the case that one or more of the participants were current or previous visitors to Cork Street, and Sam thus had a ringside seat, an advantage he shared with Sir George Lewis. Sam's own information was supplemented by Ada's awareness of what was going on, gained from her position as an important Mayfair hostess.

The Hon. George Lambton said that Sam was the ideal man to visit if you wished to hear all the latest news of the political, racing and social world. He enjoyed gossip (though never about the business affairs of those who came to him, for in that respect he was as discreet and as trustworthy as could be) and he was sought after as a fund of information. Those who entered his office could, should they so wish, pass on confidences and scandal about the upper set. Sam's charm, and the fact that they wanted to borrow from him, and so to some extent ingratiate themselves with him, must have led to many tasty morsels of scandal being imparted. Doubtless some also sought his advice as a man of the world.

James Francis Harry St Clair-Erskine, the fifth earl of Rosslyn, whose ancestors had included a Lord High Chancellor of Great Britain, was only 21 when he succeeded his father in 1890. By this time he had led a varied and fairly destructive life. At Eton he was 'flighty and self-indulgent', and he wasted his time at Oxford and in the Army. As soon as he inherited his family estate, property in Fife and Midlothian of 3,310 acres worth £9,186, as well as further income from collieries and £50,000 in securities, he set about spending it. A regular at the racecourse, he bought a string of horses, and gambled and drank heavily, and like Sam he was an habitué of the casino at Cannes. Within three years of his accession he had mortgaged the estates for £100,000 and borrowed more than £125,000 from Sam. Escott described him as a man who was amusing to those he met on a footing of equality, and the best fun in the world. 'To his inferiors he is arrogant.' One wonders what stance he adopted when he paid his visits to Cork Street.

Rosslyn deals with his relationship with Sam in his autobiography, *My Gamble With Life*, which was published in 1928. He describes how, while seeking yet further loans, he was riding in Rotten Row one morning when he met Sam, 'the great moneylender', taking his morning constitutional on horseback. He took the opportunity to discuss his business affairs and made an appointment to see Sam that evening. When he arrived he was surprised to find Sir George Chetwynd there, 'and only then knew that he was one of Lewis's touts'. This account confirms the view already expressed that Chetwynd acted as Sam's eyes and ears at the racecourse, and that his friendship with Sam was founded partly on the services he rendered. Sam told Rosslyn that he had heard that he had lost a great deal of money, and not only was he not prepared to lend him any more, but required repayment of at least £50,000 of the debt within a month, otherwise he would have to take steps to recover the whole of the £125,000.

Shocked and alarmed at being forced to face reality, Rosslyn contacted his solicitors. They told him that it was impossible to raise a further loan on the estate as it was already over-encumbered, not only with the mortgages but also with a jointure of £2,000 a year for his mother and certain provisions for the younger children. He went back to Sam to see if he would soften his attitude. 'No man', he said, 'could have been fairer.' Sam told him to sell his horses and stud and let him have the proceeds, and he would then consider the matter further. This raised £15,000. At the same time Rosslyn decided to sell Dysart House, the family home at Kirkcaldy, and his policies, which were expensive to maintain, and to use those receipts to reduce his mortgage liabilities substantially. But he was still financially over-stretched, and did not have the ready money to pay the further £35,000 which Sam had indicated he was prepared to accept for the moment.

He made an appointment to see Sam at 23 Grosvenor Square, and asked his solicitor Mr William Dundas to accompany him. For reasons of professional etiquette Dundas would not enter the house, but paced about outside hoping that the meeting would end in time for Rosslyn and himself to catch the mail train to Edinburgh. When Rosslyn went in Sam showed him 'the greatest hospitality'. Algernon Sydney was also present. Within half an hour a deal was struck. Dundas, on learning that Sam had his solicitor with him, had no qualms about joining them, and after a few perfunctory remarks as to details and the drawing up of the deed, Rosslyn and Dundas were on their way to King's Cross in good time to catch their train. 'The impossible had been done,' wrote Rosslyn, 'a mortgage of £107,000 had been arranged on the estates at 5% which was afterwards reduced to 4½%.' These were competitive rates, and no attempt was made to take advantage of Rosslyn's desperate situation in order to extort an unreasonable return.

It was a perfect example of Sam's methods, and shows just why so many of his clients spoke so highly and warmly about him and, above all, trusted him. He had not shouted or ranted or threatened; on the contrary he was courteous and hospitable to his debtor. He converted what had been effectively an unsecured debt into a secured debt. He had acted swiftly, and made his decision without having to confer with any other person, and his solicitor was on hand to deal with the matter immediately. The manner in which Sydney quickly agreed the technical details with Dundas shows that Sam had instructed him not to raise any pedantic or legalistic objections. Most remarkably, Sam found it quite possible to offer a mortgage of £107,000 on property which Rosslyn's own solicitor said would not bear any further loan. It is no wonder therefore that Sam's reputation was high among those who dealt with him, and helps us to understand why so many of them rallied to his support when attacks were made against him.

Unfortunately the loan provided only temporary respite for Rosslyn, for he was declared bankrupt in 1897. This was subsequently annulled in 1902. He divorced his first wife and took as his second Georgiana Robinson, an American lady from Minneapolis, who was described in *Debrett* as 'a member of the dramatic profession', and they had a home in Park Lane. Rosslyn too became an actor, and appeared on the London and provincial stage using the name John Erskine. Unfortunately he once more succumbed to his former vices of excessive drinking and gambling, and in 1923 the family collieries had to be sold. He fled abroad to escape his creditors, and died in 1939. Sam seems to have come through financially unscathed, and his executors' bank accounts show that payments were being received from Rosslyn or his trustees for many years after Sam's death.

A good example of Sam's intimate knowledge of the workings and scandals of the inner circle was the Aylesford episode, which illustrated the moral standards of behaviour of certain elements of high society who would have been among the first to comment adversely on the alleged shortcomings of moneylenders. It seemed for a time as though it would end in the divorce court and provide the great British public with an engrossing insight into the behaviour of its betters. None of those involved emerged with any credit.

In the years after his father's death, an effective role in state affairs was being sought for the Prince of Wales, particularly important as his mother was more and more isolating herself from the nation. In 1875 Edward suggested that he should make an official visit to India. Disraeli, who was nurturing a plan to have Queen Victoria declared Empress of India, approved, and he secured a grant of a quarter of a million pounds from the British and Indian governments to finance the expedition. Among those accompanying the prince, and especially selected by him, were his close cronies Colonel Owen Williams, then commanding the Blues, Lord Charles Beresford, a fearless hunter in

19 Hugh Lowther, fifth earl of Lonsdale. One of England's wealthiest men, but frequently in need of cash. He turned to Sam
Hulton

20 General Owen Williams, member of the Jockey Club and Tory MP, owed Sam more than £140,000 at the time of Sam's death   *Hulton*

21   The fourth marquis of Ailesbury. 'If I want money I go and ask Mr
     Lewis for some . . .'
                                                                Hulton

22   The fifth earl of Rosslyn, bankrupt before the age of 30   *Hulton*

23 England's premier earl, the twentieth earl of Shrewsbury, found it
convenient to deal with Sam. He borrowed more than £367,000

Hulton

24   Lord Charles Beresford, centre of a Society scandal   *Hulton*

25 Sir George Chetwynd, client of and tout for Sam *Hulton*

26   The eighth duke of Beaufort, Sam's highest-ranking client   *Hulton*

the fields and bedrooms of England, and the Earl of Aylesford, also known as 'Sporting Joe', who was married to Owen Williams's sister Edith. All three gentlemen were also friends and clients of Sam and met him frequently at Cork Street and at the racecourse. Indeed, it is highly probable that both Aylesford and Williams had resorted to Sam to finance the expenses of the trip.

Another member of the prince's 'fast set' who did not go with them to India was Lord Blandford, the heir to the seventh duke of Marlborough and brother of Lord Randolph Churchill. He was married to Albertha, one of the seven daughters of the Duke of Abercorn, but he treated her abominably. He had a much greater affection for Sporting Joe's wife, Edith Aylesford. At one time the prince had also dallied with her, and had foolishly written some rather indiscreet letters. No sooner had the prince's party left the shores of England than Blandford rented a house close to Edith's home at Packington Hall. He was given a key to a private entrance, and was seen to be leaving in the early hours of the morning.

In February 1876 letters began to arrive in India. Sporting Joe Aylesford received a hysterical note from Edith saying she was going to elope with Blandford; the equally highly strung Blandford wrote to Owen Williams saying that he was prepared to meet Sporting Joe in a duel; and the prince received from Randolph Churchill, who knew of the existence of the prince's letters to Edith, a *'very private and confidential letter'*. Randolph, fearing a public scandal which would harm his family's honour, implored the prince to prevail upon Aylesford and Owen Williams not to be rash or take any hasty or violent action. Another brother of Edith's threatened that if Blandford did not meet him in a duel he would shoot him down like a dog in the street. Aylesford, threatening revenge on Blandford, hurried home, as did Owen Williams, not only because of these events but also because his wife had become seriously ill.

Lord Lansdowne, later to become Edward's first Foreign Secretary, then entered the scene and muddied the waters. He was married to a sister of Albertha, and he begged Edward to restrain Aylesford because, he added menacingly, the consequences could be 'important to you as well as him'. On being pressed by the prince to elucidate, he retreated, and apologised in contrite terms, and begged the prince to make allowance for the fact that he had acted as he did because of 'the calamity which threatened the prospects and happiness of my wife's sister and of her children'.

By this time Lady Aylesford had been convinced by her family that a publicly fought divorce would lead to her bitter persecution by Society. To save the situation, Randolph embarked on a scarcely disguised blackmailing expedition. Uninvited, and accompanied by Edith, he called upon Alexandra ('Alix'), the Princess of Wales, at Marlborough House to entreat her to use her influence with the prince. Had she realised who was visiting, and their purpose, she would not have received them, but when they were announced by her butler, Alix, who was unfortunately somewhat hard of hearing, thought he had said that Lady Ailesbury was calling, and she instructed the footman to show her up. Lord Randolph told the princess that 'being aware of peculiar and most grave matters affecting the case, he was anxious that His Royal Highness should give such advice to Lord Aylesford as to induce him not to proceed against his wife'. When news of this reached the prince he was furious that his wife had been brought into such a sordid affair. He sent Lord Charles Beresford to England and gave him a letter to deliver to another of his friends, Lord Hardwicke, instructing him to obtain an apology from Randolph. At this time Sam was meeting one or other of Beresford, Owen Williams and Aylesford almost on a daily basis.

Hardwicke saw Randolph and reported back to the prince that Randolph had told him that 'he was determined by every means in his power to prevent the case coming before the public and that he had those means at his disposal'. On Hardwicke's enquiring what they were, Randolph said 'letters from Your Royal Highness to Lady Aylesford written some [four] years ago had been found, copies of which he had and which he was determined to use to prevent the case ever coming into court – that these letters were of the *most compromising* character, that he had placed them in the hands of the solicitors acting for him and Blandford and that . . . if they ever came before the public Your Royal Highness would never sit on the throne of England.' It is difficult to imagine a more serious and cruel threat to a monarch's heir. Hardwicke's view was that Randolph would stick at nothing.

Hardwicke said Randolph had argued that the prince had known of Blandford's intimacy with Lady Aylesford, and it was through the prince's influence that Lord Aylesford had accompanied him to India, despite an imploring letter from Lady Aylesford not to take her husband away, 'that in fact there was collusion between Your Royal Highness and Aylesford to throw Lady Aylesford into the arms of Blandford, that you had succeeded, but that having letters to prove Your Royal Highness's own admiration for Lady Aylesford, they would prevent any divorce by using this powerful lever in any way they might think fit'. A fine mess!

Randolph told his father that he had not mentioned the letters from the prince to Edith as a threat, but had simply said to Hardwicke that he could not guarantee that the letters would not be used in any divorce case. The kindest gloss that can be put on such hypocritical and self-serving posturing is that he had rushed to defend his family's honour without stopping to think, and that he genuinely believed that the prince had acted in collusion with Aylesford. Further, he was well aware of, and strongly resented, the prince's affection for his own wife Jennie, and the fact that the world knew of it. He was not the compliant husband so far as the prince was concerned that he was about others of Jennie's escorts.

Queen Victoria took Edward's side. He had declared to her that there was nothing in the letters that could not be 'broadcast to the world at Charing Cross', and the Queen thereupon said that his word was good enough for her and she had not the slightest doubt that the letters were not compromising.

To the relief of Edward, Sporting Joe decided not to seek a divorce, but to separate from his wife and thus avoid a public scandal. Randolph signed a grudging apology, which was grudgingly accepted, but this did not prevent the Prince and Princess of Wales from letting it be known that they would not accept invitations to houses where the Churchills were received. This effectively ostracised Randolph and Jennie from Society. As Sir Winston Churchill described in his biography of his father, 'The fashionable world no longer smiled. Powerful enemies were anxious to humiliate him. His own sensitiveness and pride magnified every coldness into an affront. London became odious to him.' It was to be eight years before there was a reconciliation, at a dinner party hosted by Lady Dorothy Nevill. Jennie's beauty and charm eventually won the day, and the prince was soon once more plying her with presents of expensive jewellery.

261

Lord Aylesford had visited Sam shortly after his arrival home, and borrowed heavily then and for several years after the Blandford incident. He emigrated to America in 1882, where he bought a ranch in Texas. Within three years, at the age of 36, having squandered his family fortune by gambling and other extravagances, he died of alcoholism, 'one of the worst examples', it was said, 'of the English peerage'.

Edith lived with Blandford for some time in France as Mr and Mrs Spencer, and she gave birth to a son. They did not marry, for Blandford, though he had been divorced by his wife, declared that Edith was a remarkable mistress but unsuitable as a future Duchess of Marlborough. When he inherited the dukedom he married a wealthy American widow, Mrs Hammersley. Edith stayed in Paris where she died in 1897. The Prince and Princess of Wales sent a wreath to her funeral.

Sam was very well acquainted with Lord and Lady Randolph Churchill's affairs. When Randolph resigned from the government in 1887 he took up racing, which involved him in expense beyond his means. Though no evidence has been found to establish that Randolph became a client of Sam, it would not be surprising to discover that he was. Not only were Jennie and Randolph neighbours of Sam and Ada in the Square, but Sam had, as one of his longstanding and most interesting clients, Jennie's closest admirer, Count Charles Rudolf Ferdinand Andreas Kinski. He was born in 1858 and was four years younger than Jennie. His father, Ferdinand, one of Austria's great landowners, was the seventh Prince Kinski, and his mother was a Liechtenstein princess. Their family tree could be traced back to the thirteenth century. The count served as honorary attaché at the Austro-Hungarian Embassy in London from 1881, and that was the year he entered Jennie's life and heart, where he stayed for 12 ardent and tempestuous years.

It was also about this time that he came to know Sam, for Kinski was very heavily involved with the racing set, gaining great popularity and becoming a national hero when he won the Grand National riding his own horse, Zoedone. Handsome, talented and brilliant, he was immediately accepted into London society, particularly by those addicted to the Turf. Even Randolph enjoyed his company, though his romance with Jennie was an open secret all over

London. Unfortunately he had no private means of his own to sustain himself among such expensive company, or to court Jennie in the manner he wished. His father made him a lavish allowance, but this was always speedily spent. Sam advanced him the cash necessary to indulge the lifestyle he sought, and must have done so, completely unsecured as it was, only in the belief that the prince would always be ready to meet his son's debts. The largest single sum recorded in Sam's bank account as paid to Kinski was £17,100 in June 1892. This was probably the last large loan Sam made to him. The prince provided the money for Sam to be paid off, but extracted a promise from his son that, whatever happened, he would never 'go to the Jews again'.

When Randolph's syphilis took a strong hold, and Jennie, who felt she could not leave him, decided to accompany him in 1894 on what was intended to be a year-long world tour, Kinski made what amounted to an ultimatum – that she should leave Randolph and make a fresh start with him or he would leave her. They had waited too long already, he said, and he would not, and could not, bear to be separated from her. He argued that the world would understand if she left Randolph, now a virtual madman. They were entitled to a life together. But Jennie felt her duty to the man she had once loved was overwhelming. He was dying, and he needed her. She turned Kinski down. Seven months later Randolph died. Kinski in the meantime became engaged to Countess Elisabeth Metternich Zur Gracht, 20 years younger than Jennie, and a cousin of the Empress of Austria. He married her just two weeks before Randolph died. On the death of his father he succeeded as Prince Kinski. He had left the diplomatic service and became Privy Councillor and Chamberlain to the Emperor of Austria. He was a regular visitor to England, coming at least once a year for the Grand National, and after his wife's death at an early age in 1910, he kept a flat in Clarges Street. His and Jennie's paths crossed from time to time, but she by now had entered on her second marriage (one which, as will be seen, may well have had an influence on Ada), and her relationship with Kinski thereafter remained entirely platonic.

The Marquises of Anglesey owned 30,000 acres in Stafford, Anglesey, Derby and Dorset producing, in 1880, about £110,000 gross, but by the end of the century their financial affairs were in a sorry state. Accumulated debts reduced the net receipts almost to nil, and they became heavy borrowers. The fourth marquis relied on loans from Sam even before he succeeded to the title in 1880, and until his death in 1898 remained heavily indebted to him. A somewhat idle man, or as *Vanity Fair* described him, 'not one of those strong-minded men who make life a burden by their own energy', he was easy-going and generous to a fault. He even increased the allowance to his younger brothers and to his sister-in-law out of his own pocket to the extent of £10,500 a year. His reward for this kind gesture was to earn for himself such a reputation for generosity that it resulted in attempts of every kind, and from all sides, to extract money from him, so that eventually, and, contrary to his natural instincts, he had to act harshly to avoid the predators. In 1896 and 1897 he repaid Sam £100,000 of his debt, but this still left more than £50,000 owing.

It would appear that his son, Henry Cecil, the fifth marquis, took the debt over, but Sam had less luck with him. This young man, born in 1875, and married to a daughter of Sir George Chetwynd, had a passion for dressing up in bizarre and extravagant costumes. He toured Europe with a theatrical company and put on ruinously expensive productions in which he appeared performing an act called 'the Butterfly Dance'. He was made bankrupt in 1904, a year before his death, with total debts of £255,969. When his trustees sold the contents of Beaudesert and Anglesey Castle they included jewelled walking sticks, paste diamonds, silken nightshirts, and 'an amazing collection of unnecessary gear', and it would seem that this was a case in which Sam and his estate lost most of the £50,000 owed to them.

Many who were engaged at the highest court levels had no compunction in going to Sam for assistance should needs require. The earls of Wemyss (pronounced Weems) and March had inherited Wemyss Castle and 7,000 acres in Fife during the eighteenth century. Francis, the eighth earl, was aide-de-camp from 1881 successively to Queen Victoria, Edward VII and then George V. He mixed in the highest circles of society, was a trusted friend of the monarch, and after he succeeded to the title in 1883, went to Sam. In January 1888, when he received a cheque from Sam for £14,875, he was already 70 years of age, well versed in the ways of the world – he had been a Member of Parliament for 36 years from 1841 to 1883 – and hardly a novice when dealing in financial matters. Yet he was quite happy to deal with Sam and accept his terms.

Another of Sam's clients became involved in a scandal which highlighted the importance of the London season to Society, and the lengths to which its members would go in order to secure their places in it. One can begin to understand why they were prepared to borrow to maintain their positions, though to most people today the object of their desires might appear unworthy of such effort and sacrifice. Lord Charles Beresford, a minor player in the Aylesford scandal, was a naval captain, later admiral. He and his brothers, Marcus and William, were sons of the fourth marquis of Waterford and all three, said Lillie Langtry, as 'handsome as paint'. Marcus became racing adviser to the Prince of Wales and manager of his stud. Charles was a great practical joker. When in command of HMS *Thunderer* he saw Lillie Langtry and the Prince of Wales slip, unnoticed as they thought, into a cabin. Charles cut off its ventilation shaft and the lack of air soon brought an abrupt end to whatever it was that Lillie and the prince were engaged in.

One of his mistresses was Frances Brooke. Frances, always known as Daisy, was born on 10 December 1861 into a world of wealth, position and privilege. Her father, who died when she was three, was the Honourable Charles Maynard, the son and heir of the third Viscount Maynard. When her grandfather died Daisy inherited the Maynard estate (though not the title), bringing her £30,000 a year, and Easton Lodge in Essex. Her mother remarried in 1866 Lord Rosslyn (father of Sam's client), by whom she had five children. Daisy's stepfather was sophisticated, cultured, intelligent and a member of the best clubs. Distinguished in appearance, with a certain swagger and insolence of manner, he conveyed the impression of being perpetually on the lookout for the main chance. His daughter Millicent became Duchess of Sutherland, and she, with Lady Wimbourne, the daughter of the Duke of Marlborough, Lady Dorothy Nevill, daughter of the Earl of Orford, and Lady Elizabeth Balfour, daughter of the Earl of Lytton, was one of the great London hostesses who shared the power, with the Prince of Wales, to set the tone of London life.

Like other girls of her class, Daisy was educated at home by a succession of governesses, in history, languages, literature and the 'use of globes'. Of outstanding beauty and intelligence, she captured the heart of the young Lord Brooke, the heir to the fourth earl of Warwick, a love she reciprocated. He approached Lord and Lady Rosslyn to seek her hand. He was persuaded, against his will, to wait until Daisy was a little older, a delay engineered by Lord Rosslyn because he had higher hopes for his stepdaughter. Through the recommendation of his friend Disraeli, Daisy was selected as a wife for Prince Leopold, the cultivated, but unfortunately haemophiliac, son of Queen Victoria. She was subjected to the scrutiny of the Queen and passed the test. But Leopold, who knew of the mutual affection of Daisy and Lord Brooke, had himself fallen in love with another, Princess Helen of Waldeck-Pyrmont. He suggested to Daisy that she should reject him, thus leaving the way free for each of them to follow the dictates of their hearts. This Daisy did, and to the fury of the Queen she promptly married Lord Brooke. At the wedding consecrated in Westminster Abbey in April 1881, Prince Leopold (who married his Helen but died after just two years of married life after sustaining a simple bump on his knee) was best man and, to foreshadow events to come, the principal royal guest was the Prince of Wales.

No sooner was she married than Daisy promptly, avidly, delightedly and with abandon engaged in the accepted norm of moral laxity which prevailed among the prince and his followers, and in upper Society generally, by attracting a retinue of admirers of her own. She succeeded during the first four years of her marriage in both bearing three children by her husband and having a series of extra-marital affairs. It was, she said, 'a great game'. Lord Brooke accepted the situation with equanimity.

The handsome and adulterously energetic Lord Charles Beresford became her most passionate lover. She even contemplated eloping with him and abandoning her husband and three children. Indeed, she took it upon herself to confront his wife and tell her of the liaison, although Lady Charles Beresford, who was older than her husband, was already well aware of it. After this confrontation Charles's ardour for Daisy waned, particularly when he learned that he was not without competition for her affection. As he cooled towards her, Daisy's jealousy of his wife grew, and when she learned that Lady Charles was pregnant she wrote a blistering letter to Charles accusing him of infidelity to herself, and demanding that he should leave his wife immediately and come to her. He had, she said, 'no right' to beget a child by his wife. Unfortunately the letter was opened not by Charles, but by his wife. Distressed at its contents, and determined to fight for her husband, she passed the letter for safekeeping to her solicitor, the obvious lawyer to instruct in such a delicate case, none other than Sir George Lewis. He wrote to Daisy warning her not to cause any further distress to his client. Daisy, realising what a dangerous piece of evidence had fallen into the hands of her rival, demanded its return; 'It is my letter. I wrote it.' Her legal knowledge was imperfect, and Sir George informed her that the letter was the property of the person to whom it was addressed.

Acting in anger, but also with malicious insight, Daisy sought advice from the Prince of Wales, believing him to be the only person who might have sufficient influence to prise the letter away from Lady Charles. She also knew that he would not welcome yet another public scandal involving one of his closest friends. Daisy had been intermittently in touch with the prince since her marriage, and had on one occasion entertained him and the Princess of Wales at Easton. The prince, faced with a beautiful woman in distress, realising what a dangerous missile the letter could be to his own well-being, and finding lustful thoughts surfacing in his mind, agreed to help. At two o'clock that morning he roused Sir George who, to his shame, quite unprofessionally allowed the prince to read the letter, though he refused to destroy it or hand it over.

Spurred into action by what he read, the prince called upon Lady Charles, but she, with commendable courage, refused to be overawed. She instructed Sir George to write to Daisy indicating that she would return the letter, but on one condition, a condition so horrendous that it struck at the very heart of Daisy's lifestyle, and at all that Society held dear. Daisy, Lady Charles demanded, should stay away from London for the entire Season! No more humiliating terms could have been proposed, an unthinkable self-imposed social ostracism.

Daisy went back to the prince, and made it clear that she would do anything, but anything, if he could only wrest the letter back. She said that the prince gave her a look which every woman would recognise and understand. When he called a second time on Lady Charles he bluntly told her that if she did not return the letter it was she, not Daisy, who would have to leave the London scene, and

267

subsequently made his threat good by openly inviting Daisy and her husband to functions he attended, and refusing to go to houses where the Beresfords were accepted. Lord Charles, who until then had been attempting to persuade his wife to give up the letter, rallied to her because of what he considered to be the ungallant interference and intrusion of the prince in his affairs. He despised the 'lickerish servility' of Sir George in allowing the prince to see the letter, and called the prince a cowardly blackguard to his face. The pair nearly, or actually, according to which account one reads, came to blows. He left vowing revenge.

Yet another letter surfaced. Lord Charles composed it while serving overseas, addressed to the Prince of Wales, but sent to his wife with firm instructions to hold it back until he told her to deliver it to Marlborough House. 'The days of duelling are past', the letter read, 'but there is a more just way of getting right done than can duelling, and that is – publicity.' Charles told his wife to show a copy to the prime minister, Lord Salisbury. Charles was advised by his brother Marcus, by the prime minister, and by Sir Edward Clarke, whom Lady Charles consulted professionally, not to send the letter to the prince. Lady Charles then told the prime minister that her sister had written out the whole story and intended to publish it, and that there were several people who wanted to make use of it at the next general election for their own purposes! There was almost no limit to the lengths people would go to ensure they remained part and parcel of the social 'scene', including threats, arm-twisting, and political and social blackmail.

Although Salisbury, with the assistance of Lord Marcus, managed to persuade Lord Charles not to have the letter sent to the prince, news of its contents inevitably leaked out, to the distress not only of the prince and his friends, but to many politicians, and most importantly to the Princess of Wales. She was abroad at the time visiting her parents in Denmark, and she decided to stay on the Continent until matters quietened down.

Lady Charles telegraphed Lord Charles to come back home to protect her. This he did, and immediately despatched a violent letter to the prince demanding an apology to his wife, failing which he would 'no longer intervene to prevent these matters becoming public'. Poor Salisbury spent a frantic week, shuttling between the prince, Queen Victoria and the Beresfords, and only just managed to prevent Lord Charles from holding a meeting with the representatives of the press at which he intended to reveal the whole story. The prince wrote a conciliatory letter to Lord Charles saying that he was upset to learn that Lady Charles believed that he had intended publicly to wound her, and assuring Lord Charles that there was no intention so to do, and regretting that she should have been led to such an erroneous impression. Daisy was temporarily excluded from Court, and Lady Charles instructed her brother to send the original offending letter back to her.

Lady Charles was the main loser. She retired to the Continent in order to avoid further humiliation; Lord Charles went back to his naval duties; and Daisy became one of the successors to Lillie Langtry as the prince's mistress, a position she was to hold for many years.

The Beresford affair caused a rift in Daisy's marriage. Lord Brooke was rumoured to be considering suing for divorce on the grounds of his wife's adultery with no fewer than 14 co-respondents, including the Prince of Wales, Lord Charles Beresford, the Duke of Marlborough and Lord Randolph Churchill, but proceedings never came about. It was not until 1897, after the exchange of carefully contrived letters of apologies had been sent to the prince and accepted by him, that a truce was called. He sent copies of the correspondence to Daisy. 'It is a great triumph', she trumpeted, but she too was relieved that the episode was closed. By then, Daisy had troubles of her own. The prince's love for her was waning; for some time their relationship had been platonic; and in March 1898, at the age of 35, she gave birth to a son, more than 12 years after the birth of her youngest child. She was replaced in the prince's affections by Alice Keppel, who kept her position until Edward died in 1910.

At one time Daisy was wealthy in her own right, and her husband had substantial estates in Warwick and Somerset, but by 1899 the family was in deep financial trouble. From 1897 there were constant sales of land. Lord Brooke lost a small fortune in several of Moreton Frewen's fruitless speculations, and Daisy was sued by her creditors. By 1914 she owed £90,000 or more to various moneylenders despite her aristocratic disdain of them. Her valuables had all been sold or impounded. Her only assets were the love letters which Edward had written her, addressed to his 'Darling Daisy Wife'. She decided to use the letters to pay off her debts. She tried to blackmail Edward's son, King George V, by threatening to write her memoirs with the assistance of the notorious Frank Harris, and publish them in America where, she said, by including the letters she could earn £200,000. She justified her actions by contending that she had come to her present parlous financial state because of the vast sums she had expended on entertaining Edward and his circle. The King and his advisers outwitted her by obtaining a court injunction in chambers, that is at a hearing not held in public, restraining her from publishing the letters or any extracts from them. She caved in and returned the letters 'with splendid generosity', she said. 'I have done nothing with these letters, and have never dreamed of publishing such things. My memoirs are my own affair, and every incident of these ten years of close friendship with King Edward are in my brain and memory . . .'. When she eventually wrote her autobiography, 15 years later, it was innocuous in the extreme. She claimed, piously, that she had not for a moment thought of revealing any confidences or betraying those who had been her close friends.

Daisy professed to be a socialist, and unsuccessfully stood as Labour candidate in a by-election in 1923. She was defeated by the future prime minister, Anthony Eden. Her husband died penniless in 1924. Daisy offered her home, Easton Lodge, which she could scarcely afford to maintain, to the Labour Party for its use, and it held various conferences there. She died in July 1938.

What is one to make of episodes such as this, and how did the behaviour of those considered to be the cream of Society, the Prince of Wales and all who looked to him as their social leader, compare with that of the worst of the moneylenders? The offence of Lord William Nevill in the eyes of Society was not that he had committed criminal fraud on his friend Spender Clay and on Sam, but that he had let the side down. Lord and Lady Charles Beresford made blackmailing threats to the prime minister of the day and to the future King of England, and then humiliatingly retreated. Aylesford and Lord Randolph Churchill were equally guilty of blackmailing intentions. Yet all were eventually received back into the fold. Moral censure was directed at the alleged excesses of the moneylenders (who were looked down upon by most of those mentioned), but should their misdeeds be considered any worse than those of the close friends of the prince?

They did not threaten to bring down governments, nor boast, as Lord Randolph did, that he had the Crown of England in his pocket.

The fortunes of some families were secured, partially at least, by timely advances from Sam, and there are living today men and women who are enjoying the fruits of the commercial transactions their ancestors entered into with him. The Cholmondeley family found themselves in particular straits in the 1880s, and the third earl failed in his attempt to dispose of their Houghton estate in Norfolk; there were simply no buyers in the market. Edward VII thought about taking a lease for his son, the future George V, but found it 'frightfully neglected owing to poverty'. The third earl was succeeded by his grandson, who sought help from Sam and took large loans in 1891 and 1893, and continued to borrow regularly until Sam's death. Somehow the estate survived, and the family's fortunes were revived when the fourth earl's heir, Lord Rocksavage, married Miss Sybil Sassoon in 1913. The Cholmondeleys thus joined the many old English families who introduced Jewish blood into their ranks, families such as those of the dukes of Norfolk, of Roxburghe, of St Albans and of Wellington; the earls of Orkney, Derby, Rosebery, Crawford and Southampton; the marquises of Mountbatten, of Crewe and of Salisbury; Viscounts Halifax and Galway; Lord Saye and Sele, Lord Grey de Ruthyn, Lord Auckland, Lord Sherborne and Lord St Davids. Perhaps if Sam had not been there to support the tottering edifice, the Cholmondeley fortune might have been dissipated beyond repair before the beautiful Sybil came along. She had received sound advice from her father. In his will he had impressed on her 'the necessity of avoiding all extravagance and gambling'. She appears to have passed the advice on to her son. When he died in 1990 he left £118 million.

Sam numbered among his clients many men holding illustrious foreign titles, including Prince Henry of Hess, Count Trautmansdorf, Count Sierstorpff and of course Prince Kinski, but the highest-ranking member of the English aristocracy who engaged in business with him was the eighth duke of Beaufort. The Beaufort family could trace their roots back to the fourteenth century, and occupied a splendid Palladian mansion in Badminton as their home from 1682, where the first duke kept a household of over 200. It was remodelled by William Kent in the 1740s and, set in a landscape designed by

Capability Brown, became and remains to this day famous as a centre of hunting and riding, and for its internationally recognised annual Horse Trials. One of the first packs of hounds in the country was bred and kept there in the early eighteenth century. In 1853, the year in which he succeeded to the title, the eighth duke hunted on no less than 102 days. But despite the ownership of vast tracts of land – even today the Beaufort estates run to more than 40,000 acres in Wales, in addition to 19,000 at Badminton – and a high annual income (at least £30,000 in the early eighteenth century), the family found themselves in the 1840s in financial difficulties. In 1848, the year in which the Duke of Buckingham fell into bankruptcy, the seventh duke of Beaufort was tottering on the edge.

Lavish expenditure, largely on the maintenance of the home and entertainment, drove the seventh dDuke to take a bridging loan of £24,000 from Hoare's Bank in 1849. It was a measure of Sam's success not only as a moneylender, but effectively as he became in his later career a private personal banker to the English aristocracy, that when the eighth duke needed money he turned to him rather than to a bank or insurance company.

Henry Charles Fitzroy, the eighth duke, was one of the most likeable grandees of his time. He married Lady Georgina Curzon, the daughter of Earl Howe. The family entertained the Prince and Princess of Wales quite frequently at Badminton. The duke became an equerry of the prince, was Master of the Horse in 1858–59 and again from 1866 to 1868, became Lord Lieutenant of Monmouthshire, and served as the Member of Parliament for East Gloucestershire from 1842 to 1856. He and his wife drove in a rather patrician way through the poorest quarter of Bristol because he believed it gave the people pleasure to see them. During the Chetwynd/Durham libel suit he joined Sam and his coterie of racecourse friends in staunchly supporting Chetwynd; indeed, he could scarce speak to those who opposed him. Altogether he was a sociable and well-known figure among the upper reaches of Society, experienced in affairs, and a far cry from the likes of the fourth marquis of Ailesbury.

The Beauforts had unfortunate experiences with two of their sons, Lord Henry and Lord Arthur Somerset, both of whom went into exile abroad to avoid scandals. Whether by coincidence or not, it was at this very time, in 1889, that the duke indulged in some of his heaviest borrowing from Sam, £29,700 in January of that year, and a further £6,000 in July. Sam would surely have lent a sympathetic ear to his problems. The duke died in 1899, and as Sam's estate had no claim outstanding in 1901, it would appear that by then the duke's debt to Sam had been repaid, and presumably their business dealings were mutually satisfactory.

If the Duke of Beaufort was the highest-ranking of Sam's clients, Reginald Baliol Brett, second Viscount Esher, was the most influential. Many considered him to be the *éminence grise* behind the throne. Certainly he enjoyed the confidence not only of Edward, as Prince of Wales and when he became king, but also of the prince's mother, Queen Victoria; his wife, Queen Alexandra; and his son, George V. He was the intimate of every prime minister from Rosebery to Baldwin, but always declined high office, preferring to manipulate events from backstage. During his quite glittering career he was asked to write Disraeli's biography and to edit the *Daily News*, but he refused. The Tories offered him the Secretaryship of War, and the Liberals the Viceroyalty of India, but he rejected the offers. He believed his gifts were best exercised behind the scenes and he could not be tempted into the public limelight.

Esher became a close friend of the fourth Earl Grey (yet another of those who suffered financially from investing in some of Moreton Frewen's more madcap schemes) and it was through him that, while still an undergraduate, he was introduced to the Prince of Wales and eventually became a frequent visitor to Marlborough House. Esher's marriage in 1879 to the daughter of the Belgian ambassador to London brought him into Queen Victoria's inner circle. He had an innate ability to advance his own career by exploiting the genuine friendships that he formed with those in the inner circles of society and politics.

He was born in 1852, the son of the first Viscount Esher, the Master of the Rolls, and succeeded to the title on his father's death in 1899. After Eton and Trinity College, Cambridge, he spent some time as a lieutenant in the Militia before becoming private secretary to the Marquis of Hartington (later the eighth duke of Devonshire), who was then the leader of the Liberal Party following Gladstone's resignation. Hartington refused the offer of premiership, and during the period that Esher served him was Secretary of State for India and then

Secretary of State for War, so that the young Esher served his apprenticeship in the very midst of those who exercised political power in the land. Esher was elected Member of Parliament for Penryn and Falmouth and served from 1880 to 1885, but he found himself unsuited to the rough and tumble of parliamentary life. In 1901 Edward appointed him Deputy-Constable and Lieutenant-Governor of Windsor Castle, and he exercised a remarkable influence over the King during the early years of his reign. It was the ever tactful Esher who, at the express request of Queen Alexandra, was selected to break the news to Daisy Brooke that her close friendship with Edward would have to cease once he was on the throne. After Edward's death he and Lord Francis Knollys (1837–1924), Edward's private secretary from 1870, undertook the task of searching out and destroying the King's personal and private correspondence, particularly that which had passed between him and his numerous lady friends. It was they who were responsible for outmanoeuvring Daisy when she subsequently tried to blackmail King George V by publishing his father's letters.

Esher was one of the small group – Sir Ernest Cassel, Lord Farquhar (Master of the Royal Household and future friend of Ada) and Sir Dighton Probyn (Keeper of the Privy Purse) being the other members – who organised King Edward's finances so successfully that he was relieved of all encumbrances and became financially stable. This was a remarkable position for Esher to have filled, because he had the greatest difficulty in managing his own financial affairs. He loved horse racing, and became an addict after seeing his first Derby in 1878. It was a mania with him, and he had several horses in training. In October 1881, after suffering particularly heavy losses at Newmarket, he wrote to his wife: 'My darling ... I *must* get it back and I shall have a plunge on *Kermesse* tomorrow. If she loses we must go to the workhouse.' He was aware of the pitfalls of the sport, and had some knowledge of the traps awaiting the unwary. Telling his wife of one particular journey by train to Newmarket, he wrote: 'When we had got half way, one of the companions produced three cards and turned out to be a Professor of the three card trick. He got about £20 out of his fellow travellers before we reached Newmarket. I did not contribute to his earnings ...'. But knowledge of the traps, and avoiding them, are two different things. In the 1890s he was persuaded to be his own trainer, but he was never very successful. He was too fastidious to contend with the coarse ways of the Turf, and in any event he was not rich enough.

Esher accumulated debts and had to turn to his father for help. But the gift of £3,000 the former Master of the Rolls gave him to settle his affairs was not enough. Indeed, it is doubtful whether his father knew the full extent of his son's debts, for Esher had turned to Sam, and had become a client of his, from at least 1891, and by 1901 he owed £30,000, more than one million pounds at today's values. No. 17 Cork Street became almost as familiar to Esher as the Houses of Parliament, Marlborough House and Windsor Castle, and there must have been many occasions when he arrived on Sam's doorstep directly from one or the other of these centres of power. Sam's estate received regular repayments of the debt, and when Lord Esher died in 1930 his estate was shown as worth £40,000.

Sir Charles Henry John Chetwynd-Talbot, KCVO, the twentieth earl of Shrewsbury, the premier earl of England and Hereditary Great Seneschal of Ireland, was born in 1860. He was educated at Eton and became a keen lover of outdoor sports, particularly riding. He drove a smart four-in-hand, and ran the Greyhound coach from Buxton to Alton Towers daily for several years, and he was a first-rate polo player. He introduced cabs fitted with noiseless tyres to London and Paris, a particular boon because the clatter of thousands of horses' hooves and the din occasioned by the contact of solid metal or wooden wheels upon cobbled roads made both towns much noisier then than they are now, despite the density and clamour of present-day traffic. When, as a mere youth, he succeeded to his title in 1877, his family owned over 35,000 acres in Stafford, Chester, Worcester, Salop and Derby worth over £60,000 a year, and that did not include the value of the minerals under 2,000 acres in Glamorgan. In 1880 *Vanity Fair* said that he was, not surprisingly, the object of much female admiration. 'What he may become no man can tell', but they described his manners as good, his disposition amiable, and said that he was a gentleman who possessed a strain of shrewdness which had already stood him in good stead. He was very sound, not one to be underestimated, and he took sensible steps to repair the family fortunes.

On the death of the nineteenth earl the family's finances were in disarray, and a receiver was appointed by the Chancery Division of the High Court to collect income from the estate to pay off a list of admitted debts. The twentieth earl proved an excellent manager of the estate, and during the 1880s and early 1890s, when most landowners were reining back on their outgoings, he expended large sums on the farms and cottages to keep them in first-rate order. It was a stark contrast to the situation prevailing at Savernake while the fourth marquis of Ailesbury was in possession.

He funded the work by taking mortgages over various properties in a somewhat piecemeal fashion. In 1894 he applied to the Royal Insurance Company for a £200,000 loan on the security of his Ingestre Estate in Staffordshire. The survey they commissioned from Messrs Lofts and Warner, a Mayfair firm who specialised in the field, gave his application glowing approval. It showed that the 8,000 acres then produced a net income of almost £13,000. All the farm buildings were modern and in good repair, and there was a good class of tenant. The neighbourhood was attractive, as the estate was surrounded by those of the earls of Lichfield, Harrowby, Ferrers and Hatherton, and there was excellent shooting and several packs of hounds. Ingestre Hall (no longer the family seat) was described as an imposing mansion standing in a fine park. The accommodation was of a very superior character with every convenience and all the luxurious appliances desirable for a nobleman's establishment, including modern sanitary arrangements, electric light service, and ample supply of water and hydrants for protection against fire. The stabling, with stalls and boxes for 50 horses, constituted perhaps the finest range in England. Messrs Lofts and Warner valued the property at £330,000 or thereabouts and considered it ample security for a loan of £200,000. They concluded their report:

> ... we think it right to refer to the depressed state of the property market at the present time, and it might be suggested it would be difficult to realise the above sum, but insamuch as the borrower is the possessor of very large entailed estates in the same county we do not think it at all probable that this property would ever come into the market, and moreover the margin both as regards rental and capitalized value is a very ample one and we can confidently recommend the loan.

It would appear that the loan did not eventuate. Instead the earl took out a mortgage of £260,000 with the Loan Trustees of the Life Association of Scotland, £35,000 with the Legal & General Society, and £30,000 with others, not only on the security of Ingestre but also on other properties. Both the earl and his wife had also, from time to time, taken loans from their solicitors at six per cent.

In 1898 he decided to bring all the mortgages under one head, and to reduce the rate of interest he was then paying if at all possible. He approached Sam. He was already a client, having borrowed comparatively small sums of £1,000 to £2,000 from 1893 or perhaps even earlier, and in July 1896 Sam had advanced him £11,000. On this occasion, however, he was seeking no less than £325,000 in order to pay off his existing borrowings and consolidate them. It was an extraordinary sum to ask of an individual lender. Very few, if any, of the banks or insurance companies would have considered such an application. Bankers tended not to lock up large sums of money in fixed loans on the security of landed property, that being a class of business more in the way of insurance companies at that period. But even such a large company as the Royal Exchange Assurance had less out on mortgage than Sam. There could not have been another person in the whole of the country who could have been approached with any prospect of receiving a positive reply. On 18 January Sam signed a contract with the earl agreeing to advance the £325,000. It was obviously a matter in which the legal formalities would necessarily take some time, and as the earl was apparently rather strapped for cash a cheque for £1,000 was given immediately, and another £5,000 a few weeks later, well before any security was completed.

There were two factors that made this large transaction even more remarkable; Sam agreed to accept repayments over ten years at the very modest rate of three per cent, absorbing the costs himself; and the deal was negotiated and completed during the period when he was heavily involved elsewhere and very much in the public eye, attracting the most extensive, and most adverse, press coverage of his career. His highly publicised civil action against Spender Clay had concluded before the Lord Chief Justice and a jury just three weeks earlier. Sir George then wrote his letter to *The Times* branding Sam as a curse to society. On 24 January just two days after the contract with Shrewsbury was signed, Lord William Nevill was arrested and made the

277

first of his appearances at Bow Street. Sam gave his evidence on 31 January and within three weeks Nevill had been sentenced to his five years' imprisonment at the Old Bailey, with Sam a prominent spectator sitting in the centre of the court. His presence there was reported in all the national and London papers. The Select Committee on Moneylending was in session, and on 10 March Sir George gave his evidence in the House of Commons and unleashed his attack on Sam. On 22 March his further letter to *The Times* was printed, inviting Sam to sue for libel. Yet all this while, Sam was quietly and confidentially arranging and completing the largest transaction of his career with an eminent and respected pillar of society. It is no wonder he could then afford to take a break in Monte Carlo, secure in the knowledge that there was nothing that Sir George could say or do which would diminish the trust Sam's clients had in him.

In 1901 the earl owed Sam's estate £367,911, making him its largest debtor. The mortgage was obviously extended beyond ten years, as the repayments continued until well after the First World War ended. From the examples of Esher and Shrewsbury, it can safely be said that there was no one in the land so highly placed, and so influential, that he might not have recourse to Sam.

18 · Retirement

For almost two years Sam had been slowly running his business down. In June 1900, at the age of 62, he underwrote his last loan and retired. There is no reason to suppose that the decision was affected in any way by the public criticisms which had been made; had they worried him to any great extent he would have left his profession long before; but it may be that, despite what he had told Blumenfeld, the parliamentary debates on the Moneylending Bill helped him to make up his mind. The comparatively short era of complete freedom for moneylending and moneylenders was approaching its end, and the new Act would make it much more difficult to engage in the profession. It would be of no avail to a moneylender that he had obtained the seal or signature of a borrower. If the court was of the opinion that the rate of interest was excessive, it would have the power to overturn the agreement, and would thereby be introducing uncertainty into every moneylending contract. This may have been an element in his thinking, but, most probably, he simply felt that he had worked long enough – almost 50 years – and that the time was ripe to bow out of the everyday hassle of business, much as he had enjoyed it.

The money he had out on loan, on mortgages, bonds, bills and promissory notes would clearly take several years to collect. But his trusted clerk, Henry William Gilbey, and the few other staff at Cork Street, were well capable of dealing with this without his presence. He was not dependent on payment of the debts owing to him to maintain his style of living; his other readily realisable assets, totalling about £1 million, and the income they generated, were more than sufficient for the purpose. He once told the Hon. George Lambton, who asked him whether he was a very rich man, 'Well, my boy' (his favourite expression) 'it depends what you call a rich man, but I can tell you this, that I have a great deal more money than I want, and if it was not

279

for Monte Carlo and Ostend, where I always lose heavily, I don't know how I should get rid of it.'

Immediately ahead of him when he retired was his social season of racing at Ascot, Goodwood and Brighton; the river at Maidenhead; the theatre; and time to be spent with Ada, her brothers and sisters, nephews and nieces (of whom he was extremely fond), with his large circle of friends and acquaintances, or, if the fancy took him, at the casino. Though the average expectation of life for a man was then 48 years and for a woman 52 years, he was in good health, and had every prospect of many happy years of retirement. He was not, however, to enjoy it for long.

That November Lord Roberts, the commander-in-chief of the British Forces in South Africa, having, as he thought, effectively defeated the Boers, left Lord Kitchener behind to complete the conquest. Roberts returned to England, and on Thursday, 3 January 1901, a triumphal procession through London was arranged. There was an ominous start to the day. As morning broke London was enveloped in a pungent yellow fog of the type happily now seen only in films or on television. There was little promise that there would be favourable conditions for the procession, which started late because Lord Roberts was delayed by the weather, both on his journey to Southampton and from there to Paddington. Fortunately the fog dispersed about nine o'clock, to be replaced by a lingering grey mist which was sufficiently thin to allow the spectators in the streets to see the passing show clearly; but the day remained very cold. He was met at the station by the Prince and Princess of Wales, the Duke and Duchess of York, Princess Victoria of Wales, the Duke of Connaught and the Duke and Duchess of Teck. The band struck up 'See the Conquering Hero Comes' and Lord Roberts left, preceded by the royal outriders and accompanied by an escort of the 10th Hussars. Immediately behind rode six Indian orderlies, 'splendid fellows whose striking uniforms and stalwart soldierly bearing attracted universal attention and admiration'. The troop-lined route to Buckingham Palace was by way of Sussex Gardens, Bayswater Road, Hyde Park, Piccadilly, St James's Street, Marlborough Gate and the Mall. Balconies, windows, even roofs, were draped in red cloth; flags, bunting and shields of every description were displayed from every vantage position. Sam, as patriotic as the next man, was watching the parade from an open window of the Berkeley Hotel on the corner of Berkeley Street and Piccadilly, when he was suddenly seized with a spasm of the heart.

His doctor, Dr Henry Dutch, had his practice in Berkeley Street, and was immediately summoned. Sam was taken home, and Dr Dutch gave him his constant attention, by day and night. Eminent consultants, Sir Douglas Powell and Sir William Broadbent, were called in. Apart from Ada and immediate family, Sam was allowed to see only Sydney and Gilby. The foggy weather prevailed for some days and caused Sam to have an attack of asthma. Despite this he rallied, and appeared to be responding well to treatment when, without warning, he succumbed and died, on Sunday, 13 January at 1.30 in the morning. Ada was with him at his last moment. Dr Dutch certified the cause of death of Samuel Lewis, financier, of 23 Grosvenor Square, as angina pectoris.

The many messages of sympathy and condolence received by Ada were remarkable both for their number and the exalted rank and position of the senders. In accordance with Jewish custom, the burial followed shortly afterwards, on the following Wednesday at the Hoop Lane cemetery of the West London Synagogue, 'a pretty little ground situated about midway between Finchley and Hendon station' (Golders Green Crematorium is now immediately opposite it). A large group of mourners gathered at No. 23, and the line of carriages stretched right round the Square. Sam had requested that everything should be conducted as privately as possible. The curtains were drawn, and no information was given to the waiting press as to the names of those who were attending the funeral. According to the correspondent of the *Star* some were moneylenders, others were dealers in *objets d'art*, diamond merchants, jewellers, stockbrokers, and some connected with the theatrical profession, mainly on its financial side. They were, he said, 'keen-looking, well-groomed, and prosperous-looking'. Apart from the mourners, there was a crowd outside consisting largely of grooms, ostlers, coachmen and gentlemen's servants, who were employed in the houses in the Square. The opinion generally expressed among them was that Sam 'wasn't a bad sort'. The cortège moved off on its journey, with Sam resting in a simple coffin of polished oak, with just one wreath of violets and lilies-of-the-valley upon it. At the cemetery the ceremony and service

281

performed by the Reverend Isidore Harris were of the utmost simplicity.

The inscription on Sam's tombstone reads:

> Farewell Good Husband and Friend
> The Lord Redeemeth the Soul of His Servants
> Ps.XXXIV 23
> Samuel Lewis
> Passed Away
> 13th Jan 1901
> In his 63rd year

Nine days later Queen Victoria died. Sam's life had matched the length of her reign almost exactly, born within months of its start and dying within days of its end.

The Times, brief and to the point, simply recorded the death 'at his Grosvenor Square residence of Mr. Samuel Lewis, the well-known moneylender'. Other papers carried much fuller accounts, and on the whole he received what would nowadays be called 'a good press', though bearing in mind the contemporary adherence of most newspapers to the motto *de mortuis nil nisi bonum*, the obituaries must be read in that context. The *Telegraph* described him as 'the most favourably-known member of the moneylending profession, as his business was, perhaps. the most extensive of the kind in this or any other country ... In the latter years of Mr. Samuel Lewis's life his name had virtually become a household word.' The *Daily Mail* and *The World* used the same headline, 'The Prince of Usurers'; to the *Morning Leader* he was 'Moneylender to the aristocrats and evader of the courts', and to the *Daily Express*, 'the greatest private moneylender in the world ... standing quite at the top of his profession'. It added that scarcely anyone was too highly placed to have escaped the reputation of having at one time or another gone to Sam Lewis for pecuniary assistance. For the *Weekly Budget* he was 'undoubtedly "uncle" – for great consideration – to the Upper Ten'. The papers unanimously took the line that though his charges were high, his methods were straightforward and honest, and tinged at times with generosity. The *Daily Mail* put it this way:

He belonged to a profession deservedly unpopular, but he was at the head of it, and not to be confused with practitioners of the Gordon type. He did not prey upon the poor and needy, but lived upon the follies of his time.

He said once that he had a million of money on paper, and every name on it in *'Debrett'*, and there is little reason to doubt the statement. He was the society moneylender, and few of the young spendthrifts who have dragged honoured family names into the bankruptcy and other courts got there without a little friendly assistance from Sam Lewis.

He was not entirely rapacious, nor altogether heartless, but when once he had established a monetary connection with a man it was not his fault if the intimacy, usually so satisfactory in its results to Sam Lewis, were broken off. When once he had made an agreement with a man he kept him to it to the very letter.

This last comment seems rather unfair on Sam, given the numerous occasions where he was quite prepared to forgo his dues if his debtor had fallen on hard times.

The *Mail* said 'he could, if he chose, be extremely engaging in a somewhat rough and ready way, but, on the other hand, if he had no desire to make himself agreeable he took no pains to disguise the fact. He had a good sense of humour and his ready wit stood him in good stead'. It then tried to analyse his motives, and considered that after he had acquired, many years before, more money than he knew what to do with, he continued to practise his 'usurious arts' not so much out of greed or gain, but from a strange and half-humorous principle he had evolved out of his 'curious and exceedingly perverse nature' of teaching a lesson to 'the rich worldling, the gullible youth'. This may well have hit the mark. So many of his clients were young men whose start in life was startlingly different from his own. They had been born with a silver, or at least a silver-plated, spoon in their mouths, and were quite unaware of the difficulties and problems facing the majority of the population; and they had no real appreciation of just how lucky they had been in their privileged birth and upbringing. Perhaps he was wreaking revenge on them on behalf of all those who, beginning as he began, never escaped from their poverty.

The *Telegraph* referred to his very wide circle of clients and of friends, and added that it was not too much to say that many of the former passed into the latter category owing largely to the direct and open character of his business transactions:

> It has been remarked that his aim was to do business with those who were thoroughly aware of the nature of the bargain they proposed contracting, and who could at the same time appreciate the risk he was incurring. Sharp man of the world as he was, he was not incapable of generosity even in a strictly business matter. As a consequence even those who paid most dearly for his help never spoke but with good-natured admiration of him, and long after they had ceased to need assistance remained on a friendly footing with him; in many instances becoming frequent visitors at his town house.

They reported that when he was asked what motto he would choose should it be necessary for him to select one, he suggested 'I lend to the Lord, and give to the Poor'.

Sam's formerly harsh critic, *The World*, which had so severely castigated him and the other 'West End Usurers' 25 years earlier, thought the news of his death would be received with mixed feelings by many who were brought into contact with him in the course of his 'undeniably useful, if not wholly beneficent career'. They compared him with the most distinguished members of another and more predatory calling – that of the old time 'knights of the road', the highwaymen:

> He brought to his profession a personal bonhomie, a spasmodic generosity, and an occasional touch of incongruous sentiment, which in a way commended him even to the most luckless victims of his peculiar financial genius ...

Perhaps the most surprising obituary was that in *Truth*, written by his one-time adversary, Labouchere:

> The late Mr. Sam Lewis was a most remarkable man, and he occupied for many years a unique position in London. I have not often had occasion to speak in favour of a moneylender, but Mr. Lewis was in most ways unlike all others of his class. It may have been his policy to make friends even of his own clients; but I can safely say that, though I have met many who have met with him

for extrication from their pecuniary embarrassments, I never heard from anybody a suggestion that he had not dealt fairly and regularly. His charges were high, and he amassed an enormous fortune out of the necessities of his fellow creatures – which is not necessarily a reproach, for all fortunes are made by the same process. But – so far as my knowledge goes – I am glad to say it is only second hand knowledge – he always made the borrower understand clearly what he had to pay and what he had to receive, which was hard cash and not cigars, jewellery or 'Old Masters'; To this he owed the fact that he carried on for many years the largest moneylending business in the West End without making enemies or creating a scandal. No doubt he also owed his success to his genial manner and his reputation for kind-heartedness, a reputation which, I think, he deserved.

Labouchere was wrong about Sam having made no enemies. He had overlooked Sir George Lewis, for one; and it could be that it was Sir George who was right about Sam, and all the others who were out of step. Sir George doubtless shed no tears on learning of Sam's death, and must have found the praise heaped on him rather galling. He probably deeply resented Sam's success in establishing friendships with so many whose company he himself enjoyed.

None of those who had dealt with Sam and who afterwards wrote about their experiences had a bad word to say about him. Benzon said he had no complaints; Lonsdale that Sam was benevolent; Lambton that he was the straightest moneylender of all time; Rosslyn that no man could have been fairer; and Nevill that he was straightforward. The various tributes to his basic honesty would have been very welcome to Sam, and no doubt were to Ada. He was well aware of, and cultivated, the reputation that he had gained for straight dealing, and he disclosed to his confidants that it was a matter of great pride to him that he was accepted as a man of his word, which indeed he was.

The most fulsome and sentimental tribute was in the *Jewish Chronicle*. Written by his solicitor and friend, Algernon Sydney, it outlined Sam's humble beginnings and led to the time when his financial dealings were on so big a scale that his name had become almost a household word in social circles. He said that Sam had accumulated a vast fortune in what was a disagreeable business at its best, but no one could charge him with ever having tried to gain a dishonest advantage of those with whom he had financial relations. Sam had risen to the commanding position he occupied by the exercise of the same qualities which would lead to success in any calling – shrewdness, enterprise, determined will, good nature, pleasant manners and absolute straightforwardness. It was not the amounts in which he dealt, nor the fortune he accumulated, which had gained him the title of 'Prince of Moneylenders'; it was the princely way in which he conducted his business. It was no wonder, Sydney said, that so many of his clients passed into the category of friends, and visited him at his town house in Grosvenor Square.

People of high position flocked to Sam Lewis because they could trust him ... Undoubtedly Mr. Lewis's terms were high. In the case of clients with large means and more especially if they tried to get the better of him, he held the debtors to the letter of their agreement. But to poor and unfortunate debtors he was generous to a degree which might seem incredible if only half of his kindness was related ...

Sam Lewis was one of the most kind-hearted and charitable of men. He had shown himself so ever since his boyhood, when, having to support his mother, he undertook to allow her a pound a week ... It was often more than he could manage, though no one travelled the country more diligently than he. On one occasion he shed bitter tears because his week's labours had brought him only 15/- and his mother would have to go short ...

I have always maintained that a man should be judged not by his calling, but by what he is in himself. His particular vocation may be due to circumstances of which the general public have no know-ledge. The spirit in which he exercises it is the chief point to consider. Therefore while I have known intimately all sorts and conditions of people from the highest communal worthies down-wards, I do not hesitate to say that there was more real goodness in Sam Lewis's little finger than in the whole body of many a man who has gone down to the grave in a halo of sanctity, and whom the world has reverenced as a combination of all the virtues.

On the same page as this obituary the *Jewish Chronicle*, quite properly, included the information that Sydney was to receive a legacy of £15,000. Obviously such a generous gift was capable of colouring Sydney's judgment, and all due allowance must be made for that; but nevertheless what he wrote has the ring of truth. As Sam's solicitor and friend for more than 20 years, he was in a good position to know.

It might perhaps be said that Sam had so much money that he could afford to be generous to those in difficulties, but there have been many men in his position who were not. But was Sydney begging the question? It is undoubtedly true that a man should be judged by what he is, but what if he adopts an immoral calling? What if he becomes a thief, or worse? How laudatory should obituaries be of a blackmailer who donated most of his ill-gotten gains to charity? The argument was over whether moneylending as practised by the West End moneylenders was inherently immoral, and whether there could be any excuse for entering the profession.

The *Jewish Chronicle*, while admitting that most of Sam's obituaries were favourable and showed that he must have had many good qualities, could not resist harking back to its long-held fears and worries about the effect of the activities of Jewish moneylenders on the reputation and standing of the Jewish community. In its editorial column it said that though they acknowledged that Sam was a philanthropist of the first rank, a friend and benefactor of the poor, none the less they would prefer for the sake of the good name of the Jewish community that there were no Jewish moneylenders at all, even of the Sam Lewis type:

For, whether practised with harshness or geniality, usury is one of the most injurious occupations. It benefits no-one to borrow for the purposes of debauchery at 60%. Lending money at commercial rates is quite another matter, and for many years the two occupations were almost the only trades open to Jews. Usury came thus to be regarded as the monopoly of the Jewish race. Under better treatment from the law, the conscience of the community has risen in protest against businesses of a demoralising character, and [Jewish] public opinion on the subject has become progressively more pronounced. In recent times institutions like the Religious Education Board have felt constrained to go to the length of refusing donations from Jewish moneylenders. A wholesome deterrent effect has thus been exercised upon the younger members of the community, which we believe will have the effect in the course of a generation or two of causing the profession to disappear from our midst.

On one score, at least, they need not have worried; there was never to be another Sam Lewis.

19 · Sam's will

Charity shall cover the multitude of sins.
First Epistle General of Peter iii: 8

He hath dispensed, he hath given to the needy,
His righteousness endureth for ever.
Inscription on memorial tablet to Samuel Lewis at
Dublin Jewish Board of Guardians

Money is required from the cradle to the grave –
yes even after the grave is closed you need money to keep
the tombstone and flowers in order, I am afraid.
Mr Mark Wilson, witness before 1925 Select Committee
of House of Lords and House of Commons

The Society of Friends gave sound advice to its members on the subject of making a will. It told them to secure the services of a skilful lawyer of good repute and recommended them to have strict regard to justice and equity, and not to be actuated by caprice or prejudice, or to carry any resentment to the grave. Wills, they added, should not be postponed to the sick bed, 'an improper season to settle our outward affairs, in the painful struggles of nature, even if we should be favoured with a clear understanding, which ought not to be diverted from a solemn consideration of the approaching awful end'. Sam had devoted much of the two years prior to his death to considering the terms of his will, and discussing them with Ada and Sydney. He signed it in September 1900 when he was in good health. Sydney had occupied the position of Sam's principal almoner and charity adviser, a role he subsequently performed for Ada. There is no doubt that he had an influence on the choices they made, and that one of the best ways to their respective charitable pockets was through him.

There were many reports, but few surviving records, of Sam's generosity during his lifetime. He was one of just 17 persons who pledged an annual subscription of £100 or more to the Prince of Wales's Hospital Fund, an obligation he honoured until his death. The *Daily Telegraph* said that as he wandered up and down Bond Street, a favourite pastime of his, every beggar who accosted him was well rewarded, and according to Sydney he always carried a bundle of bank notes in one of his trouser pockets for this very purpose. Sydney said that when asked, Sam expressed real pleasure at having the opportunity of relieving distress, and sometimes he would say, 'It is very kind of you to ask me', and his genial manner left no doubt that he meant what he said. Anyone in genuine distress who called at his office in Cork Street was given some financial help. He must have become known as a 'soft touch', because eventually he had to be protected by his clerks, otherwise the number of applicants would have prevented him from conducting his business. On one occasion when he broke the bank at Monte Carlo, he distributed half of his winnings to the poor in Marseilles. As we have seen, on his visits to Ireland during his earlier peddling days he never left without making donations to deserving charities, Jewish and non-Jewish, and we have already noted his contributions to the charity funds of the Dublin synagogue.

According to *The World*, outside his profession Sam cultivated a reputation for philanthropy, and seemed to have expended in charity a fair proportion of the profit which he extracted from the necessities of his clients, and Labouchere agreed that he had a reputation for kindheartedness. But was this reputation deserved? Was Sydney right when he said that Sam had more goodness in his little finger than there was in the whole body of many a man who had gone to his grave in a halo of sanctity? Or was his alleged generosity a shallow façade, mere show, something he deliberately encouraged and nourished for the outside world? Any doubts that anyone might have had as to his sincerity, and thoughts that he might have cultivated a reputation for philanthropy rather than practised it, were dispelled immediately the terms of his will became known.

His estate was finally sworn at £2,671,094 3s 11d, on which estate duty of just over £200,000 was paid. In current terms this is equivalent to approximately £100 million, an enormous fortune by most standards. It placed him firmly among the wealthiest men in England. The estate consisted of an almost equal division between his stocks, shares and money at the bank; and the money he had out on loan. There was comparatively little tied up in property. His share portfolio, valued at £1,100,000, was widely spread, and included bonds issued by the governments of the Argentine, Brazil, Chile, Egypt, Germany, Hungary, India, Italy, Japan, New Zealand, Portugal, Russia, Spain, the Transvaal and the United States. He held municipal bonds of Mexico City and Toronto, and shares in many railway companies including the Manhattan, the Northern Pacific, the Atcheson Topeka, the Lake Erie and Western, the Mexican Central and the Argentinian Great Western. He was modestly involved in the goldfields of Matabeleland and in South African mining companies. He was quite possibly influenced in his purchase of the gold shares by a friendship with his fellow Pelican Club member, Barney Barnato. Other miscellaneous holdings included the National Telephone Company, the Ritz Hotel Syndicate, the Hurst Park Syndicate and founder shares in Harrods.

The division of the moneys he had out on loan was illuminating. More than £1 million was out secured on the mortgage of property; another £115,000 on bonds, bills and promissory notes. This was indicative of the changing nature of his business. When he started he had placed almost complete reliance upon personal lending at high rates of interest to individuals who had expectations, or who could supply guarantors; but later he advanced most of his money against solid mortgages of land or shares. We know from the Nevill case that to some extent he was still engaged in the former right up until the end of his working life. This was comparatively short-term business; the mortgage lending would have been for a period of years, and was obviously safer, but the rate would have been much closer to that charged by the banks in similar circumstances.

Apart from his homes, Sam had a 91-year lease on some shops and dwelling houses in Kensington High Street which produced a net income of £4,000 (and which were valued for estate duty purposes at £80,000); a warehouse property in Bury Street, St Mary Axe (£4,300); a house called The Paddocks at West Moseley (£4,300); a house in Tooting (£1,900) and two at Clapham ((£1,600); a freehold in Glasgow; and a farm and cottage at Sharnbrook in Bedfordshire (£4,000). The motley character, situation and comparatively low value, of the properties suggest they were obtained on foreclosure or on compounding of debts rather than by a deliberate investment policy.

The figures provide confirmation of Sam's probable annual income during the latter years of his life. His loan book of £1,250,000, divided as it was between the short-term, high-interest loans of between 30 and 40 per cent which turned over several times during a year, and those on mortgage at between 3 and 7 per cent, probably provided an average of about 15 per cent per annum. He had no partners, so that after the expenses of his office, including the commissions he paid for the introduction of business, a reasonable assumption is that his annual income from his profession was in the neighbourhood of £150,000. The £1,250,000 in stocks and shares yielded dividends averaging about four per cent, namely £50,000 a year. Together this gave him £200,000 per annum at a time when income tax was one shilling in the pound, and each pound was worth about £35 in today's terms. He earned in a week more than his father earned during his whole working life.

Of the 36 debtors who had given security for their loans, 20 had £10,000 or less outstanding at the date of Sam's death. These included Sir George Cayley (£5,000), Count Trautmansdorff (£10,000), Lord Gerrard (£10,000) and Lord Clanmorris (£9,000). Sam had a thriving Irish connection: Clanmorris, an Irish peer, had a small estate in Mayo and he was just one of six Irishmen to whom Sam had loaned a total of £200,000. Interestingly, Lord and Lady William Nevill were shown as owing £5,000. This could have been the balance still outstanding from the time of Nevill's imprisonment, or possibly that was forgiven and a new loan advanced to help them in their time of difficulty; the latter would not have been out of keeping with Sam's character. There were eight debts of between £10,000 and £50,000: of these, Lord Esher owed £30,000, Lord Magh £35,000 and Prince Coloredo Mansfeld £50,000. Six were between £50,000 and £100,000.

Edward Wingfield-Stratford, another Irish connection, owed £51,000; Lord Lurgan, the gambling 'aristocratic tout', £52,000; the Marquis of Anglesey the same amount; Lord Essex £55,000. Lord Rosslyn, the friend of the Prince of Wales and backer of Moreton Frewen, was involved for £78,000. General Owen Williams, the Old Etonian equerry to the Prince of Wales, founder of Sandown Park, member of the Jockey Club, commander of 'The Blues', the Household Cavalry, and Conservative Member of Parliament for Great Marlow in Buckinghamshire, owed £142,768. It was not until well after the First World War had ended that this debt was fully repaid. But the largest borrower of all was the twentieth earl of Shrewsbury and Talbot, whose total indebtedness was £370,000.

The £115,000 out on promissory notes was spread over 66 accounts ranging from £100 to £20,000. Ada's brother-in-law, Saville J. Parker, Emmie's husband, owed £19,000. Sir George Lewis had referred to Parker in his evidence to the Select Committee as being one of the usurers in business in the West End, in Sackville Street. In the will Sam's executors were instructed not to call in this debt so long as interest of four per cent was paid. This was Sam's way of continuing to help finance Parker's business while ensuring that Ada received an income from the loan. Count Kinski, Jennie Churchill's lover and suitor, owed £4,000; Hwfa Williams, the general's brother, £2,400; the Hon. George Lambton, £500; the Earl of Dudley, £2,000; Lady Sykes, £5,000; Lieutenant-Colonel Legh, £9,000; Viscount Valletort, £1,300; the Marquis of Cholmondeley, £700; the Marquis of Winchester, £4,000; Baron Ecardstein, £3,700; and Prince Coloredo Mansfeld, again, £11,400. It seems that the Marquis of Downshire, who owed nearly £6,000, must have been a particular friend of Sam and Ada. He led the escort which met Her Royal Highness Princess Christiana when she opened the Ada Lewis Wing of the Maidenhead Hospital which Sam had provided for, and his wife was also a guest at the ceremony.

It is given to very few to be able to distribute such a fortune; for most of us it is an impossible dream. What a man does in his final testament for those he leaves behind can be as indicative and eloquent a testimony of his character as his acts during his lifetime. Sam's sudden death had caused consternation among some of his debtors, and left them wondering whether their loans would immediately be called in. Sam had foreseen this, and gave his executors full discretion regarding collection. They were provided with powers to extend payment of debts, compound them, or release them, and so could adopt the same attitude and spirit towards the debtors as he had done in his lifetime. Many debts were not recovered in full, or at all. On the other hand some debtors made extended payments, and the interest continued to run until the debt was liquidated. From such information as is available about the size of the eventual residuary estate, it would appear that the trustees realised approximately £2,200,000 from the estate, after allowing for the costs of administration which must have been heavy.

He gave just eight per cent of the net estate to family and friends. Ada was bequeathed the houses in Grosvenor Square and Brunswick Terrace, and all the furniture and effects, including horses and carriages, which went with them. The property at Maidenhead was already hers. In addition she received a life interest in the income of the residue of the estate. As the high-interest loans were repaid, the trustees reinvested the money received in more solid, low-interest-bearing shares, but her income from the estate and from her own resources was always more than £100,000 per annum. After her death two-thirds of Sam's residuary estate was to pass to two charities nominated in his will, and the remaining one-third was Ada's to dispose of in her will at her entire discretion. In the event she gave most of that to charity. The result was that about 90 per cent of all the money that Sam left went to charitable organisations.

The approximate breakdown of the distribution of the estate was:

	£
Estate duty	200,000
Family, friends and staff	200,000
Immediate payment to charities	5,500
Payment to named charities to take effect after Ada's death	1,000,000
Two-thirds of residue to named charities to take effect after Ada's death	540,000
One-third of residue at Ada's disposal in her will, most of which went to charity	270,000
Total	2,215,000

The magnitude of Sam's bequest can be gauged by figures given in an article in *The Times* in September 1899. In each of the previous eight years there was in England an annual average total of £1,250,000 in charitable testamentary gifts. Sam provided almost double that on his own.

Ada's brothers and sisters or their husbands, except for Alice, were given handsome legacies. Quite why Alice, who was always referred to as Dotie, received nothing is not clear. She was married to the successful composer and conductor André Messager, and perhaps was considered to be sufficiently well provided for. She was a particular favourite of Ada, and it may be that Ada had agreed with Sam that she would do anything necessary to help Dotie should the need arise.

Those who had served him well were not forgotten. His chief clerk, Henry William Gilbey, received £2,000. All his domestic servants and coachmen, 'whether first or second (including my groom known as "Charlie")' who had been in his service for three years or more were given £100 each. The love and fond memories he still retained for his mother 28 years after her death was shown by a legacy of £2,000 to Agnes Wilton, who had been her companion and nurse. Agnes was only 23 when Sarah Lewis died, and had since married and emigrated to Melbourne. That he should have thought of rewarding her after all that time, and with such a large sum, is a source of credit both to her and to him. He made the gift 'in grateful recognition of the services she rendered to my mother'.

Judaism, as all religions and secular moral codes, has charity as one of its primary tenets; the teachings of Jesus and his disciples on the subject closely parallel those in the Old Testament. Because of his schooling and family upbringing, and his regular attendance at synagogue, Sam would have had the lessons firmly rammed home. He had the added advantage of having experienced the need for charity from the other side of the fence, when he and his sister, his mother and his father, were the beneficiaries of charitable giving.

In the thirteenth century Maimonides provided a code explaining the Jewish conception. It specified eight degrees of charity in descending order of praiseworthiness. The highest was to strengthen the hand of someone in need by making him a loan or a gift, or finding him work, so that he could restore his self-confidence and dignity. The lowest degree was to give grudgingly, and only after being asked. The Jewish attitude is that the genuinely needy are *entitled* to assistance, so that the giving of charity is not a virtue, but a duty. When Leopold Greenberg was editor of the *Jewish Chronicle* during the first part of this century he made the point clear by headlining details of the wills of recalcitrants, 'To charity, nil!' It served to encourage benevolence among those who were to follow. For the Jews charity became not merely an individual matter, a question of individual choice, but one of group concern and responsibility. They recognised that their welfare as a people was involved in the proper care of the sick, the poor, the widow, the orphan and the stranger. The organisations and institutions founded by the English provincial communities of which we have spoken were the embodiments of such beliefs.

Generally speaking, Victorian philanthropists were predominantly composed of members of the commercial, industrial and financial communities. The large aristocratic landowners rarely left large sums to charity. This was perhaps not surprising, given the agricultural decline during the last quarter of the nineteenth century, but the reasons went further than that. The effect of settled estates, and adherence to the traditions of primogeniture, the need they felt to ensure the preservation of the family mansion, to provide the eldest son with the means to uphold his title and the family's honour with due dignity, to contribute to the upkeep of the dowagers, daughters and younger sons – these all necessitated the retention of the bulk of the family wealth within the family. There was little scope for testamental generosity towards strangers. Rt. Hon. William Thomas Spencer, the sixth Earl Fitzwilliam, lived at No. 4 Grosvenor Square, and when he died, just a year after Sam, his estate was of almost identical size. He left nothing to his servants, and nothing to charity; but then if Sam and Ada had had children of their own, their wills would also have been very different.

There were exceptions, of course, and above all it must be remembered that most of the landed gentry regarded support of their local charities as both a duty and a pleasure. Contributions were made towards schools, money given for church repairs, free bread distributed to the poor, and subscriptions given to fuel and clothing charities. They provided allotment gardens for the labourers, and financial, as well as sporting, support to the cricket club – indeed, all local organisations came within their ambit. It has been estimated that during the middle years of the nineteenth century the great estates annually expended between 4 and 7 per cent of their gross income on charitable work, though these contributions generally diminished as the century progressed and the agricultural depression hit hard.

But it was the bankers, the industrialists, the brewers and the large retailers, men such as Guinness, Mount Stephen, David Lewis, Whiteley, Debenham, Gorringe, Morley, Maple and of course Sam, who made the large contributions. To some extent it could be said that the new money was developing a quasi-aristocratic sense of obligation. The motives of those making charitable donations are varied. They might be driven by religious commitment, humanitarianism, social idealism, civic patriotism, personal satisfaction, a desire for self-perpetuation, or a combination of one or more of these. It is true that some sought personal publicity, and for others their driving inspiration was the opportunity it afforded to climb the social ladder. To support charities, particularly those favoured by royalty, was helpful, to say the least, to those who cherished thoughts of a title. Though Sam appeared not to seek glory for himself, he was ambitious for Ada.

Perhaps it is more worthy to dispense charity during one's lifetime rather than make charitable provision in one's will, because then the benefits the gifts bring can be accelerated. John Wesley said: 'If I leave behind me ten pounds (above my debts and my books) you and all mankind bear witness against me that I lived a thief and a robber.' Andrew Carnegie's theory was that a man who died rich died disgraced. Few can be as altruistic as that. Sam took a middle course. He was generous during his lifetime, but the bulk of his charitable dispositions were made in his will. He also believed that charity began at home, and his family and friends, and charities in the localities in which he had lived, were most favoured.

The immediate charitable legacies were small, totalling just £5,500. The remainder were to be paid only after Ada's death: she was 56 years of age at the time, and there was no way of knowing how far in the future her death might be. Eleven charities, 9 of them Jewish, were each to receive £500:

Prince of Wales Hospital Fund
Guy's Hospital
West London Synagogue of British Jews
Board of Guardians for the Relief of the Jewish Poor
The United Synagogue
Jews' Hospital and Orphan Asylum
Jews' Free School

Anglo-Jewish Association
Institution for the Relief of the Indigent Blind of the Jewish
Persuasion
Society for Relieving the Aged Needy of the Jewish Faith
Jewish Soup Kitchen

Those payable after Ada's death were:

£400,000	To his Trustees for establishing dwellings for the poor
£250,000	Prince of Wales's Hospital Fund for London
£100,000	Board of Guardians for the Relief of the Jewish Poor for establishing a Convalescent Cottage Home or Hospital on the Sea Coast in England
£20,000	London Hospital for founding and endowing a ward to be called 'The Ada Lewis Ward'
£20,000	Sisters of Nazareth, Hammersmith
£15,000	To his Trustees for such charitable institution or institutions at Maidenhead or Cookham as the trustees select
£15,000	To his Trustees to be invested, and income for 20 years to be applied for the relief of the Jewish poor in Dublin
£15,000	Homes for Working Girls in London, for establishing a Home for Working Girls in the City or Administrative County of London, to be called 'The Ada Lewis Home'
£10,000	Maidenhead Hospital for founding and endowing a wing to be called 'The Ada Lewis Wing'
£10,000	Guy's Hospital
£10,000	Charing Cross Hospital
£10,000	St George's Hospital
£10,000	St Bartholomew's Hospital
£10,000	St Thomas's Hospital
£10,000	Hospital for Consumption and Diseases of the Chest, Brompton Road
£10,000	Sussex County Hospital, Brighton
£10,000	Metropolitan Hospital
£10,000	University College Hospital
£10,000	Jews' College
£10,000	Board of Guardians for the Relief of the Jewish Poor
£5,000	Evelina Hospital for Sick Children for the purpose of founding a ward to be called 'The Ada Lewis Ward'

£5,000 Paddington Green Children's Hospital for the purpose of founding a ward to be called 'The Ada Lewis Ward'

£5,000 Jewish Soup Kitchen

£5,000 Royal London Ophthalmic Hospital

£2,000 Jews' Deaf and Dumb Home

£2,000 Jews' Hospital and Orphan Asylum

£2,000 Home and Hospital for Jewish Incurables

£2,000 Royal National Lifeboat Institution, to be applied for the benefit of the widows and orphans of men who lose their lives in lifeboat service, or of persons injured while engaged in such services

£2,000 In trust for such society or societies for providing the poor with coals as the Trustees select

£2,000 In trust for such society or societies for providing the poor with soup as the Trustees select

£2,000 Society for Metropolitan Fire Brigade Widows' or Orphans' and General Benefit Fund

£1,000 Blackrock Convalescent Hospital, Brighton

£1,000 Cabdrivers' Benevolent Association

£1,000 British and Foreign Sailors' Society

£1,000 Children's Aid Society

£1,000 Universal Beneficent Society

£500 National Refuges for Homeless and Destitute Children

£500 Home of Rest for Horses

£500 Factory Girls' Country Holiday Fund

£250 Poor Box at each of the City of London Justice Rooms and at each of the Metropolitan Police Courts

The two charities selected by him to benefit from his residuary estate were the Dwellings for the Poor and the Prince of Wales's Hospital Fund. By the time the estate was finally wound up they each received an additional £270,000. Including these payments and the gifts to individual hospitals, the result was that £670,000 was given for housing and just over £750,000 for hospital charities. We shall deal later with the use made of these funds by the main beneficiaries, and explore how far Sam's money is still today bringing comfort and relief to those in need.

In considering Sam's life and his will there is a nice point which can be argued at length by casuists and moralists. Was the greatest happiness of the greatest number served and promoted by Sam relieving the young sparks of the nobility of their wealth? The follies and extravagances of the rich ultimately led to improvement of the lot of the poor. Was Sam an unmitigated rogue with a smile on his face, or a latter-day Robin Hood?

There are clear connections between the gifts Sam made and his experiences in life. The then current popularity of housing and hospital charities were fitting reminders to him of his days spent in Lower Hurst Street; his mother's fear of eviction for non-payment of rent; his young sister's incurable illness. The provision he made for coals for the poor recalls his mother's application to the Birmingham Hebrew Philanthropic Society for this very purpose. Sam used the opportunity to help those who might find themselves in similar circumstances. The gift he made to Agnes Wilton is proof that he never forgot his early days and his humble origins, though it is also clear that he did not go out of his way to tell people about them. Only Sydney, of all those who wrote obituaries of him, knew the details of those times.

With the surprising exception of his birthplace, Birmingham, institutions in all the towns with which he had his main links were beneficiaries. At Brighton, the Sussex County Hospital and the Blackrock Convalescent Hospital; in Dublin, the Jewish poor; in Maidenhead, the Maidenhead Hospital, and £15,000 for such institutions there or in neighbouring Cookham as his trustees chose. London, of course, gained the most. There were 13 named London hospitals, the Prince of Wales's Hospital Fund for London, and the housing charity which, when formed, initially confined itself to dwellings in the metropolis. The overwhelming majority of the gifts were non-denominational. No more than ten per cent of the total was for Jewish charities, and even then the trustees were directed that the convalescent home which was to be built or purchased by the Jewish Board of Guardians 'shall not be confined to persons of the Hebrew faith although persons of that faith shall have the preference over persons not of that faith'.

Certain legacies may have been of extra significance. The £10,000 for the Maidenhead Hospital exactly matched the amount which the Honourable W. W. Astor gave to celebrate his son's coming-of-age just two or three months before Sam signed his will. The £400,000 for housing was double that which Sir Edward Guinness had given his trustees. The £250,000 for the Prince of Wales's Hospital Fund was its largest gift at that date. Perhaps in each of these Sam was trying to prove a point.

It might perhaps be thought that the terms of the will would receive universal acclaim, but some discordant voices were raised. The *Morning Leader* carried an interview with the Secretary of the Hospital Saturday Fund, who 'was in high glee over Mr. Sam Lewis's bequests to London Hospitals' but who none the less raised one mild criticism very familiar to those engaged in charity work:

The only point that marred his pleasure was the manner of selecting the fortunate institutions. Thus, St. Thomas's and St. Bartholomew's, which are fairly prosperous, and the Evelina Hospital for Children, which recently received an enormous bequest from Baron Ferdinand de Rothschild [he had founded the hospital after his wife died in childbirth], and whose revenue and expenditure almost balance, have all received big legacies, but St. Mary's which has an income of £11,000 and an expenditure of £23,000, King's College which has a deficit of some £2,000, and the West London, which serves an enormous and densely populated district, and has practically nothing from invested property, have all been ignored.

'It seems a pity,' said the Hospital Saturday secretary, 'that legacies such as those of Mr. Lewis, are not made in consultation with men who know exactly the relative needs of the various hospitals.' ...

However in many cases the money is badly needed. The Royal London Ophthalmic Hospital, which only the other day was sued for its rates, is likely to find its debts wiped clean away when it gets its legacy. University College Hospital, the Metropolitan, Guy's, and London Hospital are also in real need, and Mr. Sam Lewis's bequests will be a God-send.

There is a danger consequent upon a single very large donation to a charity, particularly if it is given for a specific purpose: it can be counter-productive, and this was touched upon in the 1906 Annual Report of the Governesses' Benevolent Institution, a substantial beneficiary from Ada's will, which urged upon its subscribers the need the institution still had for their support. 'Some during the year have ceased to subscribe on the plea that the Institution can no longer require their help, and this erroneous impression has also proved a serious handicap in gaining the sympathy of fresh supporters. Instances have been known in the history of other charitable societies where munificent gifts such as this have been followed by so general a withdrawal of support as to seriously cripple their power for good.'

There were one or two who took the same view as that adopted by the Glasgow and Birmingham synagogues and the various correspondents of the *Jewish Chronicle* who have been quoted earlier, that it was not right to accept money which had been accumulated from such a tainted source. The *Charity Record and Hospital Times* commented that they could not see why such a suggestion should even present itself, much less be given serious attention. It added:

> If rumour speaks truly, the deceased, although a money lender, did not make his millions by grinding down the widow and the orphan, but out of the follies and out of the reckless extravagancies of gilded youths who could well afford to pay dearly for the accommodation they sought. The hospitals therefore need have no scruples in taking this money and applying it for the benefit of the sick and the poor.

The *Morning Leader* said it 'could not imagine that any of the charitable societies will decline to participate in the windfall, nor is it clear that they should'. There was no report that any of the charities refused to accept Sam's money.

20 · Ada without Sam

There is nothing to suggest that the marriage of Sam and Ada, spanning more than 33 years, was other than happy, despite their disparate interests and differing family backgrounds. True, they had no children of their own, but they both embraced Ada's many nephews and nieces, and great-nephews and nieces, and the content of Sam's will was evidence of his fondness and concern for them. He did not fully share Ada's love of art, music and opera, though he owned one or two good paintings, including a rare Millais landscape, nor Ada his liking for the casino and the race track; but each comfortably accommodated the other's enthusiasms. She was by his side during the frequent attacks made upon him by Sir George Lewis and others. She mixed with high society as he did, and it must have been as hurtful for her as it was for him to see him condemned in the correspondence columns of *The Times* as 'a curse to society and a danger to the community', as a man whose transactions 'approached blackmail'; or in the *Jewish Chronicle* as a 'moneylending vampire' whose activities caused non-Jews to denounce Jews. Sharing the burden of the insults brought them closer together. She could not have anticipated Sam's death, so sudden and unexpected. Fortunately she was a practical woman, capable of dealing with the situation calmly, and with many interests, particularly in the artistic field. She was cushioned by the considerable wealth she now enjoyed, having both her own means and the income of Sam's estate. It was her money which was to be the key to her future life.

Ada had become one of the best-known and most popular hostesses in London, noted for her sumptuous dinners, but formal entertainment was out of the question, at least for the time being. She observed a period of at least six months' formal mourning and busied herself in deciding which of the three houses she would keep. Her first step was to sell the house at Hove, and she instructed her agents, Messrs

Jenner and Dell, to dispose of it. By the turn of the century Brighton was no longer the town of high fashion it had been. It was passing through a period of depression, and did not attract Society in such great numbers, at least not until it recovered somewhat with the advent of the motor-car: then Brighton was an ideal distance for a day's run from London, and the town regained some of its former distinction. Ada acquired a Sharon, and then a Krieger 'motor carriage', but she was still very much a horse person, proud that her carriages and horses were among London's finest. She and Sam had enjoyed the time they spent together in Brighton, but the facilities of the town obviously no longer fitted into the pattern of life she was setting for herself enough to justify retaining the house there. The house and its contents were sold by auction.

She made up her mind to keep 'Woodside', and continue to enjoy the summer seasons at Maidenhead. It appears that she originally also intended to stay on at 23 Grosvenor Square, despite the size of the house and the obviously high cost of living in the Square. (Some idea of the latter can be gained from the provisions of the will of the sixth Earl Fitzwilliam. No. 4 Grosvenor Square had been occupied by the Fitzwilliam family from the time of the fourth earl in 1783. In 1902 the sixth earl gave his trustees power to advance his daughters £10,000 for its upkeep for just 12 months.) There were only five years unexpired on Ada's lease, and in April Sydney called upon the directors of the Grosvenor Estates seeking an extension; but this was refused. Instead Ada turned her attention to No. 16, almost in the centre of the northern side of the Square, the house in which Spender Clay had been living with his mother and stepfather at the time of the Nevill case. The lease ran to September 1941 at a rental of £200 per annum, rising to £400, and she purchased this on 12 August 1901 from Captain The Hon. Henry Charles Denison for £26,750. For her money Ada aquired a home described by the estate agent as 'of moderate size, occupying a very choice position on the sunny side of the Square, directly overlooking the Ornamental Gardens, a few minutes' walk of Hyde Park, Bond Street and Piccadilly, and within easy reach of the Houses of Parliament, the Clubs, Theatres and the resorts of fashion'. Everything, indeed, that a man, or woman, of position could desire.

This 'moderate-sized' house had a frontage to the Square of 32 feet and a total depth of 160 feet. Ada commissioned a great many alterations, the work being carried out by Cubitts to designs by William Flockhart. It was approached through a portico entrance into a marble paved vestibule leading to the entrance hall, and was on four floors, and also had a large basement. The first three floors were serviced by an Otis lift. Sad to relate, the windows on the ground floor needed iron guard bars. There were 11 bedrooms, three bathrooms and two dressing rooms; the main boudoir had Adam ceiling decorations and walls hung in silk; there was a library, a morning room and a very large dining room. Although at that period houses in the Square mainly had white and gold Louis Quinze decorations for their intercommunicating drawing rooms, Ada preferred the Regency style. Her front and back drawing rooms were fitted with embossed recessed fireplaces with ormolu mounted dog stoves, marble mantelpieces, marble hearths and parquet flooring. The front room measured 30 by 24 feet, and the back room 30 by 20 feet. In addition to all this was the servants' hall, butler's bedroom, strong room, butler's pantry, a large kitchen (with a dressing room adjoining), a scullery, spacious wine cellarage, coal cellars, larder and tradesman's entrance. At the rear in George Yard was space for five cars or three loose boxes and a coach house for carriages. There was also a harness room, kitchen, two bedrooms and a bathroom, and stabling belonging to the property at the rear across St George's Yard. Quite adequate, really, for a family of one.

When Sam and Ada moved into the Square their neighbours were almost entirely titled personages. Twenty years later they reflected the changing nature of Society, and were a finely balanced mixture of the traditional aristocracy and the rich newcomers. There were two dukes, two marquises, three earls, six lords, three barons, seven dowagers and seven knights. The plutocrats included Jack Barnato Joel, who owned two Derby winners, a feat Sam would have willingly paid a fortune to emulate; King Edward's great friend Sir Ernest Cassel; and Sir Lionel Phillips, the Londoner who became a mining pioneer in the Transvaal and was one of those sentenced to death because of his involvement in the Jamieson Raid. (He was later reprieved and fined £25,000 instead.) Two other residents who were to play an important role in Ada's future were Sir Horace Brand Farquhar, later the first Viscount Farquhar, and his wife Lady Farquhar.

Ada spent a great deal of time on her charitable activities. She made small contributions to various charities throughout the year, but every March, about the time of the Jewish festival of Passover, she sent money to 80 or 90 charities, sums mostly ranging from three to ten guineas, though many received as much as 100 guineas. The Jewish Boards of Guardians in London and Dublin, the Jewish Soup Kitchen, the Stepney Jewish School and the Jewish Blind were regular recipients, but for the most part she covered the whole spectrum of charitable need, secular and non-secular. She made a large donation to the Building Fund for a new school of Art and Needlework, and was rewarded with a letter of thanks from Princess Christiana.

At the beginning of June 1901 she met Sir Alexander MacKenzie, the principal of the Royal Academy of Music, and funded five scholarships to be awarded annually and allotted at the discretion of the Academy's Committee of Management. The scholarships were, indeed to this day still are, open to British-born subjects of either sex under the age of 22, and the successful candidates are entitled to three years' musical education at the Royal Academy of Music with a contribution towards their fees. Among the early youthful winners were, in 1903, the 12-year-old Myra Hess, later Dame Myra Hess; in 1909 the 14-year-old Harriet Cohen; and in 1912 Giovanni Battista Barbirolli, then 13, and later, of course, Sir John Barbirolli of Hallé fame. At a meeting held on 3 July the Committee resolved to thank not only Ada for her great generosity but also the husband of Ada's niece Zilla Cliffe, Frederick, who had possibly been instrumental in encouraging Ada to make the gift. At a Committee meeting three weeks later it was resolved that Frederick Cliffe should be appointed a Professor of the Academy 'at the highest rate', an example that it was no disadvantage to be related to a favourite relative of Sam and Ada.

Ada spent June and July of 1901 at 'Woodside'. That year there was much to be enjoyed; quite apart from the annual Engineers', the Fishermen's, and the Bray Watermen's Regattas, there was a fete and garden party for the Maidenhead Branch of the Soldiers and Sailors Family Association, held under the patronage of the Scots Guards, and the most select and genteel of all the regattas, that of the Brigade of Guards. For many years there had been a strong connection between the town and the Brigade of Guards, many of whose officers were members of the foremost aristocratic and landowning families in the country. The link was the Guards' Boat Club, which was also to have a decisive impact on Ada's later life. It was founded there in 1865 because of its ideal situation, within convenient rowing distance of Windsor and riding distance of the barracks at Pirbright. At one time it occupied part of the building which is now Skindles Hotel, but in 1903 was moved to a position opposite the island between Maidenhead Bridge and Brunel's railway bridge. Its regatta days were grand occasions, and special trains brought fashionable guests to Taplow Station. The band of a Guards regiment played popular tunes of the day on the Club's lawns, and the brilliantly smart uniforms of the officers and the stylish dresses and large hats of the ladies created a colourful, and very English, occasion. Visitors to the Club included royalty and nobility, other prominent members of English society, and all the leading local families.

In June and July Maidenhead was crowded, and the 1901 season was a particularly successful one. Lord Astor entertained weekend parties at Cliveden; at Taplow Court the Grenfells' guests included Mr Arthur Balfour and the Duchess of Portland. Lady Anglesey and Lady Dudley (whose husbands had been clients of Sam), Prince Soltykoff, the Duke and Duchess of Newcastle, the Duchess of Sutherland and Lord and Lady Castlereagh were just a few of those who came to Maidenhead that year, complemented by other 'dukes and duchesses, cabinet ministers, empire-makers and bookmakers, millionaires and moneylenders, stars of society and stars of the Halls'. But that year, though resident at 'Woodside', Ada did not participate in the festivities – yet nor did she completely hide herself away. Instead, according to the *Maidenhead Advertiser*, she was regularly to be seen on the balcony of her house 'in deepest mourning'.

Despite the sad loss of Sam she had her compensations – as much money as she could possibly want; two beautiful homes; a loving family, many of whom lived close by; her charitable interests; many musical companions, including her private string quintet who regularly met at her home; not one, but two, of her own Stradivarius violins to play upon; the opportunity to travel wherever and whenever she wished; and countless friends and acquaintances. She also pampered herself, and spent several thousands of pounds with Cartier for jewellery, and with Mellier and Steinway for a grand piano.

Just as Sir George Lewis's house in Portland Place provided a welcome for talented, but temporarily impecunious, painters and actors, so Ada's house in Grosvenor Square was the refuge of many a struggling instrumentalist and composer, and practical help was never refused by her in deserving cases. She had long been a devotee of the opera and had a box at Covent Garden which she regularly attended. She was also a regular visitor to the Bayreuth festival, and was one of those who had supported it when it was not as luxurious a town to visit as it subsequently became. Jennie, Lady Randolph Churchill, was there in 1891, and recalled the occasion in her memoirs:

> We spent a delightful week, although, personally, I was suffering agonies with toothache, until I found an unexpected Good Samaritan who sat beside me and who produced cocaine. This lady was no less a person than Mrs. Sam Lewis, wife of the well-known moneylender. An excellent musician she was a godsend to innumerable artists.

Ada's youngest sister, Alice Maude, was once described as 'one of the prettiest girls I ever saw with enough talent and bewitchment in her, to promote a propensity for being betrothed to the well-known in the land of harmony'. She was successively engaged to four such, and ultimately, in 1895, she married André Messager, her final fiancé. Alice, using the *nom de théâtre* Hope Temple, was a composer of ballads with titles such as 'An Old Garden', 'My Lady's Bower', and 'Fond Heart', of the type then popular both in the concert hall and for family circle entertainment. Her husband, whose student she had been, was the music critic of *Le Figaro*, the conductor of the Opéra Comique in Paris, and a composer of note. His operetta *La Basoche* was performed by the D'Oyly Carte Company at the Royal English Opera in London in 1891, and Alice collaborated with him on *Mirette*, which was composed for the Savoy Theatre in 1894. He wrote the music for the ballet *The Two Pigeons*, which was in the recent repertoire of the Royal Ballet. His teachers, Gabriel Fauré and Charles Saint-Saens, remained two of his closest friends. Fauré visited London almost every year between 1892 and 1900 and it is reasonable to assume that Messager introduced him to his sister-in-law, and that he was an honoured guest at Grosvenor Square. Just a week or two after Sam died it was announced that Messager had been appointed artistic director at Covent Garden and the following May was to take up the position, which he held until 1907. With their shared musical interest, and given the closeness of the Davis family, Alice and André must have been a great comfort to Ada in the months following Sam's death.

Ada was the wealthiest widow in England at the time. Handsome, talented and rich – what a catch she was for someone! Neither her religion nor her late husband's notoriety nor the source of her wealth would have been a hindrance to a determined suitor. Perhaps only her age would have been a bar, for 58 then was as 80 or 85 is today, though a fortune hunter would have considered that an advantage. There must have been many eligible males, either single, or more likely widowers, who eyed the prospect, and there was doubtless considerable speculation among her family, friends and outsiders as to whether she would remarry and, if so, who her choice would be. Marriage apart, it was perhaps inevitable that someone would have designs, honourable or otherwise, on her money.

Who could have guessed that one of the first to make his move would be none other than the King of England, Edward VII, though his motive was not personal gain? Ada was shortly to take a step which was to expand her social horizons and put her into contact with the highest in the land. It would mark an advance into an echelon of society which perhaps, because of Sam's profession, she could not have hoped to enter while he was alive.

As already mentioned, Sam left the Prince of Wales's Hospital Fund for London (it changed its name to the King Edward's Hospital Fund for London on 1 January 1902 and is now known as the King's Fund) a quarter of a million pounds plus one-third of his residuary estate. However, neither the original gift, nor any interest on it, was payable to the Fund until Ada's death, and the invested capital would bring Ada approximately £10,000 a year in interest during her lifetime. The Fund was perhaps the principal and most significant contribution that Edward VII made to the welfare of the nation. He was never simply a figurehead, but took an active and prominent part from the outset. During the nineteenth century, and indeed until 1929, the choice for the sick poor in need of hospital treatment, in so far as they had a choice, was between entering a workhouse infirmary or a voluntary hospital. There is no doubt that, notwithstanding continual improvements being made at the infirmaries, the voluntary hospitals were superior in almost every aspect; in treatment, availability of medicines and equipment, ratio of staff to patients, and in the standard of their consultants, doctors and nurses. They also had the added advantage of not being tainted in the eyes of the patients with the Poor Law. Some voluntary hospitals had munificent endowments, but most London hospitals depended for the bulk of their capital and current expenditure upon voluntary contributions from the public, in the form of subscriptions, donations, payments by patients (from the late nineteenth century) and income from investments, together with support from the then two main London hospital funds, the Metropolitan Hospital Sunday Fund and the Hospital Saturday Fund, both founded in 1873.

Medical science advanced rapidly during the last quarter of the century and new techniques, medicines and equipment – such as X-rays, discovered by Wilhelm Roentgen in 1895 – became available. The expectation of patients rose, but the improvements, though welcome, were expensive. Costs rapidly outstripped income, and there never was a period when the voluntary hospitals were entirely free from financial worry; most, at one time or another, had to close beds, or wards, or even whole wings. It was becoming increasingly difficult to tap fresh sources of income. But what the ordinary mortal was unable to achieve, royalty could. When, in 1897, Edward's mother, Queen Victoria, celebrated 60 years of her reign, committees throughout the length and breadth of the land discussed plans to honour the occasion. Edward, who had for many years interested himself in hospital affairs, looked into the question of setting up a third Hospital Fund. There were rumblings among a minority that perhaps the time had arrived when the state should exercise some control over the hospital system, but that was not Edward's view, and he strongly supported the role of voluntary hospitals:

> Public opinion has shown itself upon more than one occasion, and I think wisely, in favour of the maintenance of the voluntary system for support of our hospitals ... It is obvious, however, that if these institutions are to be saved from State or parochial aid, their financial condition must be secured. We must recall that, apart from purely philanthropic work carried on in the relief of our sick

poor, we look to the voluntary hospitals for the means of medical education and the advancement of medical science.

Even the radical *Lancet* had ceased to advocate the establishment of state hospitals, believing that patients were cared for better under a charitable system, that the management of individual hospitals was better than 'local municipal wisdom', and that state control would lead to the loss of charitable donations.

In June 1897, Edward invited 22 leaders in religion, medicine, surgery, commerce, administration and industry, some of them his close personal friends, to a meeting at Marlborough House. A special committee of ten was appointed from among their number to further the scheme. The aim was not merely to assist the hospitals by paying off their current debts, it was also to increase their efficiency. The new Fund encouraged improved accounting systems, the amalgamation of small hospitals and shorter working hours for nurses. Perversely, some of the work undertaken by the Fund to fight off state participation eased the takeover of the voluntary hospitals when the National Health Service was introduced in 1948. Lord Rothschild was the treasurer, and it was hoped that money would be raised from 'persons who have not hitherto acquired the habit of giving regularly to these institutions'. As we have seen, Sam was among the first subscribers. Also involved in the early days of the Fund were Lord Iveagh, whose donation of £12,500 was the highest on the first list of contributors; banker J. Pierpoint Morgan, who became a member of the Visiting Committee; Andrew Carnegie, who later gave £100,000; and also the Chief Rabbi, Nathan Adler; the Lord Mayor of London, Sir George Faudel Phillips; Sir Ernest Cassel; and Sir Edgar Speyer. The Chief Rabbi and the Lord Mayor were involved because of the offices they held, but the last two were examples of the acceptance of Jews within Edward's circle. The Fund became an excellent vehicle for the social aspirations of German Jews. For reasons which will become apparent, Algernon Sydney was later elected to the Executive Committee.

At the beginning of 1902 Ada took herself on a prolonged holiday to Europe (including a visit to Turkey where she made a donation to the British Relief Fund). Compared with her total income the £10,000 a year from the capital which eventually was to pass to the Fund was not an overwhelmingly significant sum. To the Fund, however, £10,000 would have been of major importance; in 1901 its total receipts were just over £58,000. It was estimated at the time that the combined annual deficit of the London hospitals was £100,000 and one of the Fund's initial aims was to attract a permanent additional income of £50,000 a year from a few wealthy contributors who had money to spare. It was felt that if that were achieved it would be comparatively easy to raise the remaining £50,000 required to put the hospitals on an even keel. That, at least, was the view expressed by George Stephen, the first Baron Mount Stephen who was one of the chief fundraisers, and for many years its chief donor, his gifts and legacy eventually exceeding even Sam's. Ada, with the full knowledge and approval of the king, was designated a possible large donor. They wanted to persuade her to pass the £10,000 a year to the Fund during her lifetime. The capital, of course, was subject to the trust imposed by the will and could not be touched. Mount Stephen was one of two men given the task of parting her from her money. The other was Horace Farquhar.

In one way Mount Stephen's career was similar to Sam's, in that he started from very humble beginnings. The eldest son of a Banffshire carpenter, he spent his school holidays as a herd boy, and at the age of 14 was apprenticed to an Aberdeen draper. He moved to Glasgow, and then London, where a chance meeting with a cousin, a Montreal draper, led him to Canada in 1850. On his cousin's death ten years later he became the sole proprietor of his cousin's firm. He expanded the business, embarked upon cloth manufacture, and in 1873 became a director of the Bank of Montreal, and in 1876 its president. Finance led him into the railway business as one of a group of six who successfully completed the Great Northern Railway, which made fortunes for them all. The Canadian government then called upon Mount Stephen and his group to complete a partially built trans-continental railway line it had started but which had run into trouble. After innumerable difficulties, financial and political, and after being at one time literally within hours of bankruptcy, the task was successfully completed in 1885; the Canadian Pacific Railway was born. Mount Stephen retired from its presidency in 1888, and in 1893, at the age of 64, made his home in England. He was created a baronet in 1886, and a peer in 1891, taking his title from a peak in the Rockies named after him by railway surveyors. He lived chiefly at

Brocket Hall, Hertfordshire, devoting his time largely to charitable endeavours.

The lengthy, and mostly distinguished, career of Farquhar, the Master of the Royal Household, and one of those near to the King who ensured that his reign was relatively solvent, was not altogether untainted by scandal. A banker-cum-politician, he was made a baron in 1898 after only three years on the House of Commons back benches – a rapid promotion which he himself attributed to the fact that he had subscribed more than the 'accepted tariff' to the Conservative party. Later, in 1907, he was said to have acquired a gain of £70,000 through timely dealing in the shares of the somewhat dubious Siberian Repository Mines Ltd, of which he was a director, and of which he persuaded Lord Knollys, Edward VII's private secretary, to become a director. Farquhar became Lord Steward of the Household, and in 1917 was promoted to a viscountcy, followed by an earldom in Lloyd George's resignation honours list. For many years he was treasurer of the Conservative party, but left the post in 1923 when a sum of at least £80,000 was discovered to be inadequately accounted for. Farquhar died later that year, making lavish bequests to various members of the Royal Family in his will, but, rather unfortunately, it was said, no funds out of which they could be paid. Lord Beaverbrook's robust opinion was that 'Horace had spent the lot'. There is, however, conflicting evidence on the point, and it would appear that he left a substantial estate.

In tandem, Mount Stephen and Farquhar were a formidable combination, one that Ada would have found it difficult to withstand even if she had not been favourably inclined towards the scheme; and of course they were backed by the authority and glamour of the King. They were an irresistible force approaching a far from immovable object. At some time before Ada left for her European holiday the first steps were taken to involve her in the Fund. Whether the initiative was Ada's, though the available correspondence suggests that this was unlikely, or whether she was guided by Sydney at the instance of Lord Farquhar, is not clear. Certainly Farquhar led the King to believe that the idea had emanated from him. There always was a battle of those surrounding the King to curry favour by ensuring they received credit for good results, and to avoid blame when things went wrong.

On 5 March 1902 Farquhar wrote to the Prince of Wales, telling him that he had seen Sydney:

He accepted my proposal very favourably – and promised he would lay it before Mrs. Lewis directly she returned from abroad, in a month's time!

I had a long conversation with Mr. Sydney who promised his support in the matter – altogether I feel more sanguine of success. I will tell your Royal Highness the details of my interview when I have the opportunity [this last word was then crossed out and the word 'honour' inserted] of seeing you

Your obedt. and devoted servant,

Horace Farquhar

This news was passed by the Prince of Wales to Mount Stephen, who replied on 7 March saying he was 'very pleased at your good news from Lord Farquhar and earnestly hope all will go right with the Old Lady'. What could he have meant by this description of Ada? Was it intended to be taken literally? This is unlikely, as Ada was younger, by a few years, than both he and the King. Was it used in a friendly way, almost as a term of endearment? Or did it indicate a measure of contempt towards someone who was merely an object from which to extract money? Ada would not have been amused had she seen the letter.

Later that day the Prince of Wales addressed a meeting of potential supporters of the scheme, and the following day Mount Stephen wrote in appropriately obsequious terms:

Sir,

I hope you will not think me a tiresome old bore if I take leave to say that I think your speech is excellent and most politic in paving the way for Mrs. Lewis to take the initiative with her £250,000 ...

Now that the object your Royal Highness has in view is publicly known it will be easier to make some progress in getting the money together. I shall of course help all I can. If Mrs. Lewis should take kindly to the scheme, I feel confident you will get the sum required ... before next year's meeting takes place ...

The letter made it clear just how much importance they attached to landing Ada – the first £10,000 is always the hardest to get.

When Ada returned to England, Sydney put the proposition to her. She immediately indicated her agreement. What was her motive? She was by now worldly wise in the ways of Society, its methods of operating and its deference to money. She must have been able to foresee the benefits likely to come her way. At the same time she shared Sam's genuine charitable instincts, and bearing in mind her past work she would in any event most surely have found a charitable outlet for a great deal of her fortune.

She was speedily able to complete the delicate task of negotiation with her Grosvenor Square neighbour, Lord Farquhar. Did they meet at his place or hers? Did he make any promises to her? Did he point out to her the social advantages which were likely to accrue from becoming a substantial supporter of the King's favourite charity – or were they obvious? In the event, once she had agreed she did not have long to wait for results. She received letters on 24 April from both the Prince of Wales and from the King himself. The prince, writing from York House, expressed his thanks for 'this great act of liberality on your part, which has given me the keenest satisfaction, and which I feel certain will be heartily and gratefully appreciated by all classes of your fellow citizens in London', and he ended his letter 'Believe me, dear Mrs. Lewis, sincerely yours, George P.' The letter from Buckingham Palace was in Farquhar's handwriting, but signed by the King:

The King has heard from Lord Farquhar of the very generous act which Mrs. Lewis proposes to take in regard to 'King Edward the Seventh London Hospital Fund' by proposing to present to it an annual sum of £10,000, the interest of £250,000 which was bequeathed to the charity on her death by her late husband. The King, being the Founder of the Fund and deeply interested in its prosperity, assures Mrs. Lewis that he highly appreciates this munificent gift of hers, and he thanks her most sincerely for her generosity.

EDWARD R.   Buckingham Palace
                                                     24th April 1902

A personal letter from the King! How proud Sam and her parents would have been.

315

Ada wrote appropriate replies, saying that in making the gift she felt that she was fulfilling a part of the charitable intentions of her late, dear, husband. It gave her, she said, as much happiness to present the gift as she trusted it would to those who would benefit.

Invitations quickly followed. The first, but of course, was from Norfolk, the Earl Marshal, for Ada to be a guest at the King's Coronation at Westminster Abbey, with a seat in the north aisle of the nave; and another to witness a royal procession from the vantage point of the Royal Household Stand in the very forecourt of Buckingham Palace. In due course she received from the Keeper of the Privy Purse a medal from His Majesty the King to be worn in remembrance of Their Majesties' Coronation. Later that year Edward, who had been shooting at Sandringham, sent her a parcel containing six pheasants and six partridges – hardly kosher, but none the less welcome for all that. She was now sufficiently accepted to be able to send personal congratulations to the Prince and Princess of Wales on the occasion of the birth of their fifth child on 19 December, and for the prince to reply by telegram, signing himself simply 'George'.

She was doubtless delighted with the royal reaction to her gift – it really was astonishing just how quickly and far up the social ladder money could take you – but her vanity demanded a wider recognition. She wanted as many others as possible to know what she had done. This was referred to in a postscript of a letter dated 10 September 1902 from Mount Stephen to Sir Arthur Bigge. 'No newspaper that I have seen has said a word about Mrs. Lewis's splendid gift. It was she who set the pace and that should not be forgotten so soon.' A week later he wrote to Bigge again: 'As to Mrs. Lewis, I only mentioned the matter as I thought it would be a pity if she took it into her head that her splendid gift had been received with scant acknowledgment or notice on the part of the public; she is a woman.' What he said is, once again, open to interpretation. He may have been genuinely concerned that she should get public credit, which she deserved, or it may be that he feared lack of it would jeopardise future donations. He seemed to believe that women were innately more vain than men, yet few women could have been much more sycophantic towards royalty than he was, and his desire for royal approval was his form of vanity. Ada would have been less than delighted if she had known that whatever the royal reception was on the surface, behind the scenes she was regarded by one of the King's advisers more as a meal ticket for the Fund; a mere woman.

The importance of Ada's gift to the Fund can be measured by its annual reports for 1903 and 1904. In 1903 her £10,000 donation represented 12 per cent of the Fund's total income. In 1904 the Fund distributed grants totalling £28,300 shared (not equally) between 24 London hospitals, including Guy's, the Hospital for Sick Children, King's College Hospital, London Hospital, Middlesex Hospital, Royal Free Hospital and St Mary's Paddington. Ada's money thus accounted for 35 per cent of all the grants.

Lord and Lady Farquhar became good friends of Ada, and another charity to which they introduced her was the Governesses' Benevolent Institution. Its main aim was to assist governesses in illness, distress and old age. Lady Farquhar had been a donor since 1867, and became a patroness in 1904. Lord Farquhar was a patron and steward. It was quite well funded, and one of its oldest supporters was Baroness Angela Burdett-Coutts. This introduction was to have a considerable effect on the fortunes of the Institution.

One of the most gratifying occasions for Ada during 1902 took place on 25 July at the Queen's Hall in London. She accepted an invitation to be guest of honour at the Annual Prizegiving Day of the Royal Academy of Music. The next in line to be invited, if Ada had been unable to accept, was Dame Nellie Melba. After some of the successful students had exhibited their talents, and before presenting the prizes, Ada delivered a suitable short address congratulating them, and expressing the hope that they would bring future distinction to themselves and the Academy. This would appear to be the first time she had spoken in front of a large audience, which can be a daunting experience, and she coped well. She added that she was delighted to know that her efforts to help 'Music' had been so cordially and warmly appreciated. Mount Stephen had been right in gauging the importance to her of public acknowledgement of her good works. In this regard she was the opposite of Sam, who preferred to engage in quiet, unpublicised, charity.

One is left to wonder what would have happened if Sam had made such a gift to the Fund during his lifetime, which he could easily have afforded to do. Would, and could, protocol have allowed him to be a guest at the Coronation and be invited to the Palace? It seems highly unlikely. What would Sir George have said?

21 · The lieutenant

The year of 1904, three years after Sam's death, proved to be momentous for Ada. In May she offered the Royal Academy of Music a prize of 50 guineas for the best quintet for pianoforte, two violins, viola and cello, by a British-born composer. The work had to be specially written for the occasion and to consist of four movements. Although the successful competitor was to retain all rights of publication of the work, she expressed the wish that the first performance should be given at her home, presumably to be played by her own musicians. No note has been found of the winning entry, but it doubtless led to an evening at Grosvenor Square which provided great enjoyment to those there, and particular excitement, and a taste of luxury, for the winner.

As usual she spent June and July at 'Woodside'. The Guards Boat Club was well settled on its new site, and was housed in a much more commodious and attractive building. During Ascot Week the town was overflowing. The hotels were full, and all the available houses in the neighbourhood were let. Many well-known people arranged house parties, including the Duke and Duchess of Newcastle at Forest Farm, Lord Stanley and Lady Alice Stanley at Cowarth Park, Lord Burnham, the proprietor of the *Telegraph*, at Hall Barn, Colonel F. C. Ricardo at Cookham, Lord and Lady Esher at Orchard Lea, and, of course, Mr Astor at Cliveden. Most importantly, it was made known that the King and Queen would be spending a day with Mr Grenfell at Taplow Court.

Ascot Sunday, as always the highlight of the season – 'the Sunday of the Year on the River' – fell on 19 June. The previous Sunday was a quieter prelude, but none the less very busy. The *Maidenhead Advertiser* had cause to complain about a party of the Grand Order of

318

Water Rats, numbering about 100 music-hall artistes, some of them very well known, whose conduct 'was no credit to their profession; it was about on a par with what one might expect from a third rate bean-feast party'. Miss Marie Lloyd, they noted, was not with this 'rowdy-dowdy' company, but with some friends on the electric launch *Margie*. Also on the river that day, on the yacht *Isis Hathor* which Sam had acquired shortly after purchasing 'Woodside', were 'Mrs. Lewis, *Mr. Montagu Hill*, and others from Woodside'. Who was this man that he deserved a specific mention not afforded to the other guests?

On Ascot Sunday the weather was perfect, and under the bright sunshine the river was transfigured. Turner, the lock-keeper at Boulter's, started his day at five o'clock in the morning and the last boat did not pass through until eleven o'clock that night. One thousand punts, canoes and scullers, and 182 small and large launches were made to fit together so tightly that their eventual disentanglement seemed hopeless. So great was the pressure that many boatsmen, tired of being kept waiting for hours in the queue, turned about and went downstream. There was also, the *Maidenhead Advertiser* reported, a remarkable display of motor cars in the roads near Boulter's Lock, nearly 100 being counted at one time!

The largest gathering, on the banks and on the river, was at Boulter's. The sides of the lock were packed with spectators all day, watching the work of the conservancy men and delighting in the passing show. A rumour that the King and Queen would be seen on the river had attracted many of them there. Their Majesties visited Mr and Mrs Grenfell at Taplow Court in the afternoon and in the evening the Queen, with Mr and Mrs Joseph Chamberlain and other well-known visitors, took to the river on an electric launch, to the delight of those who saw her from the banks or on the river.

There was, as always, a wonderful display of ladies' costumes and millinery, because on Ascot Sunday, partly for the delight of the 'lower classes' who came down by train from London to witness the scene, the Society ladies wore the new frocks they had purchased especially for the Ascot races. 'Lady look-loungers found plenty of fashion fancies upon which to feast their eyes. Some of the costumes were almost as charming as the pretty ladies who wore them.' One journalist rhapsodised:

I have often said if I were an Englishwoman I would always wish it to be summer. There is something in summer weather that has the power to bring out the best of English beauty – the freshness of complexion, the fair hair, the blue eyes, the athletic and healthy figure of Englishwomen – all these things appear to their best advantage when they are clothed in the lightest of colour of all clothes – in muslins, and whites and blues. It would be difficult to find anywhere in the world a more dazzling collection of beautiful women than one saw on the Thames on such a day as I have just passed through.

What a romantic age it was! Women were publicly placed on pedestals, while privately considered inferior.

Owing to the vast crowds on the lockside, ropes were placed across the entrance to limit their numbers, and it was reported that 'from beyond "Woodside" to the Ray Mead Hotel, thousands of persons congregated in the afternoon and evening, and the promenade has never been so crowded'. The afternoon scene was enlivened by the arrival of a lifeboat in the charge of Colonel Ricardo, those on board being armed with collecting bags on long poles in which they gathered funds for the National Lifeboat Society. This could well have been the occasion which further fired Ada's enthusiasm for that charity. She later presented the National Lifeboat Institution for the Preservation of Life from Shipwrecks with two lifeboats, to be called the *Ada Lewis* and the *Samuel Lewis*, and in her will left them sufficient funds to endow the running costs. During the evening, to the delight of the crowds, the queen, with Mr and Mrs Joseph Chamberlain, went for a trip on the motor launch *Angler*. A perfect ending to a perfect day.

At the end of June, on the day after celebrating her sixtieth birthday, Ada presented, and opened, three cottage homes for the Royal Berkshire Regiment, adjoining the barrack drill-ground at Reading. They were well built and fully furnished, and all had bathrooms and gardens. The gift was made by Ada, she said, specifically as a tribute to Sam. He was obviously still very much on her mind. A large party attended, including Sydney, and after lunch Ada showed her burgeoning confidence by making a short speech. She was doubtless highly satisfied when the event was reported in the *Queen*, and the world thus knew of it. Her social credentials were now of the highest. The King's accolade must have overridden the prejudices of those who previously may have considered her unfit for acceptance. One thing she still lacked, which would have increased her delight, was a consort with whom to share her advancement. A cultured Jewish widower, well accepted in Society circles, would have been ideal, perhaps.

During the next two weeks she was frequently seen on the river in her yacht, but she went up to London on 12 July to attend a reception given by the Prince and Princess of Wales at Marlborough House in aid of the League of Mercy, another hospital charity. We also know that she was in London on 20 July, for on that day, quite out of the blue, she married – in church. Her husband was the man who had accompanied her on the yacht *Isis Hathor* two weeks earlier – William James Montagu Hill, a lieutenant in the Scots Guards, the son of a vicar. He was just 27 years old, less than half her age. She was almost old enough to have been his grandmother.

The marriage raised a host of issues. How long had she been considering this step? There was no doubting her strong Jewish background and upbringing. She and Sam were both active members of the West London Synagogue and attended Brighton Synagogue when staying in the town. What had made her decide to marry a non-Jew; why at this particular time; and why one so young? Why did she, who could so easily have chosen a person of distinction, or honour, or achievement, select him? Were they both genuinely in love, or she alone; or was it a mere infatuation, straightforward sexual desire on her part and perhaps fortune hunting on his? Or, despite all outward appearances, was she lonely, and in need of more permanent companionship? Did she simply seek an escort for social functions? Was he her charitable gift to herself? Had the prominent contemporaneous examples of Baroness Burdett-Coutts and Lady Randolph Churchill influenced her at all? And how did her brothers and sisters react to the news, with pleasure or regret, delight or amazement? And what might they fear? Had anyone been privy to her intentions and, if so, did they attempt to dissuade her? Would she have married him if either of her parents had still been alive? How would Sam have viewed the match, and the knowledge that much of his wealth was likely to pass into unexpected hands?

And what of William's family? Did they react favourably to their son marrying a Jewess, albeit in church? When the Earl of Rosebery married Hannah Rothschild, his mother, then the Duchess of Cleveland, was horrified that he had chosen a Jewish wife. Hannah's wealth was no compensation for her religion so far as the duchess was concerned:

> You can easily suppose how unhappy I must feel in finding that you have chosen as your wife, and the mother of your children, one who has not the faith and hope of Christ. I do honestly, and from the bottom of my heart, disapprove of such marriages, and I could not say otherwise without acting against my conscientious conviction.

Society too did not look kindly on that union, being particularly hostile to Rosebery. Young Reginald Baliol Brett, later to be the second Viscount Esher, confided to his diary that 'people are angry with him for marrying so much money'. The Jewish community, too, was opposed to the match. The *Jewish Chronicle* declared, 'We mourn, we deplore, this degeneracy, and we pray to God fervently to spare the community another similar grief.' And again:

> If the leviathan is brought up with a hook, how will the minnows escape ... Was there amongst the millions of brethren-in-faith all over Europe no one of sufficient talent, sufficiently cultured, sufficiently high minded, to be deemed worthy to be received in the family circle, that this honour must be bestowed upon one who must necessarily estrange the partner from her people? ... A sad example has been set which, we pray God, may not be productive of dreadful circumstances.

Ada was closer to being a leviathan than a minnow, but there was no such public reaction. She had acted speedily and circumspectly, and left little time for opposition.

Lady Randolph Churchill said of her own second marriage that it would be very quiet, but not done in a hole-in-the-corner fashion as if she were ashamed of it. Ada acted likewise. The church chosen by her was St Mark's in North Audley Street, just one minute from the Square. After its rebuilding in 1878 it had become as fashionable as the neighbourhood. A special licence had been obtained, and the ceremony, which lasted only a few minutes, was conducted 'according

27   The second Viscount Esher, a power behind the throne and government, but a frequent visitor to Sam at Cork Street   *Hulton*

28   Sir Edward Guinness, later Lord Iveagh, an important influence on Sam's decision to provide housing for the working classes

Hulton

29　Lord Farquhar, who persuaded Sam's widow to donate £10,000 a
year to the King Edward VII Hospital Fund　　　　*Hulton*

30   The dashing Lieutenant William Hill, Ada's second husband

Miss Mollie Hill

31 The *Samuel Lewis* lifeboat being launched by horses at Skegness just after the First World War. The *Ada Lewis* was based at Newbiggin-on-Sea. Together they saved more than 100 lives.

Mr Basil Major

32   The Ada Lewis drinking trough at Maidenhead   *Freddie Davidson*

33   The Ada Lewis Homes at Beckenham erected by the Schoolmistresses'
and Governesses' Benevolent Institution in 1926 and later sold to fund
the building of Queen Mary House at Chislehurst. Ada's legacy of
£50,000 to the Institution revolutionised its finances

Schoolmistresses' and Governesses' Benevolent Institution

34 Queen Elizabeth the Queen Mother opening Queen Mary House at Chislehurst in 1967. The young spectator is Lady Diana Spencer, now Princess of Wales

Schoolmistresses' and Governesses' Benevolent Institution

to the Rites and Ceremonies of the Established Church' by the rector of the parish, the Reverend R. H. Haddon.

It would have been only natural if the marriage had stirred up some resentment among her relatives and friends. They might have worried that she was making a fool of herself; that he might take her money and run. The difference of age made it highly possible that he would seek solace outside the marriage, and might do so openly. She could become a laughing-stock. More mercenary thoughts must have entered their minds too; would they be cut out of her will? Marriage automatically revokes existing wills. Would she leave everything to her new husband? They must all have assumed, and quite reasonably so, that she would have made provision for them, just as Sam had done; indeed they could have expected that their sister would leave them even more. If she was besotted by her new husband she might give him everything.

They obviously had some forewarning of the coming marriage since William had stayed with Ada at her house parties at 'Woodside', and they were seen together on the river. The probability is that they first met through the Guards Club, perhaps when she was there as a guest, or possibly from an approach by him to sell her tickets to view the annual Brigade of Guards Regatta, for he was a member of the organising committee. Her brother Ernest, who was a solicitor, acted for her in drawing up the new will which was ready for signature on the wedding day. He knew its terms, but would not have behaved unprofessionally by letting others know what it contained, unless, that is, she authorised him to do so. Representations were doubtless made to her that she should think carefully about the step she proposed to take. Those most likely to influence her were Sydney and Ernest, to whom she entrusted many of her private affairs. But whatever the innermost thoughts and feelings contained within the minds and hearts of those affected, whatever arguments there might have been against her marrying the young man, for the moment their voices were stilled. At least some of her relatives and friends were there to support her when she stood before the altar in a grey dress and white picture hat. Those specifically mentioned by the *Maidenhead Advertiser* were Ernest, who gave her away; her sister Emily and her husband Saville Parker; Zilla and Frederick Cliffe who had been so generously helped by both Sam and Ada; and Mr and Mrs

323

Andrade. The *Advertiser* indicated that other members of the family were present, but did not name them.

William James Montagu Hill was born on 13 December 1876 in Nottingham. His father James had been vicar of St Paul's in that town, and he was already 66 years old when William was born. Unfortunately he did not live to see his son's marriage, having died seven years earlier. William's mother, Marie Amelia, *née* Pilcher, had been left the income on a legacy of £12,000 from her father, and she also had a separate income from property, but clearly William was becoming involved in a realm of wealth hitherto unknown to him. At the time a private income was essential if one was to keep up one's standard as an army officer, particularly in the Guards, and in many instances the cost of doing so was almost £1,000 a year in excess of the pay. William was probably holding his own only with difficulty, and perhaps a little borrowing.

He signed the register in the name 'Lewis-Hill'. This was presumably a requirement imposed by Ada, and by this she was telling the world that she had not forgotten Sam. As she controlled the purse strings it was a condition William could painlessly accept if it pleased her. Immediately after Ada's death he dropped 'Lewis' from his name.

He had been commissioned into the Scots Guards in January 1899, and promoted to the rank of lieutenant in August 1900. He served with the 1st Battalion at Windsor, and was made adjutant to the Officer Commanding in June 1903. A frequent visitor to the Guards Club in Maidenhead, he was also actively involved in the social side of the battalion's life. A photograph of him in his high-collared scarlet uniform with its blue facings, carrying his busby in his hand, shows a strikingly handsome, slim though sturdy, young man, upright as befits a Guards officer, looking confidently towards the camera. A full, but trim, moustache, beneath a strong nose and piercing eyes, gave him a more mature look than his years warranted, and undoubtedly made him most attractive to women.

Ada was not the first wealthy woman, nor will she be the last, to marry a husband so much her junior, in her case by 33 years. Many more than have done it must have considered it, but hesitated at the last moment, because to take such a decision and carry it through requires courage and self-confidence, or a high degree of disregard for what others might think. Disraeli deliberately sought out a rich wife. Mary Anne Wyndham-Lewis was a wealthy widow 12 years his senior. They fell genuinely in love and the marriage was blissfully happy for 33 years. The intrepid, tempestuous Duchess of Montrose, who ran horses under the name 'Mrs Manton', and before whom jockeys and trainers trembled, married her third husband when she was 70 and he was 24. Both Sam and Ada knew her well.

Sir Winston Churchill's American mother, the beautiful Jennie Jerome, whom Ada had met at Bayreuth, first married the brilliant Lord Randolph Churchill. He became Chancellor of the Exchequer and was close to becoming prime minister when he suddenly resigned from the government. He died in 1895. Jennie had had many lovers during the marriage, including the Prince of Wales and Sam's good client Count Kinski. In 1900, when she was 46, she married George Cornwallis-West, who was 21 years her junior; indeed, he was the same age as Winston and his mother was the same age as Jennie. George, described by a follow-officer in the 1st Battalion of the Scots Guards as 'short of brains', had good connections but no money. The Prince of Wales was one of many who tried to dissuade her, but she was bold enough to tell him that she knew her own mind a great deal better than the prince. He wrote to her:

> You know the world so well that I presume you are the best judge of your own happiness – but at the same time, you should think twice before you abuse your friends and well-wishers for not con-gratulating you on the serious steps you are going to make. I can only hope that we shall be mistaken.

Although they were genuinely in love with each other, their friends were right. The marriage ended in divorce 12 years later. The whole episode prompted Lady Dorothy Nevill, then 70 years old, to reply, when asked by a friend what she was doing strolling among the children playing in Hyde Park, 'if you want to know, my dear, I am searching in the perambulators for *my* future husband.'

Lillie Langtry too looked for a younger man when considering her second husband. In 1899, when she was 46, she married the 28-year-old Hugo de Bathe. Poor and foolish, he had the single advantage that when his father, Sir Henry de Bathe, died he would inherit the title and Lillie would become Lady de Bathe.

Most importantly, Ada had before her the well-known and much publicised example of Angela Georgina Burdett-Coutts, Baroness Coutts, and there is good reason to think that this influenced her decision. Ada and Angela shared common interests and connections, and there were many similarities between the two women. It appears likely that they had met socially. The gossip, discussions and arguments which had raged round Angela when she married were doubtless echoed, at least in part, round Ada.

Angela, who became the richest heiress in England and enjoyed a fame which matched that of Florence Nightingale, was born in 1814, the youngest of the six children of Sir Francis Burdett, the politician, and Sophia Coutts of the banking family. When her maternal grandmother, who before her marriage had been a maid in the service of her husband's brother, died, her husband married a young actress, Harriot Mallon. He was 80, and Harriot was younger than his three daughters. The second marriage caused some misgivings and ill-feeling in the family. This riled him, and as he had already made ample provision for his daughters (having given each of them £25,000 on marriage and a further £20,000 subsequently) he altered his will and left his entire fortune, including his interest in Coutts' Bank, to Harriot. When he in turn died, Harriot married again. Her second husband, William Aubrey de Vere Beauclerk, the ninth duke of St Albans, was half her age. She found the temptation to become a duchess irresistible. She took a great liking to Angela and after making provision for a generous annuity to her husband, made Angela her heiress. The duke died in 1849 and everything then passed to Angela. There were, however, two conditions. Angela was required to adopt the name Coutts (as Ada required her second husband to acquire the name Lewis), and if she should marry an alien then her share of the banking business could, in certain circumstances, revert to her elder sisters.

Angela lived in a great house in Piccadilly and had innumerable suitors. Her choice of husband greatly exercised the public mind and it was said that she received a proposal from every young man of good family. Even Prince Louis Napoleon was mentioned. The elderly Duke of Wellington, with whom she forged a firm friendship, the one man she hoped would propose, did not. When he was 77 and she was 22, in response to her prompting he wrote to her: 'You are young, my dearest! ... I entreat you again ... not to throw yourself away on a man old enough to be your grandfather, who, however strong, hearty, and healthy at present, must and will certainly in time feel the consequences and infirmities of age.' Had he been as willing as she was, she would have accepted him despite the remarkable difference in their ages. She declined all other advances, and devoted herself exclusively to social entertainment and philanthropy, and for a long time Charles Dickens was her almoner for the latter purpose. Her many charitable interests included support for those involved in the care of neglected children – she assisted in the foundation of the National Society for the Prevention of Cruelty to Children; elementary and scientific education; protection of dumb animals; female emigration; exploration of Africa; and care of those wounded during the war. But there were two particular issues which she enthusiastically embraced which Ada also pursued – housing for the poor, and the extension of women's opportunities in commerce and the professions.

When Sam and Ada discussed the terms of their wills with Sydney and each other the buildings in Columbia Square, Bethnal Green, which had been erected by Angela for the working classes, were among those considered. We shall see that Ada also appears to have been influenced by Angela Coutts's work for improving the lot of women and enlarging the areas of work in which they would be accepted. They were both friends of the Governesses' Benevolent Institution, and there was yet a further charity they supported. In 1877 Angela Coutts made strenuous efforts to help the Turkish peasantry who were swept from their native villages by the Russian advance, and for her work and generosity she was honoured by the Sultan. Ada followed almost exactly in her footsteps. Furthermore during Ascot Weeks Angela was a frequent visitor to Maidenhead, usually staying with the Astors at Cliveden. At weekends in October and November she was to be seen taking part in the 'Church Parade' and drive along the front at Brighton and Hove. Though there is no record of Angela and Ada having met it is highly likely that they did. What is beyond doubt is that Ada must have been very aware of Angela's life story.

To organise her charitable affairs Angela employed a small secretariat at her Piccadilly home. One of its number was William

Lender to the lords, giver to the poor

Ashmead Bartlett, the son of a young American widow whom Angela had befriended 20 years before, when he was ten years old. Angela paid for his education at Torquay, then at Highgate School, and later supported him while he was at Oxford. She appointed him as commissioner to her Turkish Compassionate Fund, giving him the job of organising the unloading and distribution of stores. In the summer of 1879 after he returned from his tour of duty, Angela chartered a steam yacht for a Mediterranean cruise. There was a small party on board, which included Bartlett and a Miss Shirley who joined the boat part way through the holiday. It was during the cruise that Angela realised that she had fallen in love with him. She made up her mind to marry him, even though there was a difference of 37 years between them. She knew she could offer him luxury for life, and help him in his ambition to forge a political career. With her assistance he could get the nomination as Conservative member for Westminster, her father's old seat. He in turn would help her dispel the loneliness which, despite her wealth and position, she increasingly felt.

News of her proposed marriage began to spread through Society, and gossip ran riot. Bartlett had some charm and good looks, but few of her friends believed him worthy of her. Many considered he was an unscrupulous fortune-hunter. And what would the effect be on Coutts' Bank if she parted with her interest to an outsider? Incredulity gave way to concern for her well-being, anger that she might be making an exhibition of herself, and fear that she would too readily part with her money of which others had expectations. Great efforts were made to prevent the marriage taking place. In an attempt to stop her, the news was deliberately leaked to the Queen. Victoria thought that Angela 'really must be crazy ... she seems to have lost her balance', and she wrote to Lord Harrowby:

> ... the Queen has been told that there are circumstances which make the marriage an unusual one. She trusts that Lady Burdett-Coutts has given the fullest consideration to this step before making her final decision. The Queen knows too little respecting the subject to offer an opinion on it, but it would grieve her much if Lady Burdett-Coutts were to sacrifice her high reputation and her happiness by an unsuitable marriage.

There could hardly have been a clearer recommendation, almost a command, from the highest in the land. When Harrowby passed this on to Angela, as he was intended to, she bravely, and diplomatically, told him to reply to the Queen that he had no information on the subject alluded to.

Then, those concerned at the Bank sought to exert pressure on Angela to drop her plans. It was pointed out that as Bartlett's parents were American he was an alien, and her interest in the Bank would be at risk. Angela did not give way under this, but Bartlett did. He called at the Bank and said that finding so many difficulties in the way he had given up the idea of marriage, and had released the Baroness from her engagement to him. The affected parties scarce had time to uncork the champagne to toast the relief they felt at this news, than Angela let it be known that though he might release her, she would not release him, and that she was as determined as ever to proceed. Undeterred by this setback, they produced evidence that Bartlett had made love to the young Miss Shirley during the cruise. A friend of Angela's wrote to one of the directors of the Bank and repeated what Miss Shirley had told her:

On board this yacht this man had made violent love to her and told her over and over again that he couldn't marry her though he gladly would. He was under very peculiar circumstances. He could not explain them, but felt obliged to marry a lamp-post of a woman (his very words) repeated again and again. And that her money would help on his ambition! Miss Shirley apparently had his presents but no letters as proof of Bartlett's loving . . . she [Angela] is like a girl of fifteen. She does not *know* the storm of censure, indignation, grief, amazement that is going on everywhere. She is quite unaware of what she is going to bring on herself.

A further bombshell was dropped. In November 1880 a young woman was brought forward who said that Bartlett was the father of the child she was expecting. Angela was able to dispose of both these allegations quite easily – she simply refused to believe them.

And then she counter-attacked. She wrote that no marriage, however 'singular, or if you like eccentric', was a matter for scandal. She pointed out that her grandfather's second marriage had been very happy, and that Harriot had genuinely loved an old man, and had then been happily married to the Duke of St Albans though he was half her age. She herself would have been quite prepared to marry Wellington if she had been asked. She said that no one had the right to judge her behaviour but herself, nor had they a *right* to offer advice or remonstrance. Despite all the opposition the marriage took place in February 1881. She was 66, nearly 67, and he was just 30, their ages corresponding very closely to those of Ada and her new husband at the time of their marriage.

Angela remained in the public eye and continued her charitable work until her death in December 1906, but after her marriage her donations were on a very much diminished financial scale. This was inevitable. She had had to give up certain of her Bank income in a compromise reached with her sister over the 'alien' clause in her step-grandmother's will, and during the course of her marriage she gradually transferred most of her stocks and shares to her husband. He did very well out of the marriage, both financially and from the point of view of his career, as he became Member of Parliament for Westminster in 1885.

Was their marriage a happy one? It was said that he brought his mistresses to her home; that he made derogatory remarks about his ageing wife, and had once exclaimed aloud at a public event: 'I must go home and look after my grandmother'; and some alleged that he destroyed her happiness and wasted her inheritance. She was certainly deeply in love with him, and remained so. One friend said: 'I only knew them both when she was an aged woman and he was a man about forty or so with greying hair, but she still adored him ... she always addressed him with the utmost affection.' Friends and relations frequently remarked how well and young she looked, and the general opinion seems to be that most of the 25 years of married life they had together were contented and happy.

It is inevitable that there would have been similar discussion and criticism when Ada's plans became known. People rarely change. When young women still in their teens or their twenties express love and devotion for millionaires who are in their seventies and eighties, Society sighs, says there is no fool like an old fool, and looks to where the money is. They have a point – the same young women do not seem to fall so readily in love with 70- or 80-year-old retired bus-drivers. When the sexes are reversed, and the youngster is the man, then criticism and cynicism are even greater. Should Angela and Ada have known better? Who is to say what is good for another?

When the terms of Ada's will were made known it became apparent that she was a little more canny and less easily parted from her money than Angela. Perhaps this was because she knew that Sam had accumulated his wealth only after enduring a poverty-stricken childhood, followed by hardship when he went on the road as a pedlar; his money had been hard earned. She signed her will on the day of her marriage. Obviously it had been prepared in advance, and although detailed, showed signs of haste in its drafting, because there were important omissions which had to be corrected later. She bequeathed to William the house at Maidenhead, all her motor cars, launches, boats, carriages, horses, carriage wraps, harness and saddlery, and £300,000. This was far more than she left to anybody else, but none the less it did not include the house in Grosvenor Square, and it represented only 25 per cent or less of her total worth. The matter did not rest there, however, because before she died Ada was to change the terms of her will no fewer than seven times. These alterations, so far as they affected William, which they did in five of her seven codicils, reflected the fluctuating nature of their relationship.

They had been married no more than 11 weeks when she cut him out of her will completely. On 3 October something had occurred which caused her considerable distress. She immediately called in her brother Ernest, who prepared the first codicil for her. The very next day, without ascribing any reason in the document itself, she revoked every gift and bequest made to him. He was left nothing. Significantly, one of the witnesses to the codicil was a nurse at Middlesex Hospital. Three weeks later William was back in favour, though not to the extent of £300,000, nor was he to have 'Woodside'. She doubtless confided to her diary the reasons for the revocation and the reinstatement, but all we have are the terms of the second codicil made on 28 October. By this she bequeathed him £125,000, the two portraits of him and of herself painted by Thaddeus, a mail phaeton, a brougham, a pony cart, four horses and suitable harness: 'The change in my intentions towards my husband regarding "Woodside" and other matters must be obvious to him considering the circumstances of October 3rd, 1904. *Such impressions are not easily effaced.*'

One can only speculate what it was that had caused the rift. Had she caught him with another woman? And in 'Woodside' itself? Or was it simply something William had said? What did he say or do which then led her to change her mind? Did he promise not to repeat the offence; or did he perhaps convince her she was wrong about what she thought she saw or heard? She could not have been totally convinced, because he was now to receive less than half the previous bequest.

One of the confidantes with whom she discussed her marriage was Lady Farquhar. In this second codicil Ada also bequeathed £50,000 to Lady Farquhar's favourite charity, the Governesses' Benevolent Institution, to build and maintain residences similar to the Institution's existing homes at Chislehurst in Kent, to be called the Ada Lewis Homes.

Ada must have had a firm idea in her mind of just what it was that she expected from William. She was obviously prepared to continue with the marriage, and allow him to provide it, whatever it was, but on probation as it were. He did not remain in her good books for very long. In her fourth codicil of 12 May 1905 his legacy was again reduced, this time to £100,000, and the horses and carriages were taken away. Once again one of the witnesses was a hospital nurse. After that their relationship must have settled down, and been more to her liking. Possibly she made him, and others similarly affected, aware of the ups and downs of their fortunes in her changing will, and used the codicils as a weapon with which to keep them in order. In November 1905 she increased his legacy to £150,000 and in June 1906 to £175,000. Additionally he was given the yacht *Ailsa*, £2,000 payable immediately on her death, the black pearl out of 'my three pearl shamrock ring worn by me', also a mail phaeton and buggy, and three horses to be chosen by him and two sets of harness and gear.

Unfortunately, for more than a year Ada had had another, insoluble, problem to contend with. It was no coincidence that the witnesses to her codicils were nurses. In April 1905 it had been diagnosed that she had contracted inoperable cancer of the stomach. She needed almost constant medical attention, and it is possible that William, who had resigned his commission, did so in order that he might be able to spend more time with her. Inevitably, and increasingly, she had to take account of the reality of her situation. In the fifth codicil, made on 17 November 1905, she expressed the desire to be buried next to Sam, and she reserved a plot at Hoop Lane cemetery.

She made every effort not to allow her illness to affect her more than was absolutely necessary, and kept up her social and charitable engagements as best she could. Royal invitations continued to arrive. On 15 June 1905 Princess Margaret of Connaught, the King's niece, married Prince Gustavus Adolphus of Sweden. Playing an important part in the ceremony, in his capacity as Master of the Household, was Ada's friend and neighbour, Lord Farquhar. To honour the event the King and Queen gave a garden party at Windsor Castle on the preceding day, from 4.30 to 7. The Lord Chamberlain, at the command of Their Majesties, sent an invitation to Ada and William. It was hardly an intimate occasion – there were 6,000 guests – but nevertheless it was an honour to have been invited. Special trains ran between Paddington and Windsor, though Ada may have preferred to come direct from nearby Maidenhead. The men wore morning dress. *The Times* devoted plentiful space to descriptions of the ladies' frocks; pale lilac, white, grey and blue were the colours most favoured. The weather was bright and sunny, and guests arrived early. They gathered on the East Terrace lawn, and after the royal party entered they all sat down to tea in tents specially erected for the day. The royals were served on gold plate, the guests on silver. It was an enchanting setting for a happy occasion. On 1 June the following year Ada was at Buckingham Palace being presented to the King and Queen by Lady Farquhar. The invitation specified 'Full dress. Ladies with Feathers and Trains.'

Her charitable work was not neglected, and rarely out of mind. When she returned to 'Woodside', just a week after her marriage, she entertained the inmates of the Maidenhead Workhouse to a high tea, a treat, said the *Maidenhead Advertiser* which 'the poor folk' will greatly appreciate. In July she accepted an invitation from HRH Princess Christiana of Schleswig-Holstein to a reception for supporters of the Royal School of Needlework. She visited Turkey again on holiday, and while there organised work for the poor of Constantinople, in recognition of which the Sultan conferred the Ottoman Order upon her.

During 1905 she was actively engaged in setting up a project she had long planned, the Ada Lewis Nurses' Institute, to fill a gap she felt existed in providing home nursing for the sick middle classes who were temporarily experiencing financial difficulties. In many ways the very poor were well provided with such services. Most of London was covered by the excellent facilities supplied by organisations such as the East London Nursing Society, established in 1868 to 'provide trained nurses to nurse the sick poor in their own homes in East London'. The London Jewish community also made arrangements in this field for their poor through the work of Lady de Rothschild, Mrs Helen Lucas and Mrs Alice Model. Lady de Rothschild and Mrs Lucas paid the salaries of visiting nurses who were put at the disposal of the Jewish Board of Guardians. In 1895 Mrs Model founded the Sick Room Helps Society, later known as the Jewish Maternity District Nursing and Sick Room Helps Society. This effectively became a provident society with a contribution of one penny a week 'to encourage self-respect and thrift', and sent help into homes in which the mother was ill or had just given birth. The society had close ties with the Jewish Board of Guardians of which, of course, Sydney was the solicitor, and Ada became a much appreciated benefactor.

However, such organisations catered only for those who could pay nothing, or almost nothing, towards the cost of treatment, and not for those the *Jewish Chronicle* termed 'reduced gentlefolk and struggling professionals'. As one of that class expressed it: 'The rich can have all they want, and so can the poor. But we are the intermediate ones who occasionally need help the most, but cannot ask for it. Mrs. Hill is the first person who has thought of people in our position.' They were too well-off to be considered poor, and could not afford the full fees which a nursing institution would have to charge. With the active support and encouragement of her brother Ernest, and of her own medical adviser, Dr Henry Dutch, suitable accommodation was found for nurses at 62 Oxford Terrace, off the Edgware Road. They were all experienced in district nursing, which they started only after they had completed three years' hospital training. They were given board and lodging, and received what was considered a handsome starting salary of £30 a year, rising by £2 a year to £40. Their catchment area was a two-mile radius from Oxford Terrace. For a minimum of five shillings, and a maximum of ten shillings a week, patients obtained the daily visiting services, up to three a day if necessary, of one of these fully trained nurses. Their duties were confined to washing and dressing the patient, making the bed, and, under the direction of the medical attendant, dressing wounds, or applying surgical or medical treatment, or any nursing required for the immediate comfort of the patient. They also attended at operations, preparing the patient and the room for the purpose, assisting the surgeons, and clearing away afterwards.

The organisation was run on strictly non-denominational lines, and persons of all creeds used the service. The fees charged by the Institute were not used for paying expenses, but set aside to accumulate for the provision of similar homes in other districts. That, at least, was the original intention. The official opening was fixed for 26 October and the invitations sent out, but Ada was too unwell to attend. By January 1906 three nurses were employed, a fourth was about to start, and the target was for the engagement of a total of 12 nurses. They worked from 8.30 a.m. to 2 p.m. and again from 4.30 to 8. It was hoped that as the Institute expanded not only would they relieve some of the existing pressure on the hospitals, but they could increase employment opportunities by engaging respectable, active women who might be required for night work.

Another advantage of the scheme, it was felt, was that it would enable doctors in poor neighbourhoods to retain paying patients who would otherwise drift to the hospitals for free treatment. Indeed, its success depended upon the cooperation of those very doctors in referring cases to the Institute. But for one reason or another the doctors did not take to the proposal, and were lukewarm towards the scheme. The demand did not increase; indeed it dropped. Although such patients as they had expressed grateful thanks for the help they were given, the whole operation withered on the vine in the absence of sufficient support from the doctors. Ada was extremely disappointed, and in the sixth codicil, made on 30 June 1906, revoked the original provision in her will for its continued funding.

She kept in touch with her friends in Dublin. In April 1906 a special Passover appeal was made for the Jewish poor in the town, and a total of £59 14s 6d was raised, of which Ada contributed £10 10s 0d. She had also remained in contact with the vicar who had conducted her marriage service, Reverend Haddon, with whom she shared a common interest – music. He was a member of the Worshipful Company of Musicians and was well aware of the generous donations which Ada had made to the Royal Academy of Music, the scholarships she had founded there and the support she gave to struggling artists.

Lender to the lords, giver to the poor

Perhaps he hoped she might be equally generous to his Company. At a meeting of the Court of the Company held in July he suggested that its honorary freedom should be conferred on Ada in recognition of what she had done for music. The Master of the Company supported the motion, and it was stated that it had been discovered that there was a precedent for bestowing the freedom on a woman. After discussion it was decided on the proposition of Rev. Haddon, seconded by Sir Homewood Crawford, that the Master be authorised to ascertain if Ada would be willing to accept the honour. She wrote and told them that she would be proud of the distinction, but indicated that she might not be well enough to attend the ceremony at their Hall. It was agreed that if this were the case then the certificate would be presented to Ada at her home, or at some other place convenient to her, and that notice would be given to each member of the Court so that as many as possible might attend.

Alas, it never took place. For several months Ada's condition had been deteriorating. She was still at 'Woodside' at the beginning of September, but it was felt that she could receive better attention and treatment in London, so she returned to Grosvenor Square. On 11 September she discussed and signed the seventh and last codicil to her will, making changes which were to have an important effect on two charities in particular, the Ada Lewis Women's Lodging Houses and the Governesses' Benevolent Institution. She then lapsed into a coma and after, what had been a long and painful illness, died on Saturday, 13 October. Ernest was with her at the last.

The funeral party left from 16 Grosvenor Square on the following Monday, and she was buried next to Sam at the Hoop Lane cemetery. The Reverend Isidore Harris of the West London Synagogue, who had officiated at Sam's funeral, again conducted the service, which was simple in character. There were no flowers of any kind. There is no record of whether William was among the mourners at the burial ground. The inscription on her tombstone made no mention of him. It reads:

Hail most good one
Here at last I rest
with thee and rise
again with thee.

Ada Hannah Lewis
wife of
Samuel Lewis

Died 13th October 1906.

Was her short second marriage – it had lasted little more than two years – a happy one? It was quite within Ada's power to have ordered William out of her homes if the position had become intolerable. She could also at any time have cut him out of her will, and left him out permanently, if that is what she desired. But she did neither, and he was to receive considerably more than any other individual. The conclusion must be that she felt that she gained something from the union; sufficient to justify the very generous bequest she made to him. Perhaps, indeed, like Angela, she had fallen in love with her husband and, despite the occasional hiccup, remained so.

What was his view of the marriage? He waited a whole four months before remarrying, and took his new bride, who was a spinster and just one year younger than he was, on a Mediterrean honeymoon cruise on the yacht Ada had left him. In the marriage certificate, under the heading 'rank or profession' he described himself as 'gentleman'. They were to have two daughters, but the marriage broke up after only a few years. During the First World War he served with distinction in the Army, achieving the rank of colonel, and was awarded the Distinguished Service Order and the Military Cross. He spent some time in Africa, but then returned to England. When the Second World War began he again took an active part, and became a colonel in the third battalion of the Home Guard at Camberley. He went to live in France, and stayed there until his death on 4 January 1970, aged 94. His main assets were there and he disposed of them by a separate will. His English estate was about £13,000 and most of the income on the capital went to his daughters for life. An annuity, and his residuary estate, was left to Mademoiselle X, 'my nurse and housekeeper', because, he said, 'it is my desire that my residue should be received by a person who I know will put it to good use.'

There was much to be admired in Ada's life. She used her natural artistic talents and the worldly goods she accumulated to good effect. It must be said that though she spared no expense to surround herself in luxury, with her beautiful homes, the finest clothes, overseas travel

337

whenever she desired it, the best bred horses, and Stradivarius violins to play upon, she never forgot those in need, and throughout her life gave generously. She went further. She did not simply donate money to charity on a regular basis and consider her duty done. She also gave of her time and effort. She had proved herself a faithful and supportive wife, tough when the going was tough. She stood by Sam when criticism of him abounded, and was directed at him from all quarters. A loving sister and aunt, a steadfast friend, she deserved the praise given by those of her obituarists who said she was held in the highest esteem. To the end she remained generous and true to her family, to Sam's few distant relatives, her friends, her staff, and others who had rendered some service for which she wished to show her appreciation. She did not forget her days in Dublin, or the friends she had made there, and the needs of the city's poor.

Her estate totalled more than £1 million and, of course, she additionally had the right to dispose by her will of one-third of Sam's residuary estate. William received his £175,000, plus a payment of £2,000 for his immediate needs. Seven of her eight surviving brothers and sisters, and Annette's widower, shared £300,000 between them, though not equally. Ernest received the highest amount, £63,000, and 'Woodside'. For some reason Clara and her husband Augustus Jacobs were omitted. Sydney was given £20,000.

The *Maidenhead Advertiser* said it was pleased to learn that the indoor and outdoor servants had not been forgotten, 'handsome sums in the case of old and faithful servants being bequeathed to them'. Legacies of between £5 and £1,000 were given. Even the smallest gifts were meticulously considered, as the following extract from her will shows:

19. I BEQUEATH to the lockkeepers at Boulter's and Cookham locks twenty five pounds each and to the assistants five pounds each
To the assistants and servants of Webb the carrier at Maidenhead regularly employed by him twenty five pounds to be divided equally amongst them
To each of the gardeners regularly employed in Grosvenor Square five pounds
To each scavenger regularly employed in Grosvenor Square five pounds

To the Station Master at Maidenhead Station fifty pounds for distribution amongst the ticket collectors and porters regularly employed there
To Chapman the attendant at No. 6 box at the Royal Opera fifty pounds
To the Postmaster for the district which includes Grosvenor Square one hundred pounds for distribution amongst the postmen who regularly deliver letters at my house and the further sum of fifty pounds to be distributed amongst the messengers who regularly deliver telegrams at my house
To the Superintendents of Police for the Hyde Park and Bond Street Districts one hundred pounds for distribution amongst the policemen regularly engaged in directing the traffic in Hyde Park and Bond Street.
Where the word 'regularly' is employed in this clause it shall mean during the three months preceding my death.

In addition, the doctor who attended her during 1905 received £500, and every nurse in her service for one month before her death was given £100. It is difficult to think of anyone she overlooked, and if there were some such it must have been inadvertent.

Her 'quintette of artists' were given special rewards 'in recognition of the happy evenings of music I have enjoyed during many years through their services'. Bruno Schonberger was given £1,000, an annuity of £300, and a share of her cigars and wines. William H. Squire received £2,000 and the cello in use at the date of her will; Hobday £500 and the viola then in use; Haydyn Inwards £500. Tivadar Nachez had £2,000 and her second 'Strad' violin.

The 'first' Stradivarius, 'valued at fifteen hundred pounds', went to Sir Alexander Mackenzie, or the principal for the time being of the Royal Academy of Music for the use of the 'Ada Lewis' scholars, and it is still there. It was made by 'the Master' at Cremona in 1736 when he was 92 years old. It was valued at £65,000 in 1979 and must today be worth very considerably more. The bow was by Lanny. There are only 700 known Stradivaris, wonders of the musical world, in existence, and Ada had two of them. She also requested her trustees to allow the Academy to use her Steinway grand piano by Mellier on special occasions. Of her other musical friends, Madame Marie Roze received £3,000; Hugo Heinz, Emma Burnett, Dezso Kordy and Madame Dotti (then in America) £500 each; and Signor Ria £100.

The remainder of her estate, and the one-third of Sam's estate, went to charity. The two main beneficiaries were the Governesses' Benevolent Institution and the Ada Lewis Women's Lodging Houses which, in addition to gifts of £50,000 each, shared her residuary estate. They will be dealt with in more detail later.

There were just six legacies, totalling £17,000, to specifically Jewish charities. The Jewish Board of Guardians received £5,000. The same amount was given to what she termed in her will 'the Jewish Lying-In Hospital' to found a Sarah Davis Ward in honour of her mother. There was no organisation of that name, and the trustees of the will had to take the matter to court for a decision. There were several claimants but it was eventually decided in the Chancery Division that the intended beneficiary was the Jewish Maternity District Nursing and Sick Room Helps Society, later known as the Jewish Maternity Home or, more familiarly among the Jews of the East End who were its clientele, 'Mother Levy's'. Jewish schools in London and the surrounding districts were given £3,000. Coals for the Jewish Poor of London had £2,000, and the Jewish Lads' Brigade, 'in memory of my former husband Samuel Lewis', and the West London Synagogue of British Jews, £1,000 each. Other bequests were:

The Lord Mayor of London to found 'The Ada Lewis Winter Distress Fund'	£25,000
The Lord Mayor of Dublin for a similar purpose	10,000
The Church Army	20,000
The Salvation Army	20,000
The United Kingdom Beneficent Association	20,000
National Refuges for Homeless and Destitute Children	10,000
Royal Masonic Institution for Boys	10,000
The National Life-Boat Institution to endow the 'Samuel Lewis' and 'Ada Lewis' Life Boats (or such sum as is necessary for the purpose)	5,000
Royal Society of Musicians	5,000
Home for German Sailors at South Shields	5,000
Cabdrivers' Benevolent Association	5,000

Ham Common National Orphan Home for Fatherless Girls	5,000
The Middlesex Hospital to endow a 'Samuel Lewis Ward'	5,000
The Soldiers' Orphanage Home	5,000
Little Sisters of the Poor	2,000
The Montague Williams Blanket Fund for the Poor	2,000
The National Hospital for Diseases of the Heart and Paralysis, to endow two beds	2,000
Metropolitan Police Convalescent Home	2,000
Railway Officials and Servants' Association	2,000
National Waifs' Association	2,000
Metropolitan Fire Brigade Widows' and Orphans' General Benefit Fund	2,000
National Industrial Home for Crippled Boys	2,000
King Edward's School at Whitney	2,000
Metropolitan Police Orphanage	2,000
For distribution amongst annuitants who have been receiving periodical payments through my secretary	1,000
Gardeners' Royal Benevolent Institution	1,000
British and Foreign Sailors' Society	1,000
National Society for the Prevention of Cruelty to Children	1,000
To erect the 'Ada Lewis Cattle Drinking Trough' at Maidenhead	500
For the poor of Constantinople	500
Rev. R. H. Hadden for Church purposes	500
For each poor box at every Metropolitan Police Court	250

All the moneys that Sam had left to charity which were to come into effect on Ada's death were now payable. The combined total of their charitable donations exceeded £2 million. Distribution of the money was of course dependent on the sale of the stocks, shares, bonds, properties and, in the case of Sam's estate, collection of debts. This took a considerable time, and many debts were written off. Occasionally a debtor was made bankrupt, not necessarily by Sam's trustees, and the dividend received was less than 20s in the pound. It was not until 1917 that sufficient moneys were collected for all the original legacies to be paid, and the last payment from Ada's residuary estate was not made until 1968.

Sir Arthur Bigge, the King's Equerry-in-Waiting, wrote to Danvers Power, the honorary secretary of the King Edward's Hospital Fund, on 18 October 1906:

> I am sure the Prince of Wales [later George V] will be interested in the information you give about Sam Lewis's money. Certainly the Hospital Fund has benefited by the moneylending business – and also Captain Hill!

22 · The beneficiaries

He hath dispersed, he hath given to the needy,
His righteousness endureth for ever.
Memorial to Samuel Lewis on tablet at
Dublin Jewish Board of Guardians

Altogether 51 charities were beneficiaries under Sam and Ada's wills. They consisted of organisations established to help the hospitals, the working classes, the middle classes and the arts; and doubtless they all, from the Salvation Army to the Metropolitan Police Convalescent Home, from the London Hospital to the Home of Rest for Horses, from the Sisters of Nazareth to the Jews' Deaf and Dumb Home, put the moneys they received to good use. Moorfields Eye Hospital, for example, spent part of its legacy in providing quarters for sick nursing staff and part to install a bacteriological laboratory. The lifeboats presented by Ada to the National Lifeboat Institution gave years of service. The *Ada Lewis* stationed at Newbiggin-by-the-Sea was involved in several rescues, particularly during the First World War, including saving the lives of 22 crew members of the SS *Invergoyle*, which was torpedoed three miles east of Newbiggin Point and, most unusually for a lifeboat, rendering assistance to a stranded submarine. The *Samuel Lewis* was in service at Skegness from 1906 to 1932. Between them the boats saved more than 100 lives. We shall examine just a few of the charities in more detail to see how the money was spent.

Ada left £10,000 to the Lord Mayor of Dublin, the income to be used for the relief of the poor within the City of Dublin during the winter months and to be called the Ada Lewis Winter Fund. She left £25,000 to the Lord Mayor of London for similar purposes. Immediately the news was reported in the local press in Dublin the Lord Mayor was inundated with appeals from charitable societies. In

343

December 1908 the Master of the Rolls approved a scheme under which the capital was to be held by the Commissioners of Charitable Donations and Bequests in Ireland and the net yearly income was to be applied during the months of November, December, January, February and March in rendering assistance to the poor of the city without distinction of creed. This remains the position. The trustees, consisting of the Lord Mayor, the High Sheriff, and one other, distribute the income to local charities, mainly, but not exclusively, religious. Convents and sisters are particularly well represented. The annual income has risen steadily from IR£165 in 1909 to IR£2,500 in 1990, in which year 30 charities received allocations ranging from IR£50 to IR£300. By careful, yet imaginative, investment the capital sum had by 1985 increased to IR£25,548 and is doubtless higher today. The Dublin Jewish Board of Guardians usually receives £50, and Sam would have been particularly heartened to learn that in the early years the Board used its share to provide coals for the Jewish poor of Dublin.

The High Court in London approved the London scheme, also in 1908, and in almost identical terms to the Dublin scheme. The beneficiaries are 'poor or distressed persons residing, engaged or employed within the City of London', or former residents or their families or dependents. The records of the Fund indicate that care is taken to ensure that it is the genuinely needy who benefit. At 31 March 1987 the market value of the capital fund was £64,913, and that year there were 24 recipients of £75 each in cash plus a Christmas hamper. The trustees regularly receive letters of thanks saying how grateful the recipients are to Ada Lewis, and how appreciative they are of the help they now get through her thoughtfulness and kindness, though they can know nothing about her.

Sam's gift to the Jewish poor of Dublin was £15,000. The Jewish population of Ireland has never been large, and the majority have always lived in Dublin. In the mid-eighteenth century they numbered about 200, and there were very few more when Sam paid his first visits in the 1850s. By the date of his death, however, following the mass exodus of Jews from eastern Europe in the 1880s and 1890s, their numbers had considerably increased. The official census returns of 1881, which in Ireland included religious affiliation, showed the Jewish population of Ireland as 453; by the time of the 1891 census there were 1,779; and in 1901 there were just over 2,000 in Dublin alone. The majority of the newcomers were poor, and in need of support from their more affluent coreligionists. In 1889 the Dublin Jewish Board of Guardians was founded to cater for their needs and in 1901 its income from all sources was £298.

Sam instructed his trustees to apply the income of the £15,000 for a period of 20 years for the relief of the Jewish poor in Dublin. They were given permission to make the payments either directly to the poor or to channel the funds through existing Dublin institutions. At the end of the 20-year period the trustees could then either continue to make payments of the income, or transfer the capital and income to a local institution. The Board of Guardians, as the largest Jewish charitable organisation in the town, naturally expected to receive the largest share of the income.

Shortly after Ada died Sydney contacted John David Rosenthal (1833–1907) and asked him to elect five trustees to manage the bequest. He was an appropriate choice. A luminary of the legal profession, he had been a member of the Council of the Incorporated Law Society in Ireland and a Director of the Solicitors' Benevolent Association. He served as solicitor and honorary secretary to the congregation for 30 years and represented it at the Board of Deputies of British Jews. In February 1907 he appointed five well-known members of the Dublin community, but in doing so he, and Sydney, found that they had unwittingly stirred up a hornets' nest.

In addition to the Jewish Board of Guardians there were several other organisations in Dublin which in various ways supported the Jewish poor. These included five synagogues, the Ladies' Benevolent Society whose object was the relief of poor lying-in women, the Hachnasath Orechim, founded in 1888 for the relief of strangers, giving them shelter for three days, and the Medical Relief Society. They all felt slighted that Sydney had not dealt with them direct. After a great deal of internal quarrelling it was eventually agreed to appoint seven gentlemen representing seven different charitable institutions of Dublin to lay before Sydney the true state of affairs of the Dublin Jewish poor and the institutions which supported them. Deputations were sent to London to see him, and in due course Dublin trustees were appointed to hold the £15,000 on behalf of the London trustees of the will. It was doubtless with great relief that

Sydney passed the money and the responsibility for the distribution of the income to them, but even then individual members of the community were to write to him from time to time complaining that a particular charity was not receiving its fair share. In 1921, the period provided in Sam's will having expired, the capital sum was formally passed to the Dublin trustees who now control it absolutely.

The Board of Guardians received, and continues to receive, the bulk of the income, and it has always been put to good use. In 1901 its income from all sources was £298; in 1921 it was £1,160. Typical benefits given were fare money for people travelling to Liverpool, the loan of money to a small trader for stock, the distribution of coal tickets, help to a family during a daughter's sickness, payment of rent for widows, £4 to a deserted wife to enable her to return to America, £1 to a commercial traveller robbed by another commercial traveller. Today much of the income from Sam's legacy is used to assist the elderly of the community. A photograph of Sam was prominently displayed in the Committee Room of the Board, as was a commemorative plaque (now in the Dublin Jewish Museum) which is inscribed:

He hath dispersed, he hath given to the needy.
His righteousness endureth for ever
To the sacred memory of
MR. SAMUEL LEWIS
who has generously bequeathed the sum of £15,000 for the benefit
of his co-religionists in the City of Dublin.
Died 13th January 1901

Every year, on the anniversary his death, a memorial prayer is said for Sam at the offices of the Board.

The first salaried governesses date back to Tudor times. The much-sought-after position of governess to the children of the reigning monarch was one of the oldest appointments in the Royal Household, and the successful applicant was always of high birth, usually a duchess, a countess, or the wife of a baron. She was required to be wise, discreet, polite and eminently trustworthy. In Victorian and Edwardian England class was still the most important element in a family's selection of a governess. As she had to be upper-class, or at least genteel, the financial collapse of one part of a family meant that its unmarried and now impoverished daughters were ideal material for other members of the family seeking a governess for their older children. A teaching post, which at least put a roof over her head, was often the only course open to the middle-class spinster whose parents had died or who could not afford to keep her at home, and this continued to be the situation until the outbreak of the Second World War. The 1927 Annual Report of the Governesses' Benevolent Institution recorded that the majority of its applicants were the daughters of clergymen, doctors, lawyers, naval and military officers, and others of the professional and middle classes of the community, who through bereavement or family misfortune had been compelled to earn their own living. Their duties were largely confined to teaching the daughters of the family they served.

During the nineteenth century their working conditions and pay were poor, usually £25 to £30 a year, and many led a miserable existence. Some families treated them shabbily, and impoverishment and unemployment were their frequent companions. As early as 1829 a society known as the Governesses' Mutual Assurance Society was formed to alleviate their hardship, particularly in illness and old age. The society did not flourish, and indeed collapsed nine years later, but several of its supporters reconstituted it in 1841 under the title Governesses' Benevolent Institution. In 1843 the Reverend David Laing was appointed honorary secretary, and it was largely through his devoted efforts, organisational skills and fund-raising ability that the society obtained the substantial base from which it grew. Its stated aims were 'to raise the character of governesses as a class, and thus improve the tone of Female Education; to assist Governesses in making provision for their old age; and to assist in distress and age those Governesses whose exertions for their parents, or families, have prevented such a provision'. Within a year Laing had expanded the list of subscribers from little more than a handful to 600. No less than five members of the Royal Family and 62 of noble birth were patrons. By 1860, the year in which he died, the list had risen to 6,000.

At the first annual fund-raising dinner of the GBI held in April 1844, the guest speaker was Charles Dickens:

Take the case of those ladies in comparison with menial servants: they are worse paid than the cook: their salaries bear poor comparison with the wages of the butler: they appear but shabbily with

347

the remuneration of the lady's-maid: and they are even lower than those paid to liveried footmen ... and after having faithfully accomplished her task in one family, she is thrown upon the world, and goes forth again among strangers to educate others ...

The Society might relieve the physical sufferings of governesses in distress – it might cheer them on the bed of sickness, and soften the asperities of their condition in declining age; but, unless the society exerts its energies to render governesses *more respected*, it will fall far short of the great end which I conceive it had in view. From first to last I have had a confidence that the society would do its duty; and I hope by its means to see blotted out a national reproach, and that the profession of education will be placed on that honourable footing which in any civilised and Christian land, it ought to hold [continuing cheering].

During the first 60 years of its life the society became one of *the* national charities. Though it never reached the popularity of hospitals and housing for the working classes as a recipient of charitable funds, it none the less came high up the scale. This may have been due to some element of guilt and self-serving on the part of wealthy donors who needed the governesses' services. Royal patronage also helped its cause. Queen Victoria was its first royal patron, to be followed by Edward VII. At the time of writing the Queen Mother holds the position and Earl Spencer, father of the Princess of Wales, has been its chairman since 1963.

The question of a permanent home for retired governesses was first raised in 1844. Ground was purchased in Prince of Wales Road, Kentish Town, in 1847, and Laing said, 'Let us no longer have before our eyes the painful spectacle of the worn-out governess, still longing and striving for the employment age will no longer allow her to attain, yet destitute of all the comforts which should accompany old age – let us give her a home who has influenced the domestic character of so many houses.' The Asylum for Aged Governesses, a haven and resting-place for the homeless governess, was opened in June 1849 at at a total cost of £9,000. It was sold in 1870 and the proceeds used for the purchase of land in Manor Park Road, Chislehurst, where 12 houses for retired governesses plus one for the lady superintendent were erected. Work was completed in 1872.

Ada Lewis approved of female advancement in all fields, and the aims of the GBI would have appealed to her in any event, but her friendship with Lord and Lady Farquhar, long-standing supporters of the institution from 1867, must have influenced her. She did not make her first donation until 1902, shortly after she had made their close acquaintance.

Ada was at Grosvenor Square during the last few weeks of her life, and Lady Farquhar, who lived just a few doors away, and who had arranged for her to be presented at Court, most probably visited her and comforted her during the period she was considering the final alterations to her will. It was the seventh codicil, signed just four weeks before her death, which led to a dramatic change in the fortunes of the GBI. In the four previous years its total receipts from all sources – annual subscriptions, donations and legacies – totalled £7,995, £11,498, £6,466 and £9,620 respectively. Ada's legacy to them was £52,000 plus half her residuary estate, to be used for the purpose of building further homes similar to those at Chislehurst. By the time the very last instalment of her residuary estate was paid out, more than 63 years after her death, the society had received almost exactly £100,000 including interest. Without Ada's contribution, which transformed its funds, the society could not possibly have progressed in the successful way that it did.

Once the terms of Ada's will became known the GBI was inundated with requests for accommodation, and there was a falling-off in subscriptions. The trustees were compelled to make it publicly clear that Ada's money, when it came, had to be used solely for building and maintaining homes similar to those at Chislehurst, and that their supporters' subscriptions were still very much needed:

No portion of it will be available for the existing work of the Institution. The Board desires to give this fact the fullest publicity in the hope of saving further disappointment to would-be recipients, and also to urge upon the subscribers the need of the Institution for their continued support. Some during the year have ceased to subscribe on the plea that the Institution can no longer require their help, and this erroneous impression has also proved a serious handicap in gaining the sympathy of fresh supporters.

From time to time the institution enquired of Ernest when and how much they were likely to receive, and the difficulties of collection were set out by him in a letter written to their secretary in 1925:

> Referring to your enquiry on the telephone this morning, as to whether there was any likelihood of your Institute receiving anything further on account of the residuary estate by the end of the year, we fear that there is not much chance of anything further being paid by then.
>
> The residuary estate consists mainly of the reversion of certain trustee investments, the income whereof is payable to the various tenants for life and annuitants [whose ages] vary, we should think, from about forty to sixty-five, and the ages of four of the tenants for life vary from about forty-five to fifty-five, and the age of the remaining tenant for life is seventy-five. You will see therefore that it is impossible to say when these funds will fall in.
>
> In addition thereto Mrs. Lewis-Hill's estate consists, as we think you are aware, of part of her late husband's residuary estate, and this consists mainly of a property in Ireland and one in Glasgow. The Irish property is in course of realisation under the Irish Land Acts and it is quite impossible to say when the sale will be completed, or what the proceeds will amount to, and with regard to the property in Glasgow, the Trustees have made several attempts to sell it but without success. It is fully let, and they are in receipt of the rents and profits, but until things improve, there does not appear to be any prospect of their being able to realise.
>
> This information is not very definite, but you will no doubt appreciate the difficulty there is in not being able to give you any approximate idea as to when any further distribution will be made, but you will gather that there will be a considerable sum of money payable to the institution in the future.

In the meantime permission was given for part of the sums received to be used to purchase annuities, and by 1926 there were 31 annuities of £52 a year provided for retired governesses.

In 1924 a four-acre site at Beckenham, on the side of a hill overlooking a valley, with an excellent view of the Crystal Palace, was acquired for £2,600. Work was completed in 1926 at the cost of £20,000, and the first retired governess took up residence in May of that year. Ernest was invited to the official opening. There were ten semi-detached villas, and another for the lady superintendent. In addition to the house and an annuity of £52, each resident was granted free gas, coal, electric light and medical attention. All necessary furnishings were provided, though residents were encouraged to bring their own pieces if they so wished.

At first, all residents had to have a relative or friend living in to look after them, but it proved more and more difficult to find such companions. As time passed the usefulness of the homes became doubtful because women were living longer and retiring later. The number capable of running their own homes and doing their own cooking was decreasing, and the majority had reached the stage when they were too old to fend entirely for themselves and needed some degree of supervision. The trend was for new homes to provide at least one main meal a day and accommodation more suitable to current needs. Accordingly arrangements were made to sell the site at Beckenham for £120,000, and this sum, together with £20,000 raised by an appeal, was used to replace the original homes at Chislehurst. The new building, Queen Mary House, which opened in 1966, thus very largely owes its existence and survival to the moneys received from Ada's legacy. Today the insurance cover effected for rebuilding purposes is almost £4 milllion which gives some indication of the present value to the society of Ada's gift.

Residents are no longer restricted to retired governesses, and include women teachers and other ladies connected with the private sector of the teaching profession, and the society is now called the Schoolmistresses' and Governesses' Benevolent Institution. Queen Mary House is set in pleasant and spacious grounds and accommodates 44 residents, 10 in flatlets who look after themselves and the remainder in comfortable single furnished bed-sitting rooms equipped with every convenience. Meals are provided for all residents in the dining room. There is an extension in which medical care can be given to those not so seriously ill as to require admission to hospital.

Over the years the successive boards of trustees have invested Ada's moneys prudently and made good use of the income. Today, though facing the problems common to most charitable organisations, particularly those involved in the provision of homes for the elderly, the society's financial position is strong. Its declared policy is that as few conditions as possible shall be imposed on residents, and no visitor to the House can fail to be impressed by the relaxed and warm style of management and the combination of independence and support it gives to its residents.

We have discussed the worrying financial position of the hospitals at the beginning of this century, but there was another medical problem which proved more difficult to resolve, the question of convalescence. Because of the shortage of beds, patients were discharged from hospital earlier than was desirable, and many returned to homes which were so insanitary that much of the benefit derived from their stay in hospital was undone. A period of convalescence, preferably in an area where the air was clear and bracing, was needed to ensure that patients gained sufficient strength to face their home conditions. Some hospitals had their own convalescent homes, and there were many private homes, but overall there was a serious deficiency of such accommodation. There was an additional problem for Jewish patients. Some of the voluntary hospitals which served the bulk of the Jewish poor in the East End of London, particularly the London Hospital (now the Royal London Hospital), the German Hospital and the Metropolitan Hospital, made special provision for the needs of their Jewish patients, by providing kosher food and facilities for the observance of religious rites, but such facilities did not extend to their convalescent homes. Many orthodox Jews preferred to forgo a period of convalescence rather than break their religious codes, and as a result many such suffered in their health.

It was the Jewish Board of Guardians in London, of which Sydney was a founder member and honorary solicitor, which made strenuous efforts to fill the gaps in the system. Sir Lionel Cohen became president of the Board in 1900 and it was at his suggestion, made through Sydney, that Sam was induced to give the legacy of £100,000 to the Board 'for the purpose of establishing at some place on the sea coast of England a convalescent cottage home or hospital ... And I direct that the inmates of the said home or hospital shall not be confined to persons of the Hebrew faith although persons of that faith shall have the preference over persons not of that faith.' Soon after Ada died the Board set up a sub-committee, which included Sydney, to make recommendations. It reported in January 1907, and advised that a site should be found not further north than Felixstowe; not less than £80,000 should be set aside for investment; the balance should be used for the purchase of the site and erection of the building; it should be open to both male and female patients; no patients suffering from phthisis (tuberculosis) should be admitted; there should be room for about 50 inmates; and if possible all nursing staff should be fully qualified. They took the opportunity of repeating, on behalf of the Board and its supporters, their keen appreciation of the generous intention of Sam Lewis, which would, they felt sure, be the means of doing infinite good to those who were selected for the benefits of the trust; and they added that they were deeply aware of the honour which had been done to the Board by entrusting it with the equipment and management of an addition to the still too few institutions of the kind then existing in the country.

A suitable site of about three acres was found at Walton-on-the-Naze in Essex and purchased for £3,100. By June 1908 tenders totalling £20,000 had been accepted, and the home, to be called the Samuel Lewis Convalescent Home, was completed in 1910. At the consecration in May there were several representatives of the Jewish establishment present, conveyed there from Walton-on-the-Naze Station in brakes and wagonettes. The Reverend J. F. Stern, the minister of the East End Synagogue, delivered a special dedicatory prayer:

> Almighty and All Merciful God! We are gathered here to con-
> secrate this Home to the beneficent purpose designed by our
> departed brother in faith, to enter upon the sacred trust he has
> bequeathed to us. We will strive to perform our charge in faithful-
> ness to the living and the dead, so that the loving intentions of the
> Founder may be abundantly realised, and his benefaction may be a
> source of blessing to our brothers and sisters who will sojourn
> within these walls. May the rest and tender care which they will
> find here renew their strength, so that their health may spring
> forth speedily, and they may be enabled, on their return to their
> homes in our busy city, to support themselves and their families by
> the toil of their hands.

It is noteworthy that Reverend Stern emphasised, in Jewish fashion, that a main purpose of the charity would be to enable the recipients to support themselves and their families. Mr Louis E. Raphael, chairman of the home's Committee of Management, said that two classes of patients would be catered for. The first were those who were sufficiently cured to be discharged from hospital, but who nevertheless required careful nursing, attention and feeding, and who were not well enough to return to their own homes, where such matters could not be properly attended to. For them it was hoped that on the invigorating east coast they would be thoroughly restored to health and rendered fit to resume the stern struggle of life. The second class comprised those frequent cases where there might be no actual illness, but where men and women were enfeebled by poor or insufficient food, overwork or insanitary surroundings.

Raphael announced that some very valuable donations had been received, including a cheque for £100 from Mr Leopold de Rothschild for games, two pianos from himself, furniture from Mrs Harris Lebus, and from Sydney an enlarged photograph of Sam which was for many years displayed in a prominent position in the home. The executors of Louisa Sophia, Lady Goldsmid, allocated £1,300 for the endowment of two additional beds.

There was an income of about £3,000 a year from their investments, but it was felt that this would not be sufficient to provide free admission to all 60 beds. The committee therefore agreed to reserve 20 beds for fee-paying patients at a maximum charge of 10s 6d per week. During its first year of operation 644 patients were treated, of whom 345 were women. With the bulk of the Jewish poor living in the East End of London, it followed that the largest number of patients admitted were referred from the London Hospital. Patients originally stayed for an average of four weeks, but this was reduced to three weeks, enabling more to benefit, and gradually the numbers increased to over 1,500 a year.

During the two world wars the home was requisitioned by the military. In 1916 the men's wing was taken over for the convalescence of wounded troops, and in 1939 it was taken over by the Ministry of Health and Essex County Council for use as a hospital and first aid post. It was well attended during the 1950s and 1960s, but gradually circumstances turned against its continuation. The general improvement in living conditions and the increasing use of antibiotics meant that in the crucial few weeks after hospitalisation more and more postoperative patients could return to their own homes. Local authorities who, until then, had contributed to recuperative holidays at the home for those who had not required hospital treatment, withdrew their support. After 66 years' service to the community, the building itself required extensive and expensive modernisation to bring it up to modern standards; and due to lack of financial support, coupled with changing needs, the home was closed in 1976. More than 50,000 residents had enjoyed its benefits, and over the years its medical officers reported that more than 95 per cent left either cured or improved.

The legacy still provides comforts for the sick and needy. The home and grounds were sold for £120,000 in 1982. The Jewish Welfare Board (as the Jewish Board of Guardians was by then called, which now operates under the title Jewish Care) applied to the Charity Commissioners for consent to use the income from the Trust to provide for the benefit of elderly, frail and infirm people requiring short stay or permanent care in Jewish Welfare Board Residential Homes. This is the current use of Sam's legacy.

There are fashions in charitable giving as in everything else. At the end of the nineteenth century two of the most popular causes were support for the voluntary hospitals and housing for the working classes. The great voluntary hospital system in England, which contributed largely to the rapid progress then being made in all aspects of health care, was almost entirely funded by the donations of the rich, without whose support they could not have continued. The middle and working classes made their donations too, but in the overall picture their financial contribution was marginal. As the rate of medical progress quickened, so the expectations of patients rose, and there was an insatiable demand for cash to sustain the momentum. Hospitals were high on the list of those with money to spare for charity who looked for an avenue in which to channel it. They provided the advantage of affording easy public recognition of gifts, should donors wish it, for their names could be affixed to a bed, a ward, a wing or even a hospital.

In its early years the King Edward VII Hospital Fund, now known as the King's Fund, had a considerable impact on the financial health of London voluntary hospitals, its grants making good their annual deficiencies. Today its financial resources are minuscule compared with the cost of providing the metropolis with its medical care. Despite its income having increased to £4,500,000 in 1989, and its capital to £70 million, these sums pale into insignificance when measured against National Health expenditure. In 1985, in the London Health Districts alone, this amounted to £2,265 million.

For many years the Fund undoubtedly was a beneficial influence on the efficiency of the voluntary London hospitals. But things were changing in health care. The poor, for whom the voluntary hospitals catered, were joined by the middle classes who sought the medical treatment they could no longer afford to buy for themselves at home. As the voluntary hospital system began to crumble under the weight of ever-increasing costs it became clear that a new system was essential. By 1939 the Fund had to agree that the voluntary hospital system needed state aid. During the war the hospitals relied increasingly on the government, and when the National Health Service came into being in 1948 the Fund used its experience of 50 years' work in the field to help shape the new system.

The Fund still owes a great deal for its continued existence and present strength to its founders and those who supported it financially in its early years. By the end of 1909 Sam's trustees had passed over £258,000 and between then and 1937 a further £267,000. Small sums followed in succeeding years until 1949 when the grand total reached £527,307. Additionally, during her lifetime, Ada made contributions of £37,605 and Sam £420. In all they gave £569,328. This was the Fund's second largest source of capital and income, exceeded only by Lord Mount Stephen whose legacy totalled £815,000 and his gifts £500,000. Other generous contributors were Sir Thomas Sutherland, £483,000; Mr Claud Watney £420,000; Sir Julius Wehrner £390,000; Andrew Carnegie £100,000; and Sir Ernest Cassel £66,000. In July 1937 Dr Eardley Holland, a commissioner of the Fund, said that the Samuel Lewis Bequest was one of the main sources of its income.

After 1948 the Fund had to find a new role. Today it concerns itself with promoting good service for patients, a high standard of health for the community, and maximum autonomy for the patient, the family and the community. It considers that it is in the spirit of the founders of the Fund and the intentions of Edward VII that emphasis should be placed on helping the family and the community to choose. The Fund still seeks to stimulate good practice and innovation in all aspects of health care and management through research and development, education, policy analysis and direct grants. Its grants range from sums of a few hundred pounds to major schemes costing over £1 million. In 1989, for example, contributions were made towards the cost of a project on leadership development in nursing (£20,000); a visit to the Rand Corporation in California to look at methods of medical audit (£250); production of a video on pregnancy in women with physical disabilities (£5,000); evaluation of a venous ulcer project at Charing Cross Hospital (£20,000); towards the cost of group support for bereaved parents (£8,600); and for a research project looking into the concepts of diet and health in relation to the elderly Chinese community (£2,800). By selecting areas in which the money supplied can generate an influence beyond the confines of the work done and the research undertaken, the Fund aims to add leverage to its efforts.

As with the hospitals, so with housing. Victorian England had more than its share of filthy, crumbling, overcrowded slums. Throughout the nineteenth century the demand for houses far exceeded the supply. Demolition in the teeming town centres, particularly in London, to make way for railways, docks, warehouses and street improvements, was at its height. Many thousands were displaced, and in some areas between 60 and 70 per cent of the population were compelled to live in one small overcrowded room, in which every domestic operation was carried on. The Royal Commission on Housing of 1885 recorded one case in a London borough in which 11 families lived in 11 rooms. A medical officer of St George the Martyr, Southwark, said there were 'swarms of men and women who had yet to learn that human beings should dwell differently from cattle, swarms to whom personal cleanliness was utterly unknown, swarms by whom delicacy and decency in their social relations were quite unconceived'. In relation to the wages then being earned by the working population, even such inferior accommodation was expensive.

Clean, substantial, sanitary housing was lacking in sufficient quantity for the working classes, and the position was worse in London than elsewhere in the country. To remedy, or at least ameliorate, the situation was a task so daunting that, as was the case with hospitals, it cried out for state and municipal intervention and assistance. That this should come was inevitable, but governments and local authorities were slow to act, and the first tentative steps were taken by private eleemosynary, or at least semi-charitable, institutions.

The Metropolitan Association for Improving the Dwellings of the Industrious Classes was formed in 1841 with the aim of 'providing the labouring man with an increase of the comforts and conveniences of life, with full compensation to the capitalist'. Three years later the Society for Improving the Condition of the Labouring Classes began to take an interest in the field of housing. It proposed a series of pilot schemes on a small scale to ascertain what was the best type of accommodation for different classes of occupants, and also to demonstrate that homes which provided comfort and decency could be built and operated at rentals the working man could afford. The association raised its money by selling shares, but limited dividends to a maximum of five per cent. In the 1860s Angela Burdett-Coutts, prompted by Charles Dickens, built four blocks in Bethnal Green which set the pattern for many which followed. Four- or five-storey blocks were sited around a central open space. Sets of rooms were arranged off central spine corridors and shared lavatory and washing facilities were provided. There were covered areas for drying clothes, and these could be used as children's play space on wet days. Sir Sydney Waterlow, of the pen and printing company, founded the Improved Industrial Dwellings Company, run on similar lines. George Peabody, the American who resided in London, made £500,000 available to the trustees of the Peabody Donation Fund, and gave them complete discretion. They decided to spend most of the available capital on providing cheap, clean, well-drained and healthy dwellings for the poor. By 1890 they had built more than 5,000. Although the government, and through them the local authorities, gradually became active in the field, there was still scope for the individual philanthropist.

Two men who made handsome contributions to this work, and whose efforts particularly impressed and influenced Sam, were Lord Rothschild and Sir Edward Guinness, later Lord Iveagh. Sam of course knew Iveagh well through his connection with the Ailesbury estate and his abortive attempt to purchase Savernake. The Guinness Trust was set up in February 1890 with a gift of £200,000 and its main object was:

The amelioration of the condition of the poorer classes of the working population of London and of their modes and manner of living, by the provision of improved dwellings; by giving them facilities, should the Trustees think it desirable in any or all cases to do so, for obtaining means of subsistence and the necessaries and decencies of life; and by such other means as the Trustees may in their uncontrolled discretion think fit ... *with the hope that, should his expectation in this respect be fulfilled, the success of the experiment may lead to other efforts in the like direction.*

The administration of the Trust shall be wholly unsectarian and non-political ... and it will be a violation of the intentions of the Founder if participation in its benefits should be excluded on the ground of religious belief or political bias.

Lord Rothschild was the unquestioned lay leader of the Jewish community. Very much an 'East End man', in the sense that he was concerned for the welfare of the poor Jews who mostly congregated in the Whitechapel and Mile End area of London, he did his best to relieve the chronic overcrowding which existed there. In 1893 the Jewish Board of Guardians' Sanitary Committee's Visitor inspected 1,746 dwellings and found that nearly half of them fell below the standards laid down by the local authority under the Public Health Acts. Lord Rothschild founded and became chairman of the Four Per Cent Industrial Dwellings Company,which had similar aims to the other organisations. Significantly, its solicitor was Algernon Sydney. By 1901 the company was housing 4,600 individuals in five separate developments in the East End. Sam, concerned as he was in Jewish matters, and with further information being fed to him by Sydney, was well aware of the importance of the provision of better living accommodation for the working classes. He had also never forgotten his early days in Lower Hurst Street.

Philanthropy alone could not keep pace with the growing housing demands, but there was a contribution for it to make. The philanthropists perhaps underestimated the dimensions of the evil, and some critics have said that their activities masked it, but when all is said and done they did not simply stand and stare, but actually did something about the problem. They brought some relief, but more importantly their activities acted as a prod to local authority and

359

government to take up the cudgels and participate in this necessary work. Sam provided in his will that his trustees should use £400,000 to purchase land and erect suitable dwellings 'to be let to poor persons at low rents'. The area of activity specified was England, but until well after the Second World War all the flats and houses erected by the Building Fund, which became known as the Samuel Lewis Trust for Dwellings for the Poor, were in London.

The influence of Lord Iveagh was clear. The twin aims of his fund, that those intended to benefit were the poorer of the working classes, and that no one should be excluded from benefit on the grounds of his or her political or religious beliefs, were followed by Sam's trustees. Relations between the Samuel Lewis and Guinness trusts remained close, perhaps inevitably in view of the wish expressed by Sam that his trustees should manage the estates 'as near as may be in a similar manner to that in which the buildings belonging to the Guinness Trust (London) Fund are now managed'. Indeed, so similar were the aims and activities of the two funds that in 1920 the Charity Commission suggested that they should merge, but the idea was ultimately rejected as not representing Sam's intention or wishes. By a scheme approved by the Board of Charity Commissioners in 1958 the then trustees were to be replaced by six others, one of whom was to be appointed by the Guinness Trust. When in 1980 the Guinness Trust launched a 90th Anniversary Appeal Fund the Samuel Lewis Trust was among the contributors, and there has always been, and remains, a high degree of cooperation between the senior staff of each organisation.

The £400,000 was in the hands of the trustees by 1911, and thereafter a further £270,000 was received, although the final instalment was not paid until 1948. The first recorded meeting of trustees was on 8 December 1909, held at 44 Clifton Gardens, Maida Vale, the home of Clara and Augustus Jacobs. By June 1908 sufficient monies were in hand for land at Liverpool Road, Islington, to be purchased. The estate which was built there, at an inclusive cost of £101,000, was completed in 1910, and consisted of six parallel blocks, each five storeys in height, with 44ft-wide playgrounds separating each block. The opening ceremony took place in the presence of the mayors of Holborn, Poplar, Southwark, Marylebone and Chelsea, and many metropolitan medical officers, as well as representatives of the Guinness Trust, Sutton Trust, Peabody Trust and the East End Dwelling Company. It consisted of 151 well-ventilated flats with three rooms, 150 with two rooms and 22 single-room flats. Additionally each flat had a scullery. Rents ranged from 8s per week to 2s, inclusive of rates, chimney sweeping and venetian blinds – considerably less than those ruling in the neighbourhood for smaller and less well-equipped tenements.

Originally only married couples with young children of or under school age were offered flats, the one-room flats being reserved for female old age pensioners. Each applicant was visited at his or her home, and no one who was in arrears with rent or whose home was very dirty or verminous was accepted. The average rent charged was 2s 7d per week, and the average earnings of the head of each family was £1.3.5d per week. No flats were let to the unemployed or to those earning more than £1 5s 0d per week. The self-employed, such as waiters, taxi drivers and costermongers, were also not accepted because of the difficulty of verifying their earnings. Rents were set at a level which it was expected would produce a net return of over three per cent per annum, but this was never achieved for any sustained length of time. Over the first 75 years of the life of the Trust the estates showed a return, based on the original cost of the land and buildings, varying between three per cent down to as low as 0.93 per cent and this, of course, to some extent restricted its capital growth.

The *Morning Leader*, with perhaps only a touch of exaggeration, described the Liverpool Street flats as being built to such a high standard that a workman could have a flat equal in many respects, but not in rent, to some of the best in the West End. They added that the architecture, from the designs of Messrs Joseph & Smithen, would not have disgraced Belgravia, nor would the interior fittings. The floors were of parquet. The sculleries were described as marvels of compact design. They contained, in just a comparatively few square feet, a full-sized, enamelled, cast-iron bath, a table which was hinged to the side of the bath, a copper which supplied hot water for the bath and for laundry, a gas stove, a kitchen range, a sink, and a dresser with three tiers of shelves. In the fireplace was an ingenious device patented by the architects. There was a sliding back to the range. The fireplace in the living room backed on to that in the scullery, and when the slide was raised there was nothing between the two fireplaces. By a tilting arrangement the contents of one grate could be transferred to the other. When the cooking was finished in the scullery the tenant operated the mechanism, transferred the fire to the living room, and lowered the slide. He thus had a warm living room, and the smells of cooking were kept out. An integral balcony housed a larder, coal bunker and fully tiled water closet.

There were also some frills, missing from most similar phil-anthropically funded housing estates at that time. The site was surrounded by an ornamental dwarf glazed brick wall, there were bay windows, picturesque porches at the entrances to the blocks, the balustrades to the staircase were constructed of ornamental panel balusters instead of the usual plain bars, there were 21 domes on the slated roofs, attractive shelters in the courtyards in which tenants could sit and watch their children playing, and there was a resident porter. A separate drying room for communal use avoided the then usual sight of washing hanging on a line from balconies or windows. It was said that the rather ornate style of the building was intended as a memorial to Sam. This estate was recently modernised and now provides 250 homes.

By 1939 a further seven sites had been developed, at Ixworth Place, Chelsea (1912); Warner Road, Camberwell (1913–19); Vanston Place, Walham Green (1920–2), the first to have separate bathrooms and a supply of electricity in addition to gas; Dalston Lane, Dalston (1923); Lisgar Terrace, Fulham (1927); Amhurst Road, Hackney (1931–7); and at Amhurst Park, Stamford Hill (1938–9), though the flats there were not built until after the war. On average there have been between 6,000 and 7,000 persons living in the flats at any one time, the 2,200 tenants each paying reasonable rents, and occupying premises which were well maintained and continually being im-proved.

One problem facing such housing trusts was whether to borrow for expansion. Some felt it right to operate only within the limit of their own capital. It was not until the 1960s, for example, that the Sutton Estates seriously considered the possibility, and it worried them. The Guinness Trust on the other hand borrowed freely, and more than half of its estates were built, in part at least, on borrowed money. The Samuel Lewis trustees also believed in borrowing, and the Chelsea and Camberwell estates were funded partly by loans from the Union of London and Smith's Bank. In 1927 the Trust obtained a mortgage on two of its estates for £100,000 in order to finance part of the cost of the Fulham estate.

The Housing Act of 1974 enabled trusts such as Guinness and Samuel Lewis to obtain loans, subsidies and outright grants from the Housing Corporation and from local authorities on a very generous scale. As at 31 March 1990, Samuel Lewis had loans of £41 million and a housing association grant of £58 million. The current financial strength of trusts such as these is therefore largely due to these grants and loans, but no trust would have existed had it not been for the foresight and benevolence of their original benefactors, men such as Sir Edward Guinness and Sam. It would be pleasing to think that from time to time those enjoying the benefits provided by such trusts, and those to whom they give employment, spare them a thought.

Nepotism, perhaps justifiably, played an important part in the early years of the trust. Sam would have approved of his family and friends taking leading roles. The first three trustees were Algernon Sydney, who also became its first chairman; Ada's brother Ernest, who succeeded Sydney as chairman in 1916, a position he held until his death in 1954; and Ada's brother-in-law Augustus Jacobs. When Jacobs died in 1921 his son Ernest Lionel Jacobs became a trustee. The first secretary was Sydney's son, H. C. Sydney, who served from 1909 to 1944, and he was succeeded by Ada's nephew, Ernest's son Geoffrey Hope-Davis. On his death in 1949, Mr F. H. Stevens became secretary until 1951, but then A. V. H. Sydney, Algernon's grandson, and H. C. Sydney's son, took over and served the fund until his retirement in 1974. He was the last direct link with Sam and his circle, and his retirement thus marked the end of an epoch during the term of which it could be said that there was always someone involved in the work of the Trust who was a direct descendant of Sam and Ada or of their closest friends and advisers. There have always, even until today, been active members of the Guinness family involved in its Trust. It is somewhat sad to think that in Sam's case the chain has been broken.

Today the Samuel Lewis Group, as its review for 1990/91 discloses, consists of four registered housing associations which work together to provide good quality, affordable housing in London, Kent (at Rochester, Gillingham, Margate, Ramsgate, Dover and Folkestone) and on the south coast of England (at Hastings and Worthing). It manages 4,500 homes and has a development pipeline of 1,000 new and improved flats and houses. It employs 200 staff and has property assets (at vacant possession market value) of over £250 million net of loans. In 1988, 1989 and 1990 more than £40 million per year was invested in new housing, and priority in letting the properties is given to those who are, or who are about to be, homeless. In London more than half of all new tenancies are given to ethnic minority households – most fitting, perhaps, given the ethnic minority status of its founder.

Ada was deeply concerned about the plight of single or widowed women whose income prevented them from being able to afford decent accommodation, and she recognised that there was a great need for cheap lodgings for poor women. Men in this situation were fairly well catered for, particularly by the Rowton Houses, but Ada felt that much of the drunkenness and vice among poor women was brought about by their degradation in sordid surroundings. She left £50,000 to her trustees 'to found, endow and maintain at one or more places in London Women's Lodging Houses to be called the Ada Lewis Women's Lodging Homes'. As the charity also shared her residuary estate equally with the Governesses' Benevolent Institution, the total receipts from her estate for this purpose eventually reached almost £100,000.

A scheme for the administration and management of the Ada Lewis Women's Hostels, as the charity was first named, was approved by the High Court in 1912. For many years Ernest was a trustee, as was Miss Miriam Moses, a mayor of Stepney and an active social worker in the Jewish community. Land had been purchased by the trustees of Ada's will in 1910 at 172 New Kent Road in south London, close to the Elephant and Castle. Work began in 1911 and the hostel, under the supervision of its architect, Mr Charles Joseph, who had worked for the Guinness Trust, was completed by the end of 1912. There was accommodation for over 200 residents. It was described as a hotel for working women and girls, easily accessible at cheap rates by underground, bus or tram from all parts of London, which aimed to provide safe and comfortable accommodation at moderate rates. Each resident had a separate bedroom, and free use of the general rooms – a dining room, laundry and drying room, a reading room provided with newspapers and books, a sewing room, a large general sitting-room which had a piano and board games available, footbaths and a brushing room. Hot or cold baths, including soap and towel, cost 1d. Bedrooms were let on a daily or weekly basis, the charges being 3s for seven nights (4s and 5s for the superior rooms) or 6d per night (8d and 10d for the superior rooms). Food, subsidised from the general income, was varied and cheap: soups were 1d, egg and bacon 3d, a plate of meat 2d, kippers, bloaters and herrings 1d each, and a large pot of tea 2d.

The women's editor of the *Maidenhead Advertiser* ('Madge') paid a visit in February 1913 and was disappointed in what she saw. The public rooms she found immense. There was 'nothing in the least homelike in the aspect, whether exterior or interior':

> Everything is arranged with strict regard to hygiene and sanitation, nothing could be better planned so far as these important matters are concerned ... Amidst so much that is admirable one regrets to have to criticise the building, which looks more like a hospital or a reformatory than a place intended to be home. The size of the rooms is so enormous, and they are so lofty and lighted by so many windows, that any thought of coziness or comfort of home-like feeling is entirely impossible, except perhaps for a very small minority ... One wonders what the generous-hearted Mrs Ada Lewis would have thought of this immense barrack, forbidding of aspect, though integrally perfect so far as health and cheapness are concerned ... May it be more successful than it seems to promise!

The building was sold in 1968.

In 1989 the Trust merged with the John Beech Trust and is now called The Women's Housing Trust. It provides housing for over 250 women and is developing houses for 30 more. It is on a sound financial basis with assets exceeding £5 million. Penny Gluckstein is chairman, and a majority of the trustees and staff are women, something which would have been very pleasing to Ada, who in some respects could be said to be a pioneer in the field. As we have seen, her charitable activities always extended beyond the genteel token support given by many of her contemporaries, and she involved herself closely in the day-to-day operation of the charities she favoured. The major part of the Trust's housing consists of three

Lender to the lords, giver to the poor

hostels located in Islington, Brent and Hammersmith, each having a resident manager. Every resident has her own bedroom, and shares kitchen and bathroom facilities. A number of bedrooms have been specially converted for disabled women. There is an agreement with the Samuel Lewis Housing Trust for it to provide management and development services.

A high proportion of the 51 charities who benefited from the wills of Sam and Ada still exist and remain active. Thus today, through the instrumentality of a wide range of organisations, there are thousands of individuals whose standard of living and comfort is enhanced by their generosity and foresight. This has to be put on the balance when judgment is passed on Sam's life and character.

23 · Robin Hood?

Was Samuel Lewis a saint or a sinner; on which side of the divide did he fall?

Sir George Lewis was firmly wedded to the view that moneylending as carried on by the West End moneylenders was an evil; that its practitioners were responsible for a great deal of wanton gambling and crime; and that it was Sam who was the leader of the pack. It followed in his mind that Sam was the most blameworthy of them all. 'Sinner' was too mild a description so far as he was concerned. It must be said that not one of the major allegations he made was ever substantiated in a court of law. Indeed, the opposite is true; whenever there was an independent inquiry, Sam was exonerated. Sir George's allegations were never shown to be more than unsupported assertions, and no one else aimed such strictures at him. The overwhelming majority of those who dealt with Sam praised him.

Sir George blamed Sam for Lord William Nevill's downfall, but Nevill's behaviour before the Clay case, and his convictions after, clearly demonstrated that it was not Sam who corrupted him. Sir George quoted the case of the Australian undergraduate in which he alleged that Sam charged interest of £950 on a loan of £500. There was no law prohibiting the rate which could be charged, but if Sir George's account was accurate, then Sam's behaviour on that occasion, though not unlawful, was outrageous, and cannot be justified. But Sir George did not relate this story until 14 years after the event was alleged to have occurred, and we do not know Sam's version, which might well have thrown a different light on the affair. When Sir George made an allegation against Sam which was tested in court, for example in the Chetwynd/Durham libel action, he could produce no evidence to back it up, and his client the Earl of Durham withdrew the charge. When Sam entered the witness box in the Clay case his evidence was believed by the jury, and he was the subject of friendly comment from the Lord Chief Justice. When Ailesbury raised a claim of fraud against Lord Iveagh and Sam, it was given short shrift and unceremoniously dismissed by the court.

Sam engaged in no trickery, no underhand methods. He knew there were people who would inevitably land in debt through gambling and high living. He could afford simply to sit back and wait for them to visit him. He did not set out to ensnare them, nor did he ruin them. Any who foundered ruined themselves. No action of Sam's could have curbed Ailesbury's excesses, which were flourishing before he ever approached Sam for a loan; and the Squire and Ernest Benzon and Lord Rosslyn and others of that type could not have been reined in by anybody. There were pickings to be made from the follies of certain youths. If he had not gratified their wish for instant credit others would have done so, and not behaved half as well towards them as he did. He could convince himself that he was entitled to a clear conscience, particularly when he combined his business with generosity to individuals and to the impoverished masses. The moral ground on which he stood was no less firm than that of the Bank of England.

Lambton, Benzon, Nevill, Chetwynd and Esher all engaged in excessive gambling, and their stories illustrate that gambling fever can affect the strong and intelligent as well as the weak and foolish. Sam too gambled, but within his means, and when he won heavily at the tables in Monte Carlo or Ostend used the occasion as an opportunity to share his winnings with the poor. Other extravagant behaviour and expenditure, such as that indulged in by Lonsdale, Benzon, Ailesbury, Baird and, in his early days, Lambton, was not a phenomenon which began when they met Sam. They were already deeply immersed before they came to him for assistance. Certainly when they called on him the odds were heavily balanced in his favour. There is no question but that many of the wastrels were no match for him; their entirely different backgrounds, upbringing and experience of the world ensured that. But after the first few years of his career such clients formed a comparatively insignificant proportion of his business, both in terms of their numbers and the sums involved. Most who came to him were mature men of experience who well knew what they were about, men who were able to judge whether their advantage lay in dealing with Sam or whether they would be better off seeking accommodation elsewhere. He had no monopoly. The growth of his lending on security was obtained in direct competition with, and at the expense of, the banks and insurance companies. No one was coerced into conducting business with him. It was their free choice, and he frequently advised them to try other sources if he thought they could obtain better terms elsewhere. If they chose to put their business with him they were treated with respect and fairness, of that there can be no doubt. The testimonies to his upright dealings were too numerous to be ignored.

Sir George should have looked elsewhere to put the blame, to the society which provided some young men with fortunes, or excessive expectations of fortunes which they were ill-equipped to handle. It was their lack of gainful occupation; their acceptance that a life of idleness, gambling and excessive expenditure was a desirable end in itself; and their belief that they were *entitled* to indulge themselves in this way without regard to the sensibilities of others which led to the unhappy endings which befell some of them.

Sir George seemed to have been upset that Sam had a residence in Grosvenor Square, and said he could afford it only because he engaged in extortionate usury. He jeered that Sam, then living in luxury, had started his working life with 'his shop in his pocket', but there was no shame in that; on the contrary, it was to Sam's credit that he overcame his early disadvantages. For Sir George the trade of usury was 'shocking' and brought unwarrantable rewards to its practitioners; but it was not illegal, and there were many of Sam's clients, including the Earl of Shrewsbury and Viscount Esher, who would gladly have countered Sir George's view.

Why was Sir George so bitter? Sam was surely right when he said that there had to be something beyond his general aversion to moneylenders and moneylending. There must have been a personal element involved. Perhaps it was jealousy, or temper, or pique, or fury, that one he despised none the less moved in similar circles, shared the same clients, enjoyed a good reputation and refused to enter the lists with him in the courts. The author's verdict on the clash between the two Lewises is that the burden of Sir George's complaints was unsustained and unsustainable.

In the early seventeenth century a satirical Jewish handbook was published in Italy setting out the qualities required for the perfect moneylender. It suggested he should be a humble and modest man with an affable approach. 'Let him answer anger with soft words, let him be rather of those who are insulted than of those who insult, let him welcome people with a friendly face, and let them like to have dealings with him. If he lacks any one of these characteristics he is unsuited to the practice of his profession.' He also had to be 'well spoken, diligent, adroit, agile' and to have a fine presence. He needed to be endowed with a good memory, have a bushy beard, and to care about his appearance. With the exception of the bushy beard, Sam had all the requisite qualities. His timing, and the careful selection of his objectives, proved to be inspired. He displayed a shrewdness of judgement which established beyond doubt that his success was not due to pure chance. He chose to earn his living as a pedlar when that trade could still lead to substantial financial rewards; he entered the business of moneylending in the very period when it was free of restriction. He selected as his clients the hereditary, titled, land-owning nobility at the precise moment when their fortunes were in need of urgent sustenance and relief from the remorseless agricultural decline of the 1880s and 1890s, and when they were under attack from the advancing and super-wealthy plutocrats whose progress pushed up the price of everything the noblemen considered desirable, and who seemed set to put paid to many of the advantages that life had bestowed on the nobility. He made his upward move in society just when the Prince of Wales had eased the path of outsiders, and he found for himself a wife who was much more than just a loyal and loving adornment. This could not all have come about by mere chance or luck; he made his own luck.

Of course moneylenders were not universally popular; as we have seen, they never have been. And undoubtedly there were many cases in which Sam looked beyond the borrower to the family standing behind him, knowing that they were the true security for his loans, that they would not stand by and see their relatives face financial ruin. But this was simply one element he took into account when he calculated the risk of the loan, and was not a circumstance he used to put pressure on the family. He never bombarded them with threats, or indeed, so far as can be ascertained, ever threatened anybody. It was unfortunate for Sam that the more than justified ill-reputation of the preliminary fee men, the touts, and the Kirkwoods and Gordons of the moneylending world, brought condemnation down not only on their heads but on everyone else engaged in the profession.

Sam shared the profit he made, not just with Ada and her family, but with the thousands of unfortunates who did not know him and whom he did not know, but for whose suffering he genuinely felt a warm concern. His money circulated; he spent it, and he gave it away. The money he loaned out brought benefits even if the recipients squandered it, for it passed to others who could use it for more productive purposes. A witness before the 1925 Select Committee put this aspect into simple language: 'Let it be remembered please, that money which is borrowed is not buried in the garden; it is spent, and spent for all purposes, rent, rates, taxes, and all commodities necessary for human beings. If you are interfering with moneylending I submit you are interfering with British trade, and we know that it needs no interference just now.' It was surely better for the common good that money circulated rather than being lost and buried in large family estates.

It would seem that Sam was sincerely devout, though neither sincerity nor piety necessarily guarantee that an individual's beliefs and actions are right. A cannibal doubtless sincerely believes in his right to kill and eat other humans. None the less Sam's adherence to a religious creed which enjoins its members to follow a strict code of moral behaviour is an indication, at least, that he recognised the necessity of conducting his life with consideration for others. His widespread charitable gifts, which began when he was still in his teens, must lead to the conclusion that Sam, unlike some of the medieval churchmen who declaimed against usury while practising it, and unlike Isaac Gordon who desperately wished to be accepted in the synagogue, but whose every act flew in the face of its tenets, followed the course his religion dictated, at least its dictates about charity.

Despite this, there is no doubt that he caused great anguish to some in the Jewish community who felt that he, and his brother moneylenders, brought nothing but discredit upon them. And it was not only the Jewish community, but much of English society, which frowned on their activities. But were the criticisms of the West End moneylenders justified; were those of the Sam Lewis type morally inferior to those who condemned them? There was an abundance, a surfeit, of double standards and hypocrisy. Newspapers accepted payment for moneylenders' advertisements while simultaneously condemning their activities; bankers shared in their profits, while yet trying to disassociate themselves in the public eye; men of fashion and fortune loaned out on usury using the cloak of known moneylenders to shield their identity and retain their undeserved reputations.

The moral behaviour of high society generally left much to be desired. There were individuals, highly regarded and spoken of approvingly, part and parcel of the favoured upper coterie, who did not hesitate to lie or cheat or even descend to blackmail if their social positions or aspirations were put under threat. It could well be that Society looked down on moneylenders because they had to go to them for help, something they regarded as an embarrassing admission of failure. As Jeremy Bentham said, the moneylender is popular only at the moment he parts with his money, not from then on. Borrowers often feel hostility to those who help them. It could not be said with any justification that Sam was morally inferior, either in word or deed, to those among whom he lived and with whom he conducted business. No hint of scandalous personal behaviour was raised against him, or Ada, and such riches as he acquired were spent not solely for personal pleasure or luxuries, but with the welfare of others in mind. The evidence of their many kindnesses is overwhelming.

There would, of course, have been no story to tell if it had not been for the money Sam amassed. It was not his charm, wit, ability and hard work, nor Ada's musical talent or her skill as a hostess, which brought them power, social position and worldly goods. Many who have such qualities do not become rich. It was the wealth he acquired which brought these rewards. What would Ada's life have been without Sam's money? Would the lieutenant have married her? Would the King have invited her to the Coronation? Would Lord and Lady Farquhar have befriended her? The questions need only be asked for the answers to be apparent. The money provided her with a more interesting and luxurious life than she could ever have dreamed of when she met and married young Sam Lewis in her parents' home in Dublin.

Sam used his money for his and Ada's social advantage. But this was only a part, and a very small part, of the equation. The bulk, the overwhelming bulk, of their wealth, was given for charitable purposes and it is surely this which must be the deciding factor in appraising Sam's life work. If he had had his wish the epitaph on his tombstone would have read: 'He loaned to the rich; he gave to the poor'. That would have been an accurate description. Perhaps the fairest conclusion, an opinion which would surely be echoed by the tens of thousands of individuals who have enjoyed the benefits of his philanthropy in the past, by the many thousands who do so today, and by those still unborn who will do so in the future, is that Samuel Lewis represented the acceptable face of moneylending.

Notes on sources

I have drawn my material from the archives mentioned in my acknowledgements, contemporary newspaper and magazine reports, directories, interviews with two great-great-nieces of Ada Lewis and with the surviving daughter of Lieutenant Hill by his second marriage, and from the books set out in the bibliography.

For a researcher engaged in Anglo-Jewish studies on a subject from 1841 onwards, the *Jewish Chronicle* is often the best source at which to start. It is a first-class paper of record, and will frequently provide greater detail than many archives, for within its columns can often be found verbatim reports of meetings, whereas the minutes of an institution will record only the decisions reached. Its correspondence columns attract and reflect a wide and influential selection of views of the Jewish community. It is the source of much material throughout the book, including the early history of the Birmingham Congregation and the institutions of provincial Jewry; of the discussions within the Jewish community on the topics of the day, including public reaction to Jewish moneylenders; and of course use was made of its interviews with, and obituaries of, prominent Jewish figures. Other newspapers which I used extensively were the *Daily Express, Daily Telegraph, Daily Mail, The Times, Daily News, Morning Post*, the *Star*, the *News of the World* and the *Estates Gazette*, and local papers when the story took me there, such as the *Abergavenny Echo*, the *Maidenhead Advertiser, Aris's Birmingham Gazette* and the *Brighton Standard and Fashionable Visitors' Lists. Burke's Peerage* was invaluable.

CHAPTER 1

I drew heavily on two books, *Birmingham Jewry 1749–1914* and *Birmingham Jewry. More Aspects 1740–1930*, under the editorship of Zoe Josephs and I. A. Shapiro. These are the work of non-professional historians, and provide a fine example of what can be achieved by amateurs in the field of local history. Background material was obtained from the *Victorian County History, vol. VII*, dealing with Warwickshire. An article by S. Y. Prais on 'The Development of Birmingham Jewry' in the *Jewish Monthly*, 12 no. 11, Harry Levine's *Short History of the Birmingham Hebrew Congregation – Singers Hill 1856–1956* and *Provincial Jewry in Victorian Britain*, edited by Professor Aubrey Newman, are particularly helpful. This last publication, and Cecil Roth's *The Rise of Provincial Jewry*, were used for this and chapter 2.

CHAPTERS 2 AND 3

Two books which give an excellent base from which to consider Anglo-Jewry in the nineteenth century are Professor Lloyd Gartner's *The Jewish Immigrant in England 1870—1914* and Vivian Lipman's *Social History of the Jews in England 1850–1950.* They also, together with Frank Schlechter's article, 'An Unfamiliar Aspect of Anglo-Jewish History' and Harold Pollins's *Economic History of the Jews in England,* throw some light on the Jewish pedlar's life. Cecil Roth's book on provincial Jewry mentioned above includes the communities of Liverpool and Great Yarmouth. Bertram Benas provides an interesting insight into the Jewish institutions of Liverpool in his article on the subject in the *Transactions of the Jewish Historical Society of England,* 'A survey of Jewish institutional history of Liverpool and district'.

Mr Joe Wolfman, who undertakes the care of the Liverpool Jewish archives, and Mr Asher Benson, who does likewise in Dublin, kindly supplied information not readily available elsewhere, and both are experts on the Jewish aspects of their respective towns.

For the history of the Jews in Dublin I have referred to *A Short History of the Jews of Ireland* by Bernard Shillman, *The Jews of Ireland from Earliest Times to 1910* by Louis Hyman, and the article on the 'Early history of the Dublin Hebrew Congregation' by Lucien Wolf in the *Transactions of the Jewish Historical Society of England.* Martin H. Elias deals with the Dublin Jewish Board of Guardians in his outline of its history.

J. M. Goldstrom's *The Social Content of Education* and Cyril Hershon's *To Make Them English* consider the aims of the educators of the Jewish poor. Once again the pages of the *Jewish Chronicle* provide a forum for discussion in the Jewish community on the question of the education of its young.

CHAPTERS 4 AND 5

There are literally hundreds of books on moneylending, religious attitudes towards usury, the church's role in medieval times, the displacing of the Jewish moneylender by Christian moneylenders, and the arguments leading to the eventual abolition of the usury laws. There is nothing published, so far as I am aware, on the subject of the Jewish moneylender in Victorian England. The main works I consulted were: Bacon's essay *Of Usurie*; H. L. Bellot and R. J. Willis, *The Law Relating to Unconscionable Bargains with Moneylenders, including the History of Usury to the Repeal of the Usury Laws* and *The Legal Principles and Practice of Bargains with Moneylenders*; Jeremy Bentham, *Defence of Usury*; Arthur Birnie, *The History and Ethics of Interest*; William Cunningham, *Christian Opinion on Usury*; James Grahame, *Defence of Usury Laws against the Arguments of Mr Bentham and the Edinburgh Reviewers*; A. Hardaker, *A Brief History of Pawnbroking*; Felicity Heal, *Of Prelates and Princes*; Albert M. Hymanson, *A History of the Jews of England*; William Ingram, *A London Life in the Brazen Age: Francis Langley 1548–1602*; Richard W. Keuper, *Bankers to the Crown: the Riccardi of Lucca and Edward I*; Aaron Kirschenbaum, *Jewish and Christian Theories of Usury in the Middle Ages*; Jacques Le Gof, *Your Money or Your Life*; Robin Mundill, *The Jews in England 1272–1290*; J. B. C. Murray, *The History of Usury*; Dorothy Johnson Orchard and Geoffrey May, *Moneylending in Great Britain*; James Parkes, *The Jewish Moneylenders and the Charters of English Jews in their Historical Setting* and *The Jew in the Medieval*

Lender to the lords, giver to the poor

Community; Leon Poliakov, Jewish Bankers and the Holy See; F. W. Read, Evils of State Interference with Moneylending Considered Historically; Edgar Rosenberg, From Shylock to Svengali; Joseph Schatzmiller, Shylock Reconsidered: Jews, Moneylending, and Medieval Society; Kenneth R. Stow, Papal and Royal Attitudes to Jewish Lending in the Thirteenth Century; R. H. Tawney, Religion and the Rise of Capitalism; Thomas Wilson, A Discourse upon Usury with Historical Introduction by R. H. Tawney; Lucien Wolf, Essays in Jewish History.

I am especially indebted to Dr Robin Mundill, who read the section of the book relating to the medieval Jewish moneylender, for the corrections he made and the improvements he suggested.

For the development of banking from the sixteenth century onwards, and for a discussion of the ethical and legal implications arising from this development, I found P. S. Atiyah's The Rise and Fall of Freedom of Contract; Stanley Chapman's The Rise of Merchant Banking; Edwin Green's Banking. An Illustrated History; and R. D. Richards's A Pre-Bank of England English Banker, particularly helpful.

CHAPTER 6

The Prince of Wales's dominance of late Victorian society and his liberal attitude towards Jews are touched upon in the multitude of books which deal with his life and times, ranging from heavy academic investigations into the minutiae of his career as prince and later as king, to gossipy accounts of his many liaisons with the beauties of the day. I particularly made use of Allen Andrews's The Follies of King Edward VII; James Brough's The Prince and the Lily; Jennie Churchill's Reminiscences; Virginia Cowles's Edward VII and his Circle; Colin Holmes's Anti-semitism in British Society 1876–1939; T. S. Escott's three books England: its People, Polity, and Pursuits, Society in London, and King Edward and his Court; Philip Magnus's King Edward VII and Sigmund Munz's King Edward VII at Marienbad were especially helpful.

In this chapter details of Ernest Benzon mainly come from his autobiography, How I Lost £250,000 in Two Years, and of George Lambton from his autobiography Men and Horses I Have Known.

CHAPTERS 7 AND 8

The nature of high society, and its lifestyle which led to high borrowing, is reflected in Adam Badeau, Aristocracy in England; John Bateman, The Great Landowners of Great Britain and Ireland; J. V. Beckett, The Aristocracy in England 1660–1914; George C. Brodrick, English Land and English Landlords; J. Camplin, The Rise of the Plutocrats; David Cannadine, The Decline and Fall of the British Aristocracy; Leonore Davidoff, The Best Circles; Lady Augusta Fane, Chit-chat; Marc Girouard, Life in the English Country House; J. H. C. Morris and W. Barton Leach, The Rule Against Perpetuities; Ralph Nevill, The Reminiscences of Lady Dorothy Nevill; the Earl of Rosslyn's autobiography My Gamble with Life; G. R. Searle, Corruption in British Politics 1895–1930; Laurence Stone, The Crisis of the Aristocracy 1558–1641; F. M. L. Thompson, The Ailesbury Trust 1832–1856 and The End of a Great Estate; and Paul Thompson, The Edwardians. The Remaking of British Society.

Notes on sources

CHAPTER 9

Detailed portraits of Sir George Lewis and Henry Labouchere are in their biographies, *Lewis and Lewis* by John Juxon and *'Labby'* by Hesketh Pearson. There is a description of Sir George's office and clientele in *Recollections of a Court Painter* by H. Thaddeus. The details of the criminal libel action were largely taken from the pages of *The World*, which reported the proceedings verbatim, and from other newspaper accounts.

CHAPTER 10

Mayfair is dealt with by Mary Cathcart Borer in *The Years of Grandeur: The Story of Mayfair*; Reginald Colby in *Mayfair: a Town within London*; Arthur Irwin Dasent in *A History of Grosvenor Square*; Ralph Dutton in *London Houses*; and Charles T. Gatty in *Mary Davies and the Manor of Ebury*. For Maidenhead I made use of the *Maidenhead Official Guide of 1905* and *The Story of Maidenhead* by Luke Over. The history of Brighton is dealt with in detail in *Life in Brighton* by Clifford Musgrove and *The Open Air* by Richard Jefferies.

CHAPTER 11

There are of course many books dealing with the racing scene and particular heroes, jockeys, horses and owners, but those I found most revealing for the purposes of this book were: *Racing Reminiscences and Experience of the Turf* by Sir George Chetwynd; *The Jockey Club* by Roger Mortimer; *The Fast Set: The World of Edwardian Racing* by George Plumptre; and *The Turf. A Social and Economic History of Horse Racing* by Wray Vamplew.

CHAPTER 12

Douglas Sutherland has written a biography of the fifth earl of Lonsdale, *The Yellow Earl: Life of Hugh Lowther*. There are revealing descriptions of Moreton Frewen and his machinations in *The Splendid Pauper* by Allen Andrews, *Mr. Frewen of England* by Anita Leslie, and *Studies in Sublime Failure* by Shane Leslie, and in his autobiography *Melton Mowbray and Other Memories*. Mari Sandoz deals with British investment in the American prairies in *The Cattlemen*.

CHAPTER 13

Some relevant information is to be found in *London Clubs* by Ralph Nevill and *Fifty Years of My Life* by Sir John Astley.

CHAPTER 14

The Earl of Cardigan in his *The Wardens of Savernake Forest* fully covers the history of the Ailesbury family and its relationship with Savernake. A large section deals specifically with the fourth marquis and the court proceedings, and it is the most comprehensive work available on the subject. Charles B. Cochrane in *Showman Looks On* adds something to our knowledge of Dolly Tasker. The Ailesbury archives at Wiltshire County Record Office contain the diaries of the third marquis, though in parts his handwriting is very difficult to decipher. There are also printed proceedings of the appeal to the House of Lords with comments in the margin written by the fifth marquis. Richard Onslow has written a biography of George Baird, *The Squire*, but he makes no mention of his borrowing from Sam.

CHAPTER 15

Most of the details of Sam's relationship with Lord William Nevill are taken from newspaper reports of the cases of *Lewis* v. *Clay* and of the criminal proceedings against Lord William Nevill. Further information comes from Nevill's description of his time in prison in his book *Penal Servitude*.

CHAPTER 16

The basis for this chapter are the Proceedings of the Select Committee of the House of Commons on Moneylending in 1897 and 1898, including the evidence of witnesses. Thomas Farrow's works, *The Moneylender Unleashed* and *In the Moneylender's Clutches*, lay down the background to the inquiry, and the subsequent proceedings of the Select Committee of the House of Lords and the House of Commons in 1924/5 add to our information. There was considerable comment on Isaac Gordon's career, both before and after he gave evidence to the Select Committee in 1897, in the national press and in the *Jewish Chronicle*. His case against Street is reported in the Law Reports [1899] 2 Q.B. 641. It appears from M. J. Landa's book *The Jew in Drama* that Landa was the only friend Gordon had.

CHAPTER 17

There are references to Sam's clients, their relationships with him and with each other and their standards of conduct, in a variety of books and magazines. *Vanity Fair* provides pen pictures of many of them, and some merited biographies. Many of the books referred to above in the notes to chapter 7 include relevant material, as also do *Lord Randolph Churchill* by R. Foster, *The Royal Baccarat Scandal* by Sir Michael Havers, Edward Grayson and P. Shankland, and *The Days I Knew* by Lillie Langtry. Lord Esher's diaries are in the Esher Archives at Churchill College, Cambridge, but unfortunately do not deal with his financial affairs in detail; however, James Lees-Milne's *The Enigmatic Edwardian* throws some light on this and on Lord Esher's racing interests.

CHAPTER 18

For a discussion on English philanthropists, see *English Philanthropy 1660–1960* by David Owen. A copy of the affidavit submitted to the Inland Revenue by Sam's executors which is among the papers in the Samuel Lewis Trust archives provided a wealth of information about his estate, and included a full list of his creditors and debtors. It was from the contents of this document that I was able to follow the trail which led to so many of his clients. His will of course led to the archives of the various charities which benefited from the will; see notes to chapter 22 below.

Notes on sources

CHAPTERS 19 AND 20

The archives of the Samuel Lewis Trust contain many interesting documents relating to Ada's social life after Sam's death, for example invitations to the Coronation of Edward VII, to Buckingham Palace and to Windsor Castle; also documents relating to some of her charitable activities. Unfortunately I was not allowed to examine the documents for the time I needed to obtain the full benefit from them, or to reproduce them. However, the Royal Archives at Windsor Castle containing the correspondence quoted in chapter 20 of King Edward VII, the Prince of Wales, Lord Farquhar and Lord Mount Stephen are reproduced from the Royal Archives by gracious permission of Her Majesty the Queen (RA Geo. V. C273).

CHAPTER 21

There are two biographies of Baroness Coutts which provide a full insight into her life and particularly document the steps which led to her marriage to her young husband: Edna Healey's *Lady Unknown* and Diana Orton's *Made of Gold*. An outline of the history of Coutts' Bank can be found in *Notes on the Origin and History of Coutts & Co.* by R. Brooke-Caws.

CHAPTER 22

I inspected the archives of some of the beneficiaries of Sam and Ada's wills, including those of the Ada Lewis Dublin Winter Distress Fund, the Ada Lewis London Winter Distress Fund, the Royal Academy of Music, the Samuel Lewis Bequest for the Jewish Poor of Dublin, the Samuel Lewis Trust, the Schoolmistresses' and Governesses' Benevolent Institution and the West London Synagogue of British Jews. There is doubtless a great deal of further information to be gleaned from the archives of remaining extant charities which I did not examine, but some of them provided me with copies of documents they held.

The following books provided me with guidance for this chapter: Brian Abel-Smith, *The Hospitals, 1800–1945*; J. W. Beattie, *The Story of the Governesses' Benevolent Institution*; G. D. Black, *Health and Medical Care of the Jewish Poor in the East End of London 1880–1939*; Maurice Bruce, *The Coming of the Welfare State*; Ernest R. Dewsnup, *The Housing Problem in England*; Martin H. Eliasof, *The Dublin Jewish Board of Guardians: an Outline of its History*; R. Kirkman Gray, *A History of English Philanthropy*; F. D. Long, *King Edward Hospital Fund for London 1897–1942*; Geoffrey Rivett, *The Development of the London Hospital System*; A. V. H. Sydney, *A History of the Samuel Lewis Housing Trust 1901–1974*.

Bibliography

Abel-Smith, Brian, *The Hospitals, 1800–1945* (1964)
Andrews, Allen, *The Splendid Pauper* (1968)
—, *The Follies of King Edward VII* (1975)
Ashley, Sir William, *An Introduction to English Economic History and Theory* (1893)
Asquith, Margot, *The Autobiography of Margot Asquith* (1920)
Astley, Sir John, *Fifty Years of My Life* (1894)
Atiyah, P. S., *The Rise and Fall of Freedom of Contract* (1979)
Bacon, Francis, *Essays: of Usurie* (1625)
Badeau, Adam, *Aristocracy in England* (1886)
Bateman, John, *The Great Landowners of Great Britain and Ireland* (1876)
Beattie, J. W., *The Story of the Governesses' Benevolent Institution* (Private circulation, 1962)
Beckett, J. V., *The Aristocracy in England 1660–1914* (1986)
Bellot, H. L. and Willis, R. J., *The Law Relating to Unconscionable Bargains with Moneylenders, Including the History of Usury to the Repeal of the Usury Laws* (1897)
—, *The Legal Principles and Practice of Bargains with Moneylenders* (1906)
Benas, Bertram B., 'A survey of Jewish institutional history of Liverpool and District', *Transactions of the Jewish Historical Society of England*, xvii (1951)
Bentham, Jeremy, *Defence of Usury* (1787)
Benzon, Ernest, *How I Lost £250,000 in Two Years* (1889)
Birnie, Arthur, *The History and Ethics of Interest* (1952)
Black G. D., 'Health and medical care of the Jewish poor in the East End of London 1880–1939', unpublished Ph.D. thesis, University of Leicester (1987)
Blumenfeld, R. D., *R. D. B.'s Diary 1887–1914* (1930)
Borer, Mary Cathcart, *The Years of Grandeur. The Story of Mayfair* (1975)
Brodrick, George C., *English Land and English Landlords* (1881)
Brooke-Caws, R., *Notes on the Origin and History of Coutts & Co.* (1950)
Brough, James, *The Prince and the Lily* (1875)
Bruce, Maurice, *The Coming of the Welfare State* (1968)
Burke's Peerage
Camplin, J., *The Rise of the Plutocrats* (1978)
Cannadine, David, *The Decline and Fall of the British Aristocracy* (1990)
Cardigan, Earl of, *The Wardens of Savernake Forest* (1949)
Chapman, Stanley, *The Rise of Merchant Banking* (1984)

Chetwynd, Sir George, *Racing Reminiscences and Experience of the Turf* (1891)
Churchill, Jennie, *Reminiscences* (1908)
Cochrane, Charles B., *Showman Looks On* (1945)
Colby, Reginald, *Mayfair: a Town within London* (1966)
Cowen, Anne and Roger, *Victorian Jews through British Eyes* (1986)
Cowles, Virginia, *Edward VII and His Circle* (1956)
Cunningham, Peter, *Handbook of London* (1850)
Cunningham, William, *Christian Opinion on Usury* (1884)
Cyclopaedia of Music and Musicians, 7th edn (1956)
Dasent, Arthur Irwin, *A History of Grosvenor Square* (1935)
Davidoff, Leonore, *The Best Circles* (1973)
Dewsnup, Ernest R., *The Housing Problem in England* (1907)
Dictionary of Business Biography (1984)
Dictionary of National Biography
Dutton, Ralph, *London Houses* (1952)
Encyclopaedia Britannica, 11th edn (1911)
Endelman, Todd M., *The Jews of Georgian England* (1979)
Eliasof, Martin H., *The Dublin Jewish Board of Guardians: an Outline of its History* (Dublin 1926)
Elleray, D.Robert, *Brighton. A Pictorial History* (1897)
Elman, Peter, 'Jewish finance in thirteenth century England', *Transactions of the Jewish Historical Society*, xvi (1952, talk originally delivered 1940)
Escott, T. S., *England. Its People, Polity, and Pursuits* (1879)
—, *Society in London* (1885)
—, *King Edward and His Court* (1903)
Fane, Lady Augusta, *Chit-Chat* (1926)
Farrow, Thomas, *The Moneylender Unleashed* (1895)
—, *In the Moneylender's Clutches* (1895)
Foster, R., *Lord Randolph Churchill* (1981)
Frewen, Moreton, *Melton Mowbray and Other Memories* (1924)
Galbraith, J. K., *Money, Whence it Came, Where it Went* (1975)
Gartner, Lloyd P., *The Jewish Immigrant in England 1870–1914* (1960)
Gatty, Charles T., *Mary Davies and the Manor of Ebury*, 2 volumes (1921)
Girouard, Marc, *Life in the English Country House* (1978)
Goldstrom, J. M., *The Social Content of Education* (1972)
Grahame, James, *Defence of Usury Laws against the Arguments of Mr. Bentham and the Edinburgh Reviewers* (1817)
Gray, R. Kirkman, *A History of English Philanthropy* (1905)
Green, Edwin, *Banking. An Illustrated History* (1989)
Grunwald, K., ' "Windsor Cassel" – the last court Jew', in *Yearbook of Leo Baeck Institute* (1969)
Hardaker, A., *A Brief History of Pawnbroking* (1892)
Havers, Sir Michael, Grayson, E. and Shankland, P., *The Royal Baccarat Scandal* (1977)
Heal, Felicity, *Of Prelates and Princes* (1980)
Healey, Edna, *Lady Unknown* (1978)
Hershon, Cyril P., *To Make them English* (1983)

Lender to the lords, giver to the poor

Holmes, Colin, *Anti-semitism in British Society 1876–1939* (1979)

Hyman, Louis, *The Jews of Ireland from Earliest Times to 1910* (1972)

Hymanson, Albert M., *A History of the Jews of England* (1908)

Ingram, William, *A London Life in the Brazen Age: Francis Langley 1548–1602* (1978)

Jefferies, Richard, *The Open Air* (1875)

Josephs, Zoe and Shapiro, I. A. (eds), *Birmingham Jewry 1749–1914* (1980)

—, *Birmingham Jewry: More Aspects 1740–1930* (1984)

Juxon, John, *Lewis and Lewis* (1983)

Kaeuper, Richard W., *Bankers to the Crown: the Riccardi of Lucca and Edward I* (1973)

Kirschenbaum, Aaron, 'Jewish and Christian theories of usury in the Middle Ages', *Jewish Quarterly Review* 75 no. 3 (1985)

Lambton, George, *Men and Horses I Have Known* (1924)

Landa, M. J., *The Jew in Drama* (1926)

Langtry, Lillie, *The Days I Knew* (1925)

Law, Frank W., *History of Moorfields Eye Hospital* (1975)

Lees-Milne, James, *The Enigmatic Edwardian (Lord Esher)* (1986)

Le Gof, Jacques, *Your Money or Your Life* (1988)

Leslie, Anita, *Mr Frewen of England* (1966)

Leslie, Shane, *Studies in Sublime Failure* (1932)

Levine, Harry, *A Short History of the Birmingham Hebrew Congregation – Singers Hill 1856–1956* (1956)

Lipman, Vivian, *Social History of the Jews in England 1850–1950* (1954)

Long, F. D., *King Edward Hospital Fund for London 1897–1942* (1942)

MacAlpin, Daniel Rankin, *The Law Relating to Moneylenders and Borrowers: a Treatise on Bills of Sale, Personal Security, and Monetary Dealings with 'Expectant Heirs'* (1880)

Magnus, Philip, *King Edward VII* (1964)

Maidenhead Official Guide (1905)

Margouliouth, Rev. Moses, *The History of the Jews in Great Britain* (1851)

Martin, Ralph G., *Lady Randolph Churchill*, 2 vols (1974)

Maugham, Robert, *Outlines of the Jurisdiction of all the Courts in England and Wales* (1838)

Middleton, Tom, *Yesterday's Town* (1980)

Morris, J. H. C. and Leach, W. Barton, *The Rule Against Perpetuities* (1962)

Mortimer, Roger, *The Jockey Club* (1958)

Mundill, Robin R., 'The Jews in England 1272–1290', unpublished Ph.D. thesis, University of St. Andrews

Munz, Sigmund, *King Edward VII at Marienbad* (1934)

Murray, J. B. C., *The History of Usury* (1866)

Musgrove, Clifford, *Life in Brighton* (1981)

Nevill, Ralph (ed.), *The Reminiscences of Lady Dorothy Nevill* (1906)

—, *London Clubs* (1908)

Nevill, Lord William (under nom-de-plume W. B. N.), *Penal Servitude* (1903)

Newman, Aubrey (ed.), *Provincial Jewry in Victorian Britain* (1975)

Onslow, Richard, *The Squire* (1980)

Orchard, Dorothy Johnson and May, Geoffrey, *Moneylending in Great Britain* (New York, 1933)

Orton, Diana, *Made of Gold* (1980)

Over, David, *The Story of Maidenhead* (1894)

Owen, David, *English Philanthropy 1660–1960* (1964)

Parkes, James, *The Jewish Moneylenders and the Charters of English Jews in their Historical Setting*, Jewish Historical Society Miscellanies III (1932)

—, *The Jew in the Medieval Community* (1938)

Pearson, Hesketh, *'Labby'* (1936)

Pevsner, Nikolaus, *The Buildings of England* (1963)

Phillips, Hugh, *Mid-Georgian London* (1964)

Plumptre, George, *The Fast Set: the World of Edwardian Racing* (1985)

Poliakov, Leon, *Jewish Bankers and the Holy See* (trans. from the French by Miriam Kochin) (1977)

Pollins, Harold, *Economic History of the Jews in England* (1982)

Prais, S. Y., 'The development of Birmingham Jewry', *Jewish Monthly*, 12 no. 11 (1948)

Read, F. W., 'Evils of state interference with moneylending considered historically', *The Liberty Annual* (1892)

Richards, R. D., *A Pre-Bank of England English Banker, Edward Blackwell* (1928)

Rivett, Geoffrey, *The Development of the London Hospital System* (1986)

Rose, Kenneth, *Superior Person* (1969)

Rosenberg, Edgar, *From Shylock to Svengali* (1960)

Rosslyn, Earl of, *My Gamble with Life* (1928)

Roth, Cecil, *A History of the Jews in England*, 2nd edn. (1949)

—, *The Rise of Provincial Jewry* (1950)

Sandoz, Mari, *The Cattlemen* (1961)

Schatzmiller, Joseph, *Shylock Reconsidered: Jews, Moneylending and Medieval Society* (1990)

Schechter, Frank I., 'An unfamiliar aspect of Anglo-Jewish history', *Transactions of the American Jewish Historical Society*, xxv (1917)

Searle, G. R., *Corruption in British Politics 1895–1930* (1987)

Select Committee on the Usury Laws, Report, PP 1818, vol. VI

Select Committee on Bills of Sale Act (1878) PP 1881, vol. VIII

Select Committee of the House of Commons on Moneylending, PP 1897 XI 405; 1898 X 101, Report with proceedings, evidence, appendix and index

Select Committee of the House of Lords and the House of Commons on the Moneylending Bill (House of Lords) and the Moneylenders (Amendment) Bill, Report, proceedings, minutes, evidence and index, PP 1924/5 viii 31

Sheppard, Francis, *The History of London 1808–1870: the Infernal Wen* (1970)

Shillman, Bernard, *A Short History of the Jews of Ireland* (1945)

Smith, Adam, *Wealth of Nations* (1776)

Smith's Postal Directory of Maidenhead (1897)

Spring, David, 'The English landed estate in the age of coal and iron', *Journal of Economic History*, 2 (1951)

Stone, Laurence, *The Crisis of the Aristocracy 1558–1641* (1967)

Stow, Kenneth R., 'Papal and royal attitudes to Jewish lending in the thirteenth century', *Association for Jewish Studies Review*, 6 (1981)

Supple, Barry, *The Royal Exchange Assurance: a History of British Assurance 1720–1970* (1970)

Sutherland, Douglas, *The Yellow Earl: Life of Hugh Lowther, 5th Earl of Lonsdale 1857–1944* (1965)

—, *The Landowners* (1968)

Sydney, A. V. H., *A History of the Samuel Lewis Housing Trust 1901–1974* (privately printed)

Tarn, John Nelson, *Five Per Cent Philanthropy* (1873)

Tawney, R. H., *Religion and the Rise of Capitalism* (1926)

Thaddeus, H., *Recollections of a Court Painter* (1912)

Thompson, F. M. L., 'The Ailesbury Trust 1832–1856', *Economic History Review*, 2nd series, 2 (1949)

—, 'The end of a great estate', *Economic History Review*, 2nd series, 8 (1955)

—, *English Landed Society in the Nineteenth Century* (1963)

Thompson, Paul, *The Edwardians: the Remaking of British Society* (1975)

Vamplew, Wray, *The Turf: a Social and Economic History of Horse Racing* (1976)

Victoria County History, A History of Warwickshire, vol. VII (1964)

Vincent, John, *Later Derby Diaries (Diaries of 15th Earl of Derby 1826–93)* (1976)

Warren, Samuel, *Ten Thousand a Year* (1841)

West London Synagogue of British Jews, *Minute Books 1860–75; 1888–98.*

Weinreb, Ben and Hibbert, Christopher (eds.), *The London Encyclopaedia* (1983)

Wilson, Thomas, *A Discourse upon Usury (1572), with historical introduction by R. H. Tawney* (1925)

Wolf, Lucien, *Essays in Jewish History* (1934)

—, 'Early history of the Dublin Hebrew Congregation', *Transactions of the Jewish Historical Society of England*, xi (1924)

Index

Aaron of Lincoln, 40
Aaron of York, 41
Abergavenny, William, 1st marquis of,
92, 94, 185–6
Ada Lewis Nurses' Institute, 333–5
Ada Lewis Women's Lodging Houses
(now Women's Housing Trust), 336,
340, 364
Ada Lewis Winter Distress Fund,
Dublin, 340, 343–4
Adler, Dr Nathan, Chief Rabbi, 15, 16,
128, 311
Ailesbury, Charles Brudenell-Bruce,
1st marquis, 162
Ailesbury, Ernest Brudenell-Bruce, 3rd
marquis, 163, 165–7
Ailesbury, George Brudenell-Bruce,
2nd marquis, 162
Ailesbury, George William Thomas
Brudenell-Bruce, 4th marquis, 92,
161–84, 255, 368
Ailesbury, Henry Augustus Brudenell-
Bruce, 5th marquis, 174, 176–7, 182,
183
Ailesbury, Julia (wife of 4th marquis,
née Haseley, aka Dolly Tester), 164,
165, 168, 173, 181, 182–4
Alexandra ('Alix'), Princess of Wales
(later Queen), 163, 260, 261, 262,
267, 268, 272, 273, 274, 280, 319,
333
Anglesey, 4th marquis of, 264
Anglesey, 5th marquis of, 264
Asquith, Margot, 72
Astley, Sir John, 83, 157
Astor, William Waldorf, 129, 300, 318

Audley, Hugh, 118, 124
Aylesford, Heneage, 7th earl of, 57,
255, 258–62
Aylesford, Lady (Edith), 259–62

Badeau, Adam, 90
Bank of England, 55
Baird, Alexander ('the Squire'), 141,
165, 168–70, 255, 368
Barnardo, Dr Thomas John, 25
Barnato, Barney, 158, 291
Bartlett, William Ashmead, 328–30
Beaufort, Henry Charles Fitzroy, 8th
duke of, 141, 143, 255, 271–3
Bernadi, John Michaelis, 24
Bentham, Jeremy, 31, 42, 43, 66
Benzon, Ernest, 63–8, 139, 141, 146,
159, 285, 368
Beresford, Lady Charles, 266–9, 270
Beresford, Lord Charles, 57, 255, 258,
260, 265–9, 270
Beresford, Lord Marcus, 71, 141, 157,
268
Beyfus, Henry, 103
Bigge, Sir Arthur, 316
Birmingham Hebrew Congregation, 6,
10, 24, 208, 209, 225
Birmingham Hebrew National School,
7, 11–16
Birmingham Hebrew Philanthropic
Society, 7–9, 17, 19, 300
Birmingham Sabbath Meals Society,
4
Blandford, Marquis of (see
Marlborough, 8th duke)
Blumenfeld, R.D., 64, 165, 253

Boss, Albert, 103–15
Brighton, 79, 124–8
Boulter's Lock, Maidenhead, 117, 128–31, 319
Brooke, Frances ('Daisy'), later Countess of Warwick, 58, 98, 265–70, 274
Brooke, Lord, 266, 269
Buckingham, 2nd duke of, 85
Burdett-Coutts, Baroness Angela, 317, 321, 326–30, 358

Cahorsins, 38, 39
Cassel, Sir Ernest, 59, 60, 274, 305, 311, 356
Cayley, Sir George, 292
Chetwynd, Sir George, 64, 80, 138–44, 149, 169, 186, 256, 264, 272, 367
Cholmondeley, George Henry, 4th earl, 255, 271, 293
Churchill, Lady Randolph (Jennie), 70, 124, 156, 261–3, 293, 308, 321, 322, 325
Churchill, Lord Randolph, 57, 124, 259–63, 270–1, 325
Clanmorris, Lord, 292
Clay, Henry Spender, 123, 187–202, 270, 277, 304
Cliffe, Frederick and Zilla, 306, 323
Cork Street, 54, 61, 68, 70, 124, 136, 165, 187, 255, 279, 290
Coutts' Bank, 49, 64, 328, 329
Cowley, Lady Violet, 130, 186, 190

Dublin, 19, 23–7, 344–6
Davies, Mary, 118–19
Davis, Alice Maude ('Dotie', aka 'Hope Temple'), 23, 295, 308–9
Davis, Annette, 21, 26, 27
Davis, Charles, 23
Davis, Clara Emma, 21, 26, 237, 338
Davis, David Marcus, 20–2, 26–7, 55
Davis, Emily Emma, 21–6, 323
Davis, Ernest Henry, 23, 28, 323, 334, 338, 349, 350
Davis, Frank Isaac, 21
Davis, Joseph Mayer, 21, 23

Davis, Sarah (née Mordecai), 20–1, 27
Davis, Montagu, 21
Downshire, Arthur Willy, 6th marquis of, 293
Dudley, William Humble Ward, 2nd earl of, 159, 186, 293
Dundas, William, 257
Durham, John George, 3rd earl of, 68, 71, 138, 142, 272
Dutch, Dr Henry, 281, 334

Ecardstein, Baron, 293
Edward I, 39–40
Edward, Prince of Wales (later Edward VII): 2, 97, 99, 127, 129, 131, 135–6, 158, 264, 265, 266, 271, 272, 274, 280, 319, 333, 370; king of the social scene, 57; enjoyed company of Jews, 58; patron of the turf, 132–4, 163, 169; and the Aylesford affair, 258–62; and the Beresford affair, 267–70; and Sam's legacy, 309–17, 325, 348, 356
Edwardes, George, 157
Escott, T.H.S., 57, 132
Esher, Reginald Baliol, 2nd Viscount, 60, 70, 255, 273–5, 292, 318, 322, 368, 369
Essex, Lord, 292

Falmouth, Zender, 4
Farrow, Thomas, 205–8, 210, 211, 228, 229, 231, 245, 249
Farquhar, Lady, 305, 317, 332, 333, 348–9
Farquhar, Horace Brand, Lord, 60, 123, 274, 305, 313–17
Field Club, 52, 64
Fitzwilliam, William Thomas Spencer, 6th earl of, 296, 304
Flower, Peter, 72
Frewen, Moreton, 147–53, 273

gambling, 79, 1333
George, Prince of Wales (later King George IV), 125
George, Prince of Wales (later King

George V), 100, 264, 270, 271, 273, 274, 314, 315, 316, 342
Gerard, Lord, 143, 292
Gilbey, Henry William, 279, 295
Goldsmid, Sir Isaac Lyon, 21, 128
Goldsmith, Francis, 21, 128
Gordon, Isaac, 208–26, 241, 252, 371
Governesses' Benevolent Institution, 301, 317, 327, 332, 336, 340, 346–51
Gower Street, 27
Graham, Sir Reginald, 167
Grosvenor, Sir Thomas, 119, 120
Grosvenor Square, 83, 117–24
Guinness, Edward Cecil, 1st Baron Iveagh, 172, 174, 180, 297, 301, 358, 363
Guinness Trust, 358, 360

Haddon, Rev. R.H., 323, 335–6, 341
Hardwicke, Lord, 260
Hill, William James Montagu (Lewis-Hill), 319, 321, 324, 336–7, 342
Hirsch, Baron Maurice, 59–60
Hope-Davis, Geoffrey, 28, 363
Hove, 117, 124–8
Huntly, 10th marquis of, 146
Hyde Park, 60, 81, 120, 121

interest, rates of, 35, 39, 41–4, 46, 47, 93, 209, 219, 220, 229, 238

Jacobs, Augustus, 28, 237, 338, 360
Jay, Daniel, 235–7, 247, 248
Jewish Board of Guardians (now Jewish Care), 7, 63, 298, 306, 334, 340, 352
Jewish pedlars, 4, 17–19
Jockey Club, 134, 137, 143, 164

King Edward VII Hospital Fund (now King's Fund), 290, 297, 298, 309, 355–7
Kinski, Count Charles Rudolf, 70, 255, 262–3. 292, 325
Kirkwood, John, 208, 218, 227–35, 241, 252, 371
Knights Templar, 37, 38
Knollys, Lord Francis, 274, 313

Labouchere, Henry, 96, 101, 145, 202, 223, 235, 284–5, 367
Lambton, Hon. George, 68, 70, 121, 255, 279, 285, 293, 367
Langton, Walter, Bishop of Coventry, 41
Langtry, Lillie, 98, 138, 169, 170, 265, 269, 325
Lansdowne, Henry Charles, 5th marquis of, 259, 260
Legh, W.J., 143, 293
Lewis, Ada Hannah: birth, 21; 26; marriage, 27; fine horsewoman and musician, 28; social aspirations, 124; legacy under Sam's will, 194; her income, 294; after Sam's death, 303; sells home at Hove, 303; purchases 16 Grosvenor Square, 304; charitable gifts during lifetime, 306; founded scholarships for Royal Academy of Music, 306; supported impecunious musicians, 308; approached on behalf of King, 309; invited to coronation, 316; presented cottages to Royal Berkshire Regiment, 320; second marriage, 321; influences leading to her second marriage, 322–8; alters will seven times, 331; illness, 332; at Windsor Castle garden party, 333; presented at Court, 333; awarded honorary freedom of Worshipful Company of Musicians, 336; last changes to will, and death, 336; her estate and will, 338
Lewis, Elizabeth (wife of Sir George), 100
Lewis, Frederick, 3, 5, 8, 9, 61, 173
Lewis, Sir George Henry, 26, 45, 58, 75, 96, 97–116, 127, 140, 141, 144, 159, 186, 187, 193, 194, 197, 207, 235, 238–46, 249, 255, 267–8, 285, 293, 307, 367, 369
Lewis, Gertrude, 3, 10, 13
Lewis, Samuel: birth, 2; schooling, 14–16; as a pedlar, 17–19; visits to Dublin, 19, 24–6; donations to

Dublin Synagogue, 26; marriage, 27; becomes a moneylender, 28; supported by Bank of England, 55; his strategy, 57; his clients as friends, 61; death of mother, 61; method of business, 62; Lambton's description, 68–9; involved in Boss's action against *The World*, 105; moves to Grosvenor Square, 117; purchases 113 Brunswick Terrace, Hove and 'Woodside', Maidenhead, 130; frequents the turf, 133; enjoyed gambling, 135; social advance promoted by General Williams, 136; accused by Sir George Lewis of breach of Jockey Club rules, 141; and the 5th Earl of Lonsdale, 149–54; Moreton Frewen's description of Sam, 153; described as 'benevolent', 154; not cultured, 156; membership of the Pelican Club, 157; a theatrical angel, 158; arrested at the Field Club, 159; and the 4th marquis of Ailesbury, 165–84; and Lord William Nevill, 185–204; cross-examined by Sir George Lewis, 194; Select Committee House of Commons 1897, 207, 237; attacked by Sir George Lewis, 240–2; responds to attack, 243–4; invited by Sir George Lewis to sue for libel, 244, 248; knew all the current gossip, 255; and 5th Earl Rosslyn, 256–8; the Aylesford affair, 258–62; and Count Kinski, 262; and 4th marquis of Anglesey, 263–4; and 8th earl of Wemyss, 264; and 8th duke of Beaufort, 271–3, and 2nd Viscount Esher, 273–5; and 20th earl of Shrewsbury, 275–8; retirement, 279; illness and death, 281; obituaries, 282; will, 289–302; the size of his estate, 290; 90 per cent to charity, 294; collection in of his estate, 341; memorial prayers for him still recited in Dublin, 346; saint or sinner?, 367–73

Lewis, Sarah (née Lyons), 3, 9, 17, 19, 27, 61, 173

Lind, Jenny, 15

Liverpool, 21–3

Lombards, 38

Lofts & Warner (surveyors), 276

Lonsdale, Hugh Lowther, 5th earl of, 62, 138, 139, 145, 158, 169, 285, 367

Lurgan, Lord, 139, 141, 159, 292

MacKenzie, Sir Alexander, 306, 339

Magh, Lord, 292

Maida Vale, 28

Maidenhead, 79, 117, 128–31, 318, 319, 320

Mallon, Harriet, 326

Mansfeld, Prince Coloredo, 292–3

Marlborough, John Spencer Churchill, 8th duke of, 259–62

Melton, William, Archbishop of York, 41

Messager, André, 295, 308–9

moneylenders: Jewish, 34–40, Christian, 37; Italian, 38–40; Riccardi of Lucca, 39; net profits, 46; preliminary fees, 50; agents, 51; small loans, 51; West End moneylenders, 52–4; hidden, 52

moneylending: early history, 29–42; outlawed in middle ages, 32; church as borrowers, 36–7; defaulting borrowers, 74

Montefiore, Sir Moses, 14, 15, 25, 105, 128

Moore, Abraham, 235–6

Mordecai, Anne (Sarah Davis's mother), 21

Mordecai, Henry (Sarah's grandfather), 20

Mordecai, Isaac (Sarah's father), 20–1

Mount Stephen, Baron George, 312–17, 356

National Lifeboat Institution, 320

Nerwich, Abraham, 24

Nerwich, Meyer, 24

Nevill, Lady Dorothy, 261, 292, 325

Nevill, Lord William, 130, 161,

185–203, 270, 285, 292

Paulet, Lord Henry, 159
Parker, Saville J., 293, 323
Pelican Club, 62, 157–9
Probyn, Sir Dighton, 60, 274

Raphall, Dr M.J., 13, 15, 16
Rosebery, Archibald Philip, 5th earl of, 128, 137, 322
Rosslyn, James Francis St. Clair-Erskine, 5th earl of, 79–80, 149, 152, 255, 256–8, 285, 292, 367
Rothschild, Hannah, 128, 322
Royal Academy of Music, 306, 317, 318, 335, 339
Royal Exchange Assurance, 277
Russell, Lord Chief Justice, 189, 191, 192
Russell, T.W., MP, 251

Salisbury, 3rd marquis of, 268–9
Samuel Lewis Convalescent Home at Walton-on-the-Naze, 352–5
Samuel Lewis Trust for Dwellings for the Poor, 359–64
Saunders, Scott, 178
Select Committee of the House of Commons on Moneylending (1818), 45
Select Committee of the House of Commons on Moneylending (1897–8), 46, 207–54
Sherrard, Buck, 139, 141
Shrewsbury, Charles Henry John Chetwynd-Talbot, 20th earl of, 70, 91, 255, 275–8, 292, 369

Smith, Adam, 88
Soltykoff, Prince, 141, 307
Sydney, Algernon Edward, 17, 63, 69, 140, 194, 243, 244, 257, 285, 286, 289, 290, 304, 311, 313, 320, 322, 327, 334, 338, 352, 354, 359, 363
Sydney, A.V.H., 363
Sykes, Lady Tatton, 141, 293

Thaddeus, H., 98
Trautmansdorff, Count, 292

Valletort, Viscount, 293
Victoria, Queen, 13, 57, 97, 100, 125, 128, 133, 150, 163, 258, 261, 264, 266, 269, 273, 282, 310, 328–9, 348

Walton, Lawson, QC, 197, 198, 251
Wemyss and March, 8th earl of, 255, 264
West London Synagogue, 28, 128, 281, 297, 340
Williams, Hwfa, 293
Williams, Colonel (later General) Owen Lewis Cope, 92, 135, 139, 141, 143, 146, 258, 292, 293
Wilton, Agnes, 27, 295
Winchester, Marquis of, 293
Wingfield-Stratford, Edward, 292
Wolfe, Schreiner, 20, 22
Wood, Charlie, 139, 141
The World, 101–14
Worshipful Company of Musicians, 335–6

Yarburgh, Robert, MP, 205, 208
Yarmouth, 20
Yates, Edmund, 96, 107